Henrietta Barnett
Social Worker and Community Planner

Henrietta Barnett
Social Worker and Community Planner

Micky Watkins

Acknowledgements for illustrations

I thank the Hampstead Garden Suburb Trustees for the use of most of the photographs which appear in this book. Toynbee Hall kindly gave permission for the publication of Plate 29; Plate 57 is reproduced by permission of the Rev. Alan Walker, St Jude's Church; Plate 86 is reproduced by permission of the University of Kent, Solosyndication; the Hampstead Garden Suburb Institute kindly gave permission for reproduction of two portraits of Henrietta Barnett (Plates 78 and 79).

ISBN: 978-0-9549798-7-4

Published by Micky Watkins and Hampstead Garden Suburb Archive Trust

Printed in Great Britain by CMP (UK) Ltd, Poole

Available from **mickywatkins@gmail.com**

Cover: Henrietta Barnett laying a foundation stone of the Free Church in Hampstead Garden Suburb, 1911.

Preface and Acknowledgements

Dame Henrietta Barnett is well remembered as the creator of the Hampstead Garden Suburb, a distinctive area of housing in North London. She wanted her Suburb to be an ideal community where all classes of people could mix and affordable housing was provided for old people, widows and single women. Culture and community life were provided by schools, churches, a Club House, an adult education Institute and many open spaces. Today, many of the communal facilities have been lost but the Suburb remains a great success financially and architecturally. Residents are certainly grateful to Henrietta for providing their well designed houses and pleasant landscape.

Surprisingly, Henrietta only embarked on building the Suburb after she had reached the age of fifty. Previously she had been committed to work in London's East End, trying to improve the lives of the poor, especially women and children. It was her experience of the poverty and degradation of the East End which inspired her to create an ideal community. But how did she have the influence and administrative ability to turn an ideal into bricks and mortar? Why was she able to recruit well-known architects, churchmen, aristocrats and rich benefactors?

Henrietta was always called "Yetta" by her family and friends; perhaps this was her childish abbreviation of her own name. However I have called her Henrietta throughout this book, even though she was Dame Henrietta from 1924.

Our knowledge of her life after her marriage comes mainly from her biography of her husband, *Canon Barnett, His Life, Work, and Friends*. For her life before marriage the best source is the *Quasi-Autobiography* by Marion Paterson, her faithful friend and companion. Henrietta was often asked to write her own autobiography and she did collect material for a book *People I Have Known*, but she never found time to write it and so, as Marion Paterson said, "all that can be done is to let her own words speak as gathered from her diaries, notebooks, speeches, publications, making her memoir autobiographical". Marion arranged this material together with many tributes from friends and linked it all together with her own account of events. She was already eighty when she undertook this work and the result is sadly incomplete. However the chapters on Henrietta's childhood and youth are invaluable and include quotations from notebooks and diaries which have been lost.

I would like to thank the Trustees of the Hampstead Garden Suburb Archive for supporting this publication. The staff of the London Metropolitan Archive have helped me with their efficient and cheerful service. John Coulter, Lewisham Local Studies Librarian, has been a great help, sharing his knowledge of the history of the Rowland family and of Sydenham. I have had valuable help from Jonquil Griffiths and from Harry Cobb, Delores Baron, Honor Sharman, Betty Law and Professor Ben Roberts.

I am particularly grateful to Julia Kellerman and Dorothy Ravenswood for editing and commenting on my typescript and encouraging me to publish.

Natalia Wilkoszewska, Anne Joshua and Charlotte Darwin have been very helpful with preparing the typescript for publication, for which I am grateful. The art work has been beautifully prepared by David Barton.

Long ago I was inspired with an interest in 19th century social history by my teacher at the London School of Economics, Lance Beales. Always, I was encouraged by my husband, John.

Contents

Contents

PART ONE

Henrietta Barnett
Social Worker
1851–1901

Chapter 1

Family, Childhood and Growing Up

Henrietta Octavia Weston Barnett was born on 4th May 1851. Sixteen days after her birth her mother died, perhaps not surprisingly considering the hazards of childbirth at that time and the fact that she was the eighth child born to her mother in ten years. The baby was named Octavia to signify that she was the eighth in the family. Weston was the name of one of her aunts. She was named Henrietta after her mother.

Henrietta's parents were Alexander William Rowland and Henrietta Monica Margaretta Ditges. In 1851 when Henrietta was born the family was living at 96 Queens Road, Clapham Park, a fashionable area of large houses.[1] Her father was 42 years old and her mother 32. They had three daughters aged five, four and three and a son, Frederich aged one, living with them at the time of the Census. Two other children, probably aged between six and nine, must have been away and their oldest son Alexander had died at the age of eight in 1849. The family employed two nurses, two housemaids and a German cook.

The Rowlands were wealthy, indeed Alexander William was the third generation of Rowlands to own a successful business in perfumery and toiletries, with premises in Hatton Garden. Rowlands Macassar Oil was so much used that furniture was protected from the oil by anti-macassars. It was used by the highest in the land, even royalty. As one of Kipling's characters said:

"Being kissed by a man who did not wax his moustache was like eating an egg without salt." Kipling (1865–1936) was a contemporary of Henrietta, dying in the same year.

Rowlands also produced hair dye, Odonto toothpaste and Kalydor, an after-shave said to eradicate pimples.[2] As Alexander William inherited his business he did not have to spend all his time striving for his wealth. He enjoyed life, took an interest in art and found time for his children. Henrietta remembered him as "being occupied in enjoying every aspect of life with his children and his worldly art-loving friends, taking his pleasures with a careless generosity which may have been reprehensible but which was very endearing."[3]

Henrietta has told us nothing about her mother but we know from records that she was German and came from Cologne.[4] She was only 32 years old when she died and we can imagine that as she lay dying after the birth she must have suffered agonies of anxiety about the future of her young family and especially her baby. Fortunately a very loving nurse was found to look after baby Henrietta. Mrs Mary Moore was 27 years old, and the fact that she was a married woman suggests that she may have been a wet nurse. Mary Moore stayed all her life with Henrietta, who always called her "Nurse" and regarded her as her foster mother. Alexander Rowland did not marry again as far as we know so the children must have felt that all his affection was for them, and from his letters it seems that "his special darling was 'Baby'".[5] So despite the loss of her mother, Henrietta had secure and loving care. Mr Rowland needed someone to run his large family and household, and he called in one of his unmarried sisters, Sophie, to take over this responsibility. Sophie Rowland was only 28, but perhaps regarded as too old to be likely to marry. She may have resented having so much work thrust upon her. It seems "Auntey" was not a very lovable person, Henrietta always disliked her and when she was older she described Auntey as "cold".

The Rowland children were educated at home, as was often the case with well-to-do families in those days. They had governesses to teach them in the early years and later the boys went to school. But Henrietta was a sickly child and perhaps not expected to live, so it was thought that she did not need to attend the classes with the governess and she was left to play with her mentally deficient sister Fanny. This neglect was probably due to Aunt Sophie who did not agree with girls being educated. Henrietta demanded at least to be allowed to sit in on the lessons and must have learnt from listening and teaching herself. When she was older, Henrietta was indignant that her early education had been neglected. Later she was taught by the governess and proved to be very good at arithmetic, particularly mental arithmetic. Marion Paterson said "Her little account books, of very limited pocket money were scrupulously kept – one satisfactory year ends with a balance 'I have 2d too much'". However she did not like French and had an inability to learn languages. Her diary entry for January 24th 1863 was "I burnt the little French book"!

She had marked preferences within the family. She loved Alice, who was four years older than Henrietta and these two sisters remained very close when they were grown up. Henrietta was also very fond of Fritz (Frederich), who was only a year older – "the brother I love best."[6] However she was not fond of her eldest sister: "Tessy came home. I am rather sorry as she is so interfering." Henrietta was physically weak but was already showing a vigorous independence.

In June 1864, when Henrietta was 13, the Rowland family moved to Champion Hall, Lower Sydenham. This was only a couple of miles south of the house where Alexander Rowland's parents lived in their large house named Rosenthal in Lewisham. The area was semi-rural with cottages, some farmland and some large houses, "gentlemen's residences", mostly occupied by successful merchants who worked in the City. There were large grounds round Champion Hall, and this was a big household with lots of children and servants, plenty of activity and interest. The children spent much time out of doors and were all taught to ride: "The children, even when quite young, rode, not on ponies but on horses, not always on the same horse, as we read in her diary of Firefly, Peggy, Paris, Charger, Buffer, all in turn being ridden by Alice Tessy and herself."[7]

Henrietta liked to be outside and always loved gardens. Her grandfather helped her to learn about flowers: "She tells too of a grandfather (whose world famed roses took many prizes at the Exhibitions) who taught her to love gardens and flowers. He gave her a little writing desk, its lid and decorations being made of compressed rose leaves, as hard as, and the colour of, ebony."[8]

On Sundays, Alexander Rowland taught his children art appreciation: "We were called down to the Drawing-room every Sunday evening after tea, not to sing hymns, but to be shewn beautiful engravings (the copies of famous pictures) chiefly those of early Italian painters. These our father explained to us and taught us how to look at a picture." It was to her father's early training that Dame Henrietta "traced her love of pictures, architecture, and also her never-failing joy in watching sunsets and indeed in colour and whatever grows."

It seems that religious practice was kept at a low key in this family, compared with the many middle class Victorian families where there were family prayers and a pious observance of Sundays. Henrietta's mother was Catholic[9], but this did not seem to have any influence on Henrietta. Presumably the children all attended church, probably at St Mary's, Lewisham, the Rowland family church, but there was not much religious teaching in this household: "What religious teaching the children had was given by Nurse who as she brushed their hair expected them to read the Bible to her." "It is Nurse," the Dame would say, "who taught me to know my Bible so well". Nurse saved up for many years to buy a large family Bible which she gave to Henrietta when she went away to school.[10]

During the winter months the family lived in Brighton, at 18 Brunswick Terrace, facing the sea: "How she loved the South Downs! To the very end of her life, when nearing Brighton, whether by train or motor car, she eagerly looked for the first glimpse of them, revelling in the light and shade playing over them; delighting in their contour, their expanse revealing to her the very touch of heaven."[11] It was to Hove (the west end of Brighton) that Henrietta took Samuel during his final illness, and eventually their ashes were buried in the churchyard of Hangleton Church in the Downs.

As a child Henrietta was frightened of the sea, but when she was 13 she overcame her fear as her diary entry shows: "Feb. 10 1864. Went for a walk on the Pier. I walked under-neath and conquered my fear." From this and from her insistence on attending lessons with the governess we see that she was a determined and independent child. But as the youngest of the family, she suffered from some bullying:

"A long time has passed since I was a girl, but I still recall, with gratitude, a Miss Sarah Howard who was the first person to believe in me. I was the youngest of a family of eight, a weakly child, and often told by my brothers and sisters that I was no good. I could not run so fast; nor climb so high in the trees; nor wheel heavy loads in the barrow; nor go such long black-berrying walks. Indeed I was made to feel myself a very inferior person. Then, one day when the brothers and sisters were ragging me, Miss Sarah Howard said 'That may all be true, but she can think better than any of you.'
That lady by her belief in me, gave me a great gift – she gave me hope to go on and faith that I should attain."[12]

Her health was a worry throughout her life. She was a "weakly child" from infancy and as an adult she was frequently ill. She had her first serious bout of pneumonia in 1865 and she was so ill that her father was recalled from abroad and Alice fetched home from school. Looking back at her life we see that her intelligence, will-power and nervous energy carried her forward despite her physical frailty. The extraordinary will-power and self-confidence which she developed later may have been rooted in the compassion her father felt for his "Baby," his motherless child. As the youngest child in the family she still had his attention when the others had grown up. She wrote an account of a journey with her father in a school copybook, quoted by Marion Paterson:

"My Tour to Buxton in Derbyshire
I am thirteen years old and a month, and I am making my first tour with Papa and Auntey
There was a gentleman in the train who showed us just before we got to Matlock, where Mr Nightingale lives, the father of the lady who went to Crimea.
Every morning she went a walk with her Father before breakfast, noticing all and everything.
Saturday June 11th Papa and I had a walk in a wood. It is quite un-cultivated and the ferns grow as thick as they can. I had read that seeds of ferns grow at the back of their leaves, and as I felt curious to see it, I looked and found the seeds in abundance.
Sunday June 12th I walked to Church with a young lady staying here. There was a child christened. It was the first christening I ever saw.

Monday June 13th Papa and I went to see Poole's Cavern. When Mary, Queen of Scots, was here she visited the cavern & as there is a pillar of Stalagnite that she went as far as, it is called the Mary, Queen of Scots, pillar.

There is also a Stalactite called the Flitch of Bacon

Saturday June 18th Today we came home. I never was so glad to get home, for though I have enjoyed myself very much indeed, yet we have so few more days at home I feel glad to be home." (They were moving to Champion Hall)

What a delight it must have been for her to be travelling with her father and to learn about nature from him during their morning walks. It seems he was a good teacher as well as a fond father. Henrietta was deeply influenced by his interest in art and nature and through her the same interests were awakened in thousands of other people.

When Henrietta was 16 she went to a boarding school where she was very happy:

"When I was sixteen and a half years old, namely in 1867, I went for three glorious terms to a boarding-school at Dover kept by three ladies, the Misses Haddon. A fourth sister had married Mr James Hinton, the aurist and philosopher, whose thought greatly influenced Miss Caroline Haddon, who, as my teacher and my friend, had a dynamic effect on my then somnolent character."[13]

Henrietta was most especially fond of Caroline Haddon, perhaps she had a schoolgirl "crush" on her and fell in love with her idealism. Miss Carrie, as she was called, gave Bible classes and on Sunday evenings she held a special "Goodnight Class":

"On Sunday after supper, the girls assembled, and having lowered the gas, started a hymn, during which Miss Carrie entered. She spoke for twenty minutes on some great thought of Life and Duty, sometimes illustrating what she said from various School events she had noticed during the past week. We often felt rebuked for little deeds we thought no one had noticed; or encouraged when we felt our feeble efforts towards goodness were recognised."[14]

The charismatic James Hinton who had so much influence was the son of a Baptist minister. Sent to work in a drapery shop in Whitechapel at the age of sixteen, "the degradation of Whitechapel life, especially in regard to the relations of the sexes, made an indelible impression on his mind."[15] By studying in the evenings he became sufficiently educated to enrol as a medical student at St Bartholomew's and he eventually became an ear surgeon. He was also interested in philosophy and believed in a universal spirit or vital force, and that man could only become his true self through good works. He was always preoccupied with saving fallen women and went to the music halls to talk to the prostitutes and try to save them.

Like their brother-in-law, the Haddon sisters were very interested in social work. They founded an orphanage at Ewell which the girls were encouraged to visit. They inspired the girls in their school to take an interest in social matters and do some practical social work:

"One day 30–40 boys from the Dover Workhouse were invited to tea at our school, and the girls were allowed and encouraged to entertain them. As I watched their low faces, their irresponsive ways, their sly unkindness to each other, their choice of brutal games, my girlish heart ached, and my ignorant mind revolted against the social injustices made evident by boys, odorous of institutionalism, dulled into inanity."[16]

Henrietta went on to say that this experience inspired all her later work for children, as a Poor Law Guardian, helping the "Feeble-Minded", as a member of the Departmental Committee on Poor Law Children and as founder of the State Children's Association.

School life was not all serious. A fellow-pupil who wrote to Marion Paterson after Henrietta's death remembered her as "a very clever girl; not interested in any sort of game, but with a good sense of fun". With her new sense of purpose she found great happiness in life; in her notebook she wrote:

"This half year I have been as happy as I could possibly be. Indeed the more I learn, and the older I grow, the happier I seem to become. I heartily thank you, dearest Miss Carrie, for all your boundless goodness to me which has been the foundation of my happiness."

An entry in her diary shows her in a state of euphoria:

"May 6 1868. Miss Haddon's Birthday. We went to Ewell; the orphans sang to us; thousands of wild hyacinths, a clear bright sky, and joy, joy in everything."

Certainly this time at the school came in the moment of adolescence when she was ready for a spiritual and emotional awakening. Many people can remember a conversion experience in their youth when they were filled with conviction – Socialism, Communism, or the dawn of freedom in the sixties – some belief which gives purpose to life. For Henrietta this conversion was religious in a general sense, an awakening of the spirit, an awareness of social problems and a desire to deal with them.

Chapter 2
Independence, Social Work and Marriage

Not long after these happy schooldays, disaster struck, for in 1869 Henrietta's father died and at 18 years of age Henrietta was bereft of both mother and father. The Rowland family had been living at a high standard in their Sydenham house, and when Mr Rowland died he left £45,000, the equivalent of nearly three million pounds today. His maccassar oil business was shared with his brother, and as his son Edward was already working in it, he left his share of the business to Edward. He divided the rest of his estate among his many dependents – his children and his two sisters. To Aunt Sophie he left £5,000 and to his other maiden sister £3,000 for annuities. To five of his children he left £5,000 each plus the residue. All the legacies amounted to £33,000, so the residue from £45,000 would have been £12,000, or £2,400 each. So Henrietta inherited £7,400 at most (about £480,000 today). The interest on this was enough for a middle-class standard of living, but she was not a wealthy heiress as has sometimes been supposed. There was delay in administering the will, and in her diary entry for September 5th 1869 she writes: "the money seems to diminish £30,000 gone already and our legacies not yet realised". Thus it is uncertain whether Henrietta received as much as £7,400.

Mr Rowland specifically left £5,000 in trust for Fanny, evidence of his kindness and surprising at a time when the mentally disadvantaged were often ignored or hidden. As we shall see, Henrietta undertook the care of Fanny and so her income may have been augmented by the income from Fanny's trust. Further evidence of Mr Rowland's views was that in his will he laid it down that if the girls married they should retain sole control of their money, but the law prevented this.

Henrietta with her sisters Alice and Fanny, together with Nurse and Auntey Sophie, moved from the big house in Sydenham to a modest house at 20 Westbourne Terrace Road, Bayswater. Living together, they should have been quite comfortably off, but from the Census it seems that they had a young barrister and his wife lodging in the house, presumably to help with expenses. The whole household employed just one maid.[17] So it seems likely that they did not receive the expected legacies.

Today the bow-fronted house in Bayswater looks a charming town house, but then it must have seemed a very humble place compared with the big house in its own grounds. The loss of her father was a terrible blow and Henrietta was very unhappy – "I dread the future so dull, dreary and weary does it look," she wrote in her diary in September 1869.[18] Added to her deep distress for her father's death was the loss of their pleasant life style in Sydenham. It was in this unhappy state that she made a will on a scrap of paper, making Auntey, Alice, Barham (a brother-in-law, husband of Tessy), and Nurse, executors. She left Auntey the small diamond ring that had belonged to her mother, to Nurse she left £300, and the rest of her property she left to Alice.[19] In her misery, she sought consolation in religion, and in January 1870 she wrote "Scales fell off my eyes and I saw God, in part, how he worked with me,

Plate 2
Henrietta about
18 years old.
Her mother died at
Henrietta's birth and
her father died when
she was 18.

and I blessed Him." Henrietta's spiritual feelings had been awakened by Carrie Haddon, and now she was plunged into a period of intense religious belief.

Since her schooldays, religion and charity had been fused in Henrietta's mind, and this would be so throughout her life. Henrietta attended St Mary's Church, Bryanston Square, and it was here that she took up her charity work. In the 19th century, most churches and chapels ran charities, and the denominations vied with each other in giving the poor small sums of money, mixed with much moral and religious advice. A church or chapel would collect voluntary contributions, the regular contributors would elect a committee which organised the parish into districts and small neighbourhoods and appointed volunteers to visit the poor in their homes in each area. The committees were mainly composed of men, but the visitors were usually women. They visited each of their families once a week, gave advice on domestic management, avoidance of drink, and moral improvement, together with material help such as blankets, clothes and tickets for purchasing groceries and coal. From the mid-19th century there were many manuals to help the lady visitors. They were advised to wear plain black clothes to make them recognizable and protect them from "indignity", and to keep notebooks in which to record their visits, gifts, and details of the families visited. This was the beginning of social casework.[20]

There were hundreds of these charities in London, and together with other, non-religious, charities they overlapped and created chaos. Some applicants exploited the situation by applying to many different charities. Also, as the lady visitors preferred to do their voluntary work near home, there was a shortage of visitors in areas such as the East End where there were few middle-class women. In 1860 the Society for the Relief of Distress was founded to try to bring order to this chaos, but the society which really achieved some success was the Charity Organisation Society founded in 1869, only a year before Henrietta took up visiting. The COS principles were based on the belief that poverty was largely the result of indiscriminate charity which made people dependent on "doles" so that a stern refusal of relief to the able-bodied would help them to find work and become independent. Charity should only be given to the old and the ill, and then only after a careful review of each case by a committee and home visitors. The stern and repressive policies of the COS became accepted in the 1870s and Octavia Hill and the Barnetts were keen supporters of these views.

The first district committee of the COS was founded by the Rev. W H Freemantle, Rector of St Mary's, Bryanston Square. In 1870 Octavia Hill undertook the organisation of the Walmer Street district of this parish and she built up a "staff" of 35 lady visitors.[21] Unusually for a woman, Octavia was made a committee member. One innovation made by the COS committee was to exchange information on cases with the Poor Law officials in Marylebone. It was to this well-organised charity that Henrietta came. In January 1870 she joined Octavia's staff as a volunteer, and "found her life's work". In her diary she noted "Wednesday January 19th, 1870. Went on my first mission in Marylebone. Very busy. God grant it success."

The charity was concerned with housing as well as poor relief. By 1870, Octavia had considerable experience of housing improvement and management of tenants. For the past five years, Ruskin, her friend and patron, had provided Octavia with the finance to buy

Plate 3
Champion Hall, Lower Sydenham, where the Rowland family lived from the time Henrietta was 13 in 1864 until her father's death in 1869. The house later became the nucleus of a hospital and was demolished in the 1990s.

Plate 4
20 Westbourne
Terrace Road where
Henrietta lived with
her sisters Alice and
Fanny, her old Nurse
and Aunt Sophie
after her father
had died.

and improve property near where she lived in Marylebone. In 1865 she tackled her first slum, Paradise Place (!), organising structural repairs, cleaning houses and providing clean water and a communal playground. Next, Freshwater Place was given the same treatment. Lady visitors insisted on payment of rents and gave tenants advice on managing their homes and finance. There seem to have been no limits to the interference and moralising to which the poor were subjected.

Octavia must have recognised Henrietta's determination and ability for, although she was only 19, Octavia soon put her on to the local COS committee and allotted her a district of her own, Barrett Court. The housing in Barrett Court was filthy and decrepit and the road notorious because, lying between Oxford Street and Wigmore Street, it was seen by wealthy Londoners as they passed by. After renovation it was named St Christophers Place and today it is a charming pedestrian way, lined with cafes and boutiques. Only the dip in the paving stones reminds one that there was once an open sewer running down the middle.

By now there had been a considerable drain on Ruskin's resources for although he had inherited a fortune from his father he was spending it very generously on charity. For Barrett Court, Octavia turned to other wealthy friends. The court was bought by Lady

Ducie in 1869, with further financial help from George Eliot, Tom Hughes, John Frederick Maurice and Princess Alice.[22] Henrietta was in charge of the visiting and rent-collecting of the renovated court and worked very hard.

Octavia Hill opened a new world to Henrietta. She was her mentor in social work and passed on her enthusiasm for social and moral reform combined with a belief in the uplifting power of great art, following Ruskin's teaching. Octavia took Henrietta to her home to meet her mother and sisters and the older girls in the school which they ran in their house in Marylebone. Moreover, Octavia generously introduced Henrietta to wealthy and famous people who wanted to support social reform and some of these people are mentioned in her diary, (see below). Henrietta certainly grew to have a strong affection for her, which was returned by Octavia. Her affectionate feelings for Miss Carrie when she was at school seem to have transferred to Octavia Hill when she started her parish work. Her high regard – perhaps love – for Octavia was shown at the Barnett's marriage, when Henrietta gave Octavia a diamond ring which was a family heirloom. Later, Henrietta feared that Octavia disapproved of this gift, for she never wore the ring and never mentioned it to her family.[23] Did Octavia feel the ring was too extravagant when they were working to combat poverty? Was she embarrassed by a "crush" which Henrietta may have conceived for her?

Throughout this period she was fortified by intense religious feelings. A long entry in her diary on New Year's Day gives us an invaluable glimpse into her mind. Her strong emotions are suffused with piety. She seems to be recovering from the shock of her father's death. She is looking outward to other people and is full of hope for the future.

> "Jan 1 1871 This New Year came in with, to me, an over-whelming sense of awe and responsibility. We sat round the table, for we had been playing cards, and a few minutes before twelve we joined hands and made the resolution never to be angry. Then out rang the bells and we all kissed each other and felt love grow and arise in our hearts. God keep it there and multiply it till it extends in <u>all</u> our hearts and <u>all</u> the world.
>
> The last year has been a lifetime. I feel it has borne fruit in many ways. Auntey is still cold, cold as ice to me; but the love of old Nurse grows and grows, and I value it. Miss Hill, too, has become my friend, and we have been introduced to many nice people – the Broughtons, Naftals, Lewes's (G. Eliot), Hills, Radleys, Godwins (George MacDonald's sister and her Husband) and to many others.
>
> I begin this year with [?] and with rejoicings for all God's great goodness and love to me during the past year. He has taught me very much, and led me so gently and tenderly; opened my heart, enlarged my capabilities, and made me know both in head and heart that He wills what is best for me.
>
> What is his will for me this year. Work, health, great and renewed love and respect for Alice; success in my work, travel and enlargement of idea, and may, might I add Love: God please grant Yetta these, if good for her."

Henrietta was always very intense and emotional and expressed her feelings not only to her diary but also to other people and in public. The Victorians were openly emotional to the extent of sentimentality. Perhaps the horrors of the First World War resulted in the English "stiff upper lip", and emotionalism has only broken through again with the growth of counselling and public displays of grief.

Despite this seriousness, Henrietta and her sister Alice seem to have had a full social life. Marion Paterson commented: "Hard as the work was, and long the hours, her diaries show that neither the home, nor their social life, were neglected. Nor were admirers absent. 'Bother the men, why can't they let me do my work,'"[24] Henrietta wrote in her diary. The two attractive young women in Westbourne Terrace probably had many invitations to dinners and parties. Her lifelong friend Walter Webb records that in 1870 Henrietta came to a picnic which he gave in Burnham Beeches, and in the following winter a friend who lived in Guernsey invited Henrietta to stay and Walter Webb and a man friend were fellow-guests. The four young people made many excursions, and went to call on Victor Hugo. Walter Webb was a frequent visitor at Westbourne Terrace, and Henrietta gave him *Carlyle's Sartor Resartus* and his *Heroes*: "These were the high class books she enjoyed." He later wrote "Her character and demeanour were of the highest order and much impressed me." Possibly he was one of her suitors.

Henrietta and Alice, with only Auntey to supervise them, must have been regarded as independent and "advanced" by their contemporaries. During 1870 they were very concerned with the Franco-German War, and offered their services as nurses, but they were not accepted because of their youth. Henrietta was determined to make some contribution to the Germans: "War ringing in my ears, and wringing my heart. I have decided to sell my ring for the Prussians … the ring is sold." This enthusiasm for the Germans is not surprising. The two young women were remembering their mother and perhaps thinking of their German relatives.

Writing in her diary in February 1872, she was more optimistic, though still very religious.

> "I am rather late in writing about this last year, but I have been much engaged and not at all inclined to do so. Spent the last hour of the old year alone in my little garret room at Hampton (her Uncle Fritz's home) and there begged God to bless me and keep me pure and good, but my temptations are many and strong.
>
> There have been blessings in this past year. First we spent a delightful month in Guernsey; then Auntey fell ill, but she pulled through and it seemed to make her more loveable to us. Then my darling decided to be a doctor. At first it was a very great disappointment to me for her to give up her painting, but soon it appeared to me to be a more real work to be a doctor. I fear though she has no steadfastness of purpose, or why should she change her work in life so often?
>
> My work went on as usual, full of life and pleasure. In April I took Circus Street to work it on Octavia Hill's plan. I felt it a great responsibility, but there is much pleasure in it.
>
> I then got to know Mr Barnett
>
> Later I was ill and had to ask S.A.B. to do my work for me
>
> Thank God most heartily for His past mercies and pray He will give me reason to guide me."[25]

Although Henrietta was four years younger than her sister she was evidently very confident in her own judgement and perhaps tried to dissuade her sister from studying medicine. However Alice persisted, qualified as a doctor, and married Dr Ernest Hart.

In her diary Henrietta made a very brief mention of her meeting with Samuel Barnett. As the curate of St Mary's, he had been drawn into Octavia's circle and it was through this connection that Henrietta and Samuel met. We know from her biography *Canon Barnett* that they first met on 3rd December 1870, Octavia Hill's birthday. Henrietta had arrived early to help Octavia dress her hair. Poor people and social workers came to the party. The Miss Harrisons sang a duet, everyone joining in with the chorus of "Quack, Quack" to put them at ease, and then the parishioners and social workers sat down together to a simple meal. Henrietta found herself sitting next to the curate, Samuel. He saw this girl of 19, a "'child' with brown curls down her back, handsome furs, and a Tyrolese hat," and he wondered what she could be doing among the social workers and the rough tenants.[26]

It seems Samuel fell in love with her at that first meeting, and throughout 1871 he wrote letters to her on parish affairs, long and detailed letters showing a passion for social and religious matters. In February 1872 he wrote to ask her to marry him. She was very surprised, for she had thought their correspondence was simply about parish matters and had not realised that it was really inspired by his love for her:

> "He looked so very much older than his age – twenty seven – that I had accepted his interest as that of a kindly elderly gentleman, with small sensitive hands, a bald head, and shaggy beard. Indeed both in appearance and manner, he was far removed from a girlish idea of a lover … He dressed very badly, generally obtaining his clothes by employing out-of-work tailors in the district. He always wore a tall silk hat which, as he purchased it by post, never fitted, and so was rammed on at the back of his head. His umbrella was a byword, and he always bought his black cotton gloves two or three sizes too large."[27]

Samuel's unprepossessing appearance was remarked on by (then Potter): "Mr Barnett, a queer ugly little man with no attraction of body or manner, but with a certain power."[28] In *My Apprenticeship* she described him as having:

> "A diminutive body clothed in shabby and badly assorted garments, big knobby and prematurely bald head, small black eyes set close together, sallow complexion and, a thin and patchy pretence of a beard, Barnett, at first sight, was not pleasing to contemplate. Yet, with growing intimacy you found yourself continuously looking at him, watching the swift changes of expression, detached but keen observation of the persons present, followed by a warmly appreciative smile at something said … an utter absence of personal vanity, an almost exaggerated Christian humility, arising perhaps from what the modern psychologist calls a permanent 'inferiority complex' – an attitude especially marked towards his adored and gifted wife!
> What charmed his comrades at work in the East End, and I speak from personal experience, was Barnett's fathomless sympathy; his 'quickness at the uptake' of your moral and intellectual perplexities; his inspiring encouragement for your strivings after the nobler self."[29]

It is surprising that Samuel had the courage to propose to her. Such a beautiful girl, with her small trim figure and pretty face, and she was better off than he could ever hope to be as a parson. It is surprising that Henrietta did not turn him down, young and attractive as she was. She asked him to give her six months to reflect on his proposal. She could not make up her mind and became increasingly anxious about the decision. In May she went to stay at a school in Boppart in the Rhine Valley, a retreat to seek the peace she felt she needed to make up her mind. Samuel continued to write her long letters, sharing his spiritual thoughts with her and keeping her in touch with the parish problems. The letters increased the pressure on her to share in his life's work: she was far away, but still in close contact. She felt torn between her work and the offer of marriage:

> "I went to a school at Boppart, where among the quiet valleys to fight the devil, and try to see what was right. My work pulled me one way, the knowledge that God had bade me save some of my poor sisters; and yet my heart honoured Mr Barnett above all men. At last one fine day on the Rhine, God spoke and bade me love him and my heart obeyed."[30]

This period of retreat was curtailed when she had a letter from her sister on 18th June saying that she was soon going to marry her fiancé, Ernest Hart, and asking her to come to the wedding. Henrietta was back home on 24th June, having spent only a month away in Germany. The day after Henrietta arrived home, "Mr Barnett and I plighted our troth, for I had realised his gift of love was too holy to refuse."[31]

To celebrate their engagement, the couple spent a day on the river at Cookham. But on the very next morning Samuel went off with his brother for a holiday in Switzerland. Henrietta was undoubtedly hurt by this but excused it by refering to "his perfect self-control" and respect for plans. He wrote to her almost daily, but when his brother, Frank, suggested curtailing their holiday, Samuel refused to change their plans!

Henrietta was only 21 when she consented to marriage. It is clear that in her busy social life she met many other young men who must have been more attractive. She was anxious and perplexed about the decision, but seems to have made up her mind suddenly, perhaps influenced by the news of her sister's marriage. It must be remembered that she had lost her father only three years previously, and now she was going to lose the sister who had been living with her, and perhaps she feared loneliness. Samuel seemed to her to be a great deal older than herself, and he offered stability and secure affection. She did not find him physically attractive, but she was very immature and ignorant in all sexual matters and probably did not understand the importance of the physical side of marriage. The most positive aspect of their relationship was that they were both on the same wave-length in thought and spirit. Henrietta was living in a state of intense religious feeling and in Samuel she found a fellow-spirit. They both believed that their social work was an important expression of Christian love and Samuel would allow Henrietta to continue with the social work which had become so important to her. She must have seen beyond his unattractive appearance the deep power of his magnetic personality, his humility, his great gift for sympathy and understanding and encouragement of others. He would not fetter her with the "ties and obedience" of conventional marriage: their marriage was to be a partnership. Most husbands expected their wives to give up voluntary work and apply themselves to house management and the children, but Samuel promised he would encourage her work and he would share his work with her. Samuel respected women and had views far in advance of his contemporaries, and in 1894 wrote: "The State should repeal all laws and abolish all customs which tempt men to lord it over women, or which interfere with the complete development of women's nature." In reply to a question whether the legal and clerical professions should be thrown open to women, the Canon said:

> "I would abolish all laws which prevent women developing themselves as they choose. I do not think St Paul's prohibition of women speaking in the churches was intended to be of perpetual obligation.
> I am in favour of the removal of legal restrictions on the occupation and voting powers of women. They should have the same liberty as men to follow any calling and to vote at any election. Their present position of subordination develops the more brutal and selfish instincts of men, and at the same time provokes women to do acts and make claims which are unwomanly."

She had found a man who would encourage her in her social work and give her secure and lasting love.

Before they could get married, it was essential for Samuel to find a living. A real proof of the partnership nature of their marriage was that they decided together where Samuel should work. In the autumn of 1872 he was offered a living near Oxford which their families hoped they would accept, especially as they both had health problems which might be eased by country air. Samuel had "frequent attacks of unaccountable fatigue" and Henrietta had unexpected bouts of ill health, which, as she grew older, became "severe and prolonged periods of nerve failure, and many attacks of pneumonia".[32] But despite their poor health the Barnetts had set their hearts on finding a living in the East End in order to carry on with their social work, so they turned down the country living and Octavia Hill used her influence to get the Bishop of London to find a living. He offered Samuel the parish of St Jude's in Whitechapel, although he warned "it is the worst parish in my diocese, inhabited mainly by a criminal population, and one which has, I fear, been much corrupted by doles."[33]

They went to look at the St Jude's vicarage which they found uninhabited and dilapidated, and in the area around "the people were dirty and bedraggled, the children neglected, the streets littered and ill-kept, the beer-shops full, the schools shut up". Despite all this they decided together to take on the task.

On 28th January 1873 Henrietta and Samuel were married at St Mary's, in the parish where they had worked and met. The wedding was very simple, for despite her family's wishes, Henrietta insisted there should be no bridesmaids, jewels or bridal bouquet. Henrietta wore a white silk or satin dress with a long lace veil. The church was full with many of the poor parishioners as well as all the parish social workers. The wedding breakfast was held at the house of her sister Alice – now Mrs Ernest Hart. They left for a five-week honeymoon in southern England. They spent much time visiting cathedrals – Winchester, Salisbury and Exeter. They had hoped to go riding, but the weather was very cold so they spent much time indoors with Samuel reading aloud Maurice's lectures on the *Epistles*, Lecky's *History of Rationalism* and "stiff treatises on Political Economy". Though Henrietta evidently found the economics heavy, she would have enjoyed the Lecky, which was a very broad-ranging book and challenging to authority. The last week of their holiday was spent at Clifton with Samuel's parents, then on 6th March 1873 they returned to London to take up the work at St Jude's. In her diary Henrietta wrote of their honeymoon "the happiest and most beautiful five weeks of my life".

Henrietta's German Connections

Although Henrietta never knew her mother, her brothers and sisters must have had many memories and spoken of her. Henrietta and Alice wanted to serve as nurses on the German side during the Franco-Prussian War, and when Henrietta wanted a retreat to reflect on Samuel's offer of marriage she went to the school at Boppart. Perhaps her German relatives recommended this school? Perhaps Henrietta made other visits to Germany? We do not know because she tells us nothing about her German relatives, although she tells us a great deal else about herself in her biography of her husband. It is also surprising that Marion Paterson in her *Quasi-Autobiography* does not even mention that Henrietta's mother was German. She must have supressed this information because she was the ever faithful companion and knew Henrietta did not want to publicise her German origins.

This reticence may be explained by the fact that Marion Paterson was assembling her life of Henrietta just before or during the Second World War. Also Henrietta wrote *Canon Barnett, His Life, Work and Friends* during the First World War, when anti-German feelings were even more strong. War is particularly painful to people with relatives on the other side. Whereas other active and intelligent women threw themselves into war work, Henrietta occupied herself with writing the lengthy biography of her husband.

1870s

Chapter 3

St Jude's and Whitechapel

The idea of living in the East End to help the poor was not new. General William Booth began his Salvation Army meetings in a tent on the Mile End Waste in 1865 and the Salvation Army has worked with the very poor ever since that time. In 1863, John Richard Green, a young clergyman inspired by Carlyle, took on a derelict parish in Hoxton. Ill health forced him to leave but the next year he returned to the East End and was a mission curate in Stepney until 1869. He is famous as the first social historian. Edward Denison settled in lodgings on the Mile End Road in 1867: he built a school, taught working men and became a radical MP. In 1868 Ruskin summoned Denison, J R Green and the Reverend Brooke Lambert to his house in Denmark Hill, where they discussed the idea of organising settlements of middle-class men who would live in the slums. However these three young men became too ill to carry on with their work. Green contracted tuberculosis, Denison's health was ruined and he died in 1870. Lambert also was very ill by 1870, though he later recovered sufficiently to continue with his East End parish, St Marks Whitechapel. Social workers in the East End needed courage to live with the dirt, pollution and vermin, with crime and degradation. It is not surprising that the Barnetts' friends were worried about them going to Whitechapel and urged them to take the parish offered them in Oxford.

When Samuel started work at St Jude's, the newly-wedded couple could not live in the Vicarage, for the previous vicar had been ill and had left the house in very bad repair. For the first few months they lived in dingy, insanitary lodgings in Eldon Street, Finsbury. The lodgings were squalid and the landlady careless. One Sunday evening when Samuel came home tired it was found that a mouse had drowned in the rice pudding – his favourite supper dish. They must have been happy when the Vicarage was made habitable, and they moved there in May 1873. Auntey had gone to live with her brother, Harry Rowland, probably to Henrietta's relief. Nurse and Fanny came to live at the Vicarage, for Samuel agreed that they should undertake the care of Fanny. Indeed Henrietta took responsibility for Fanny for the rest of her life, with Nurse acting as her carer.

Though Henrietta and Samuel had seen the Vicarage and the parish before their marriage, they must have been dismayed by all they found as they came to know it better:

"The whole parish was covered with a network of courts and alleys. None of these courts had roads. In some the houses were three storeys high and hardly six feet apart, the sanitary accomodation being pits in the cellars: in other courts the houses were lower, wooden and dilapidated, a standpipe at the end providing the only water. Each chamber was the home of a family who sometimes owned their indescribable furniture, but in most cases the rooms were

31

Plate 5
St Jude's Church
and Vicarage,
Whitechapel, 1873,
when the Barnetts
started their work.
They lived in the
Vicarage until 1892
when they moved to
Toynbee Hall.

let for eightpence a night, a bad system which lent itself to every form of evil. In many instances broken windows had been repaired with paper and rags, the banisters had been used for firewood, and the paper hung from the walls which were the residence of countless vermin."[34]

The men living in the area worked in the docks, in casual employment with no reliable wage, or they were unemployed and trying to cadge a living by hawking, begging and stealing. Together with the dilapidated church and vicarage the whole scene was enough to dismay the most stout-hearted social reformer.

Samuel and Henrietta plunged into the work and at the end of the first year, in March 1874, it was possible to report that

"The congregation had risen to about thirty in the mornings, and fifty to one hundred in the evenings; that a children's service has been started, and that a mixed choir is under training; that the schools have been opened for boys and girls together, of whom 142 are on the register; that adult classes have been started in French, German, Latin, arithmetic, composition, and drawing, which have attracted fifty students; that a mothers' meeting has been begun, a nurse and a mission-woman engaged, a girls' night school carried on, a maternity society

Plates 6 & 7
Henrietta and
Samuel at the time of
their marriage, 1873

initiated, a penny bank opened, a lending library organised, a pension scheme inaugurated, a flower show held, concerts and entertainments given, oratorios rendered in Church, lady visitors set to work, and last, but not least, a system of relief for the poor thought out and established." [35]

This was an amazing achievement in one year, particularly as much of what they were creating was innovatory. A primary school with mixed sexes was unusual at the time. Languages and art were accomplishments of the middle-class, and working-class people were not expected to enjoy flower-shows, concerts and oratorios. The Barnetts were already initiating plans which were to come to fruition in Toynbee Hall. It is difficult to disentangle the separate contributions of Henrietta and of Samuel, for they discussed everything and supported each other. However Henrietta organised the women and girls, the flower-show, and probably the music and entertainments and played at least an equal role in organising the school. Henrietta did not like organising boys, but fortunately Samuel enjoyed this: "to boys Canon Barnett was ever a willing host. Indeed his relation with boys was one I could never fathom. Personally I dislike them, their noise, greed, restlessness and want of manners; but he went below all these objectionable traits and was at once their respected comrade." [36]

They were only able to initiate so many schemes in the parish because they were able to attract helpers and draw people together into a community. When Samuel was asked how they kept their workers together he answered: "Hospitality … St Jude's and Toynbee Hall and the Exhibition are all built on my wife's tea-table." [37] At first they invited people into the Vicarage drawing room, and soon they had larger parties in the schoolroom. Henrietta particularly enjoyed their evening conversaziones. There were light refreshments – tea, coffee, bread and butter and cake. The parish workers talked with members of the congregation and local people who were drawn in to attend the classes and clubs. Sometimes there were entertainments, such as singing some Gilbert and Sullivan, but the Barnetts preferred people to talk so that the rich would get to know the poor. Unfortunately conversation was somewhat stilted, but Henrietta persisted in trying to mix the social classes. It must have been a relief when at 9.45 the Vicar announced: "We are going to dance 'Sir Roger de Coverley', and Mrs Bullwinkle and I will lead off the young people."[38]

Poor Relief

Poor relief was one of the Barnetts' first concerns, for parishioners had been in the habit of coming to St Jude's in the expectation of getting handouts of money or tickets for groceries and fuel. A West End parish donated £500 annually to St Jude's and this had been distributed unsystematically to people who asked for it.[39] Trained by Octavia Hill in the rigorous principles of the Charity Organisation Society, the Barnetts refused to give handouts and instead told people to apply to the Friday evening committee meeting of the COS – both Henrietta and Samuel were on the committee. Here case histories were taken and the old and ill were "thoroughly" relieved, but the unemployed were given short shrift, though helped to find work if possible. Not surprisingly the casual workers and

Plate 8
The drawing room of St Jude's Vicarage where rich and poor were invited to take tea and converse together. Simple furniture, but a de Morgan vase stands on the table, probably a gift from the potter.

unemployed hated this new system, and sometimes when relief was refused an angry crowd assembled outside the Vicarage, banging on the door, pelting the windows and sometimes breaking them.

Housing

At one time the Barnetts thought of living in one of the slum dwellings to experience life as their parishioners lived it, but dropped the idea when they realised that their lifestyle would still be different as they would have the option to leave. However they had an intimate knowledge of housing conditions gained from visiting their parishioners and were determined to try to initiate change. They wanted to apply the methods they had learnt from Octavia Hill to the problems of Whitechapel.

Many of the houses surrounding St Jude's had been condemned by the Medical Officer of Health, but the Metropolitan Board of Works did not demolish the houses and people continued to crowd in to them. Efforts had been made to provide housing for the poor, first by Miss Burdett-Coutts in Bethnal Green and from 1862 by the Peabody Trust, which built blocks of flats, but as the Peabody Trust required tenants to produce references from employers, the really poor – casual labourers, pensioners and the unemployed – had no chance of finding a new home. The fundamental problem was that the costs of the land and of new building were too high to make it possible to build new housing to let at really low rents – "affordable housing" as we call it now. In 1875 the Whitechapel Guardians sent a petition to Parliament, probably instigated by Samuel.[40] In the following years Samuel put great effort into the housing problem: meeting, lobbying and letter-writing; using their growing number of influential friends and his position as president of the Whitechapel Liberal Party. Octavia Hill was ever ready to help and give advice, and brought in her lawyer friend, Edward Bond, to help with the acquisition of condemned buildings.

Meanwhile Henrietta took practical steps to advance in a small way. She combined with Edward Bond to buy three slum houses which were occupied by prostitutes. The prostitutes were turned out, the houses were improved and let to respectable families. Henrietta had difficulty finding her half-share of the money (although it could not have been much), for since her marriage her capital had been tied up in a trust as required under the Married Women's Property Act of 1882 – so she sold her jewels to make the purchase.[41]

Philanthropists were persuaded to take an interest and provide finance to replace the slums. In 1876 a friend of the Barnetts and of Octavia Hill, Mr A G Crowder, built a tenement block providing a room for each family at 2/6d per week. By 1879 a thousand people were living in property bought by philanthropists, with lady rent-collectors supervising the inhabitants. They aimed to clear out the brothels as well as provide better housing for the poor. In 1883 there was a meeting at the Vicarage between A G Crowder, Alfred Hoare and other philanthropists and they formed the East End Dwellings Company. They tried to provide housing for the very poor, building flats with minimal space. For instance Katherine Buildings (named after the nearby dock) was five floors high, had 281 rooms and about 600 tenants; there was no running water in the rooms, and only 18 closets in common use. Katherine Potter was the lady rent collector, and when she married, her sister Beatrice (Webb) took over the task. Beatrice was critical of Crowder: he was a "cut and dried philanthropist, with little human nature, determined that tenants should like nothing but what was useful." He wanted to paint and finish all rooms alike, in a red colour reminiscent of a butcher's shop, despite Beatrice and Katherine suggesting that tenants did have individual taste.[42]

The housing reforms were attracting attention and Princess Alice of Hesse on a visit to England was brought by Octavia Hill to see Whitechapel housing. Samuel showed her round and as she came incognito he was able to take her everywhere – into the slum property as well as the new tenements.[43]

The Home Secretary, Sir Richard Cross, also came to visit, and promised to legislate to get the authorities to clear condemned properties. By the late 1880s large areas had been cleared and many new blocks of low-rent flats built. In later years Henrietta came to hate these tenement buildings, but at the time they seemed to be the only way of providing low cost housing. A similar policy was followed in the 1960s to solve the housing crisis, followed by a rejection, even hatred of the tower blocks.

Besides better housing, the Barnetts wanted to provide open space and leisure facilities. They helped to acquire land for two playgrounds which were opened within a short distance of St Jude's. They asked the People's Entertainment Society to provide a band for the playground on Thursday evenings during the summer. However the people of Whitechapel had their own ideas about what to do when they heard music: "a crowd of the abandoned girls of the neighbourhood with their 'chaps' came in, pushed the children aside, and rushed into lawless dancing. A Bacchanalian scene ensued. We tried talking, Mr Barnett to the lads, I to the girls, but excited evil was in the ascendancy and they would not desist. So the band was stopped, the playground cleared, the gate locked … "

The crowd hooted and howled and threw stones at them on their way home. Henrietta commented that the stone-throwers' aim was bad, which seems to suggest that they did not want to harm the Barnetts, but only express their distress at having one of their rare bits of joy cut short.[44] The conflict arose because the Barnetts, like Octavia Hill, wanted to impose their ideas of culture and fruitful leisure on working-class people who had their own rough, vibrant culture.

Schools

At the time when the Barnetts moved into Whitechapel, state education was only just beginning. Before 1870, elementary schooling was provided by the two religious groups: the Church of England Society for Promoting the Education of the Poor and the nonconformist British and Foreign Schools Society. These two societies had received small state grants since 1833. In addition there were numerous dame schools, usually run by a working-class woman who would teach children in her own home for a few pence a week. The 1870 Education Act gave localities the right to elect local school boards, levy a local rate and open schools wherever the provision made by the voluntary societies was inadequate. But attendance was not made compulsory until 1880, and even then fees had to be paid, though poor children could get exemption, and it was only in 1891 that primary schooling was made free as well as compulsory.

One of the Barnetts' first actions when they moved into St Jude's in 1873 was to open the derelict school behind the Vicarage. The building was small, cramped and had a horrible smell, but it was gradually transformed. "We began with soap, towels, and a looking-glass (unheard-of luxury) for the cloakroom; bunches of flowers were distributed to all the children through the summer months, and by degrees all sorts of nice things were added."[45] The boys and girls were taught together so that the girls would have an equal education and the boys would become more gentle. However this idea had to be abandoned after a year because the boys were too rough. Samuel and Henrietta wanted to give the children a much wider and more cultural education than was provided by the standard curriculum. In 1876 they decorated the schoolrooms with a dado of Walter Crane's coloured illustrations to Aesop's Fables. Walter Crane became a friend and they founded an Art for Schools Association in order to provide decorations for the nation's schoolrooms, which were usually bare apart from the occasional map. Another innovation in St Jude's school was the teaching of clay modelling and carpentry for two afternoons a week, but this was censured by the inspector and they were refused a grant because technical education was not in the narrow Code (the National Curriculum of the 1880s). Volunteers were found to teach geography, physiology, French, history and literature. School excursions were

Plate 9
'A court in Whitechapel and some of its children inhabitants'. Henrietta's title for this photograph. She recognised the power of the image and used slides to move her audiences and photographs to show to patrons.

started, and later, perhaps following pressure from the Barnetts, John Gorst when Minister of education made excursions count as part of the school day.

Outside school hours, volunteers ran play classes from 5 to 7 in the evening providing care for children who came from cramped homes. Afternoon classes were started to continue the education of the girls over 13, for, though most children left school when they were younger, tradesmen and skilled workers could afford to keep their children longer at school.

Samuel Barnett thought it essential to arouse the interest of parents and get their cooperation. They were invited to see the children's work at the end of term and to meet the school managers. In 1888 the parents were invited to elect two school managers, and even to make a very important decision about fees:

> "The cost of such schools as ours is large, and this year the repair of the drains amounted to over £50. It occurred to us that it might be well if we took the parents into counsel as to the amount of fee which should be charged. A conference of fathers was summoned, and it was pleasant to hear the approval expressed of our methods. After a long talk it was agreed that every parent should be left to fix the fee he thought he ought to pay. Papers were sent round, and four assessed themselves at 6d., fourteen at 4d., and forty at 3d. a week, instead of the old 2d. fee. If this plan be persistently pursued, it may be that the deficiency of income will be met."[46]

In many ways the Barnetts' innovations at St Jude's school were a century ahead of their time. Both Henrietta and Samuel became managers of other local schools. Samuel was involved in the politics of education in the East End, went on to found the Education

Reform League in 1884 and became an educational thinker of national importance. Henrietta helped, and perhaps led, in forming their ideas about a wider curriculum, in finding volunteers and in applying their ideas to St Jude's school.

Marion Paterson

Marion Paterson was just nineteen years old when she came to work for Henrietta and she remained her secretary and close companion all her life. Marion was born in 1858, one of seven children of an affluent middle-class family living in Birmingham. They lived in "a comfortable, middle-class, ten-roomed house with domestic servants' quarters, conservatory, carriage house and generous kitchen facilities". This was very much the same trade background from which Henrietta came, although Marion's father was employed as representative of Canon Iron Foundries whereas Mr Rowland owned his business.

In 1876 Marion must have been visiting London, possibly staying with a relative, when she went to the Marylebone church where the Reverend Haweis was vicar. Samuel Barnett came to talk to the congregation and on hearing him, Marion was inspired. She wrote to a friend:

> "It was so nice at Mr Haweis's this morning. He brought in a clergyman from the East End who talked to us about all the poor sinners in the wretched courts and alleys of his parish, for he says they are more sinners than sufferers and want our friendship more than our money. I want to go and be their friend: I know they are drunkards and a worse class of people than I have ever seen, but I would try so hard to help them if only Papa and Mamma will let me … I feel I must go to them. I know it will be hard work and most likely seem a failure and their lives will seem so dreadful to mix with, still I feel I can and ought to do it."[47]

Marion went to a service at St Jude's to volunteer her help. Henrietta met her in the vestry and saw a girl "whose childish face and violet eyes spoke of innocency. 'How foolish of Mr Haweis to send such a baby as this to Whitechapel' was my thought; 'I can't let those eyes see evil'". But Henrietta could always find work for people and she set Marion to tidy the clothes cupboard.[48]

At first Henrietta felt much older and wiser than her young helper: even in 1883, Henrietta addressed her as "Dear Childie".[49] In fact Marion was only seven years younger and must have quickly gained experience and knowledge of the East End. Henrietta wrote of Marion in glowing terms: "A life of service that has lasted from 1876 even to this day; a contribution to moral forces that has uplifted ideals; an offering of sympathy to the hidden depths of all and sundry; a self-surrender that was so complete in its unconsciousness as often to be unrecognised; and a gift of devotion to us both that 'passeth understanding'".[50]

This fulsome tribute tells us nothing at all about what Marion did. In fact she became Henrietta's personal assistant, companion and dogsbody. The task grew more onerous as Henrietta engaged in more and more public work: when she was appealing for support for the aquisition of Hampstead Heath Extension, Marion helped her to send 13,000 letters![51] But she was much more than a secretary. She helped Henrietta in the worst of tasks, such as cleansing the rough girls of vermin.[52] When Henrietta's ward, Dorothy, was ill, Marion helped to nurse her[53] and during Samuel's last years Marion was always at his service.[54] She went with them on holiday both in England and abroad, to Egypt, to Italy and round the world. At the close of Worship Hour, Henrietta and Marion gave flowers to people who wanted them as they left the church.[55] Marion accompanied Henrietta at her public appearances, a meek little shadow as she was described later by a Hampstead Garden Suburb resident[56]. In photographs of Henrietta at special events in the Suburb, Marion is usually included in the line-up.

Henrietta had complete trust in Marion. In 1933 Henrietta wrote: "Marion takes entire control of all my spending, & a great deal of the incidents (with Mr Baily) of my investing".[57]

At first Marion was living with the Barnetts in the Vicarage but it seems that in the 1890s she was living in the East End independently of the Barnetts, for she is mentioned as having one of the nine 'normal homes near Toynbee Hall'.[58] It seems likely that she would have left the Barnett household when they moved in to Toynbee Hall and possibly she was sharing with Ella Pycroft, a senior rent-collector who lived in one of the new buildings. Henrietta did not usually acknowledge the contribution made by Marion to the effective administration of her many projects. Perhaps this was due to the fact that she was employed. In 1936 at the time of Henrietta's death it appears that she was paid £25 per month and so it seems likely that she was paid from the start of her service in 1876.

Marion was a pretty, petite woman, and letters which she cherished and stored reveal some emotional involvements. Before coming to Whitechapel she seems to have had an admirer named Rudolf who lived in Hampstead, but after he moved away to teach in his father's school he seems to have disappeared from the scene. Meanwhile Cousin Nellie Cunningham, who lived in Totteridge, was writing love-letters to her before she moved to Whitechapel and continued to do so up to 1890. This clearly seems to be some sort of lesbian relationship.[59]

Marion's devoted service may arouse suspicions that she had a lesbian relationship with Henrietta, but there is no evidence of anything of the sort. Of course it is possible that Marion's remarkable self-abnegation in serving Henrietta may be partly accounted for by lesbian feelings which Henrietta exploited. But this is mere speculation, and the devoted lady companion-cum-secretary was a familiar figure at the time. Moreover Marion was devoted to Samuel too. In any case, when we imagine Henrietta engaged in her many good works, we must also imagine Marion accompanying her, into the wretched slum housing, moralising with girls and fallen women, organising picture shows and concerts, and writing innumerable letters to elicit support. After the death of Henrietta, Marion dealt with her numerous bequests and with the funeral arrangements. Marion wrote of her profound grief to one of Samuel's nephews: "I look back on 59 years of unbroken, unblemished friendship and I realise afresh as I have so often done before how much I owe to them both. What would my life have been without them? … I feel scarcely able to bear it. No one but myself can know what it is to me."[60]

It is so sad that when she tried to write a biography of Henrietta, age overtook her and she only produced a fragmentary account.

Chapter 4

Henrietta's Work for Women and Children

Henrietta and Samuel worked closely together in organising charity in the parish, in making a success of St Jude's elementary school and trying to improve the housing. But they were also developing in separate spheres. For instance Samuel was very interested in politics and became chairman of the local Liberal Party, while Henrietta always kept out of politics and focused her attention on the welfare of working class children, girls and young women, taking this interest beyond the parish boundaries and eventually to the national level. Samuel encouraged her in developing this work of her own, and there is no doubt that she did this work independently.

Whitechapel Girls

Victorian children are often depicted as strictly disciplined and well behaved. This was true of some children of the middle class and of the industrious working class, but the children of the casual labourers, unemployed, beggars and criminals who abounded in Whitechapel were sometimes rough, dirty, wild and uncontrolled. In 1888, when Margaret McMillan tried to provide music classes for factory girls in the East End she had to admit defeat: "They were terrible lessons: shouts, laughter, cat-calls. My hat was never on my own head, and my coat was often missing when I wanted it. Squirts of water reached me and worse things."[61] Henrietta taught poor children at a night school and must have suffered the same challenges and indignities.

When she started to work in the parish of St Jude's and got to know the people, their homes and the life of the streets, there is no doubt she was deeply shocked by the sexual behaviour of the underclass, particularly of the women and girls. She was greatly moved by the poverty, squalor and cultural deprivation, but her greatest concern was with the moral degradation. To try to empathise with her, one must consider the contemporary situation. Girls of the middle class and respectable working class were protected from having sex before marriage, and only allowed to spend time alone with a young man if they were engaged. They did not know what sex was, but they did know that it meant babies and that an illegitimate child was the worst social disgrace. Whitechapel girls of the under class did not abide by the same mores. In the absence of strong discipline or any effective birth control many of the Whitechapel girls must have become pregnant when still single. Most must have been saved from further difficulty by marrying their young man. Others were kept by their own families, sometimes the girl's mother pretending that she herself had another baby. But if a single mother had no family support, her fate could be almost "worse than death". Back-street abortion might fail or even kill mother and baby. Infanticide was a way out for the desperate and baby farmers would oblige for a small sum by starving and drugging baby into a quick death. The single mother might place the child in an orphanage or for adoption, but a better choice was the workhouse from where she would hope to reclaim her child when times got better for her. She might somehow find enough money to rent a room in a lodging house by applying for charity, begging and doing odd jobs. Prostitution was the easiest way of surviving and keeping the baby.

Family life in the underclass was extremely stressful, whole families very often living in one room. Social workers knew that incest was not infrequent and factory girls used to jokingly enquire from their mates whether it was the father's or the brother's. Drunkenness was a scourge and on Saturday nights it was common to see drunken men beating their wives in the street. Because of the cramped accommodation much time was spent on the streets, as it is today in developing countries. Among the crowds of labourers and housewives, hawkers and beggars, prostitutes were very much in evidence.

It was when Henrietta was helping Miss Carrie at the school in Dover that she first saved two girls at risk by taking them out of their bad homes. Once settled in St Jude's Vicarage, Henrietta devoted herself to helping young girls, and particularly the girls who were in danger of falling into prostitution. She had a horror of prostitution and saw it all around her in Whitechapel. Police returns showed that there were 8600 prostitutes in the Metropolis and of these 1,803 were within the Spitalfields – Houndsditch – Whitechapel – Ratcliff area, far more than in any other district of London.[62] Moreover, these women would be the most wretched of "fallen women", living in squalor, able to charge very little but paying a high rent for a room in a lodging-house.

Sometimes Henrietta tried to "save" a particular woman but usually she left this work to others. Henrietta's aim was to prevent prostitution by positive action to keep girls off the streets. To Henrietta, as well as the other women who were doing social work with girls, it seemed that the only solution was to separate the girls from their "evil environment" by finding them a place in service. No other job would provide accomodation and food. It was not possible to place these rough, untrained girls in middle-class households, but "respectable" working-class housewives could be found who would mother them and train them as maids. This policy of finding girls in need of protection and placing them in domestic service was being carried out by many charitable groups, Dr Barnardo's for instance.

In 1876 the Metropolitan Association for Befriending Young Servants (MABYS) was founded by Mrs Nassau Senior, who was an inspector of education in workhouse schools. She had found that when workhouse girls were placed in service they were often in unsuitable homes, but if they left their jobs they had nowhere to go and so could easily take to prostitution. "This Association was formed by persons who were much impressed by the difficulties and dangers which beset friendless girls in London, when thrown upon the world at an early age without adequate guidance and protection."[63] The society was better organised and provided more after-care than charities had previously offered. This was in accord with the developments taking place in social work at the time. MABYS recruited volunteer lady visitors to select suitable households where the girls could work as maids, and then continue to pay visits to them to monitor their progress. The association also opened several homes to train girls and accommodate them if they were out of a job.[64] In 1877 Henrietta began placing girls at risk in service and was helped by Marion Paterson and Pauline Townsend, and soon a group of women gathered to join in the work of placing and guiding the girls. In the first year 192 girls were placed out. In 1878 they formed the Whitechapel branch of the Metropolitan Association for Befriending Young Servants, with their office at 28 Commercial Road and Pauline Townsend as their secretary.[65] The main object was to deal with local girls but they also found places in service for some of the workhouse girls.

After-care was very well organised. Two ladies befriended each year's group of girls so that they could keep in personal touch and get to know them well as they grew up. Henrietta also organised a social club to entertain and educate the MABYS girls: many meetings were arranged in the schoolroom behind the Vicarage, there were parties and days in the country and each year a united service in the church. A circular letter was sent to all, dealing with such improving subjects as confirmation, saving and purity. By 1889 they had placed 2,350 girls.

Dealing with these girls and their problems was very hard work. Once a girl had been persuaded to make a move from her own home, she would have to be cleaned up and re-clothed before she could be acceptable in a respectable working-class family. It was essential to comb the vermin from her hair and give her a good bath, a duty which Henrietta and Marion Paterson personally undertook.[66] The girls were lent the money to buy new clothes in the expectation that it would gradually be paid back from their wages. However, despite the preparations, some of the girls were so rough and undisciplined that they turned on the housewives who employed them. One girl threw the baby at its mother, another attacked her mistress with a knife, Clara Madge tried to set fire to the house, and all the girls used bad language. No wonder that some of them had to be moved to many new situations. Sometimes mothers brought their daughters to Henrietta and asked her to place them away from the harmful influences of the area. Once a girl who was living with her mother in a brothel came to her very frightened when she realised what was expected of her; Henrietta gave her shelter for the night and early the next morning Samuel took her to a place of safety in the country.[67]

Henrietta wrote a pamphlet for MABYS, issued in 1881, describing the work and giving very practical advice. The Central Council of the Association kept in touch with the pauper schools and informed local Associations of girls placed in their area. A lady volunteer would write to the girl's mistress and visit her. She should meet the girl for the first time away from the mistress by inviting her to a class or to come to tea, and they would find it easy to make friends with her because the girls were starved of love. She should ask about the girl's daily life and the children she had to look after. She should help her to plan her money, which was £7 to £10 per annum, and to buy materials and a pattern for a new dress. She should suggest she should buy a magazine to encourage reading: *Day of Rest* or *Sunshine* were suitable. Girls had a day's holiday once a month when they could go to the zoo and the volunteers might give them supper before they went home to their mistresses at 10 pm; hanging about in the streets with no aim was dangerous. A group of girls could be taken for a country walk or go to the waxworks. Sometimes a volunteer might ask a girl to spend her holiday with her own children and maids. If she was asked to leave her place, it was essential to find her a new job. She should speak openly to the girl about her lover and the possibility of temptation he might lead her into. Tell her to avoid larking with men or taking up with men who speak to them in the street. Encourage her to bring her lover to meet you. "Prostitution is the great sin of our cities, and it is from this class of young servants that it mostly takes its recruits. This is our enemy. Friendship is our weapon."

It is easy to criticise the work of these women for their limited ambitions for the girls, and their tedious moralising. They could be seen as providing drudges for the wives of the tradesmen and skilled workers, who were becoming more affluent and house-proud in the late 19th century. In our own time with birth control, abortion and a welfare state, it takes an effort of imagination to realise the terrible problems met by single mothers if they were not kept and protected by their own families.

As well as the work for MABYS, Henrietta set out to civilise other girls in the parish and impart Christian moral values. She started parish clubs of all sorts: the Girls' Club for working girls, a Guild of Hope and Pity for children "who need to be lovingly taught the virtues of purity and honesty, temperance and mercy." The Guilds of Pity were for sexually abused children. She also started a guild for older girls who had left school, the Daisy Guild for "working girls and servants, who each do something to purify life, and help the weak or fallen," and a lunch-time club to keep the factory girls off the streets.[68]

Henrietta had very puritanical ideas about suitable leisure activities for girls. One of the helpers at the St Jude's Girls' Club was Margaret Nevinson who, with her husband, Henry, lived in Whitechapel for a time. She found that many of the girls were wild and ill behaved and she had little success in teaching them arithmetic and other subjects. She started a dancing class which was very popular and a great success, but it was "prohibited as insufficiently elevating," presumably by Henrietta, after which Margaret stopped working at the club.[69] Henrietta wanted the girls to learn about art and music with a moral purpose, about the countryside and flowers and about health and housekeeping. She approved of dances such as Roger de Coverley, but disapproved of the modern style of holding partners!

Single Mothers in the Workhouse

Since the 1834 Poor Law Act, local authority relief for the poor at home had been severely restricted. The Guardians of the Poor sent applicants to the workhouse, the dreaded refuge where families were divided and the men had to live separately from their women and children. Old people would be there for life but people pauperised by unemployment, child-bearing or illness would get out of this bleak and hated place at the first opportunity. The workhouse masters did not welcome visitors, but from the 1850s more and more lady visitors got admission and a Workhouse Visiting Society was formed. By the late 1870s there were thousands of these visitors in England.[70] They provided comforts and diversion – libraries, tea-parties, entertainments, toys – along with a great deal of moral and religious personal advice. They trained women and girls for domestic service, and provided after-care schemes to keep them on the straight and narrow path of "purity". The large contribution of women to the management of workhouses was recognised in 1874 when Mrs Nassau Senior (an acquaintance, perhaps friend of Henrietta) was appointed by the Local Government Board as an inspector of workhouse schools, the first woman to hold such a post.

When the Barnetts moved to St Jude's, Samuel was appointed a Poor Law guardian in Whitechapel, and he got permission for Henrietta to visit the workhouse. In 1875 Henrietta was appointed as a guardian, the first woman appointed to that post. She regularly visited the Whitechapel workhouse once a week. She left two very different accounts of her work: the first was her article, "The Young Women in our Workhouses" published in *Macmillan's Magazine* in 1879; the second was her account in her biography of Canon Barnett.

"The Young Women in Our Workhouses" was Henrietta's first publication – she was now 28 years old. She wrote that there were three reasons which brought young women into the workhouse:

> "First, in order to seek shelter when about to become mothers; secondly, because they are driven thither by the evil results of profligacy; thirdly, because having failed in life they choose to enter there rather than to sin or to starve. It is of the first and third classes that I now write, for the second class is being dealt with, if not efficiently, at least earnestly, by many societies founded for that purpose."[71]

Profligacy – prostitution and venereal disease – was not a suitable subject for *Macmillan's Magazine* and it was daring for Henrietta to write about about illegitimacy, however, she proceeded to describe the problem. In the year 1877–8 in the seven unions of East London, 253 "young girl-mothers" entered the infirmaries. After three weeks in the infirmary these girls had to go to the main part of the workhouse, unless they could return to their own parental home. Henrietta considered that returning home was a bad option as their immoral behaviour might have a bad influence on younger children in the family! Evidently the best solution was for lady visitors to visit the infirmary, see the girls individually, find them positions as servants and place the babies with foster-mothers. If the girls were trained they might be paid £15 per year, from which they could give £10 to the foster-mother. Henrietta described this social work as very suitable for ladies; even those who were tied by their domestic and social responsibilities might help by finding situations and foster-mothers, which could be done by letter writing in their own drawing rooms. Henrietta's account for *Macmillan's Magazine* was tailored to appeal to genteel lady readers who might volunteer their help and the article cast a discreet veil over the more sordid aspects of workhouse visiting. This account minimized the stresses of the work and made it seem most ladylike.

Forty years later, Henrietta's description of her visits to the workhouse wards gives a very different impression:

> "Into these I plunged with the ignorance and enthusiasm of twenty-four years, dominated by the faith that no girls liked being wicked, that they had only adopted evil ways inadvertently or under compulsion, and that they would gladly suffer hardship and enjoy discipline so as to become good. Slowly I learnt the truth. I had arrived at woman's estate in a condition of almost incredible innocence, and sins, now known, alas! to all playgoers and novel-readers of any age, were to me unimagined. To learn the facts of sex lawlessness through the channel of the rude words and impure minds of the women in the underground Lock wards of the Whitechapel Infirmary made me ill, but I was absorbingly interested in the individual girls and never missed my weekly visit."[72]

The Lock wards contained not only single mothers but also many prostitutes detained under the Contagious Diseases Acts of 1864 and 1866. Under these acts, police could arrest any woman suspected of prostitution; then they were medically examined and if found to be diseased could be detained for up to six months while they were treated. There is no doubt that Henrietta was deeply shocked, but also fascinated by the "fallen" women.

At first she did this work without official recognition but in 1877 she wrote a report for the Guardians. Though the report was not printed, the Guardians expressed "their grateful appreciation of the noble work". During 1876/7, 81 women and girls had been seen and 60 placed out – presumably in domestic service – the babies usually being fostered, although 12 were reported as supporting their own children. Henrietta took a personal interest in these women, and if they "flung themselves back into their ungodly lives" she pursued them.[73]

The idea of separating the single mothers from their children now seems preposterous, although even now our government policy is to get single mothers to go out to work and put their children with carers all day. When Henrietta was older and more experienced she had a completely different and much more compassionate suggestion, which was that as the mothers could care for their children better than anyone else, they should be paid to do so.

For nine years Henrietta worked with the young women in the Whitechapel workhouse. She sometimes persuaded girls to come into the workhouse rather than continue a sordid life of prostitution in a common lodging-house. She describes waiting hour after hour in a cold passage for a girl she hoped to "save": "The people surged up and down the street shouting drunken songs, quarrelling, laughing, screaming, making hideous human noises provocative to hopelessness. At last the knocker gave the single rap, which is what the poor give, and Selina was won." Henrietta was helped by Lady Monteagle, Mrs John Rodger and Mrs Frederick Greene. They formed a committee and extended their work from Whitechapel to other unions in East London.[74]

Henrietta put tremendous emotional energy into her work to save women and girls from prostitution. This work helped her to develop independently of Samuel, for he was never engaged in rescue work. After his death, George Frampton was commissioned to sculpt a memorial in Westminster Abbey. Henrietta made him change his design for he included a girl who looked like a prostitute. She suggested there should be sculptures of children instead of the girl.[75]

Children in Barrack Schools

Meanwhile, Henrietta was also helping pauper children, and this was to become a major interest in her life. The harsh Poor Law introduced in the 1830s stopped outdoor relief and decreed that the poor must enter the workhouse to get support. At first all the children were kept in workhouses with their mothers, but when it was realised that they were getting no education, boarding-schools for pauper children were opened. These were officially called district schools because they held children from several Poor Law districts, but they were commonly called barrack schools on account of their large, grim buildings. Samuel was one of the managers of the district schools, and he thought a woman was needed to help in the management. He persuaded the Local Government Board to nominate Henrietta as a guardian of the district school at Forest Gate. So in 1875 she became the first woman ever appointed to this position.[76] Hundreds of children were crowded into these schools; some were orphans, some had been wandering in the streets, but most of them had parents in the workhouse from whom they were kept separate by the harsh requirements of the Poor Law. The school at Forest Gate held 216 children from Whitechapel and 344 from Poplar in buildings which were large, well constructed and clean. In fact the children must have been much cleaner and better fed than they would have been at home, but they were shut away from the world, allowed no visitors, strictly disciplined and treated in the most unloving and institutional way:

> "The children were dressed in a uniform, and no one had his or her own clothes. They wore any that happened to fit, as they were handed out on the day of the weekly change … Silence reigned at meal times. The regulation weight of food was handed out to each child according to its age, but regardless of its size … The hours out of school were not play hours. The girls scrubbed vast areas, I had almost said acres, of boarded rooms, but they were not allowed even to do it together. Each child was placed a few yards off the other. The children were not called by their names. Each was commonly addressed as 'child'. They had no toys, no library, no Sunday school, no places in which to keep personal possessions, no playing fields, no night garments, no prizes, no flowers, no pets, no pictures on the walls, no pleasures in music, no opportunities for seeing the world outside the school walls."[77]

Henrietta was deeply moved by what she saw, and for the rest of her life she was very much concerned with the welfare of children in care. Her immediate aim was to brighten their lives, treat them as individuals and give them love. "Many were her talks with the Matron, Miss Perfect, whom she gradually prevailed upon to treat the children more individually, calling them by their Christian names instead of 'Child' as was Miss Perfect's name for one and all." Henrietta started a lending library for the children; she chose and bought the books and found a friend to be librarian and distribute the books once a week. This was "the first thin wedge of getting visitors admitted to the School".[78] Henrietta got her West End friends to provide entertainments, "one of the special joys being a catch-song (a sort of vocal musical chairs led by Miss Flo Beeton, an inimitable actress and a charmer of young children) in which the audience joined. Even a summer days excursion to the sea-side was initiated, a most un-dreamed of innovation." Toys, games and pets were provided and the discipline was relaxed so the children could enjoy life.

This transformation must have involved much hard work, organisation and persuasion, and Henrietta frequently visited the School. She remained a manager until 1897. By the mid 1880s she felt that the school was excellent. But now she realised that the system was fundamentally wrong and that children should not be herded together in such large numbers. The girls who were brought up in these big district schools had to do housework, but they emerged from the schools quite unable to run homes of their own. In the school they had to scrub large areas of floor, peel quantities of potatoes and do other tasks on an institutional scale, but they could not cook a family meal or clean a small house and had no idea of shopping. Henrietta became convinced that the children should not be confined in these barrack schools but should be given the individual treatment they needed, and in the 1890s she was able to promote this idea.

Meanwhile, eager as always to make a practical reform, though on a small scale, Henrietta started a home for girls leaving the district schools, a home where 3 or 4 girls at a time could be trained for domestic service and given love and attention. In 1880 "Harrow Cottage", facing the Whitestone Pond at Hampstead, was bought, and the furnishing was financed by a bequest from Leonard Montefiore, who left £50 each to Henrietta and Samuel in his will.[79] Mrs Moore (Henrietta's Nurse) was matron and taught the girls "to cook, to sow, to wash, to wait at table, and the biggest lesson of all to love".[80] Henrietta and Samuel drove up from Whitechapel every Friday to have a day of leisure in the fresh

Plate 10
St Jude's Cottage, Hampstead. Henrietta's 'hold-all' where she could entertain friends, care for convalescents from the East End and train girls from Barrack Schools for service.

air, visit Fanny and Nurse and encourage and advise the girls. In the vicarage at St Jude's there was now just a small household – Henrietta and Samuel with their three maids.[81]

In 1889 the Barnetts bought Heath End House near the Spaniards and renamed it St Jude's Cottage. It was much larger than Harrow Cottage, indeed it was a large house and not a cottage. There was room for the Barnetts to spend their weekends, to continue training workhouse girls as domestic servants, and to accommodate convalescents from the London Hospital. Mrs Moore retired from her work with the girls, but presumably continued to care for Fanny.

Chapter 5
Off to the Country

The Barnetts were distressed by the poverty and slum housing in Whitechapel, but they were even more distressed by the cultural poverty of the people. Writing in the *Cornhill Magazine*, Henrietta tried to give her readers an understanding of this cultural wasteland:

> "It is difficult for those of us to whom the world seems almost too full of interests to realize the deadening dullness of some of these lives. Let us imagine, for an instant, all knowledge of history, geography, art, science, and language blotted out; all interests in politics, social movements and discoveries obliterated; no society pleasures to anticipate; no trials of skill nor tests of proficiency in work or play to look forward to; no money at command to enable us to plan some pleasure for a friend or dependent; no books always at hand, the old friends waiting silently till their acquaintance is renewed, the new ones standing ready to be learnt and loved; no opportunities of getting change of scene and idea; no memories laden with pleasures of travel; no objects of real beauty to look at. What would our lives become? And yet this is a true picture of the lives of thousands of the poorer classes, whose time is passed in hard, monotonous work, or occupied in the petty cares of many children, and in satisfying the sordid wants of the body." [82]

Henrietta and Samuel took many holidays in the country and believed that nature had a renewing and spiritualising effect. They wanted the people of Whitechapel to have the same experience, and so from 1873, as soon as they had settled into St Jude's Vicarage, they took out groups of 50 or so people to visit wealthy friends who lived on the fringes of London in Wimbledon, Hampstead or the home counties. At first the East Enders behaved badly: "They pushed and scrambled, pocketed the viands, picked the flowers, stole the fruit, made unseemly noises, and rudely frolicked."[83] The journeys were made in horse-drawn vans, and when there was a stop to water the horses, some of the party slipped into the pub! Gradually behaviour improved, and the journeys were made by train, so everybody arrived sober. On arrival they were given a splendid tea in the host's garden, and played games, listened to music and admired the flowers.

Henrietta described these outings in "At Home to the Poor", an article published in the *Cornhill Magazine* in 1881. As in her other articles, she appealed to more people to offer hospitality and join in the good work. To judge from Henrietta's account, the visitors from Whitechapel were very well behaved, grateful, and very likely to make naive and amusing remarks – she made no mention of vandalism or gatecrashing. The article elicited many offers of hospitality, among them a response from a Mrs Leon.[84] The Leons owned Bletchley Park as well as a house in Surrey and were to prove very generous hosts.

The Barnetts also organised summer outings for the St Jude's congregation. These were more civilised affairs and they would go for a whole day and were entertained by their distinguished friends, for instance by Jowett, the master of Balliol, and by Sir John Gorst when he was Dean of Christ Church. They went to Canterbury, St Albans and to various aristocratic houses. Each member of the congregational outing would contribute to the cost what they felt they could afford.

In believing that birds and flowers and trees would have a good moral influence on slum dwellers, the Barnetts were following in the wake of Octavia Hill and Ruskin. Their conviction that mixing with the upper classes would civilise the working class remained a principle of all their work, from St Jude's drawing room teas and Toynbee Hall to the design of the Hampstead Garden Suburb. How I wish one could hear Henrietta rebuking those who "rudely frolicked"! The poor people who accepted patronising attitudes as the price of a day in the country reveal how much they loved fresh air and nature.

The Children's Country Holiday Fund

In the summer of 1877 the Barnetts took a holiday in Devon and Cornwall. Samuel had been ill during the winter so they did not want to go abroad and instead spent a long summer at Egloshayle near Wadebridge, where Samuel took over the church duties of the vicar and they lived in the vicarage – an economical way of taking a holiday. Their holidays were not just for relaxation, they were busy:

> "Every morning after an early breakfast we had three hours' steady reading – it was Jowett's Plato that year – and then, having loaded the tiny two-wheeled chaise with provision basket, oats-bag, sketching things, and bathing gowns, we trotted off to spend the day out-of-doors, returning to the evening meal with old Nurse and little Fanny."[85]

Usually they did not holiday alone, but had friends and family and sometimes parishioners staying with them. While in Cornwall, Octavia Hill came to stay, and Henrietta's sister Alice with her husband Ernest Hart. Then they invited more friends, including parishioners from Whitechapel with their children. All this generous hospitality made them both very weary. They found the children particularly tiring with "their uncontrolled laughter, and lawlessness of habits and customs, so innocent for them, but so trying for us". One day the Barnetts were walking past a cottage with a "comely woman standing by the door" when, "Like a flash from heaven came the idea to me … Why should they not go there instead of to us? They would like it better, relieved from the restrictions of continual best manners, and we should get the quiet we need. We could meet them on the sands every day and give them a 'good time' and a tea picnic."[86]

Samuel wrote a letter to the *Manchester Guardian* appealing to the country clergy to find willing cottagers, and that same year 9 children were given holidays. The next year a Mr Atkinson [87] was put in charge of developing the scheme and 33 children were sent to the country, and 433 in 1880. As more and more children were given holidays the organisation grew and in 1884 joined with similar charities to form the Children's Country Holiday Fund. The paid secretary was usually chosen from the young men at Toynbee – R H Tawney was one such. Volunteers selected children and visited their homes to assess how much their parents could pay. The country organisers found cottagers, paid them five shillings a week for each child, and organised games, nature study and parties. The children were from 7 to 13 years old and usually stayed a fortnight. Samuel was the chairman from the beginning until he had to resign because of ill-health in 1913. The CCHF had prestigious support: the Prince of Wales, Princess Louise, other royals and aristocrats, politicians, Sir Arthur Conan Doyle, Gerald du Maurier, Israel Zangwill and many others lent their names. It was extremely well organised and successful: in 1903, 34,000 children from the slums were given holidays.

What part did Henrietta play in the CCHF? It is clear that it was her idea in the beginning, but she does not seem to have had any official role. In his letters Samuel Barnett sometimes mentions that he has attended a committee meeting while Henrietta has gone elsewhere. Moreover, Marion Paterson, who also attributes the idea to Henrietta, makes no mention of her having any further involvement in the main organisation. The organisation quickly grew so big that the administration was put in the hands of professionals. However Henrietta did use her increasingly frequent public-speaking engagements to appeal for volunteers and funds. Also she organised nature studies. During 1898 Henrietta and Samuel spent part of their summer holiday bicycling to visit children in the country. They found the children were playing their town games and not taking an interest in nature. When they returned to the East End, Henrietta got the children who went away with the CCHF to write letters about "the birds and flowers, the sky and animals" that they saw on holiday. The following summers she gave them questions to make them think about the countryside around them. This provoked some criticism that the so-called holidays were being spent in instruction. Henrietta wrote to *The Times* to say that the children did not have to do countryside studies and the questions were very simple: "Tell me about the chickens. Does the mother feed them, or do they find their own food? Does she call them to rest under her wings and do they always obey? How many were in the biggest brood you saw?"[88]

Chapter 6

Henrietta's Mentor – Octavia Hill

Writing in later years, Henrietta described Octavia's appearance:

> "She was small in stature with a long body and short legs. She did not dress, she only wore clothes, which were often unnecessarily unbecoming; she had soft and abundant hair and regular features, but the beauty of her face lay in her brown and very luminous eyes, which quite unconsciously she lifted upwards as she spoke on any matter for which she cared. Her mouth was large and mobile, but not improved by laughter. Indeed Miss Octavia was nicest when she was made passionate by her earnestness."

Henrietta found her strong-willed and persistent, and that her enthusiasm was infectious, attracting many helpers. But she was sometimes impatient and dictatorial and she would not allow other people to alter her plans. She wanted to impose her own high moral standards on others and she lacked any sense of humour.[89] Curiously enough, much of this description could be applied to Henrietta's own character.

During the 1870s the Barnetts had laid the foundations of their future work. They owed a great deal to the training and ideas of Octavia Hill: in housing management and poor relief they were following her, putting great emphasis on the importance of getting to know and influence tenants. Already in the 1860s Octavia had organised readings, plays and parties for her tenants in Marylebone, and brought them flowers from the country.[90] The Barnetts followed her example by trying to introduce Whitechapel people to cultural experiences: music, art and nature were as important for people as better housing and living conditions. The influence of Ruskin came to them through Octavia.

Many of the Barnetts' friends and helpers had been introduced to them by Octavia. Mrs Nassau Senior, Harriet and Emily Harrison, Mrs Godwin, Florence Davenport Hill, Emma Cons, Katherine Potter were all helpers in Marylebone in the 1860s who became friends or helpers in Whitechapel. In 1875 Octavia wrote to Henrietta urging her to take on Kate Potter: "Dearest Yetta, I can't help thinking you would be very wise to see Miss Potter & interest her quickly. She is taking up one thing & another here with vigour and energy & naturally won't like to give them up for East End work when once she has begun them." [91]In this way Whitechapel acquired a valuable social worker, and later her two sisters, Margaret and Beatrice (Webb) also came to work there. By the late 1870s Octavia was so well known that large sums of money were being raised for her to provide houses for the poor and she was extending her work to the East End. For instance when Lord Pembroke gave her £6,000 to invest, she asked Samuel Barnett to send her names of slum courts which needed redeveloping.[92]

In 1873, A G Crowder gave Octavia £500 for housing. She wrote of him to an old Quaker friend: "Did I tell thee that his father is dead? He comes into a large fortune, and is full of schemes for his future work … If he comes alone to London he says that it would be to me; but I should try to transfer him to Mr Barnett." [93] Sure enough, by the following year Mr Crowder, who lived in Portland Place, was teaching at St Jude's Sunday school, and was soon providing finance for the Barnett's housing schemes. So the Barnetts were also indebted to Octavia for helpers, and financial supporters. When the Barnetts married and decided to work in the East End, Octavia's sister wrote: "Octavia thinks it such a splendid thing to have such a man at work down there … she thinks it quite a nucleus of fresh life; and Mrs Barnett, of whom Octavia is very fond, is admirably fitted to the work too."[94]

Octavia started life as an artist and she undertook the decoration of St Jude's when the church was restored in 1874. She was helped by Alice Hart, Emma Cons and the Miss Harrisons. In particular, Octavia helped to design the wall panels.[95] When they decided to hang pictures in the church, Octavia asked the Barnetts to come to the National Gallery with her to choose pictures and get copies.[96] She helped Henrietta with the art shows and introduced them to her artist friends such as Walter Crane, the illustrator and socialist. His work was used to decorate the walls of St Jude's school.

They were close friends, wrote frequently to each other and Octavia often dined at the Vicarage. Of course there were disagreements; for instance, when a benefactor gave tickets for poor children to attend the Crystal Palace pantomime, Henrietta at first agreed to organise a party of 50 children starting from Aldgate, but then she backed out of the commitment, to Octavia's dismay.[97] It seems likely that Henrietta disapproved of the pantomime on moral grounds. Somehow Octavia found someone else to take the children and she forgave Henrietta. There were probably other clashes between these two strong-minded women, but when in need they were loyal. In January 1874, when Samuel was very ill with phlebitis, and he became depressed and Henrietta was finding it very difficult to cope, Octavia wrote her a very long and kind letter.[98] Later that year Octavia was in difficulties: after a disagreement with St Mary's charity committee she had handed in her resignation and in her distress she confided in Henrietta.[99]

In the summer of 1877 Octavia came to stay with the Barnetts on holiday near Wadebridge. Henrietta records this briefly: "Miss Octavia, then both ill and unhappy, came to stay with us, and in spite of our reverence for her we made her sit 'bodkin' in the little chaise, and compelled her to join in our most frivolous pleasures."[100] To judge from one of Octavia's letters, she was in a sad state, writing that she was "frightened at everything". After being disappointed in love she was having a nervous breakdown and must have been a most trying guest.[101] When she went abroad to recuperate, she wrote frequently to Henrietta and no doubt had many letters in return. When she recovered she thanked them: "… never can I forget all you have been. You have stood by me as few have – or could." In 1879 she wrote: "Oh Yetta dear how can I ever thank you both for your goodness and faithfulness and for all you have done and are doing for me."[102]

However, during the 1880s Octavia and Henrietta drew apart. On recovering from her nervous breakdown, Octavia became a strictly observant member of the Church of England and in a letter to Samuel criticised the Barnetts for their unorthodox religious views in a tone which must have been hurtful. Also the Barnetts became disillusioned with the harsh strictures of the Charity Organisation Society and broke away from this organisation that meant so much to Octavia. By 1890 they were rarely seeing each other, so that when Henrietta sent Octavia a book as a Christmas present, Octavia thanked her saying:

"We do indeed see little of one another now, & it is doubly good of you thus faithfully to keep memory of the old days – I suppose these outward separations, & even differences of view if not of ideal are appointed in life, but it always seems to me as if the love, & knowledge of what old friends are at the heart, went so much deeper than these small outside separations."[103]

Changing interests also drew the two friends apart. Octavia became increasingly concerned with the Open Space movement which grew into the National Trust and when Henrietta became involved in the Hampstead Garden Suburb, Octavia wrote that she was too busy to help: "I fear I must not think of looking at 'Garden Suburb' questions – I have more than I shall do to follow the work before me."[104] Octavia had been the Barnetts' guide and inspirer in the 1870s. Probably her breakdown ended her role as their mentor and they drew apart in interest and beliefs.

Attracting New Friends and Helpers

In the 19th century, middle- and upper-class women were not expected to do paid work. There were thousands of women of ability, freed from domestic work by servants and wanting something worthwhile to do. They welcomed the chance to become lady visitors and get out of the house, have new experiences, and as Christians know that they were saving themselves by helping others. There were many willing helpers to be found by any charity or clergyman with the ability to organise them.

Volunteers certainly flocked to help the Barnetts. Henrietta had extraordinary energy and was developing a great ability to organise people. Samuel, when people got to know him, was recognised as a wise counsellor: he had kind eyes and gave his full attention to each person, trying to bring out the best in their character. Though St Jude's was in such a rough neighbourhood, it was not very far from the West End, and the Barnetts continued to dine out and widen their circle of friends. Whenever they met interesting or helpful people, Henrietta would ask them to come to dinner or tea at the Vicarage and so involve them in the work. All this entertaining might have been very expensive, but as Henrietta said: "We dared to give only simple, not to say frugal fare, so that none should be embarrassed."[105] She disapproved of rich tables. Philanthropists and volunteers would find themselves trying to converse with the worthy poor of the parish, fortified by glasses of lemonade. Quickly they would be drawn in to help.

In 1877 Miss Pauline Douglas Townsend applied to central committee for the job of secretary. She was not accepted, but Samuel who was chairman of the committee, directed her to Whitechapel where she met Henrietta and "was captured at once by the bright, piquante, fascinating personality, which was to inspire and refresh my life for many a long year to come. I never forget the picture she made in her somewhat unusual dress – what we called "aesthetic" in those days – her pretty girl-secretary still her closest friend, bending over the back of her chair."[106] Pauline Townsend helped Henrietta to form a new branch of MABYS with an office at 28 Commercial Street, just round the corner from the Vicarage. She was made secretary and for 22 years spent four days a week there, helping young girls. She was a "highly cultivated lady and accomplished musician"[107] and played the piano at the schoolroom parties. In 1884 she went on holiday to Ilkley with the Barnetts. They went on long walks on the Yorkshire moors, discussing their plans for Toynbee Hall.[108] While on holiday in the summer of 1885, Samuel wrote several letters to her which reveal that he respected her intellect and judgement. The following year she made a new hymn book, 500 copies were made and it was used at St Jude's for Worship Hour. These hymns were "both rational and reverent". Henrietta was very critical of the standard hymn books:

"The words of hymns are answerable for many of the misconceptions which lie at the root both of superstition and infidelity. For the sake of tune, false sentiment and morbid fancy have been allowed a place in worship. It is no light gain that St Jude's has now a book of poems which the thinker may study and which all may sing with understanding."[109]

Pauline Townsend helped with the pupil teachers association and with the picture shows and became a Trustee of the Whitechapel Art Gallery.[110] Her brother, C. Harrison Townsend, was the architect who designed the Gallery.[111] An able and dedicated woman, Pauline was a great support for Henrietta.

In 1875 Katherine Potter was sent by Octavia Hill to work as a lady rent collector. Kate evidently confided in Henrietta: when she was worrying about her possible marriage to Leonard Courtney MP. She blurted out her anxiety and misery to Henrietta who must have been very sympathetic as she had suffered similar uncertainties before marrying Samuel. Kate was keeping her feelings a secret from her family and in the following May when she decided not to marry him she asked Leonard's agreement to tell her family – and to her amazement she found Henrietta already seemed to know about it too![112] Eventually Kate consented to marry Leonard. Their dedication to Whitechapel and regard for the Barnetts was shown by the choice of St Jude's for the wedding and the schoolroom for the wedding breakfast! By this time, March 1883, Leonard Courtney as Secretary to the Treasury, was a well known Liberal politician, and so the event was given prominence in the newspapers. Amongst the news of Oxford and Cambridge Boat Race crews and Irish dynamiters, the *Pall Mall Gazette* gave good coverage to the wedding. Kate wore a dress of cream satin, with tulle veil and wreath of orange blossom, luxury in the bleak East End. A large part of the church was occupied by poor people of the parish by whom Kate was "much respected for her kind and sympathising work amongst them".[113] All the tenants in a large block of buildings where she collected rent were invited to the breakfast. A Society marriage in Whitechapel gave great publicity to the Barnetts' work. Leonard Courtney resigned from the Cabinet in 1884 (on the issue of proportional representation!) and never held a government office again, however he was regarded as a great statesman and led opinion against imperialism and the Boer War. Kate Courtney became a well known Society hostess and the Courtneys' house in Chelsea was a centre for progressive Liberal thinkers to which the Barnetts were often invited.

Kate brought her sisters, Theresa and Beatrice Potter (later Beatrice Webb), to help with the work in Whitechapel. After Kate's marriage, her work as a rent collector was carried on by Beatrice who came to live in one of the new Buildings near St Jude's. This was the beginning of her work of social investigation. Beatrice admired the Barnetts, particularly Samuel who understood her spirituality.

Some other people who gathered round the Barnetts decided that they too would live in the area. Henry and Margaret Nevinson were a young couple with a baby who lived for a time in one of the new buildings (blocks of flats) in Petticoat Lane. Henry was a journalist, and Margaret along with Beatrice Potter, helped Ella Pycroft with rent collecting in Katherine and Lolesworth Buildings. The Nevinsons rented two adjoining flats to make room for themselves, the baby and maid. Margaret described how the St Jude's volunteers living in the neighbourhood helped each other like early Christians: "The poverty and want, the drink and shiftlessness around were, at times terribly depressing, and we were only upheld by the sympathy and good-fellowship of our little band of pioneers."[115] After a time living in Whitechapel the baby got ill, but quickly recovered when sent to the Kent countryside. The Nevinsons stayed for two years, and continued to be inspired by the Barnetts' views:

> "We all met in Whitechapel with some ill-defined notion of sharing what we had of knowledge, art, music and beauty with those who had so little; some had definite theories of social reform but on the whole few of us were prigs or self-righteous, we were not above laughing at ourselves and our ideals."[116]

Ella Pycroft was Manager of the East London Dwellings Company and came to live in the same building as the Nevinsons.[117] Her helpers included Katherine and Beatrice Potter as well as Margaret Nevinson, all of them living for a time in the new buildings and experiencing East End life at close quarters. Ella Pycroft was a dedicated professional social worker, but after many years she became disillusioned and changed to teaching.

Some people attracted to the Barnetts were very wealthy and no doubt gave financial support. A G Crowder who lived in Portland Place had been introduced by Octavia Hill, came to St Jude's as a Sunday School teacher in 1874, became a Poor Law Guardian, and provided the money to build a block of model dwellings. The Reverend S A Thompson Yates took a house in Commercial Road from 1877 to 1889 where he lived in style, with footman, Chippendale furniture and his cellar, giving hospitality to the Vicarage workers.

Princess Alice of Hesse, a daughter of Queen Victoria, was an admirer of Octavia Hill's work. Her interest in housing was genuine and by no means merely a matter of duty. Indeed when a collection of Octavia's magazine articles, under the title "Homes of the London Poor", was published in America, Princess Alice translated it into German.[118] It was Octavia who brought her to Whitechapel to see the Barnett's work. This was the first of their many contacts with the Royal Family.

At first the Barnetts attracted support by word of mouth, through friends and churches. Then Henrietta's brother in law, Ernest Hart, "burst out with the rapid utterance of indignation at the folly of missing opportunities of sympathy and helpfulness by neglect of the Press". Dr Ernest Hart worked in public medicine and was a medical journalist and had already had success in drumming up support for public causes. Henrietta and her sister Alice Hart remained very close. The two couples often dined together and went on holiday together, so Ernest Hart's experience, knowledge and advice must have been a considerable help to the Barnetts.

Ernest Hart (1836–98) was a brilliant pupil at the City of London School. When offered a scholarship at Cambridge he was unable to take it up for he was a Jew, so he went to St George's Medical School. At the age of 24 he was co-editing the *Lancet*. He specialised in ophthalmology, and when he was only 28 became the Ophthalmic Surgeon to St Mary's Hospital and Dean of its Medical School. In the 1860s he became very influential in public medicine and as Chairman of the Parliamentary Bills Committee of the BMA he secured a reform of the treatment of ill people in workhouses by legislation setting up a Metropolitan Asylums Board. He also fought against baby farming, resulting in the Infant Life Protection Act. From 1866 to the 1890s he was Editor of the *BMJ*, and he also edited the *London Medical Record* and the *Sanitary Record* (concerned with public health). He wanted safe milk supplies and was an early advocate of clean air in cities. In 1876 he formed an Association for the Establishment of Coffee Taverns, which led to the re-founding of the Royal Victoria Theatre as a coffee tavern cum music hall. As well as all this, he somehow found time to reform the role and training of ships' surgeons!

When Henrietta's sister Alice married him in 1872 he was 36 years old and already a well known public figure with many contacts in Parliament and in the Establishment, and he certainly knew how to reach and influence people through the press. Moreover his public health interests, particularly in workhouses, were very much in the same area as the Barnetts'. In 1877 he helped the Barnetts to found a Medical Club: for a subscription of one penny a week members got attendance and medicine from a group of local doctors. Having this remarkably intelligent and active man as a family member must have been a great help, particularly in learning how to mobilise public opinion and contact influential people.

Samuel had occasionally written letters to *The Times*, but only about one letter a year, and they were addressing attention to problems rather than appealing for help. It was Henrietta who saw the importance of Dr Hart's advice and who led the way in using the monthly magazines to enlist help. In 1879 her first article "Young Women in the Workhouse" was published in *Macmillan's*. In 1881 "At Home to the Poor" was in the *Cornhill*, in 1882 "Passionless Reformers" was in the *Fortnightly Review* and in 1883 "Pictures for the People" was in the *Cornhill*. Then Samuel recognized the effectiveness of this method of reaching public opinion and from 1883 he wrote numerous articles. These magazines were read by the middle and upper classes and were the best vehicle for reaching people with time and money to spare.

Travel

The Barnetts lived very economically. They did not have to pay rent, for their housing came with the job, whether they were living in St Jude's Vicarage, Toynbee or Westminster. We can see from photographs that their furnishing was extremely inexpensive, with the exception of gifts of pictures and ceramics from their friends. They were teetotallers and even when they were entertaining they only provided "frugal fare". Their one luxury was foreign travel, for they were both eager to see the world.

Their first tour together was to Switzerland in the summer of 1873, when Samuel introduced Henrietta to the scenery and walking which he so much enjoyed. They walked from six in the morning until ten and from four to six in the evening, covering fifteen miles a day. "We went to Lucerne,walked up the Rigi, and by Goschenen, over the Furka, to the Grimsel, across to Meiringen, on to Lauterbrunnen, and by Wengern Alp towards home." This seems exhausting and in the summer of 1874 when they returned to Switzeland they overdid it and Henrietta became ill. She thought walking had become a fetish with her husband. In August 1876 they were again in the Alps, but now Samuel simply enjoyed the scenery while Henrietta made sketches. After a time they were joined by Ernest and Alice Hart, B F C Costelloe and three Balliol undergraduates.[120]

By the end of 1879, the Barnetts were exhausted by their hard work in Whitechapel. Henrietta had been seriously ill with pneumonia in March, and they decided to spend the winter in a warmer climate. The Rev. Brooke Lambert came to live in the Vicarage and take on the parish duties from November 1879 to March 1880, enabling the Barnetts to go to Egypt. As usual, they did not holiday alone. Kate Potter set off with them from Liverpool to Port Said, and at Cairo they were joined by Margaret Potter and the famous philosopher Herbert Spencer. Evidently the kindly Mrs Potter had decided that Herbert Spencer was in poor health and that a holiday in the company of her daughters and the Barnetts would do him good. [121] Unfortunately the Barnetts' views on having Herbert Spencer as a companion do not seem to have been invited.

Spencer was a renowned philosopher, but he was cantankerous and his habits were extremely irritating. He was only 59 years old, but his behaviour was that of an elderly eccentric. He wore ear-stoppers and if he was in company and was irritated by some frivolous remark he would press the spring which closed his ear holes so that he would not hear any further conversation. He was a great believer in the importance of thorough mastication. He detested cushions but had difficulty in finding a comfortable chair with a hard seat – "as a last resource, he had a seat covered with some inches of soft plaster of Paris, and sitting on that, made an impress from which a wooden seat of an exactly fitting pattern was cut".[122]

Henrietta was fascinated by the colourful street life of Cairo, the gardens and the palm trees. In December they embarked to sail up the Nile – a very slow journey sailing against the stream. Samuel sat on deck reading, sometimes aloud, while the ladies passed the time with sketching. They made excursions on donkeys to see the Tombs of the Kings, Karnak and many other sites. At Aswan the boat was hauled up the cataract and they continued to Wadi Halfa. For the return journey to Cairo, the sail was hauled down and the crew rowed on the current. The Barnetts' pleasure was marred by Herbert Spencer, who, Henrietta complained, was extremely egocentric and so preoccupied with fitting everything into his own theories that he was unable to enjoy the sights and sounds, the tombs and temples, which enthused everyone else. His behaviour became very erratic and he seems to have had a nervous breakdown. He went back to Cairo for treatment, but then rejoined the party again after a week. However he became so agitated when they reached Aswan they persuaded him to leave the party to have further medical treatment.

Spencer's own account of this expedition is, not surprisingly, somewhat different. He appears to have been suffering from a stomach upset as well as a nervous breakdown. He and Margaret Potter travelled overland via Paris, Turin and Brindisi and so arrived in Egypt two days before the Barnetts and Kate Potter. They played a prank on Kate. Margaret was dressed as a Turkish lady with a veil and Kate was told she would have to share a room with this strange lady. She was astonished to find it was her sister. "We had an immense joke," wrote Spencer. Henrietta said that he took no notice of his surroundings, but he was not entirely unobservant for he wrote: "The population here shocks me greatly. Very picturesque, but poor, ragged, dirty, and diseased." However he did not like passing time by buying knick-knacks in the bazaars, whereas Henrietta enjoyed buying mementoes from the crowds of traders who thronged about them. He blamed his troubles on "an imprudent meal" in Alexandria. The dyspepsia produced "a state of depression which prevented me from entering with due zest into sight-seeing – I had experience of a state, not uncommon with nervous subjects, in which fancies, afterwards seen to be morbid, took possession of me".[124] Henrietta seems to have been quite unsympathetic, and no doubt Spencer's agitation was spoiling the holiday. Also Spencer's extreme laissez-faire liberalism, once so persuasive, was going out of fashion and it was irritating to have to listen to his dogmatic principles. The new guru was T H Green. Fortunately whatever ill-feeling there was between the Barnetts and Spencer was soon forgotten, for in June 1880 Henrietta asked him to dine with them and in accepting the invitation Spencer wrote that he would "be glad to renew our Nile recollections".[125]

The party was back in Cairo in March 1880, where they were joined by Henrietta's sister Alice and her husband. They rode out to the Pyramids and saw the Sphinx. Then they all returned to England via Smyrna, Constantinople, Greece and Italy. It was quite usual for the Harts to join them for part of the holiday and Henrietta remained very close to Alice. It seems that the two sisters were very different. Henrietta described her sister:

> "She is very clever, generous-minded enough to forgive injuries, humble enough to forget them, full of the passion of pity and self-forgetful enthusiasm, with a child-like confidence in everyone which none of the disappointments she has suffered ever quenches. She narrates brilliantly but dislikes discussion, the best of her mind being assertively scientific, and her interests being those of chemistry applied to industrial enterprises. She reads voraciously, sketches dramatically, has a sunny temper, and is a trained doctor and an observant nurse."[126]

It is difficult to describe a person to whom one is very close and Henrietta says "to describe her is perplexing". We are left with so many generalisations and so many unanswered questions. Alice, living in "Fairlawn", the large family house in Totteridge, was busy with her children and with entertaining, but she found time to help Henrietta to teach physiology and baby care to mothers, she had helped decorate St Jude's and was interested in arts and crafts. She may have been doing other work on her own, but it is clear that there was much love and mutual support between the two sisters. In the late 1880s Alice gave the Barnetts a new pony for their cart at St Jude's Cottage, perhaps a suggestion that they should trot up to Totteridge more often.

1880s

Chapter 7

Horrible London

During the 1880s there was a growing public interest in the condition of the East End. There were lurid accounts in the press and discussions of how improvements could be made. "Horrible London" was the title of *Daily News* articles which sensationalised the savagery, poverty and squalor of the East End.

> "In these pages I propose to record the result of a journey into a region which lies at our own doors – into a dark continent that is within easy walking distance of the General Post Office … the wild races who inhabit it will, I trust, gain public sympathy as easily as those savage tribes for whose benefit the Missionary Societies never cease to appeal for funds."[127]

George Sims who wrote this also wrote long articles on "How the Poor Live" which appeared in the *Pictorial World* in the summer of 1882. His lurid accounts reached a wide public and stimulated a prurient interest, and a fear of the working class, though also making people realise the need for reform.

Another investigator, Andrew Mearns, wrote a pamphlet called "The Bitter Cry of Outcast London" in 1883, which was serialised in the *Pall Mall Gazette* and painted a similar alarming picture. As Henrietta said, the pamphlet "in spite of its exaggerations, aroused many to think of the poor".[128] Now a "slumming craze" started and visits to the East End became a fashion and a subject for conversation.

Dickens, George Eliot, and Disraeli had raised social consciousness and now new novelists revealed the miseries of slum life. Walter Besant's "All Sorts and Conditions of Men" caused a considerable stir and much of the material for his book was gathered in Whitechapel. Henry James roamed the London streets at night in preparation for writing "The Princess Casamassima", a novel which contrasted lives of luxury and poverty. He wrote of London as "the huge tragic city, where unmeasured misery lurked beneath the dirty night," and terrorists were plotting the overthrow of government. George Gissing wrote about his own experience of growing up in poverty and hating the degradation and depravity. He fell in love with a prostitute, tried to save her and married her, but she was an alcoholic, did not respond to his care and finally committed suicide in 1888, the year before the publication of "The Nether World" his book on London slum life.

The intellectual climate was also changing as there was a move away from laissez-faire and a growing interest in idealist philosophy. Thomas Hill Green, the exponent of idealism in England, was a friend of the Barnetts. T H Green was a brilliant student and when he was 24 he was elected a fellow of Balliol, though he was not given a full teaching post until six years later. This gave him a gap period when he experienced life away from the ivory towers. From 1865 to 1866 he was assistant to a Royal Commission investigating school education in England and Wales, working mainly in the Birmingham area. In 1866 he started to teach at Balliol and was the first tutor who was not a cleric.

This was at the time when Jowett was the master and Balliol was the most renowned college. In 1878 Green was made professor of moral philosophy.

As a philosopher, he claimed that the ultimate aim of moral action should be the common good. In 1881 he published an influential essay on "Liberal Legislation and Freedom of Contract" which criticized laissez-faire liberalism and perhaps pointed towards the idea of the welfare state. Meanwhile he took an active part in social work and local politics and in 1876 was the first university teacher to be elected to Oxford town council. He helped to found a new high school in Oxford, and he also worked for the temperance movement. He had a great influence on students and produced hard-working, serious young graduates who were aware of social problems.[129] The individualism of Herbert Spencer's "Man versus the State" had little appeal in the new intellectual climate.

The Barnetts themselves were undergoing a change in their views about the causes of poverty. As we have seen, in the 1870s they were strongly influenced by Octavia Hill, and in Whitechapel they applied the severe principles of the Charity Organisation Society, giving charity to the deserving poor – the old and the sick – but refusing the able bodied on the grounds that they should be encouraged to find work. But the Barnetts found that despite cutting down the "excessive doles", poverty was increasing. In 1883 Samuel Barnett published an article in the *Nineteenth Century* entitled "Practicable Socialism," setting out his new views. He argued that the problem of poverty must be tackled in a new way and that the state should provide for the poor, particularly housing, education, medical relief and pensions. At a COS meeting in Kensington, Henrietta criticised the Society for lacking heart and being unable to assimilate new ideas. How could man live the highest life in a country where there was great wealth, great poverty and unequal laws so that bread-stealing was declared more wicked than wife-beating? Poverty could be caused by social conditions:

> "It should be a matter of man's free will alone that determines which life he lives. Social conditions, over which as an individual he has no power, now too often determine for him, for there are forces in and around society which crush down the individual will of man."[130]

The Barnetts' views had changed with the times and with experience, and in 1886 they seceded from the Charity Organisation Society, a move which caused a considerable stir.

Today it seems to be an exaggeration to label Henrietta's views as "socialism", but they were certainly "practicable". She compared the worker's usual wage of £1 a week with the real cost of maintaining a family, publishing her findings in *The Poverty of the Poor*.[131] She went into great detail about the cost of feeding a family of eight children, allowing them porridge, treacle and tinned milk for breakfast, Irish stew for dinner, and bread, coffee and tinned milk for supper – The daily cost was 2/5d. She knew the diet had inadequate "nitrogenous substances" [protein], but even so it only left about three shillings a week to pay for rent, schooling, lighting, clothing, boots and doctors' bills. As the rent of two rooms in London was six shillings a week, Henrietta conclusively demonstrated that £1 a week was totally inadequate. She also said that a widow earning half a man's wage would have to send her children to the workhouse. From this detailed evidence it was quite plain that wages must be raised or help given to large families and that the COS principles of self-help and refusal of charity to those in employment were too harsh. The fault was with the economic system.

The Barnetts' approach to poverty was empirical and based on Christian charity. The term "gradualist" seems totally inappropriate for Henrietta, who no sooner thought of a good idea than she was putting it into practice, but they were certainly in favour of peaceful means – "the superiority of quiet ways over those of striving and crying".[132] However the decade of the 1880s was a time of turmoil. The economy was depressed, with the slump at its worst in 1886 when there was high

*Plate 12
Henrietta and
Samuel when
Toynbee Hall
was founded in
1884. They look
exhausted from 10
years hard work
in the unhealthy
living condition in
Whitechapel*

unemployment and great poverty. There were strikes and demonstrations. After a mass meeting in Hyde Park the angry crowd broke shop-windows in Oxford Street. In 1887 came the Trafalgar Square demonstration when the police lost control and soldiers were called in. A demonstrator was killed and his funeral provided another show of discontent and turned him into a martyr. Socialists were organising – the Fabian Society was pacific, but the Social Democratic Federation could be seen as a threat, with Hyndman and John Burns meeting Kropotkin, the anarchist, in Wedde's Hotel in Greek Street. In Hammersmith, William Morris held meetings of his Socialist League. It is no wonder that there were fears of revolution at this time. The Paris Commune of 1871 was still vividly remembered, and the Tsar was assassinated in 1881. Irish terrorists murdered two British Ministers for Ireland in Phoenix Park in 1882, and during the 1880s bombed railways and public buildings in London. At the end of the decade, the Dock Strike showed the determination of organised labour. The first of the many volumes of Charles Booth's Life and Labour of the People in London was published and revealed that no less than 30% of the population were living in dire poverty.

Some of the interest in the East End was an unhealthy fascination with the degradation and squalor, but many people were moved to take positive steps towards reform. Colleges and public schools began to found missions in the East End to provide education and boys clubs. University Extension classes brought adult education and in 1882 an important meeting at the Mansion House, chaired by the Lord Mayor, raised money for an East End College to accommodate the extension classes – a university for the working class.

It was at this Mansion House meeting that Professor Huxley revealed that, as a medical man, he had worked in the Docklands, and then sailed from there on a voyage round the world, "where I had an opportunity of seeing savage life in all conceivable conditions of savage degradation, and I can assure you in this experience of mine I found nothing nearly so degrading, nothing so hopeless, nothing nearly so intolerably dull and miserable, as the life I left behind me in the East End of London".[133] Huxley's speech made a great impression.

Today we also feel challenged by a sub-culture of violence and degradation, drugs and child neglect. The state is held responsible for tackling these problems, and there is little optimism that solutions will be found. In the 1880s there was less reliance on the state, and a confidence that a committed group of people could make changes. Vast areas of the globe were being civilised, and given law and order and education, so surely people could civilise the East End. Poverty could be overcome, housing improved and above all there was a firm belief in the beneficial effect of culture, particularly the high culture of the educated middle class. A knowledge of art, music and Shakespeare would raise moral standards.

Chapter 8

Toynbee Hall

By 1880 the Barnetts with their many friends and helpers were undertaking a great deal of work. Henrietta must have been extremely busy with work for the Charity Organisational Society and the Metropolitan Association for Befriending Young Servants, besides her workhouse visits, all the parish duties and constant entertaining. But despite this work-load, they took important new initiatives: together they mounted Art Exhibitions every Easter, and Henrietta on her own started the Worship Hour, a Home for the 'Feeble Minded' and the Girl Pupil Teachers Association. But their most important venture was the founding of Toynbee Hall in 1884.

Toynbee would be known by social workers throughout the world, be copied in many cities and its alumni would play leading roles in 20th century society. Samuel had been a student at Wadham, and it was not surprising that Samuel and Henrietta turned to Oxford in search of more support for their work in the East End. In 1875, soon after they were established at St Jude's, they stayed with Gertrude Toynbee, a friend of Henrietta and sister of Arnold Toynbee, a young history don who was influencing many students to feel a concern for the poor. Toynbee introduced them to Jowett and to his circle of progressive thinkers. The Barnetts became frequent visitors to Oxford. They were invited to stay at the house belonging to Dr Freemantle – 3 Ship Street. Many students were eager to learn about the East End and came to hear Samuel's accounts of East End life and his appeal for the interest and help of the young men.

The Barnetts invited the students to visit St Jude's during their vacations, participate in the social and educational work and get real experience of the life of the poor. A few of these men settled in the East End when they left Oxford, living in the new buildings, but most just stayed for a short time at the Vicarage or visited from wherever they lived in London. In 1883, Samuel spoke at St John's College on his vision of a settlement for young men so that they could live in the East End instead of just visiting. The idea was quickly realised: the money was raised; the architectural plans were drawn up by Elijah Hoole (who had worked for Octavia Hill on slum clearance), and in January 1885 Toynbee Hall was opened to the first residents. Soon they were deeply involved in education, social work and local politics. Activities which had all been started at the Vicarage could now expand. Samuel hesitated before accepting the task of warden, for they were both tired and often unwell from the strain of working in Whitechapel, but he was so evidently the right person that he was persuaded to take on the job. The salary was £250, but when Samuel's father had died in 1883 he had inherited £10,000 and so he felt sufficiently affluent to give the salary back to Toynbee Hall funds. Samuel had to continue with his work as vicar until a new job in the Church was found for him.

A photograph of Toynbee residents in 1885 shows Henrietta, rather serious and saintly looking, and Samuel looking at her, and they are surrounded by a dozen vigorous, moustachioed young men.

Henrietta, now 34, must have immensely enjoyed their respect and attention. Toynbee was a very masculine institution, indeed this was part of the purpose for hitherto the social work in the East End as elsewhere had been woman's work. It should not be forgotten that apart from a few clergy and other religiously motivated men there were thousands of unknown women involved in social work. Now young men of promise, the probable future leaders of the nation, were being given a first-hand knowledge of social conditions which they would never forget. Samuel gave a great deal of time to inspiring and helping these young men: his belief in working "one-to-one" with people led him to spend half an hour each week counselling each resident. This was in addition to all the administration and the planning of numerous activities.

There have been two excellent histories of Toynbee Hall, one by J A R Pimlott, published in 1935, and the other by Asa Briggs and Anne Macartney, published in 1984. Pimlott, writing when Henrietta was a very old lady, devotes half a page of his book to paying tribute to her remarkable character and her ability to spur on her husband: "She possessed a vigorous self-confidence and determination which, added to his qualities, made the combination fully equipped and well-nigh irresistible."[134] Apart from this tribute, he gives scant recognition to any particular role played by her. Even when writing about the picture exhibitions, he attributes all the success to Samuel. Asa Briggs and Ann Macartney also devote a page to describing Henrietta's strong character, quoting Archbishop Lang's remark: "Samuel was but the mouthpiece of

Henrietta and had the courage of her opinions," but except for mentioning her strong interest in the Children's Country Holiday Fund, they tacitly attribute everything to Samuel.

Toynbee was much like an Oxbridge college and the residents were all men, so Henrietta's work was necessarily peripheral and social, but as at the vicarage, she made the social life so important that her role was very significant. At first Henrietta undertook the housekeeping and with all the social occasions and visitors this was rather like running a hotel. She had a large staff, and the organization must have been very demanding. It was thought that with all the young men it would be necessary to employ male servants as at Oxford colleges, but Henrietta decided to employ girls and there was no serious trouble – though residents were "warned that offers to carry the heavy trays or fetch the coals were liable to generate mistaken notions." No doubt employing maids was a good deal cheaper than employing men, and Henrietta was proud of her economical housekeeping and confident of her control over the girls' morals.

The residents invited Henrietta to dine with them in the Hall whenever she wished, and she usually dined with them twice a week. Residents donated to an Entertainments Committee fund so that each resident could bring a Whitechapel 'friend' to attend dinner free of charge. Samuel planned the table seating for these Toynbee dinners, sometimes sitting on the floor to see the plan more easily. When Henrietta and Samuel moved to the Warden's Lodge in 1892 they continued to do a great deal of entertaining, inviting the local working class people, residents, social workers and their important and aristocratic friends from the West End, preferably all together. They believed that social mixing would bring about friendships between the social classes and a cultural awakening of the working

Plate 14
Henrietta and
Samuel with
the young Oxbridge
men who lived
at Toynbee Hall.
Henrietta advised
them not to help
the maids with coal
scuttles.

class; this one-to-one contact was more educational than lectures. Thus social events were at the core of the Barnett's efforts.

Each September there was a conversazione when over a thousand students, teachers, residents and associates would be invited to a big party to celebrate the start of the academic year. Henrietta, perhaps clad in her green plush aesthetic dress, would help receive the guests. Though she was economical, Henrietta was always beautifully dressed, as her photographs reveal. During the year there were frequent receptions in the drawing room for classes, societies and local organisations and including everyone who might be visiting Toynbee at the time. Some days the Barnetts were attending two or three parties. In her biography *Canon Barnett*, Henrietta gives a list of over 50 parties given in one year, including parties for mothers' meetings, the ambulance brigade, the Jews' Free School Teachers, and trade unionists.[136]

These very different people could mix when there was a lecture, concert or trade union meeting, but when the meeting was purely social it was difficult to find anything to talk about. Working men and women must have been intimidated by the essentially middle class occasions – the hand-shakings and polite talk over a cup of tea. Despite all these embarrassments, Henrietta persisted in giving socially mixed tea parties and dinner parties.[137] Twenty years previously, Octavia Hill had initiated this custom of mixing rich and poor, but she sometimes felt the artificiality. When she invited Henrietta to her annual party in 1876, she excused herself for not inviting the poor, as in past years, explaining at length that she only wanted to have fellow workers and friends, people for whom she felt a real friendship.[138] Henrietta was less sensitive to her guests' feelings and was determined to force social relationships.

Many societies flourished at Toynbee as well as the regular classes and Henrietta played a leading role in some of them. The Nursing Society visited children in schools and helped in dispensaries, the musical societies gave classical concerts on Sunday afternoons. At the Art Students Club, Henrietta organised talks on pictures. The Travellers Club took clerks and teachers to Italy, Paris, Spain and many other places which hitherto had been visited only by the rich.

They founded a library at Toynbee Hall which grew quickly and had many readers. A Free Public Libraries Act enabled local authorities to build libraries if the majority of voters wanted them. In 1890 Samuel canvassed the voters and succeeded in getting a majority of four to one in favour. He managed to raise £5,000 for the building and Passmore Edwards gave over £6,000. In 1891 the foundation stone was laid by the Lord Mayor. Henrietta helped Samuel to plan the new library, providing accommodation for lectures and a special room for children.

Toynbee was a very masculine place, and Henrietta enjoyed working with men. She saw the need for educated women to live as well as work in the East End and in 1887 she read a paper to the Cambridge Ladies Discussion Society which led to the proposal to found the first womens' settlement; the Women's University Settlement in Southwark.

Toynbee Hall was a tremendous responsibility and a great deal of work. But, as a clergyman, Samuel had to continue with the work as vicar of St Jude's and the Barnetts stayed on at the vicarage. This double burden was too much and friends began to seek a less onerous appointment in the Church for him. At last in 1892 he heard that he was to be made a canon of Bristol Cathedral and they were able to move into the Warden's Lodge at Toynbee, where they lived until 1906 when Samuel became a Canon of Westminster Abbey.

Henrietta and Beatrice Webb

Beatrice Webb was nine years younger than Henrietta and perhaps younger in experience for Henrietta made an early start to both her social work and her married life. In the 1880s Beatrice came to live close to Toynbee Hall because she was working on Charles Booth's great *Survey of Life and Labour of the People in London*, and the East End section was organized in Toynbee. In August 1887 Beatrice made a long entry in her diary:

"Mrs Barnett is an active-minded, true and warm-hearted woman. She is conceited; she would be objectionably conceited if it were not for her genuine belief in her husband's superiority – not only to the rest of the world (which would be another form of conceit) – but to herself. Her constant flow of spirits, her invigorating energy, is incalculably helpful to her husband. Her nature is saturated with courage and with truthfulness; her sympathies are keen and her power of admiration for others strong. Her personal aim in life is to raise womanhood to its rightful position; as equal though unlike manhood. The crusade she has undertaken is the fight against impurity as the main factor in debasing women from a status of independence to the one of physical dependence. The common opinion that a woman is a nonentity unless joined to a man, she resents as a 'blasphemy'. Like all crusaders, she is bigoted, and does not recognize all the facts that tell against her faith. I told her that the only way in which we can convince the world of our power is to show it. And for that it will be needful for women with strong natures to remain celibate; so that the special force of woman-hood – motherly feeling – may be forced into public work. In religious faith Mr Barnett is an idealistic Christian without dogma, and Mrs Barnett an agnostic with idealism; in social faith, the man a Christian Socialist, the woman an individualist. The woman is really the more masculine-minded of the two."

Much later, long after Beatrice had given up celibacy and married, she wrote about the Barnett's partnership:

"The Barnetts were an early example of a new type of human personality, in after years not uncommon; a double-star-personality, the light of the one being indistinguishable from that of the other.

At nineteen years of age, pretty, witty, and well-to-do, Henrietta Rowland married the plain and insignificant curate who was her fellow-worker in the parish of St Marylebone; not solely, so I gather from her own account, because he had won her admiration and affection, but also as a way of dedicating her life to the service of the poor. In many of her characteristics she was the direct antithesis of her husband, and, exactly on this account, she served as complement to him, as he did to her. Assuredly she was not hampered by the 'inferiority complex'! A breezy self-confidence, a naïve self-assertion – sometimes to the border-line of bad manners – was her note towards the world at large. Lavishly admiring, loving and loyal towards friends and comrades, her attitude towards those whose conduct she condemned – for instance, towards the heartless rich, the sweating employer, or the rack-renting landlord – was that they required 'spanking,' and that she was prepared to carry out this chastisement, always assuming that she thought it would lead to their reformation! She may have been influenced by her husband's mysticism, but her native bent was a rationalist interpretation of the facts of life. The emotion that was the warp of her weft was not the merging of self in a force that makes for righteousness, but the service of man, or rather of the men and women in her near neighbourhood. To this vocation she brought a keener and more practical intellect than her husband; a directness of intention and of speech which excited sometimes admiration, sometimes consternation, in her associates; and, be it added, a sense of humour which was

Plate 15
Henrietta dressed for dinner. The Barnetts entertained frequently though 'frugally'. They were frequently invited out to dinner, often with wealthy people and politicians. Hundreds of East Enders came to their 'Conversaziones' at the Vicarage and Toynbee.

'masculine' in its broadness, offensive to the fastidious and invigorating to those who enjoyed laughter at the absurdities of their own and other people's human nature. For all the business side of philanthropy, for initiation, advertisement, negotiation and execution, her gifts rose at times to veritable genius."

Beatrice seems to have been fascinated by Henrietta and by her partnership with Samuel. It is probable that when she married the unattractive Sidney, she had as an example the Barnetts' happy marriage of a charming woman with an unattractive man, united by their common interests and aims and belief that it led to the equality of husband and wife.

Chapter 9

Exhibitions

When the Barnetts returned to Whitechapel after their holiday in Egypt, they showed their mementoes to the Vicarage parties, and this created such interest that in the Easter holidays they opened an exhibition in the schoolrooms behind the vicarage. The rooms were far from ideal for surrounding buildings obscured the light, access was through a narrow passage and the doorways were narrow and the staircase crooked. But they made the best of it by decorating the rooms. They borrowed cases and exhibits from South Kensington, and pictures, ceramics and other exhibits from their owners and sometimes from the artists. All this required a lot of organizing, so the Barnetts formed a committee which divided the jobs between sub-committees for hanging, decorations, advertising, cataloguing, finance and watch.[140] Members of the Watch Committee guarded security and also explained the pictures to visitors. The explanation was very important in awakening interest in people who were quite unused to looking at paintings. The first exhibition in 1881 drew 4,000 people on the threepenny days and and 5,000 people on the two free days. From the next year entry was free and each Easter more and more people crowded in. In 1882, 26,000 came and the three schoolrooms had become so crowded that friends raised money to build three further rooms behind the school for the 1886 exhibition, when 55,000 people came. It was a great success.

All classes of people came to the Easter exhibitions, but the Barnetts were most delighted to attract the working-class East Enders. The exhibitions were open in the evening and on Sundays, including Easter Day, for the Barnetts knew that men working long hours all the week, including Saturdays, were only free on Sunday. Samuel succeeded in getting his bishop's tacit agreement to the Sunday opening – Bishop How was a reformer too – but this did not prevent supporters of the Lord's Day Observance Society from mounting a vigorous protest, standing in front of the exhibition and threatening future punishment on those who entered.

As the school holidays were brief and the exhibitions lasted a fortnight, the preparation had to be crammed into four days: "On the Thursday before Maundy Thursday the school broke up. On Friday and Saturday the pictures were collected. On Saturday afternoon and Sunday the catalogue was written. On Monday the pictures, 300 to 350, were hung. On Tuesday morning the Press was admitted, and on Tuesday afternoon the public opening was held."[141] All this could only be accomplished because there were many helpers. Samuel, Henrietta and the Toynbee men (after the Hall was built) all wrote descriptions of the pictures and Edmund Cook combined them into a catalogue, his wife providing apt poetic quotations. The catalogue was sold for one penny. Henrietta had to correct Samuel's descriptions, "for his colour-blindness made him unable to discern beauties that needed to be indicated, and his extravagant optimism tended to endow some artists with intentions other than their own".[142]

From reading a few catalogue entries it seems that aesthetic and technical qualities were not of great importance:

> 'A Ray Of Sunshine' by Israels.
> The sun's rays reach everywhere; artists often follow those which light up beautiful places and rich houses. This artist has followed a sun-beam which has lighted up a home where there is no beauty of colour or form, and he has shown that there is a better beauty.
> What is beauty? Not the show
> Of stately limbs and features. No,
> 'Tis the stainless soul within
> That outshines the fairest skin."

Samuel was delighted that many catalogues were sold (16,000 in 1885),[143] so that people were carrying home these thoughts. For Samuel every picture told a story, and held a moral as well, and he spent many hours at the exhibitions holding forth to the people on the meanings of the pictures. The exhibition required a great deal of organisation, and Henrietta played a large part in its success. She organised the hanging of the pictures, along with a Mr Chevalier. Policemen, firemen and caretakers had to be hired, and then about twenty gentlemen volunteers were found who took it in turns to guard the pictures, describe them for the public and prevent "unseemly conduct". Henrietta also acted as a guide, particularly for the children and the groups of pupil teachers and of mothers. She knew a great deal more about art than her husband, for as we have seen, her father began her artistic education at an early age, and she was an amateur artist herself and enjoyed making sketches and took up oil painting in later years. As it was difficult to find more people willing to act as guides, Samuel and Henrietta took round groups of teachers and other volunteers and taught them about the pictures so that they could teach others.[144] They had amazing confidence in their moral and cultural mission. A sample of Henrietta's comments shows how she felt art could uplift people:

> "... such a picture as Richmond's "Sleep and Death," which depicts the strong, pale warrior borne on the shoulders of Sleep, while being gently lifted into the arms of Death – simple in colour, pure in idea, rich in suggestion – is good for the poor to see. Death among them is robbed of none of its terrors by the coarse familiarity with which it is treated; with them funerals are too often a time of rowdiness and debauch. But death thus shown to them is a new idea, which may produce, perhaps, more modesty about the great mystery of our existence."

Here we have Henrietta in her most self-assured and patronising mood. Samuel, who was colour-blind, dwelt more on the positive pleasure and spirituality given by the pictures. Both of them were capable of finding moral meanings which were not intended by the artists. Walter Crane wrote to Henrietta: "You give a beautiful description of my design in St Jude's, but I can only be reckoned as belonging to the Household of Hope – hope rather than Faith."[145] The Barnetts' pious sentimentality, which we find difficult to take, sometimes produced ribaldry at the time. Henrietta herself relates that Miss Paterson overheard a man saying in a friend's drawing room: "It was worth a journey to East London, for the joke of hearing Mrs Barnett point out the motherhood in a cow's eye, to a crowd of Whitechapel roughs."[146]

Borrowing the pictures was the work of everybody who would help, but Henrietta was very successful in persuading people that it was their charitable duty to lend their pictures to enlighten the poor. The pictures were borrowed from artists, dealers and wealthy owners. Henrietta gives an account of persuading a wealthy lady to lend. She travelled to Blackheath to Mr and Mrs Young's house, where she found picture-lined rooms. Mrs Young offered to lend a few of her pictures and was startled when Henrietta refused them! Why? "Because they are not your best ... The best must be lent for the service of the poor." Henrietta then pointed to the gems of the collection which she wished to borrow. She told the lady about the "drear barren lives" of the people of East London and "how we had found that beautiful pictures spoke to the deepest natures of even the most ignorant, and that to many souls, deaf to the preacher, the artist whispered God's eternal truths." Mrs Young was softened and Henrietta got the pictures.

The exhibitions were always of contemporary art, and many artists who are famous today exhibited their work – Watts, Holman Hunt, Alma Tadema, Rossetti, Millais, Burne-Jones, Herkomer, Leighton, Crane and de Morgan to name a few. Many of the artists were already dedicated to social reform and influenced by Ruskin. They supported the idea of Art for the People, though not necessarily agreeing with the Barnett's moral and religious programme. The Barnetts' enthusiasm and ability to get things done must have brought in support. Moreover some of the artists were friends. William Morris had designed the colour scheme for redecorating the interior of St Jude's: "East End: apple green stencilled in darker shade; curtains red and gold; pillars scarlet; dado for aisle walls of stronger tone; walls above stone apple green around clerestory windows; abolish cornfield and hedge frieze." [147] The cover of the St Jude's parish magazine was designed by Walter Crane and his illustrations were used in the school.

They were particularly friendly with George Watts, who, besides designing massive murals, had now become portrait painter to the great and the good. The Barnetts were introduced to Watts by Octavia Hill. Apparently Henrietta asked her advice and knowing well what they wanted, Octavia replied:

"Watts might be the best man to go to. He cares for idealisation, personification, Time, Death, struggle between Death and Love, mistake of a woman's life, & all sorts of modern abstract & really noble ideas, cares for them earnestly … Of course it is a great deal to ask, but he cares more than almost any man I know for art to be used to teach great lessons, he would care for a great & a new field, he has given largely to help beauty for the people. He is a member of our Kyrle, & was a dear friend of Mrs Nassau Senior … He gets up at day break feeling life short for what he has in his thoughts, & may not help. If you ask him take care he gives you nothing the world would think unfit. His high art goes toward undraped figures sometimes."[148] (for Kyrle societies see below)

Watts received many visits in his studio from various groups organised by Henrietta, lent many paintings to the exhibitions, and painted a portrait of Samuel which he gave to Henrietta. His "Time, Death and Judgement" was the Barnetts' favourite painting. Henrietta's description of it was that "Time and Death walk hand-in-hand, followed by Judgement, who, with hidden face, holds the scales."[149] Samuel was much impressed by the picture's moral message and wrote to the Bishop of London:

"Never in my eight years' intercourse with my neighbours (who are, as your Lordship said, people of the lowest type) have I been so conscious of their souls' needs as when they hung around me listening to what I had to say of Watts' picture, Time, Death, and Judgement. Never have I received such gratitude as I did for the use of the school-rooms to see pictures on Easter Sunday."[150]

In 1884 the Barnetts' friends and admirers subscribed to place a mosaic reproduction of the painting on the west wall of St Jude's church so that it could be seen by the passers-by on Commercial Road. The mosaic was unveiled by Matthew Arnold. When St Jude's church was pulled down in 1926 it was decided to move the mosaic to the outside of St Giles' School, Endell Street, where, at the juncture of five roads it could be seen by many people. The firm entrusted to remove the mosaic "made a mess of it," but Boris Anrep relaid it, a very considerable labour of love.[151] The mosaic is now in the porch of St Giles Church.

Watts was pleased to help the Barnetts, and in 1888 gave them copies of four of his paintings to hang in St Jude's; these were "Love and Death", "The Messenger of Death", "Death Crowning Innocence" and "The Good Samaritan". Henrietta described how he "sketched the subjects direct on the canvases, dictated the colouring to one of his assistants, closely watched the work (which was carried on in the studio at the bottom of his garden), and added his own finishing touches. Thus, although unsigned, the pictures have been through the hands of the 'Signor', and were his gift to us."[152]

Later incumbents of St Jude's evidently did not want the pictures, and in 1914 Henrietta lent them to the Hampstead Garden Suburb Institute. One old girl of Henrietta Barnett School, Frances, remembers her dread and dislike of the enormous, gloomy pictures hanging on the walls of the hall where she attended school prayers in the 1930s. They were eventually sold in the 1960s to raise money for the Institute building fund. It is unfortunate that the paintings were sold at a time when Watts' work was not appreciated.

Henrietta probably played a more important role than Samuel in initiating the exhibitions, and she played the major part in selecting and hanging the pictures. During March each year Henrietta threw herself into the preparations. In a letter to Elizabeth Cadbury she wrote: "The Exhibition is a very great affair & I have to spend a good deal of time picture hunting," so it was not possible to accept an invitation to stay with the Cadburys until after Easter.[153] She had a lifelong interest in art, influenced at first by her father, and then by Octavia Hill who introduced her to many contemporary artists. However, in her biography of Canon Barnett, Henrietta does not admit that the whole idea of art for the poor was very much the fashion at the time; she writes as though no one else had ever had such an original idea. She ignores the other efforts made to bring pictures to the people.

Frances Borzello in her interesting book, *Civilising Caliban*, gives prominence to the role of the Barnetts, but she shows that they were not the first to attempt to teach the poor by means of art. Even in 1846 the *People's Journal* published printed reproductions of paintings which they hoped would take the place on the walls of artisans' dwellings of "the coarse daubs which appeal only to the worst passions – pictures of prize fighters, of Battles, of Jack Shepherd and Dick Turpin, made heroes by those who should have elevated instead of degraded our taste".[154] In 1877 the Kyrle Society was formed, named after John Kyrle, the "Man of Ross" who had worked with the labourers on his farm and tried to give them a better life. The society's aim was to bring beauty home to the people by encouraging house decoration, window boxes and by putting murals and pictures on the walls of working men's clubs and mission halls. A musical section brought concerts and oratorios to working-class districts and another section beautified parks and open spaces. William Morris, Walter Crane, Burne-Jones and Octavia Hill were leading members.

By the late 1870s the Sunday Society, which aimed to bring culture to the poor on their only free day, was suggesting art exhibitions in poor areas, and in 1879 they put on a show in Aldersgate, very close to the East End. Also in 1879 William Rossiter opened a loan exhibition of paintings in his South London Working Men's College. Borzello shows that the Barnetts knew about these previous exhibitions, for Samuel had supported them. Moreover, Lord Rosebery, who performed the opening ceremony of the first exhibition at St Jude's was president of the Sunday Society. The Barnetts' exhibitions were better in every way. The pictures on loan were from the most famous of contemporary artists, the shows were well hung and well managed and were given great publicity. Henrietta could be proud of her role in all this, and in the foundation of the Whitechapel Art Gallery.

Chapter 10
Worship Hour

We have seen how devoutly religious and prayerful Henrietta was when she lost her father at the age of eighteen. As she matured her views on religion changed and she became very critical of the Church of England. Samuel was attached to the accepted liturgy of the Church, though he wished it could be modernised, while Henrietta wanted a far more drastic change: "I being one of those unfortunate people who, while passionately spiritually hungry, cannot find food in the old forms and time-hallowed words, which have to me lost their significance by a reiteration which pays no regard to changing conditions."[155] Some said that she was not religious. "I am too reverent to be religious," was her reply. "My life is often hurried and crowded, and prayer, that communing with one's ideal, and realizing one's failings, is often pushed out altogether." Family prayers she counted "too sacred for every day, as they then become a routine".[156]

The Barnetts were moving away from the strict observance which might be expected from a vicar and his wife. When Samuel Barnett applied for a living in Stepney, Octavia Hill wrote to the Bishop recommending Samuel. But to Samuel she wrote somewhat censoriously:

> "I thought he would choose a man who, while he cared for definite work, gave a larger share of his time & strength to distinct Christian teaching in words ... I do not think that many people know the special difficulty you have in St Jude's, partly because of the Jews & Catholics, partly you lose those who go to Church consciously or unconsciously for what they get, & partly from the fact that there is little stamina from the people there ... But when all is granted I suppose that you have not succeeded – have you? – with the distinct question of faith among either your workers or parishioners. Yours has been rather a preparing of their lives & hearts for a more distinct sight to come to them ... I should like to talk to you and Yetta about it someday. I am not myself sure how far it is the world's fault & therefore a necessary stage; how far it is due to Yetta's own want of real affection for the Church, & a certain uncertainty in her own grasp of the facts about God; how far – & this I believe it is largely – to your own intense desire not to separate yourself by criticising or mocking, or dwelling on, differences between yourself & any single human soul you come in contact with."[157]

Octavia seems to be blaming Henrietta for leading Samuel astray, and very probably she did influence her husband. Beatrice Webb went even further in throwing doubt on Henrietta's belief when she wrote in her diary in 1887: "In religious faith Mr Barnett is an idealistic Christian without dogma; Mrs Barnett an agnostic with idealism."[158] Her idealism was unquestionable, but did she base this idealism on belief in God? The Archbishop of Canterbury, speaking at the funeral of Dame Henrietta said:

"Let me say a final word which must be spoken with fitting reticence about her religion. Her ardent spirit may not always have found its natural expression in the symbols of faith and worship which are a help and strength to others. But most certainly her faith was that God Himself is the Eternal Source and Perfection of all the ideals which filled her soul, and she found in Him the inspiration of all the endeavours by which she sought to realise them. To her the Good, the True, the Beautiful were not mere abstractions. They were the very life of God. Her loyalty to them was her conscious worship of Him …"[159]

Attendance at Church services at St Jude's was very disappointing. East Enders were not, and probably never had been, churchgoers. Moreover, many Irish Catholics had settled in Whitechapel and after the Russian pogroms of 1881, more and more Jews arrived, so that the number of local people who could be attracted to the Church was diminishing each year.

Also Samuel preached sermons which were too complex for a working-class congregation, and indeed his strength was in personal relations and not in public speaking. Henrietta thought that people were bored by sermons and Bible stories, and her dissatisfaction with the Church of England ritual gave her the idea that an hour of music, poetry, hymns and prayers might work. To introduce this into the church required permission, and fortunately Bishop How, the Bishop of East London, was open-minded and gave his tacit permission: "On the whole Barnett, I think the best I can do is to wink"! So in 1881 Henrietta went ahead, and, by now well aware of the importance of publicity, had posters pasted on hoardings in the East End entitled "The Buried Life", advertising the Worship Hour, 8.30 to 9.30pm on Sunday evenings, when people might find the peace and spirituality buried within themselves. In order to attract passers-by, the doors from the church on to Commercial Street were opened during hymns and people who stopped to listen were persuaded to come in. The centre of the church was for the regular congregation, but the side pews filled with tawdry girls, tramps and the very poor, the light being kept low so that they would not be ashamed of their clothes.[160]

Samuel only occasionally attended Worship Hour, and other clergy who attended did not wear their robes. Henrietta selected the readings and invited singers, often professionals who willingly sang free of charge in the East End. Sometimes choirs from West End churches came to help. There was no sermon but always a short reading from the Bible and one from an English author, anthems by a special choir, organ and violin solos, hymns and a few simple prayers. Marion Paterson helped and as the congregation left, Henrietta and Marion gave the church flowers to the people to take home.

In an article in the *Fortnightly Review,*[161] Henrietta made public her belief that flowers, music, art and the countryside were greater reformers than preaching and Bible stories. She even advocated knowledge of other religions! She said that when she was giving a talk on Egypt she related the story of Isis being slain but rising again from the Nile, to which one hearer said, "They thought the same then, did they? Only called them different names". Henrietta commented:

"Would it not be helpful if our religious teachers, instead of spending their precious time denouncing the errors of other religions, would take the truths running through the great stories common to them all, and in a historical attitude of mind show the growth of thought, the development of spirituality till his hearers are brought face to face with the Founder of our own religion, who set the noblest example; taught the purest doctrine."

This may have been a passing enthusiasm soon after the visit to Egypt, but still it was a challenging and surprisingly modern view coming from the wife of a clergyman.

The Worship Hour did attract the people of Whitechapel, and though it must have involved a great deal of organising it was a success. Henrietta continued with this work until 1893 when Samuel became Canon of Bristol and the Reverend Ronald Bayne became Vicar of St Jude's. However Marion Paterson continued to organise a Worship Hour until 1905 when the next incumbent stopped it. This had been a remarkable and successful innovation and, as Marion said, it was "entirely in the hands of Mrs Barnett", implying that Samuel made no contribution.[162]

Was Henrietta anti-Semitic?

Henrietta has been accused of anti-semitism, but there is much evidence to the contrary. Henrietta was always very fond of her sister Alice and she and her husband Ernest Hart were frequent companions of the Barnetts. The Harts lived in a pleasant house, Fairlawn, in Totteridge which was an easy ride in a pony and trap from St Jude's Cottage in Hampstead. The Harts joined them on their tour round the world and they went on many other holidays together. Ernest Hart helped Henrietta with her book on physiology and with her work for children. When he died Samuel wrote to Dorothy that Henrietta was very sad at losing Uncle Ernest, he was one of her closest friends.[164] The Barnetts also had many friends who were Jewish. The Leons had houses at Bletchley Park and at Haslemere where the Barnetts visited them and Samuel referred to them, as "old and valued friends".[165] Mrs Leon and her husband were generous hosts to the Whitechapel parties which Henrietta brought to experience the country and have a good time. When Henrietta wrote her biography of Samuel, she was helped by Mrs Leon and Henrietta entrusted Mrs Leon with the task of selecting the obituary notices from the papers to include in her book,[166] which seems to show real affection and trust. Leonard Montefiore was another friend. He was mainly involved in starting University Extension classes, but he also organised the annual flower show at St Jude's, and "amid the crowds of eager people, noisy children, discontented plant-owners, he kept the peace, and rained the sunshine of his happy laughter on all alike, Jew or Gentile, old or young". The flower shows brought a "bond of union to those divided by their creeds". It might be argued that Henrietta was being hypocritical in order to get the support of rich people, but I think she was too honest and outspoken for that and they would have detected hypocrisy.

When the Barnetts moved into Whitechapel there were many Irish Catholics in the parish but during the 1880s the pogroms in the Pale resulted in thousands of the persecuted Jews landing at the docks and settling in the districts nearby. There were no immigration restrictions or passports and England had a tradition of accepting refugees. There was hostility to these new and strange people who did not speak English, just as there was to the Irish previously and recently to the Bangladeshis and to other new groups. It must be said that at Toynbee Hall they tried to help the newcomers. H S Lewis, who spoke Yiddish, worked at Toynbee for eighteen years and gave legal advice to the poor Jews, mainly helping with their tenancy difficulties.[167] His name became widely known. Later he became a Minister of the Reformed Synagogue in New York. Toynbee Hall, unlike other settlements, was definitely not a religious foundation and Jewish people came to the picture exhibitions and the debates. In 1905 Beveridge estimated that a quarter of the Toynbee students were Jews. Samuel Barnett wanted Christian love to embrace all people. In a letter to his brother he wrote very critically of Australia for excluding people who could not write English, such as Indians or French Canadians: "They are going to keep pure their convict blood and keep clean their land from the Empire".[167] This acerbic comment was of course made privately to his brother and not intended for publication. However, Henrietta probably was dismayed by the rapid increase in the proportion of Jews in the population of Whitechapel. It undermined the parish, for with fewer Christians living locally, church attendance was very low. Eventually St Jude's became redundant and it was demolished in 1926.

Chapter 11

Teaching the Teachers and the Feeble-minded

The Pupil–Teachers Association

In the late 19th century, much of the teaching in elementary schools was done by pupil teachers, young people of 14 to 18 years old who started to teach as soon as they finished the elementary grades themselves. These poor young people had to teach a class of from 60 to 70 children all day, then spend the evening studying or attending a class. On Saturday, the morning from 8 am to 1.30 pm was spent at the Pupil Teacher centre, and in the afternoon they would have to prepare the next week's lessons. In London they were more fortunate, for from 1885 they were only expected to teach half each day and attend the other part of the day at a Pupil Teacher centre. They had to concentrate on arithmetic and grammar which were so important in the curriculum. At the end of their gruelling apprenticeship of 'cramming and being crammed' they could achieve the Acting Teachers' Certificate. Even in 1895 half the certificated elementary teachers had qualified through this route, and only half had been to Training College.[170]

The Barnetts were very concerned about the poor quality of the teachers. Samuel, who was usually so generous in his judgement of people, was scathing: "Thursday we had a party of elementary teachers, they are a set who need culture – We had 30 conceitedly ignorant, comfortably ugly men and women to whom is entrusted the power once held by students and priests."[171] Henrietta and Samuel saw that teachers needed a much better education, including some knowledge of great art, literature and music. Later, Samuel recommended that they should all go to university and have a year's vocational training after graduation – a reform that was eventually made after 1945.

When the London Pupil Teacher centres were started, Samuel offered space at Toynbee Hall to accommodate one of the centres. This arrangement only lasted a short time until new premises were found, but it led to the formation of the Pupil Teachers' Associations. These Associations were really clubs for the young people and they continued to meet at Toynbee. The boys and girls were separately organised: E B Sargant ran the Boys' Pupil Teachers Association, which had debates, lectures and outings as well as sports. Samuel had a guiding influence, and through his connections contrived to get Oxford Colleges to give scholarships to the most promising pupil teachers.

In 1886 a meeting of women in the drawing room of the Warden's Lodge at Toynbee formed a Girls' Pupil Teachers' Association. Similar Associations were started in the other centres and they were coordinated into a London Association. Henrietta founded the Toynbee group and played the most important part in the London Association. Mrs Fawcett was the first President, but during the Barnetts' journey round the world – 1890–91 – the governing body elected Henrietta as President.[171]

Henrietta thought that this work was tremendously important. In her biography *Canon Barnett* she says: "If I were writing my own life I should want at least two chapters to tell of the Girls' Pupil Teachers' Association". Her great desire was to influence the moral and cultural life of girls: by teaching the teachers she would be influencing thousands of girls in the future. No wonder that she threw herself into the work.

There were twelve centres in London, each organising lectures on subjects outside the curriculum to widen the girls' culture. There were also reading parties, tennis, hockey and swimming, and rambles in Surrey and Kent. There were explorations in London and visits to artists' studios – to Watts, Frederick Leighton, Hubert Herkomer – Henrietta enrolled the help of her artist friends. Henrietta also started a "peripatetic picture gallery, autotypes of famous Italian pictures, which she had framed and circulated among the Twelve Pupil Teacher Centres."[173] The pupil teachers' choirs competed in the Queen's Hall and were judged by Hubert Parry and there were musical parties in various aristocratic houses. There were visits to Oxford, where they were received by Jowett at Balliol, and to Newnham College, Cambridge,[174] though the girls, unlike the boys, evidently were not awarded scholarships. Henrietta organised a reading club which met in her drawing room in Toynbee Hall in the winter and in St Jude's Cottage in Hampstead in the summer.[175] She must have worked very hard at the organisation, and as usual persuaded her circle of artistic and wealthy friends to help.

In 1896 they founded a magazine to keep the Associations in touch with each other. Unfortunately the magazines, like the other records, seem to have been lost or destroyed. The British Library does have a few copies of the Journal of the Chelsea Pupil Teachers.[176] The Chelsea girls came second in the tennis competition between the London centres of the Girl Pupil Teachers Associations and were going to enjoy a social gathering with music and dancing in February. One wonders whether the boys would be present – almost certainly not. The boys had a mock Parliament, but not the girls. The journal is written in a jolly and readable style and it is apparent that these associations brought new experiences and a lot of fun to these over-worked young people.

Public Speaking and Publications

The first time Henrietta spoke to a public meeting she was very frightened and turning to Marion Paterson she said "I can't do it – I can't – you must read it for me." Her voice was filled with tears and she looked a pathetic girlish figure standing outside the hall. But she did speak and immediately she began she recovered her confidence. By the 1880s she was an accomplished public speaker addressing large meetings. When she gave a talk to the Charity Organisation Society, Samuel wrote to his brother: "There was a good audience – she looked very simple and nice as she read her earnest soul into chaff of the clumsy methods of the COS. I think her words will do good in rousing the Society to a fuller appreciation of its work. It is useless to go on today with the methods of 15 years ago and the COS must lead if it wld. organise the charity wh. doeth all!"[177]

In 1885 she was speaking at the Mansion House, and though this was to a poor audience, it was a very prestigious place.[178] In a letter of 1886, Samuel mentioned that Henrietta had gone to Manchester to give a lecture, though we do not know whether it was on children in the workhouse, pupil teachers, or another of Henrietta's numerous causes. She thought her big advantage was her strong voice." Writing in 1930 she said: "My voice is my chief asset. I have made a huge crowd in the Albert Hall hear every word, or I can whisper clearly to invalid ears through the Wireless. This God-given voice is the main reason why I receive so large a number of invitations."[179]

She enjoyed speaking to large audiences. Samuel wrote in a letter to his brother: "Yetta came home last night in quite high spirits. She made 4 speeches & had felt the joy of power. It seems that 1,200 women were present. She was elected a Vice President."[180] This was probably a meeting of the National Union of Women Workers. Henrietta was a member of this organisation from its beginning in 1897. (It was not a trade union but a federation of voluntary and professional social workers, somewhat dominated by bishops' wives and the Lyttleton family, according to Beatrice Webb.) She learned how to play on an audience, for as Marion Paterson wrote "She had a vivid delivery; & quickly, & accurately gauged her audience, knowing when to arouse them with an amusing story, when to guide their thought to which was serious, often prayerful."[181] There was always a strong moral tone and one wonders what the audience thought when she addressed the 1887 meeting of the Social Science Congress on "The Duty of Serious Living".[182]

Plate 19
A photograph
probably taken by
Henrietta, revealing
her compassion
for the children
of the slums.

Meanwhile she was reaching a large audience by her publications. Between 1879 and 1888 she had eight articles published in magazines such as the *Macmillan*, the *Cornhill* and the *National Review*. In 1888 the first edition of Practicable Socialism came out, a joint publication with Samuel, largely a reprint of their magazine articles.

During the 1880s Henrietta also wrote books for women and girls, written in simple English and packed with sensible advice. The Making of the Home was subtitled "A Reading-book of Domestic Economy for School and Home Use". She stressed the importance of home-making: "A woman's mission is a high one. On her, to a large extent, depends the good and happiness of the family and, through the family, of the nation."[183] When choosing a house, she advised women should look for one with good drains (still a major problem in the 1880s), and ventilate the rooms well. There is advice about cleaning the house and washing clothes and details of economical meal-planning. A family of six could be fed for one shilling and sixpence farthing a day using herring, lentil soup and porridge with stews of tripe and cowheel. Spirits and beer were poisons. The golden rules of health were good food, heat, cleanliness, exercise, rest and self-control. The book makes a strange contrast with Mrs Beeton and her lavish recipes, but Henrietta knew the sort of life that her girls would have to cope with.

Her next publication for women and girls was in 1887. It was a short pamphlet for mothers on "How to Mind the Baby". A doctor had said that five out of ten babies died before they were five years old. She identified four causes of illness; impure air, improper food, unwise clothing and uncleanliness, and gave directions as to how babies should be treated. Impure air was one cause of illness, so take baby out of doors and ventilate the room. Improper food was another so give only milk until the eye-teeth come through, do not give grown-up food until all the teeth are through and do not give children tea. Do not overheat or let baby get too cold, and do wash clothes frequently. Wash baby all over twice a day, clean bottles thoroughly. Do not give soothing syrup or sleeping powders. (At this time syrups such as Gregory's Treacle contained opiates). This was excellent advice. Although Henrietta herself never had a baby it is clear that her experience as a social worker had given her an insight into contemporary practice of child care and its failings. She was always interested in child health and was delighted by the excellent health statistics of children in her Garden Suburb.

During the 1880s Henrietta was teaching physiology to the girls in St Jude's school, to their mothers and to the pupil teachers and young women attending adult classes. At this time, learning about hygiene and home nursing became an accepted part of the programme of girls' guilds and clubs. But when she tried to teach rules of hygienic and healthy living, people asked "Why", and this made her realise their need for an understanding of physiology. Her teaching seems to have been very effective: "… the girl students had been achieving special distinction. For two terms in succession the best papers in physiology had been written by them. In this fact may be traced the influence of Mrs Barnett, who, it may be mentioned here, is a sister-in-law of that eminent medical man and travelled scholar, the late Dr Ernest Hart."[184] Was the immediate mention of Ernest Hart meant to show that Henrietta's knowledge was well founded or was it meant to qualify her success? Henrietta was sufficiently confident to write on the subject and in the spring of 1888, after a holiday in Italy, she embarked on writing a substantial book, "The Making of the Body, A Children's Book on Anatomy and Physiology for School and Home Use."[185] The book was published in 1894, with an introduction by Ernest Hart. It has 288 pages packed with information about the parts of the body and their working. She attributed the weak and stunted bodies of the poor to their ignorance more than to poverty.

She had a talent for communication and used any means available. From the 1890s, and perhaps before, she took photographs, and she used lantern slides to illustrate her talks and lectures. She understood the power of the visual image and was to use photographs a great deal when appealing for support for Hampstead Garden Suburb.

The "Feeble-minded"

When her father died in 1869, Henrietta took over the responsibility for her mentally handicapped sister Fanny (Frances Rowland). This was indeed a considerable responsibility, for "Aunt Fanny" lived to the age of 79 and always had the mentality of a child. The day-to-day care was in the hands of Nurse, and after her death in 1907, a Miss Gale became her carer. Nevertheless, Henrietta gave her time to Fanny, sometimes included her on social occasions and treated her as a member of the family who was to be shown respect by calling her "Aunt". On the death of Fanny in 1926 an anonymous friend wrote:

> "In no sense was she able to be a companion to her sister. Before her birth her mother was in a carriage accident which affected the babe, and all her life 'Fanny' had to be treated and tended as if she were a child of seven years old. She was always polite, sweet-tempered, generous, anxious to please, and kind to all who came into contact with her; but deformed in body, frail, incapable of thought, and unable to learn.
> When fifty-eight years ago Dame Henrietta undertook the responsibility of her she gave infinite efforts to teach her afflicted sister to knit and sew and play simple games; and surrounded, as she was, by the loving and thoughtful care of her 'guardian', poor Aunt Fanny lived a long and happy life. Those who witnessed the devotion given by an exceptionally able woman to such a case of arrested development must have often been helped by the example, among whom was,
> 'ONE WHO KNOWS'."[186]

Possibly this letter was written by Pauline Townsend, who must have helped with Fanny and seen Henrietta's loving attitude to her sister, which was the more remarkable because of the contemporary treatment of the "feeble-minded". The appropriate vocabulary for naming the less fortunate in society seems to change very rapidly. The term "feeble-minded" was first used in 1875 by Sir Charles Trevelyan when he proposed that these people should be in special institutions and not in lunatic asylums or workhouses.[187] This idea was at last realised in 1913 when the Mental Deficiency Act was passed. Meanwhile a movement had been growing for the better care of the mentally handicapped: voluntary homes were set up, some local authorities reformed their treatment and pressure groups worked to achieve the legal change.

Of course Henrietta saw the need for reform and did not limit her activities to helping her sister. She was very distressed to see similar people shut up in the workhouse or being teased and tormented in the streets. "It was heart-breaking to hear the uncontrolled laughter of the mentally deficient as they wandered aimlessly in the streets or stood idly in the courts. It was worse still to hear the cruel merriment of those who tormented them, to see their vacant faces in the Lock ward beds."[188] The sexual exploitation of the handicapped was especially worrying. As always, once alerted to a problem she would think of a solution and work to realise it. In the late 1870s it seems that she had already decided to open a home, but it was 10 years later in 1887 that Henrietta and Pauline Townsend opened the Home for Day Servants, Aubert Park in Highbury. Miss Jennings, who was a St Jude's parish social worker, and a matron lived with twelve girls in the home. The girls, who were all over 14, were taught domestic work so they could earn a living. Independently of Henrietta, a few other lady guardians saw the need to keep the mentally defective away from the workhouse and the insane asylum and started homes for girls. They came together to found a National Association for Promoting the Welfare of the Feeble-minded and Henrietta was made the vice president of this Association. Dr Ernest Hart took up this cause in the press and municipal and charitable homes were built. By the end of the century there were six voluntary schools and six special homes for girls, financed partly by voluntary subscriptions and partly by the boards of guardians who used them.[189] A departmental committee was set up to investigate the education of defective and epileptic children; Pauline Townsend was a member of the committee.[190] In 1899 an Act was passed enabling the education authorities to provide schooling for the mentally and physically disabled, either in special classes or in special schools.[191] Schooling should continue to the age of 16 and "guides or conveyances" to school could be provided. Probably this legislation was only applied by the more enlightened authorities such as Birmingham and London. Nevertheless it was an important recognition of the rights of disadvantaged children, a change for which Henrietta and her State Children's Association had worked hard.

A Petition to the Queen

By the mid 1880s the poverty and degradation of the East End were becoming well known, but now new horrors were revealed and the problems of prostitution came to the fore. In 1885 W T Stead's sensational story "The Maiden Tribute of Modern Babylon" had awakened the public to child prostitution and made it possible to write about the subject in the press. In 1888 Whitechapel was the scene of Jack the Ripper's gruesome murders of prostitutes, many taking place in alleys close to St Jude's. Local people felt menaced by the prostitution in their midst and were terrified by the murders. Samuel Barnett used the occasion to write a letter to *The Times* urging that there should be slum clearance, and that the streets should be better lit and better policed. For Henrietta this proved an opportunity to use her skills in public relations and she organised a petition from the women of Whitechapel to Queen Victoria –

> "To Her Majesty the Queen[192]
> MADAM, – We, the women of East London, feel horror at the dreadful sins which have been committed in our midst, and grief because of the shame which has fallen on our neighbour-hood. By the facts which have come out at the inquests, we have learnt much of the lives of our sisters who have lost a firm hold on goodness and are living sad and degraded lives.
> While each woman of us will do all she can to make men feel with horror the sins of impurity which cause such wicked lives to be led, we would also, your Majesty, beg that you will call on your servants in authority and bid them put the law which already exists in motion to close bad houses, within whose walls such wickedness is done and men and women ruined in body and soul.
> We are, Madam, your loyal and humble servants."

With the help of board-school teachers and mission workers Henrietta obtained 4,000 signatures from the women of Whitechapel. Kate Courtney undertook the sending of the petition to the Queen, presumably through her husband who was a leading politician. The reply to the petition was an official one from the Home Office, but the Queen herself gave a message through a Mr Ritchie of the Local Government Board as to how much she sympathised with the petitioners. Henrietta's stated objective was to stop loose gossip about prostitution and "to help the women to feel ashamed of such talk, to exercise self-control in their gossip, and to range them on the side of order". But one must also suppose that she saw this as a moment for publicising her cause and herself. The whole incident did help the drive for new housing and in the following years the Industrial Dwellings Company built large blocks of flats, pulling down the lodging-houses which had been used as brothels.

Perhaps Henrietta hoped for more from Queen Victoria and that she would play a more positive part in ridding London of slums and brothels. Henrietta always had a very high regard for the royal family. Her Nurse 'treasured in her memory all their births, marriages and deaths and everything pertaining to their lives' and fostered her interest. When she was eleven she was taken to see a royal procession and was very impressed. In her diary, Henrietta wrote: "March 7th 1863. Went to London to see the Procession. It was a very long procession, one mile altogether. The Queen was not there. The Princess was very pretty, very fair; the Prince is very fair also.

Friday January 8th 1864. The Prince of Wales has a little son."[193]

Samuel did not share his wife's adulation of the royal family and was very critical of Prince Edward. When the prince visited Bethnal Green in 1884, Lord Rosebery introduced Samuel to him. Samuel described the prince as "a heavy, coarse person who has been taught what to say". However he added "The meeting will I hope help our scheme."[194] They both knew the advantage of royal patronage, which was so important in gaining publicity and further support. Queen Victoria lent a painting to one of their exhibitions (Leslie's picture of her coronation) and the CCHF counted Princess Louise and several other members of the royal family as patrons. Princess Alice of Hesse took a real interest in the housing problem in the East End. The Jubilee in 1887 occasioned a surge in loyalty and enthusiasm and the Barnetts were swept up in the celebration. In Hyde Park 30,000 children were entertained at a Jubilee fete, and there were massive fetes at the Crystal Palace and at the People's Palace in Mile End. At Toynbee they had a flower-show and grand dinner for the poor, even the "lowest examples of humanity" from the common lodging-houses. On the night of the illuminations, Samuel and Henrietta with old Nurse, Alice Hart, Marion Paterson and a bodyguard of twenty Toynbee men spent the night walking about the streets, admiring decorations which were brilliantly lit by gas flares. In June 1887 Samuel wrote to his brother;

> "Jubilee has captured us body and mind. Day after day we have been gazing and gadding: gazing at decorations, processions; gadding among crowds of sightseers from eight in the morning, till two the next morning. Gradually our carping, criticising radicalism has faded, we feel that only the monarchy can express national feeling." [195]

Henrietta felt that conventional barriers were broken down and there was a universal communion of goodwill. She thought it was a pity to throw away all the decorations after the celebration and wrote a letter to The Times asking people to send the most beautiful ones to her so that they could be used for decorating clubs in the East End: "Could you suggest to your readers to send some of the Flags, Banners, Shields, bright coloured mottos & devices to East & South London, for Clubs & kindred institutions, where walls are bare for want of money to decorate them."[196] The idea was ridiculed in the comic papers but Henrietta did not mind, for that gave more publicity.

In the 1880s Henrietta was in her thirties and it had been a decade of immense activity for her. Helping to found Toynbee Hall and organising a busy social programme of conversaziones and dinner parties would have been enough to occupy most active women. But Henrietta had also initiated the Sunday evening Worship Hour, organised exhibitions, spent much time with the Pupil Teacher Association, besides making speeches and writing articles and continuing with her social work in the parish and with poor-law children and girls. The workload seems impossible, but she had immense vitality. Moreover, the uncertain, self-questioning girl of twenty had now turned into a supremely self-confident woman. As a mature woman, self-doubt seemed to disappear and she became confident in her own judgement, assertive and adept at self-publicity, and publicising her causes. She was not such a pioneer in social work as she sometimes seemed to think, for many others before her had tried to help the women and children in workhouses or to interest the working class in art. But whatever she took up she pursued with gusto; she could attract other helpers, delegate work and she was an excellent organiser. Above all, she understood the role of public relations and the importance of gaining the support of the rich and the famous.

1890s

Chapter 12

Round-the-World

Health Problems

Henrietta had a very strong will and once decided on a project she threw all her energies into achieving success. After her death, a friend and co-worker, Lady Sydenham, wrote:

> "Once an ideal had taken form in her brain she worked ceaselessly and with great courage and dauntless determination on the task of its fulfilment. Whatever she undertook she put her whole soul and spirit into the adventure to bring it to success. Dame Henrietta was a wonderful character and had a magnetic personality which inspired all the members of her Committees to do all they could to help her."[197]

She pushed herself beyond her physical and mental powers and had frequent spells of illness. Sometimes the illness was physical, including pneumonia – very dangerous before the age of antibiotics. More often she suffered from nervous exhaustion. She wrote: "All my life I have had uncertain health, so good, so bad; like a child rapidly very ill, and, as he used to say, like 'Mother Hubbard's dog' so unexpectedly recovering; and these quick disorders alternated as I grew into middle life, with severe and prolonged periods of nerve failure, and many attacks of pneumonia."[198] She had severe headaches. In January 1888 Samuel wrote to his brother "Yetta got a headache on Sunday & is hardly well today … Headaches are tyrants & force their servants to give in entirely".[199] Headaches are mentioned again in the same year and by October, Samuel was worried about her nervous state. He wrote to his brother:

> "I have Yetta laid up with bronchitis. This fact overwhelms all else for me & it will I know for you. She is not very bad, has herself well in hand & looks to be up in a day or two. It all comes f. worry & she is not to be blamed because folks who love her get troublesome & give her the privilege of bearing their burdens. Two or three of such folks have been troublesome & she has had them on her heart till her nerves cld not bear the strain & so she caught cold."[200]

In the winter of 1888/9 she had a severe attack of pneumonia which brought her "in sight of death". Even in April the nurse was still keeping her "wrapped in cotton wool". In May she was stronger but still not allowed out at night, and at last in June she had recovered.[201] It was this particularly severe illness which led to the Barnetts taking their remarkable round-the-world trip – a break from work and a chance to recover. However Henrietta was again plagued by illness in the 1890s. Marion Paterson tells us: "One year Mrs Barnett was very ill the whole three months [while in Bristol] – and underwent the 'Weir Mitchell' treatment to 'encase the nerves with fat'. Rather too drastic a treatment for one who believed

Plate 20 Henrietta and Samuel (recumbent) with a walking party of Toynbee Hall social workers in Guernsey. The Barnetts loved the country and enjoyed walking, horse riding and bicycling.

in whatever you do do with all your might her added weight being very burdensome."[202] Marion seems somewhat sceptical of the treatment. A photograph of Henrietta taken when she was fifty reveals that she had become plump, but this may have resulted from her age as well as the treatment. Samuel's views on the treatment are not recorded, but there is no doubt that he was very worried about her nerves. He wrote to his brother from St Jude's Cottage: "Yetta has much enjoyed the garden and is better that is to say she is less nervous but the improvement is very little." They needed to get away from work.[203]

Henrietta had cyclical mood changes, bipolarity, but it was triggered by overwork. She must have been a difficult person to live with. She was certainly very warm and loving, but she was also hyperactive and bossy. Samuel was a gentle, reflective soul, and although he undoubtedly loved her deeply and drew on her energy, he must have been exhausted by her at times. I feel it is here that Marion Paterson fits in. Henrietta was more than enough for one person and in Marion she had a companion on whom she could expend some of her restless energy – and some of her moods of nervous exhaustion.

Toynbee Travellers Club

During the 1880s the Barnetts had some enjoyable holidays. In 1887 they joined a party visiting Norway, travelling partly by steamer and partly in pony-traps.[204] Henrietta was always an eager sightseer: once, when sailing through the Mediterranean, their ship docked briefly at Gibraltar, where Henrietta was so keen to see everything that they nearly missed the liner and had to be hauled aboard the moving ship![205] In 1888 they went to Italy to help with the first tour of the Toynbee Travellers Club. Bolton King led the party of 81 to Florence at a cost of only £10.6s.7d each. They had taken classes at Toynbee on Italian history and art during the previous winter and were very appreciative of all they saw. The low cost enabled schoolteachers and artisans to join the tour, people who never imagined they could afford such an experience. It was the beginning of popular foreign travel.

In fact, during the previous year a party of eight students had visited the chief towns of Belgium. Their example inspired another small class who were studying the writings of Mazzini with Bolton King to "visit the scene of their hero's life and work".[206] They found that there would be big savings if they formed a large group, and so the Travellers Club started.

Henrietta claimed that foreign travel for the students was her inspiration. When travelling home from Egypt in 1880 they came via Rome, Florence and Milan. It was while standing under the dome of St Peter's that she thought of the people in Whitechapel and said to Samuel, "let us start them on saving, and one day when they have got enough we will bring them all out here to see Italy's wonders and be glad".[207] Samuel said "What a good idea," and in 1884 his article in the *Nineteenth Century* drew attention to the need for popular travel.

Round-the-World

By 1890, the Barnetts were exhausted by their life in Whitechapel and they decided to have a long break. In October, Henrietta and Samuel, with Marion Paterson and a nurse for Henrietta, embarked on a long journey round the world, visiting India, Ceylon, the Far East and America. Henrietta and Marion were both good sailors; however Samuel was sick in stormy seas[208] and must have suffered at times during these long voyages. They set sail for India on October 4th, arriving in Bombay on October 26th, and spent the next four months travelling all over India "from Ceylon to Darjeeling, from Madras to Bombay, from Cale to Poonah, from Hyderabad to Rajputana," as Henrietta said.[209] Marion Paterson kept a typescript journal of their travels, of the sights and landscapes and of people they met. When she arrived in Bombay she was overwhelmed by the life and colour and felt she was in fairyland. After a few days they went to Poona, where they stayed for three weeks with Indian missionaries – the Sorabjis. Then to Agra to see the Taj Mahal and to Delhi where Henrietta was in bed for a few days feeling poorly. But soon they went on to Cawnpore, Lucknow and Allahabad and spent Christmas in Benares, seeing the thousands of people by the Ganges. In Calcutta they attended a meeting of the recently founded Indian National Congress, then spent New Year 1891 in Darjeeling. Returning to Calcutta they set sail for Ceylon, but they only stayed there a week before sailing to Madras and taking the train all the way back to Bombay, from where they once more sailed back to Ceylon, arriving at Colombo in mid-February. Throughout this marathon journey, Marion Paterson kept her enthusiasm; writing from Colombo to a friend, she said:

> "Its a heavenly morning, hotter than ever but very glorious. The air is alive with the voices of many birds, and the flitting of beautiful butterflies, the palms more graceful every time one looks up, majestically graceful, the plantains, the coffee in full bloom, the roses, the sea, the red roads, the neat huts, the picturesque people – oh! that you could see it all and that I could tell you one half of the loveliness. But I can't so goodbye, and soon to be once more on board the Oriental this time to Japan. All quite well and been through all India without seeing one snake!"

Marion's description has a lightness and gaiety; she must have been very happy.

In her biography, Canon Barnett, Henrietta gave only a brief account of their Indian journeys, but she tells us that when they arrived in a town they would stay in a hotel and use letters of introduction to get in touch with Indians first. They had "verandah conversations with the native gentlemen," which gave them an insight into many Indian problems. Presumably their Indian friends were not admitted to hotels. After two or three days they would get in touch with English officials and quickly they would be invited to stay in their homes, or in the homes of missionaries. In every town they visited schools, the mission station, bankers (with an introduction from Lord Rothschild), and women's hospitals. People "of all degrees" gave them hospitality, from the Viceroy, who invited them to join him on tour, to "a native missionary in the Deccan" (the Sorabjis).[211]

They were most unusual globe-trotters, particularly in staying with an Indian family, talking with prominent Indians and visiting Congress. When they were at Bombay, visitors crowded to see them and among them Mr Gandhi, "dressed as a young Englishman, shortly back from Oxford or Cambridge, anxious to learn from the Vicar rather than to expound to him the problems of India".[212] But when Henrietta reflected on their experience, she was most impressed by the British officials:

> "Thus we gained some knowledge of that fascinating, absorbing, disappointing, alluring, glorious portion of our Empire, and the result of our experience has been to speak more doubtfully of its problems and more admiringly of its official servants – that splendid body of men who, loving truth and pursuing justice, accept service away from home in terrible climates, where misunderstandings are prolific and the sense of duty achieved is, in the majority of cases, the sole reward."[213]

Samuel and Henrietta also wrote an account of their travels for publication in St Jude's parish magazine.[214] Their first letter was sent from Port Said in October describing their voyage from England. Five more letters from India were published in the magazine, then one from Japan and one from America. Henrietta justified this long holiday by saying that they would share their experiences of the world with their friends at home.

At Colombo, Alice and Ernest Hart joined the party and they sailed on the "Oriental" to Penang and Singapore, arriving in Hong Kong at the beginning of March. They went into China to see Canton and meant to go further but the plague was rife so they embarked again and after a stormy voyage they reached Nagasaki on 11th March. They stayed five weeks in Japan, travelling by ship or train to Tokyo, Kobe, Kyoto and Yokohama, the government providing them with an official guide. Henrietta was asked to speak to the daughters of the nobles on what English women did for the poor. The princesses were present and Henrietta and Marion duly curtsied to them. One can only wonder what the Japanese princesses and "debutantes" made of these strangers. Meanwhile Ernest Hart was indulging in his hobby of collecting Japanese works of art.

In May they arrived in San Francisco and stayed in the Palace Hotel. At this point, Samuel and Henrietta began to relate the story of their journey in a volume called "Our Diary".[215] This is fascinating, for while most of the text is written by Samuel, comments are added in brackets by Henrietta so we have the two viewpoints and there can be no doubt as to the authorship of either. Samuel's account of the scenery and people they met is a lucid and serious account, while Henrietta chips in with more enthusiastic description of landscape and opinionated comments on the lifestyle of people they met. In California they were both amazed by Yosemite, but critical of the irreligious, materialistic people. However they were soon travelling north to Canada and on May 30th they met the prime minister of the province of British Columbia, and the next day Samuel preached in Victoria Cathedral.

Henrietta took a poor view of the lack of culture: "The banjo is their favourite instrument … Browning had never been heard of."[216] But when they were taken up Cedar Hill to see the view, she was astonished by the natural beauty: "Can you imagine Lucerne, the Italian Riviera, the islands and broken coast of Molde, the rocks and moss of South Devon, the firs and undergrowth of the northern slopes of Mont Blanc, and sweet briar bushes of nowhere else, all combined, and add to it the brilliant white light of Rome and you will have some faint idea of the marvellous beauty of that hill view."[217]

They were surprised by the high standard of living – the lowest wage being eight shillings per day. In Vancouver they met Mr and Mrs Ashworth whom they had helped to emigrate from Whitechapel three years previously. This couple had been poor when they lived in London, but now they had their own house and had saved up enough to buy a boarding-house.[218]

They took a train through the mountains and Henrietta "kodaked" the splendid views as they travelled via Banff and Manitoba to Chicago, where they arrived in mid-June. Here they stayed with Jane Addams at her settlement, Hull House, which she had been inspired to open by visiting Toynbee Hall. Henrietta gave a talk to the boys and girls at Hull House, while Samuel preached at various churches in Chicago. In her biography, *Canon Barnett*, Henrietta relates an incident which happened during their stay at Hull House. Naughty boys kept on knocking at the door, so in order to help Jane Addams, Henrietta lay in wait by the door and "next time that the troop of little demons appeared I administered an argument which they quite understood". (Possibly she smacked them.) When she told Jane Addams, Jane's eyes filled with tears and she said: "You have put my work back, perhaps years. I was teaching them what is meant by 'resist not evil'."[219] Henrietta did not sympathise with this point of view although she knew that her husband did.

They travelled on eastwards visiting Ann Arbour, the Niagara Falls, Toronto, Boston, Newport and New York. Here they visited Coney Island, which Henrietta condemned for providing shallow amusements for the working classes. Throughout their journey through the West and Mid-West, Henrietta commented on the low price of land and the prosperity of the people and found that many of the settlers who arrived as labourers soon became farmers. She was convinced of the benefits of emigration for the poor of London and even on the journey she was preparing a lecture for the MABYS ladies at home on helping people to emigrate.[220] On 8th July they embarked on the "City of New York" for the seven-day voyage to Liverpool. "We have had a glorious holiday, nine months of unbroken rest," concluded Samuel.[221] If this was rest, what were the demands of their working lives? Travelling at that time was physically demanding and risky, for there were no injections to give protection against the infectious diseases of the East. The fact that Henrietta could travel like this and enjoy it supports the view that the nature of her previous illness must have been more psychological than physical.

Chapter 13
Family Life

Dorothy Woods

A few months after returning from the round-the-world tour a great change took place in Henrietta's life. She became the foster mother of Dorothy, a seven-year-old girl whose parents had died. Her mother had been a voluntary teacher of French and Latin at Toynbee as well as secretary of a branch of the London Pupil Teachers Association and had died in 1890 while the Barnetts were in Japan. Her father asked Henrietta to be Dorothy's guardian and then he died very suddenly in November 1891, leaving Henrietta with the sole responsibility for her ward.

Dorothy was a delicate child, and very backward; at seven she looked like a five-year-old. Her health was the main concern, "so education was ignored until riding, dancing, porridge, cream, and Hampstead air had made her more robust".[222] She lived in St Jude's Cottage at Hampstead with Aunt Fanny, various invalids from Whitechapel, maids who were in training and Nurse, who cared for her. Henrietta and Samuel were with her when they went to the Cottage at weekends. Occasionally they took her to visit Toynbee, where the young men would make much of her and play hide-and-seek. They hired a French governess at the Cottage, with instructions to teach her out of doors as much as possible. She liked botany and drawing, but disliked other lessons. She was an unintelligent child, but very affectionate and the photograph of her with Henrietta reveals a strong emotional tie. She called Henrietta "Guardey" and Samuel was "Pater", a very usual term for fathers at that time. Their affectionate name for her was "Dolloms". Samuel had great fun with her, would pretend that he too was a child and puzzle about the ways of grown-ups and run around with her. Sometimes they took her to see the sights of London. In May 1897 they took Dorothy and Nurse to see the Prince of Wales open the Blackwall Tunnel. In 1899 they took her to see Beerbohm Tree in a performance of King John. The three months every year spent at Bristol were especially happy, for there Dorothy lived with Guardey and Pater and could play with the four children of Frank Barnett, Samuel's brother:

> "Every morning Dorothy scrambled to be the first down, and to place on the breakfast table by the side of each one's plate, a little button-hole picked from the strip of garden … After breakfast she walked down from Clifton with Pater to Bristol for lessons and play with her three playmates."[223]

Dorothy's health remained a worry. At sixteen she seemed to have outgrown her weakness and was able to go to a school where she was very happy until, while they were in Bristol in the summer of 1900, she caught diphtheria. Henrietta and Marion Paterson nursed her and she recovered sufficiently

*Plate 21
Henrietta with
her ward, Dorothy
Woods, 1890s.
Henrietta acted as
Dorothy's mother
after she was
orphaned and until
she died at the age
of 17*

for them to take her back to Hampstead, but then she developed rheumatism and after months of illness died in March 1901. The Barnetts missed the opening of the Whitechapel Art Gallery to attend the funeral. Looking back on her ten years of motherhood, Henrietta wrote: "To us both, my little ward was an uninterrupted joy, and she took a place in our lives as nothing else did before or since." These are simple words. Henrietta did not indulge in sentimentality when describing her own sorrows.

Bristol

In 1893 Samuel Barnett was at last made a canon of Bristol Cathedral, a promotion which many people felt was long overdue. His work in the East End and his spiritual leadership made him an outstanding clergyman, but his Liberal politics, Christian Socialist ideals and his assistance to trade union causes delayed his preferment while the Conservatives were in power. When the Liberal Government was formed in 1892, Jowett, the master of Balliol, saw there was a chance to help the Barnetts and he brought pressure on Lord Herschel, the Lord Chancellor, to give Samuel a canonry. Now he was able to resign from being vicar of St Jude's but continue as warden of Toynbee Hall. Samuel and Henrietta moved out of the Vicarage and lived in the new Warden's Lodge. In those days the duties of a canon were very light, and certainly a great relief after ten years of being both vicar of St Jude's and warden of Toynbee.

It was agreed that Samuel should spend three months a year in Bristol and the rest of the year at Toynbee. In 1894 they spent April, May and June in Bristol, but in the following years they went there in the summer months when absence from Toynbee Hall was easier. The Bishop lent them his house, 8, Royal York Crescent, Clifton, a spacious house with wonderful views of the River Avon, the Bedminster Downs and the Cotswolds. What a change from the cramped and drab outlook in Whitechapel! For Samuel this was a homecoming, for his childhood had been in Bristol and his happiest memories were of his grandparents' house and garden in Clifton. Moreover it meant that they could spend time with his brother Frank and his family. Frank was a local councillor and Samuel discussed local social and economic conditions with him. He soon became involved in local issues and even during his first residence was giving evening lectures to workmen in the Chapter Room of the Cathedral on unemployment, the sick and old, education and wages.

Meanwhile, Henrietta enjoyed organising their social life. They bicycled to the country nearby and with pony and trap they went on drives into Gloucestershire and Somerset. There were frequent picnics in Leigh Woods, close by the Clifton Gorge. They would set out in a party with Dorothy, her friend Phyllis, the governess and Marion Paterson and stop for a village tea. There was room to have weekend guests to stay and time to entertain them. Then there were many dinner parties and garden parties. Henrietta thoroughly enjoyed the social whirl of provincial society, where occasions were less grand than in London and she and her husband were important visitors.

Henrietta carried out social duties such as opening sales of work, making speeches at women's meetings and presenting prizes. She met the organizers of the local Pupil Teachers Association. But her chief public work was for the preservation of the beauty of the river gorge. The gorge was defaced by stone-quarrying, bare expanses of stone overtaking the woodland. Henrietta, with Dorothy, her friends and Marion Paterson scattered flower seeds on the cliffs: "First the seeds had to be collected; and then, in the back garden, the children and I mixed them with earth, stirring all sorts together in the bread-pan in Christmas pudding style. Then the packets were made about the size of a tennis ball and tied up in newspaper, and in the evening, in the gloaming, we went out like four conspirators to throw them down over the rocks."[224] Samuel carried the heavy baskets for them but would not throw the parcels because it was illegal. They were all delighted when "the bare rock produced antirrhinum, valerian, yellow alyssum, wild convolvulus, and, undoubted proof that they were the babes of our balls, Iceland poppies of the same strains as grew in our garden."

Henrietta was passionate in her delight in nature, and had a rebellious streak in her character which came out when her feelings were aroused. She was not interested in demanding votes for women for she thought the status of women and children could be raised by doing, in particular doing social work. Her example showed that a married woman need not be subject to her husband and could develop her own interests. Looking back over a century of amazing change in the status of women, it is impossible to know how much is due to political action and how much is due to individual action – women doing more and more jobs, from plumber to prime minister, and asserting their place in the home.

The three months a year spent in Bristol from 1894 to 1906 were times of great pleasure for Henrietta, especially during the 1890s when Dorothy was alive and Henrietta could be with her and her cousins every day and enjoy family life and the role of mother. It was so relaxing compared with London, where Henrietta was preoccupied with her many causes and only saw Dorothy at weekends. After Dorothy's death in 1901 many of the activities in Bristol must have been tinged with sadness. However the move to save the gorge gathered pace from 1903 with the work of local pressure groups and the National Trust. The town council could not be persuaded to act, but in 1909 George Wills, the cigarette manufacturer, bought Nightingale Valley and the surrounding woods for the public.

Fame and Influence

By the 1890s the Barnetts were well known and had many contacts in the Establishment. They both came from families who were "in trade" and so definitely not from the "top drawer", but now they were dining with wealthy and aristocratic people. During the 1870s Octavia Hill had introduced them to many people and they were such a charismatic and unusual couple that they were taken up by people and welcomed as interesting dinner-guests. The fascination with the East End in the 1880s brought their work into prominence and from the opening of Toynbee Hall they were constantly entertaining wealthy and influential people who came to give support. They wrote hundreds of letters to famous people asking them to give lectures at Toynbee. Many of them refused, but always in a courteous and friendly manner. They were successful social climbers in an age when all effective action was through the Establishment.

In March 1890 they stayed with the Rothschilds[225] – and probably found generous support. Once on the dinner-party circuit, one introduction would lead to another. When they visited the Courtneys, they met Balfour, Morley, Asquith, the Duke of Devonshire and Hobhouse.[226] They gave many dinner parties themselves, at first in the Vicarage and then in the Warden's Lodge. Many famous people appppeared on their dinner-party list – Jowett, James Russell Lowell, H M Stanley (the explorer), Walter Besant, Asquith (the future prime minister), the Duke of Devonshire, Tom Mann, Herbert Spencer, William Morris, Ben Tillett, John Burns and Lord Bryce. There was good conversation, but the Barnetts offered only "frugal fare" so that poorer guests would not be embarrassed.[227]

Henrietta was now well known and not only through her husband, for all who met them must have realised that while he was a man of vision who inspired people, she had dynamism, drive and conviction and the ability to put good ideas into practice. She was one of the people who really knew about the East End and with magazine articles and books to her credit, she was seen as an authority, particularly on children and girls.

One proof of her organisational ability was her success in promoting an independent candidate in the local school board election of 1892. At Toynbee Hall they liked the residents to participate

Plate 22
Henrietta and
Samuel in the 1890s,
now widely respected
for their social work.
Henrietta is wearing
a beautiful day dress.

in local government and George L Bruce stood as an independent candidate for the school board with Henrietta as his agent. She gathered together a band of 268 canvassers and they were successful despite the opposition of the political parties.[228] There must have been embarrassments in this hard-fought campaign, for another Toynbee resident was standing for the Church Party and Samuel was prominent in the local Liberal Party. Henrietta herself very much disliked party politics. Years later, after Henrietta's death, Bruce wrote:

"In 1891 Mrs Barnett & the Vicar made up their minds that two of us, Jackson & myself, ought to be members of the School Board. The political organisations were against us both. Quite undismayed by their opposition Mrs Barnett set to work to rouse an incredible number of her friends to give up their party ties, to give up their comfort, to risk the loss of their own friends & supporters, & to work as they had never worked before for a candidate they knew nothing of except that Mrs Barnett said he should be elected, & elected he was … She was one of the very few who 'what they dared to dream, they dared to do'. Whenever help was needed, & she thought it deserved, she gave it abundantly, I would almost say, ruthlessly; & her sheer efficiency was astounding. If she felt a thing ought to be done, she got it done, though eggs were broken in the process."[229]

Chapter 14
Pauper Children and Barrack Schools

Meanwhile, the more Henrietta saw of the poor-law children in district schools, the more critical she became of these big barrack schools. She and her friends had tried to humanise the Forest Gate school by introducing toys, books and personal clothing and by softening the rigid discipline, but she was becoming convinced that these these large institutions were fundamentally flawed. Now she thought that the only way the children could be treated as individuals and given the affection they so much needed was to place them in small homes or better still, with foster-parents.

Several tragedies occurred in the schools which were reported in the press and shocked the public. The first was a case of cruelty. Ella Gillespie was imprisoned for five years for physical abuse of the infants in the Hackney Pauper Schools. She had beaten them with stinging nettles, made them kneel on hot water pipes, banged their heads against the wall until their ears bled. Her fellow-officers knew this was going on, but had kept quiet.[230] Another tragedy occurred on New Year's Eve 1890. The children had been locked up in their night wards and the officers had gone out to celebrate New Year's Eve when a fire broke out and 22 children died.[231] Next there was an outbreak of food poisoning in one of the District Schools; 141 children fell ill and two died. This might have been passed off as accidental, but the odd-job man spoke out and it was revealed that the soup had been made from fly-blown meat and that the children were often fed on waste meat from the officers' table.

Inquests were held on these deaths and particular officers were blamed or exonerated, but Henrietta saw that the real problem was the inhuman crowding together of masses of children in the barrack schools, and she was determined to change the system. Henrietta and Dr Ernest Hart organised a deputation to meet Shaw-Lefevre, President of the Local Government Board. Marion Paterson says that Henrietta organised the deputation, while Henrietta in her biography, *Canon Barnett,* says it was organised by Ernest Hart. Probably Ernest Hart, as a man, was better placed to secure the appointment, but it was Henrietta who gathered such a large number of supporters that they overflowed the rooms into the passages and stairs of the Local Government Board offices. Sir John Gorst, Ernest Hart and Henrietta made speeches: "Of my own utterance I cannot report. I only know that I was in a terrible fright, and worn down with the labour of arranging the monster deputation."[232]

As a result of this lobby, Shaw-Lefevre appointed a Departmental Committee on Poor Law Schools in 1894. Henrietta was a member of the committee – the first woman ever to be appointed to a government committee. This committee was fairly congenial to Henrietta's views. Mundella, the chairman, was Liberal MP for Sheffield and for the last two years had been President of the Board of Trade; previously he had been concerned with education as vice-president of the Committee

*Plates 23 & 24
Pauper children in a
barrack school.
 They had no
individual clothing
and instead of being
called by their
names they were all
called 'Child'*

of the Council on Education from 1880 to 1885 and also as president of the British
and Foreign School Society. Sir Joshua Fitch had been principal of a teachers training
college, an inspector of schools and a Special Commissioner on Education in the Great
Towns. The Reverend Brooke Lambert was the vicar of St Marks, Whitechapel, the
friend of the Barnetts who had carried out the parish duties at St Jude's when Samuel
had taken holidays. Dr Edward Nettleship edited the works of T H Green in the late
1880s and was probably sympathetic. Lyulph Stanley was a dinner-guest of the Barnetts.

Sir John Gorst (1835–1916) was the most supportive member of the committee.
He was an outstanding and independent-minded politician. After a brilliant start at
Cambridge he decided to go to New Zealand where he met and married his wife. While

there, he became inspector of missionary schools and made friends with the Maoris; however, he got involved in their quarrels and had to flee from the area where he was working. Returning to England, he became Conservative MP for Cambridge. He was asked by Disraeli to reorganise the Conservative Party machinery on a more popular basis, and this brought success to the party in the 1874 election. He was one of the founders of the Primrose League. From 1885 he held various junior ministerial posts and was Minister of Education from 1896 to 1905. The health and education of children had become his chief interest and in 1906 he wrote a book on *The Children of the Nation* which, surprisingly, was dedicated to "Labour Members of the House of Commons in token of my belief that they are animated by a genuine desire to ameliorate the condition of the people". He was disillusioned with the Conservative Party and in the 1910 election he stood as a Liberal candidate but was defeated. He was a maverick, too independent to reach the highest political offices.

The Committee on Poor Law Schools worked for nearly two years, sat 50 times, saw 73 witnesses, and asked 17,566 questions. Besides hearing evidence, each of the members inspected some schools, workhouses or village communities, and probably Henrietta was the most conscientious. Samuel went with her to visit the institutions outside London, while in the London area Sir John Gorst accompanied her. Indeed Sir John Gorst seems to have come under Henrietta's spell. He was now sixty years old and a well-known and experienced politician, but for the next two years he devoted much of his time to helping Henrietta. He lived mainly at Toynbee Hall, coming to stay on Mondays, attending the committee meeting on Tuesday, inspecting schools with Henrietta all day on Wednesday; then on Thursday, Henrietta went to the Forest Gate board meeting and on Friday the committee met again. Henrietta found Sir John lacked will and perseverance, and perhaps he was exhausted by her energy and drive. There is no doubt that Henrietta was the driving force on the committee. Samuel commented: "She has done most of the work, thought out the recommendations, executed the form, and then, more than all, by a mixture of tact and temper, has made the men sign. If one thinks of the opinions with which some started, the change is wonderful."[233] Evidently Henrietta had difficulties in persuading the men, despite her unrivalled knowledge of the problems. Gorst was on her side, but she had difficulties with Mundella, the chairman. In 1895 Samuel wrote:

"Yetta has had a very trying week on her Commission. Mundella is so ignorant and such a bully. Gorst is so able & is so busy that the elements soon make a blaze. They parted hotly on Wednesday but I hope they may still so far come together as to get out a good report."[234]

The committee reported in 1896 and unanimously condemned the barrack schools both on account of the dangers of disease, especially ophthalmia and skin infections, where so many children were crowded together, and they condemned the emotional results of isolating children from the community and depriving them of individual care and affection. The alternatives of village communities, scattered homes and boarding out with families were all recommended as preferable. The committee criticised the organisation by the separate boards of guardians and unanimously recommended that a central authority should be given the organisation of all pauper children. The majority of the committee wanted this central authority to be drawn from the boards of guardians. But Henrietta and Sir John Gorst recommended that the guardians and Local Government Board should have no control of children: in their opinion the new authority should be the Education Department.[235]

The report was a press sensation. *The Times* gave a full summary, spreading over three columns, and the leader reiterated the condemnation of barrack schools and advocated the boarding-out system. On central control, the Times leader commented that "a central authority entirely disconnected with the Poor Law system is advocated on the ground that the children will be thus separated from the associations and traditions of pauperism. This aim may or may not be realised, but it must be kept in

VANITY FAIR.

July 9 1880

Vincent Brooks, Day & Son, Lith.

"Tory organisation"

Plate 25
Sir John Gorst, a
friend of Henrietta
and co-funder of
the State Children's
Association.

view, if we are not to train up a whole class of hereditary and professional paupers." This endorsement of her recommendation delighted Henrietta, who would have been accustomed to the rather aloof and guarded style of *Times* leader-writers. Samuel wrote to his brother: "Once more the wife's thoroughness told, and as a reward she got the first-rate article in *The Times*. Did you read it? The thing is really good. All yesterday she was in ecstasies."[236]

Well aware that reports were often shelved and forgotten, in 1896 Henrietta, Dr Ernest Hart and Sir John Gorst founded the State Children's Association "to obtain individual treatment for children under the Guardianship of the State". This was a pressure group which aimed at persuading government and Parliament to adopt the recommendations of the report. Henrietta was the honorary secretary of the SCA and spoke to numerous public meetings about the work of the association. They had three very specific aims:

"1. To obtain the dissolution of large aggregated schools, so that the children may be brought up when possible in families, or in small groups, where they will be in daily touch with the various interests and activities of social life;

2. To dissociate the children from all connection with the Workhouse and the officials who have to deal with a pauper class;

3. To obtain for the State further powers of control over neglected children."[237]

The SCA was chaired by an impressive series of Lords – Lord Peel, Lord Herschell, Lord Grey, Lord Crewe, Lord Burghclere and Lord Lytton. These were men from the very top of the political establishment. Lord Crewe, a coal owner of immense wealth, had to resign from the chairmanship of the SCA in 1905 when he became a minister in the Liberal government. Lord Herschell had been Lord Chancellor. Lord Lytton was to be Viceroy of India. Later Henrietta used these aristocratic contacts to form the Hampstead Garden Suburb: Lord Grey, Lord Crewe and Lord Lytton were chairmen of the Hampstead Garden Suburb Trust.

The association issued pamphlets, drafted bills and held many public meetings. Throughout all this, Henrietta was the mainspring of the association. In a footnote in her biography, *Canon Barnett*, she quotes a clerk of a board of guardians being overheard in the National Liberal Club to say: "We could of course crowd the children, but one can't put two in a bed without Mrs Barnett and her Society coming down on us with a question in the House, or a note to the Local Government Board."[238]

Henrietta lobbied Parliament, where she gained the support of a group of MPs. The parliamentary committee of the SCA was very strong and engineered debates in the Commons every year when the Local Government Board estimates were considered. They amended legislation and drafted bills, despite being strongly opposed by thousands of guardians of the poor and the Local Government Board, who had their entrenched interests. Henrietta claimed that in the first year, by constant pressure, no less than thirteen of the recommendations of the departmental committee were adopted by the Local Government Board.[239] Henrietta wrote an impressive letter to *The Times* in 1897[240] which showed her extraordinary grasp of the administrative confusion of the control of children in care. The Home Office, the Education Department and the Local Government Board were responsible at the centre, supervising four local authorities – the London School Board, the Metropolitan Asylums Board, the guardians and various committees controlling homes and reformatories. Henrietta recommended that all the children's homes, hospitals and schools should be controlled by the Education Department. Anyone reading *The Times* that day would have been impressed by that long letter. Henrietta now had a national reputation for her work for child welfare.

In 1897 the SCA obtained an amendment to the Infant Life Protection Act – which had abolished baby-farming, a cloak for infanticide. Ernest Hart played an important part in this reform, which is not surprising as he had instigated the original Act. Unfortunately he died in the same year and so Henrietta could no longer turn to him for advice and support. However Sidney Webb was an active member of the SCA Committee. In March 1898, Samuel Barnett mentioned in a letter: "At this moment my wife, under the leadership of Sidney Webb, is attacking the Asylum Board. Her Bill was introduced yesterday, and is down for second reading on Thursday. It looks as if it would pass."[241]

A common interest in Poor Law reform brought the Barnetts and Webbs together. Writing to his nephew in January 1899, Samuel said Henrietta was much occupied with Dolloms (Dorothy) who had a high temperature, "but yesterday got away for a few hours to a SCA meeting where a lot of Guardians blessed the plan of scattered homes. This afternoon we expect the Webbs to lunch."[242]

Henrietta had made a lasting friendship with Gorst. When he was piloting the great Education Act of 1902 through Parliament, he came under attack and confided: "When the Bds. of Guardians abused you and me for the Poor law Children Report, we were not hurt: why should we be hurt because the S.B.s [School Boards] abuse me under circumstances very similar – But all the abuse in the world will not divert me from my purpose."[243] He signed this letter with his initials – very informal at that time. He continued to look to Henrietta and the SCA for help. In a letter to Samuel he wrote: "Give my kindest love to Mrs Barnett & say that I expect Sca to brief me for a speech on P.L. Children next session on the address".[244] (This was one of the most important parliamentary speeches of the year.) He continued to visit the Barnetts: "Will you have me for Sunday?" he wrote, "The 3rd class bedroom will do. I would cycle up on Sat. morning."[245] He was going to join them at St Jude's Cottage in Hampstead.

The SCA promoted other legislation dealing with children. They secured the passing of a Vagrant Act in 1903 which gave better protection to vagrant children. Samuel wrote that while Yetta was working on raising money to extend Hampstead Heath, "She is also concerned in getting a Vagrant Bill thro the House. Gorst is bringing it in, perh the Govt will support it."[246] Henrietta was very concerned with the treatment of juvenile offenders. Back in 1895 she had written a letter to *The Times* about the treatment of children on remand who were kept in the workhouse. At the Islington workhouse she had seen six boys kept in one small room:

> "There were no tables, no chairs, and they were eating their dinners on the floor. There were no books, pictures or playthings; only six beds which during the day were turned up on end. – In this room the boys live, wash, eat, sleep, sometimes for three weeks, sometimes longer. Last week there were 15 lads there, and then, the matron told us, they slept three in a bed."

In the same workhouse three girls aged twelve, nine, and ten were sharing a very small room with a prostitute and a "half-wit". These children had been arrested for begging, truancy or other minor offences. Henrietta asked that their cases should be heard in a special court and that "they should be treated when under remand as naughty children, and not subjected to degrading and contaminating associations".[247]

When the Conservative government was replaced by the great reforming Liberal government, the probation system was initiated by the Probation of Offenders Act 1907, and juvenile courts were introduced with the Children Act 1908. Lord Lytton, who was chairman of the SCA, claimed that both these important reforms were due to the association's work.[248] Lord Lytton said he owed much of his knowledge of the "child question" to Henrietta. This was indeed an important pressure group and it is a pity that their full records cannot be found.

Despite some reforms, a great deal remained to be done for poor-law children. The Royal Commission on the Poor Law reported in 1908, revealing that there were few improvements in the care of children. This was one of the great reports of the previous century but it was very lengthy and too detailed to be widely read. Henrietta made a summary of the parts concerning children in simple and readable English which was published in the *Cornhill Magazine*.[249] According to the report, there were still 22,000 children in workhouses and 12,000 in the hateful barrack schools, compared with only 8,600 boarded out in families and 17,000 in village communities or scattered homes. Details of the care given in workhouses make horrific reading: "The whole nursery has often been found under the charge of a person actually certified as of unsound mind, the bottles sour, the babies wet, cold and dirty … one feeble-minded woman was set to wash a baby; she did so in boiling water, and it died." In some workhouses the babies were never taken out of doors. In one, the babies unable to feed themselves were placed in a row and all fed from one plate of rice pudding with one spoon! It is not surprising that the mortality rate was very high.

Despite the protests of the SCA, the Local Government Board was still the department responsible for most of these children. Although John Burns was now the President of the Board, it had so many duties that the welfare of children was neglected. In the Minority Report of the 1896 Departmental Committee, Henrietta had recommended that the Board of Education should be in control and now she strongly reiterated this opinion for, as she said, "This Board's one concern is children."

The State Children's Association was wound up in 1937 following Henrietta's death. At that time Lord Stanmore was the chairman and Marion Paterson was the honorary treasurer. The association was short of funds and the main objectives had been achieved, as the barrack schools had been abolished and children were not kept in workhouses. "State children" are now called "children in care", but this may be a misleading term, as shown by revelations of child abuse by foster-parents and in children's homes. It seems a pity that the SCA did not continue.

Writing of her work for the SCA, Henrietta said: "In all this work my husband did his share by counsel and comfort, the latter of which was often wanted, for I am one of the women who are not fit for public work, and dislike and distrust all forms of conflict." The first part of this quotation seems an indirect way of claiming that though Samuel gave his support, the work was all her own, which indeed it was. But to claim she was not fit for public work seems false modesty. By the turn of the century Henrietta was a skilful lobbyist. Samuel mentions in a letter: "Yesterday she was at the H. of C. preparing her committee wh. meets there on Tuesday to plan a campaign agst. Chaplin."[251] Evidently she knew the scheming, preparatory work and influence needed. It is true that she had always remained aloof from party politics, but she was a most effective campaigner and certainly able to "handbag" anyone in her way.

References for Part One

1. Birth Certificate.
2. Pigot's Directory 1834.
3. HB *Canon Barnett I*. p. 38.
4. From monumental inscription, St Mary's Church, Lewisham.
5. Paterson, Marion ms. Quasi-Biography of Henrietta Barnett, LMA/4063/006 Chap. I.
6. Paterson, Marion ms. Chap. I. The diary and notebooks have not survived.
7. Paterson, Marion ms. Chap. 1.
8. Paterson, Marion ms. Chap. I. Henrietta bequeathed this desk to her godchild, Vera Gilchrist Thompson.
9. HB *Canon Barnett II* p. 378. I am indebted to Jonquil Griffith for drawing my attention to Henrietta's very brief mention of her mother's religion.
10. The Bible is in the HGS Archive.
11. Paterson, Marion ms. Chap. I.
12. Paterson, Marion ms. Chap. XXVII.
13. HB, *Matters that Matter* p. 144.
14. Paterson, Marion ms. Chap. II.
15. Hopkins, Ellice *Life and Letters of James Hinton* Kegan Paul, 1878.
16. HB, *Matters that Matter* p. 144.
17. 1871 Census.
18. Paterson, Marion ms. Chap. III.
19. LMA/4266/A/181.
20. Prochoska, F.K. *Women and Philanthropy in 19th Century England* Clarendon Press, 1980 pp. 110–13.
21. Prochoska, F.K. op cit. pp. 130–1.
22. Thomson Hill, William *Octavia Hill* p. 76.
23. HB *Canon Barnett I*. p. 72.
24. Paterson, Marion ms. Chap. III.
25. Paterson, Marion ms. Chap. III.
26. HB *Canon Barnett I*. p. 35.
27. HB *Canon Barnett I*. p. 37.
28. Mackenzie, Norman and Jeanne *Diary of Beatrice Webb* Vol. 1. p. 170.
29. Webb, Beatrice *My Apprenticeship* p. 236.
30. Paterson, Marion ms. Chap. IV.
31. HB *Canon Barnett I*. p. 53.
32. HB *Canon Barnett I*. p. 67.
33. HB *Canon Barnett I*. p. 68.

34. HB *Canon Barnett I*. p. 74.
35. HB *Canon Barnett I*. p. 75.
36. HB *Canon Barnett I*. p. 141.
37. HB *Canon Barnett I*. p. 115.
38. HB *Canon Barnett I*. p. 155.
39. HB *Canon Barnett I*. p. 89.
40. HB *Canon Barnett I*. p. 129.
41. HB *Canon Barnett* I. p. 131. The three houses were eventually pulled down to make room for Toynbee Hall tennis courts.
42. MacKenzie, Norman and Jeanne *Diary of Beatrice Webb*. Virago, 1982.
43. HB *Canon Barnett I*. p. 136.
44. HB *Canon Barnett I*. p. 142.
45. HB *Canon Barnett I*. p. 284. Description by a pupil teacher.
46. HB *Canon Barnett I*. p. 286.
47. HB *Canon Barnett I*. p. 105.
48. HB *Canon Barnett I*. p. 104.
49. HB *Canon Barnett I*. p. 265.
50. HB *Canon Barnett I*. p. 104.
51. HB *Canon Barnett II*. p. 313.
52. HB *Canon Barnett I*. p. 116.
53. HB *Canon Barnett II*. p. 145.
54. HB *Canon Barnett II*. p. 373.
55. HB *Canon Barnett I*. p. 278.
56. Oral evidence of Mrs Ailsa Hoblyn.
57. Letter in HGS Archive. Barnett file.
58. HB *Canon Barnett II*. p. 35.
59. *The Youth of Miss Marion Paterson*. Ms. in HGS Archive. Author unknown.
60. Letter of M. Paterson to Uely Barnett in *Quasi Biography of Henrietta Barnett*. LMA ACC/3816/02/01/010.
61. D'Arcy Cresswell *Margaret Macmillan*.
62. Greenwood, James *The Seven Curses of London* London: Stanley Rivers, p. 282.
63. Metropolitan Association for Befriending Young Servants. *Leaflet*. 1876. BLPES.
64. Young, A F and Ashton, E T *British Social Work in the Nineteenth Century*. Routledge.1956. p. 145.
65. HB *Canon Barnett I*. p. 120.
66. HB *Canon Barnett.I*. p. 116.
67. HB *Canon Barnett I*. p. 119.
68. HB *Canon Barnett I*. pp. 122–3.
69. Nevinson, Margaret *Life's Fitful Fever* A&C Black.
70. Prochoska, F.K. *Women and Philanthropy in 19th Century England* Clarendon Press, 1980 p. 181.
71. Henrietta Barnett *The Young Women in our Workhouses* Macmillan's Magazine, August 1879.
72. HB *Canon Barnett I*. p. 209.
73. HB *Canon Barnett I*. p. 211.
74. HB *Canon Barnett I*. p. 212.
75. LMA/ACC/3816/02/01/003.
76. HB *Canon Barnett I*. p. 124.
77. HB *Canon Barnett I*. p. 289.
78. Paterson, Marion ms. Chap. V.

79. HB *Canon Barnett I*. p. 124 Leonard Montefiore died in 1879. He was a friend and supporter during the1870s, providing flowers for the Flower Shows.
80. Paterson, Marion ms. Chap. V.
81. 1881 Census.
82. HB *At Home to the Poor*, Cornhill Magazine, May 1881. Reprinted in S.A. and H.O. Barnett, Practicable Socialism 1888 pp. 76–7.
83. HB *Canon Barnett I*. p. 157.
84. HB *Canon Barnett I*. p. 158.
85. HB *Canon Barnett I*. p. 177.
86. HB *Canon Barnett I*. p. 178.
87. Aitken, W. Francis, *Canon Barnett*. S.W. Partridge. London. 1902.
88. Letter to *The Times* 2 June 1899 p. 13.
89. HB *Canon Barnett I*. pp. 30–31.
90. C. Edmund Maurice, *Life of Octavia Hill as told in her letters*. 1913.
91. C. Edmund Maurice, *Life of Octavia Hill as told in her letters*. Letter to Mrs Barnett, 20/11/1875.
92. C. Edmund Maurice, *Life of Octavia Hill as told in her letters*. p. 347.
93. C. Edmund Maurice, *Life of Octavia Hill as told in her letters*. p. 290.
94. C. Edmund Maurice, *Life of Octavia Hill as told in her letters*. p. 281.
95. C. Edmund Maurice, *Life of Octavia Hill as told in her letters*. Letter to Canon Barnett, 11/9/1874.
96. C. Edmund Maurice, *Life of Octavia Hill as told in her letters*. Letter to Mrs Barnett, 26/1/1875.
97. Letter of Octavia Hill to Mrs Barnett. 29/1/1877. BLPES Archive.
98. Letter of Octavia Hill to Mrs Barnett. 21/1/1874. BLPES Archive.
99. Letter of Octavia Hill to Mrs Barnett. 1/11/1874 et seq. BLPES Archive.
100. HB *Canon Barnett I*. p. 177.
101. Letter of Octavia Hill to Mrs Barnett. 24/8/1877. BLPES Archive.
102. Letter of Octavia Hill to Mrs Barnett. 5/9/1879. BLPES Archive.
103. Letter of Octavia Hill to Mrs Barnett. 20/12/1890. BLPES Archive.
104. Letter of Octavia Hill to Mrs Barnett. 13/2/1905. BLPES Archive.
105. HB *Canon Barnett I*. p. 217.
106. HB *Canon Barnett I*. pp. 119–120.
107. HB *Canon Barnett I*. p. 105.
108. HB *Canon Barnett I*. p. 314.
109. HB *Canon Barnett I*. p. 282.
110. HB *Canon Barnett I*. p. 176.
111. HB *Canon Barnett I*. p. 175.
112. Letter from Kate Potter to Leonard Courtney. 19 May 1882. Courtney Coll. 3/10. BLPES Archive.
113. *Pall Mall Gazette*, 15 March 1883. p. 8.
114. *Diary of Beatrice Webb* p. 214.
115. Nevinson, Margaret, *Life's Fitful Fever*. p. 79.
116. Nevinson, Margaret, *Life's Fitful Fever*. p. 79.
117. Nevinson, Margaret, *Life's Fitful Fever*. p. 79.
118. Maurice, C. Edmund, *Life of Octavia Hill as told in her letters*. 1913. p. 264–5.
119. HB *Canon Barnett I*. pp. 221–2.
120. HB *Canon Barnett I*. pp. 81, 92, 148.
121. Duncan, David *Life and Letters of Herbert Spencer*. 1908. p. 205.
122. Clodd, Edward *Memories*. London: Watts 1926. pp. 50–52.

123. Paterson, Marion ms. Chap. IX.

124. Spencer, Herbert *An Autobiography*. 1904. p. 335.

125. LMA/4266/A/110.

126. HB *Canon Barnett I*. p. 149.

127. Sims, George R *How the Poor Live and Horrible London*.1889. p. 1.

128. Canon S A Barnett and Mrs S A Barnett, *Practicable Socialism*. Longmans 1915, p. 116.

129. ed. Edwards, Paul *The Encyclopedia of Philosophy*. Macmillan N.Y. 1967.

130. HB *What has the Charity Organisation Society to do with Social Reform?* Published in Barnett, *Practicable Socialism* 1888. p. 158.

131. HB *The Poverty of the Poor* Published in Barnett, *Practicable Socialism* 1888. p. 4.

132. Barnett, Rev. and Mrs Samuel A *Practicable Socialism, Introduction*. 1888.

133. Quoted in Aitken, W. Francis, *Canon Barnett*. S.W. Partridge. 1902. p. 109.

134. Pimlott, J A R *Toynbee Hall*. J M Dent: 1935.pp. 74–75.

135. HB *Canon Barnett II*. p. 41.

136. HB *Canon Barnett II*. p. 84.

137. Pimlott., J A R, *Toynbee Hall*. J M Dent 1935. pp. 74–75.

138. Letter to Henrietta Barnett. BLPES 12.11.1876.

139. HB *Canon Barnett II*. pp. 151–179. This section is largely drawn from Henrietta's full account.

140. HB *Pictures for the People*, 1883 in Cornhill Magazine, reprinted in *Practicable Socialism*, 1888.

141. HB *Canon Barnett II*. p. 160.

142. HB *Canon Barnett II*. p. 160.

143. LMA F/BAR 24.

144. HB *Canon Barnett II*. p. 164.

145. Letter from Walter Crane to HB dated 30 Jan 1889. LMA/4266/A/180.

146. HB *Canon Barnett II*. p. 160.

147. HB *Canon Barnett I*. p. 218.

148. Letter to Mrs Barnett. BLPES. 1880.

149. HB *Matters That Matter* p. 20.

150. HB *Matters That Matter* pp. 18–19.

151. HB *Matters That Matter* p. 30. Boris Anrep made mosaic pavement for the National Gallery and Tate Gallery. He worked free of charge for Henrietta, as had so many other people.

152. *The Record* Hampstead Garden Suburb. Nov. 1914.

153. Birmingham City Archives MS466/69/4.

154. Borzello, Frances *Civilising Caliban*, The Misuse of Art 1875–1980, pp. 40–41. Routledge and Kegan Paul. 1987.

155. HB *Canon Barnett II*. p. 273.

156. Paterson, Marion ms. Chap. VI.

157. Letter from Octavia Hill to Mr Barnett. BLPES Archive. Coll Misc 512. 1880.

158. *Diary of Beatrice Webb* p. 214.

159. Address given by the Archbishop of Canterbury at the Funeral of Dame Henrietta Barnett, D.B.E., on June 15th, 1936 at St. Jude's-on-the-Hill, Hampstead Garden Suburb. HGS Archives, Barnett file.

160. HB *Canon Barnett I*. p. 276.

161. HB *Passionless Reformers* Fortnightly Review 1882, reprinted in *Practicable Socialism* 1888, p. 57.

162. Paterson, Marion ms. Chap. VI.

163. HB. The *Place of Women in the Established Church*, reprinted in Dame Henrietta Barnett: *Matters That Matter*. 1930.

164. HB *Canon Barnett II*. p. 123.
165. HB *Canon Barnett II*. p. 183.
166. HB *Canon Barnett I*. p. xiii. II. p. 385.
167. HB *Canon Barnett II*. p. 65.
168. Pimlott, Ben, *Toynbee Hall*. p. 155.
169. HB *Canon Barnett I*. p. 183.
170. Lowndes, G A N *Silent Social Revolution*. 1937. pp. 21, 25.
171. LMA. F/BAR/60.
172. HB *Canon Barnett I*. p. 345.
173. Paterson, Marion ms. Chap. X1X.
174. LMA/ACC/3816/02/01/005.
175. HB *Canon Barnett I*. pp. 346–7.
176. Journal of the Chelsea Pupil Teachers. 1892.
177. LMA. F/BAR 2.
178. LMA. F/BAR 27.
179. HB *Matters That Matter* p. vii.
180. LMA/F/BAR/153.
181. Paterson, Marion, Chap. XIII p 73.
182. HB *Canon Barnett I*. p. 382.
183. HB *The Making of the Home* p. 2.
184. Aitken, W. Francis, *Canon Barnett*. p. 100.
185. Barnett, Mrs S A *The Making of the Body*, 1894.
186. HGS Archive. Press cutting in Barnett file.
187. Bosanquet, Helen *Social Work in London, 1869–1912*. John Murray 1914. p. 195–204.
188. HB *Canon Barnett I*. p. 123.
189. Bosanquet, Helen *Social Work in London, 1869–1912*. p. 198.
190. Report of Departmental Committee on *Elementary Education of Defective and Epileptic Children* 1898 c8747, xxvi.
191. Report of Departmental Committee on *Elementary Education of Defective and Epileptic Children* 1899 c32.
192. HB *Canon Barnett II*. p. 306.
193. Paterson, Marion ms. Chap. I.
194. LMA/F/BAR/14.
195. HB *Canon Barnett II*. p. 75.
196. Paterson, Marion ms. Chap. VII.
197. Paterson, Marion ms. Chap. V. p. 26a.
198. HB *Canon Barnett I*. p. 67.
199. LMA. F/BAR 61//65, 68.
200. LMA. F/BAR/82.
201. LMA.F/BAR/91–93.
202. Paterson, Marion ms. Chap. X11.
203. LMA/F/BAR/225.
204. HB *Canon Barnett I*. p. 380.
205. Paterson, Marion ms. Chap. IX.
206. Pimlott, Ben, *Toynbee Hall*. p. 155.
207. HB *Canon Barnett I*. p. 255.

208. Paterson, Marion ms. Chap. X.
209. HB *Canon Barnett II*. p. 131.
210. Paterson, Marion, *Journal*. 18 Feb.1891. LMA/4063/005.
211. HB *Canon Barnett II*. p. 131.
212. Paterson, Marion ms. Chap. IX.
213. HB *Canon Barnett II*. p. 131.
214. LMA ACC/3816/02/01/004.
215. SAB/HB *Our Diary*. Canada etc 1890–91. Typescript. LMA: ACC/3816/02/02/001.
216. SAB/HB *Our Diary*. p. 31.
217. SAB/HB *Our Diary*. p. 30.
218. SAB/HB *Our Diary*. p. 38.
219. HB *Canon Barnett II*. p. 31.
220. SAB/HB *Our Diary*. p. 82.
221. SAB/HB *Our Diary*. p. 145.
222. HB *Canon Barnett II*. pp. 141–145 Henrietta's account of the life and death of Dorothy.
223. Paterson, Marion ms. Chap. X11.
224. HB *Canon Barnett II*. p. 211.
225. LMA/F/BAR/102.
226. LMA/F/BAR/122.
227. HB *Canon Barnett I*. pp. 216–7.
228. HB *Canon Barnett II*. p. 39.
229. Paterson, Marion ms. Chap. VIII.
230. HB *Canon Barnett II*. p. 291.
231. Paterson, Marion ms. Marion gives 1894 as the date.
232. HB *Canon Barnett II*. p. 293.
233. HB *Canon Barnett II*. p. 294.
234. LMA F/BAR 133 7.12.1895.
235. HB *Canon Barnett II*. p. 294.
236. *HB Barnett Canon II*. p. 294.
237. *Annual Charities Register and Digest*. 1901.
238. HB *Canon Barnett II*. p. 296.
239. HB *Canon Barnett II*. p. 295.
241. Letter quoted in HB *Canon Barnett I*. p. 296.
242. LMA/F/BAR/190.
243. LMA/4266/A/046.
244. LMA/4266/A/047.
245. LMA/4266/A/048.
246. LMA. F/BAR/298.
247. *The Times* 30 October 1895.
248. *The Times* 12 February 1897. Interview with Lord Lytton in *The Record* (Hampstead Garden Suburb) March 1914 p. 102.
249. HB *The Babies of the State* The Cornhill Magazine, July 1909, and in *Practicable Socialism*, 250. LMA/F/BAR/219252.

PART TWO

Community Planner
1900–1936
New Century – New Energy

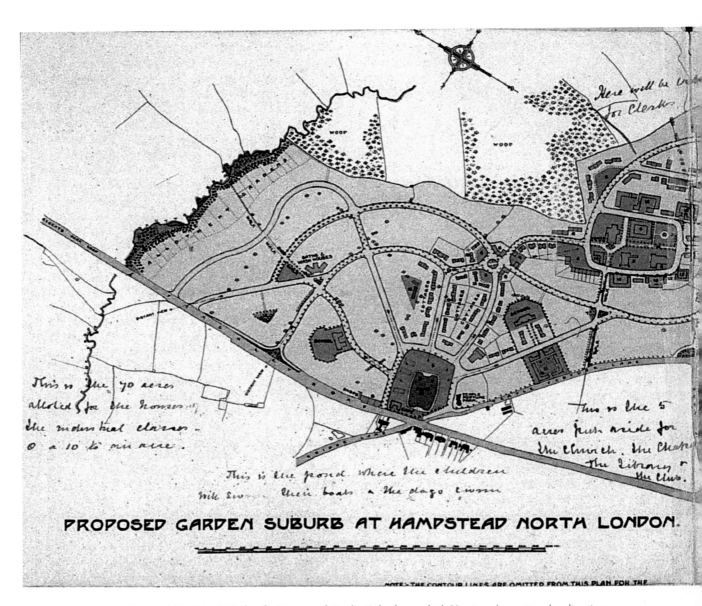

Raymond Unwin's 1905 plan for Hampstead Garden Suburb, on which Henrietta has written her directions as to the siting of her numerous community projects.

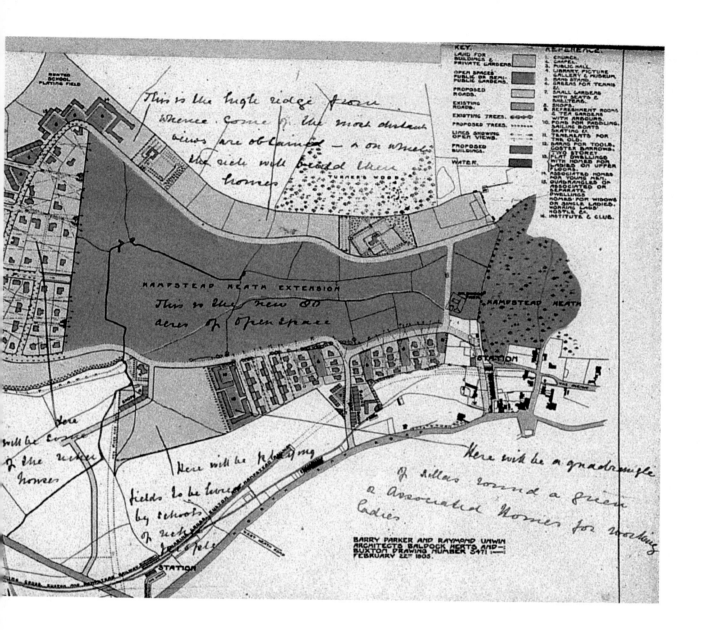

This is the high ridge from
whence come of the most distant
views are obtained — & on which
the rich will build their
homes

HAMPSTEAD HEATH EXTENSION

This is they new 80
acres of open space

HAMPSTEAD HEATH

STATION

Here
will be some
of the richer
homes

Here will be playing
fields to be turned
by schools
& rich
people

STATION

Here will be a quadrangle
of villas round a green
& associated homes for working
ladies.

BARRY PARKER AND RAYMOND UNWIN
ARCHITECTS BALDOCK HERTS, AND
BUXTON DRAWING NUMBER 341
FEBRUARY 22ᵗʰ 1905.

Chapter 15

The Heath Extension and the Founding of the Hampstead Garden Suburb

Living in the polluted air of Whitechapel, the Barnetts longed for the country and as we have already seen, in 1889 they bought Heath End House, close by the Spaniards Inn in Hampstead. The house is now marked by a blue plaque. They re-named the house St Jude's Cottage, although it is a very big cottage. They usually spent Friday and Saturday there, often with invalids from Whitechapel and nearly always with relatives and friends visiting or staying. Their visitors book includes the names of many eminent people: Canon Rawnsley, a founder of the National Trust, William Beveridge, famous for welfare reform, Adrian Boult the conductor, a nephew of Marion Paterson, Henry Ward, an LCC alderman who lived in Toynbee Hall and lent his car to Henrietta, Sir William and Lady Markby from Oxford, Charles Aitken, first director of the Whitechapel Art Gallery, Harrison Townsend, the Art Nouveau architect who designed the Whitechapel Art Gallery and 2 Temple Fortune Lane, and Sir John Gorst MP who stayed very frequently and must have been very welcome for his humour.[1] One of Gorst's remarks was "Do nothing hastily except gripping fleas."[2]

The Barnetts delighted in the unspoilt countryside spreading northward from their house. They travelled often, and in 1896 on a voyage to Russia a fellow-passenger, an American railway magnate, told them that there was a plan to build the Northern Line Underground, to run from Charing Cross to Golders Green. He intended to build a station at the Wyldes, less than half a mile from St Jude's Cottage. They realised that a new station would result in the building of thousands of new houses for commuters, and the precious countryside with its fields and hedgerows would be ruined by dreary rows of houses such as they saw in Willesden. In 1902 Charles Tyson Yerkes formed the Underground Electric Company and an Act of Parliament sanctioned the extension of the Hampstead Tube to Golders Green.[3]

From 1901 Henrietta was trying to raise money to buy the fields beyond the woods below their house, and save them from building. She hoped to make them an extension of Hampstead Heath so that they would be preserved by the London County Council. Henrietta found her feelings were shared by Emily Field, secretary of the Hampstead Heath Protection Society. Emily lived at Squire's Mount, Hampstead; she gave the carved stone drinking fountain which is near the top of the Heath Extension. In 1903 they brought in other sympathisers to form a committee: "Miss Field and I, especially, moaned in concert, and so on Palm Sunday a few of us came together in St Jude's Cottage drawing room and formed ourselves into the HAMPSTEAD HEATH EXTENSION COMMITTEE."[sic][4] They obtained an offer from the owners, Eton College Trustees, of an option on the purchase of 80 acres at the low price of £600 per acre. They gathered a large group of supporters, collected promises

Plate 26
The Field Fountain,
erected by Emily
Field in memory
of her father, a
water-colour artist.
Jack Whitehead and
Marjorie Clift
of 108 Willifield Way
are taking a drink,
1912.

of £3,000 in only two weeks, opened a bank account and, as Henrietta said: "We have interested the press, without whom one can now do no public work."[5]

A more formal organisation was needed and so the Hampstead Heath Extension Council was created with the Rt Hon G J Shaw Lefevre as president. He must have been invited by Henrietta who had met him in 1894 when he was president of the Local Government Board and he had appointed her as a member of the Departmental Committee on Poor Law Schools. Also she knew his family for when the Barnetts visited Oxford to get support for Toynbee Hall, Miss Shaw Lefevre would lend them the Somerville pony so they could drive out to the countryside.[6] The council had 179 members and included five bishops and twelve peers and many people who lived in Hampstead. Sir Robert Hunter and Edward Bond were the treasurers and Henrietta was honorary secretary.[7] The previous committee was to continue as the executive committee. Henrietta explained the scheme at the first meeting and stressed the importance of open space to London and especially East London, for which the Heath was the nearest open space: "Personally I do not care for this scheme as one who sometimes rests in a cottage at Hampstead, but as one who works in a Hall in Whitechapel." But she did care deeply about the view, for one of the Potter family who visited St Jude's Cottage relates that as he was leaving,

> "… in her friendly way she walked with me, as she often did to the gate in the garden fence, but on this occasion instead of leaving me she took my arm and led me under the fir trees to the brow of the hill. At the foot of the slope lay Tooley's Farm, now the Heath Extension; further on Temple Fortune Farm, then being farmed by a Mr Yells; on the right Bourne's farm, and beyond, fields, woods and hedgerows, stretching away to Harrow and to the Stanmore and Elstree ridge of hills. Waving her hand across the beautiful scene she asked: 'What is to become of this? Are those fields to be replaced by slate roofs? Is all this to be a second Kentish Town?' and then after a pause: 'We must do better than that.'"

They needed to raise £48,000 to buy the 80 acres, and Henrietta was the major fund-raiser: "Mrs Barnett reported that she had been crying after these fields for over two years, and written to Lord Iveagh, Lord Hobhouse, Mr Carnegie and other wealth owners."[8] Henrietta and Marion Paterson signed "thirteen thousand letters, not circular, but individual letters". There were street and shop collections and house visits, drawing-room meetings and public meetings. The approach to the press was carefully planned. Members of the Committee undertook to interest various newspapers – *The Times, Chronicle, Daily Graphic, Spectator, Telegraph, Standard, The Builder, The Field, St James's Gazette, The Echo.* Henrietta approached the *Morning Post, Daily Mail, Westminster Gazette, Express, Today* and Hampstead papers.[9] By March 1904, 159 press notices had appeared. They tailored their articles to fit the different papers: "17 articles had been written in the various styles of the various newspapers," Henrietta reported.[10] For the *Hampstead and Highgate Express* she chose a poetic style:

> "It is delightful to those of us who know the lives of town workers, the stress and pain of heat, and crowds and noise, to think that the Tube will soon bring swiftly and cheaply hundreds and thousands of them to the clean air and verdant loveliness which the heath affords. But unless the eighty acres of the neighbouring fields are secured the large numbers will destroy the beauty they go to seek, and the streets of small houses that it is proposed to build will spoil the far famed view, and defile the bright, high air with smoke."[11]

They were certainly getting a great deal of support. They must have been very pleased when they heard from a lady-in-waiting that the Princess of Wales (later Queen Mary) was much interested, and also Princess Louise, Duchess of Argyll, a daughter of Queen Victoria.[12] They discussed making use of this royal support in publicity, but decided that they could not because it had been given to them privately. However, Princess Mary was to take a lifelong interest in the Suburb, and in Henrietta, who soon had no hesitation in mentioning royal patronage whenever it was useful. They gathered £22,000 from private donations, including £1,000 each from Lord Rothschild, the Goldsmith's Company and Andrew Carnegie. They hoped to raise the rest from the London County Council, Hampstead Borough Council, and other adjacent local authorities, but the councils were slow and gave less than was hoped. After much negotiation, the boundaries of the 80 acres were changed to allow for building to the south-west of the Extension and the price was reduced to £43,000. Eventually the Heath Extension was bought and conveyed to the London County Council in March 1907. The story reveals how Henrietta could start with a strongly held idea, gain support with a drawing-room meeting, set up a committee of notable men, appeal for money, use the press, persevere and work long and hard to triumph in the end.

Founding the Suburb

Around 1900 the garden city idea was in the air. Ebenezer Howard had set forth the basic ideas in his *Garden Cities of Tomorrow*. Letchworth, New Earswick, and Brentham in Ealing were being built and the model factory towns of Port Sunlight and Bournville had proved successful. In 1897 Henrietta visited her friends, the Cadburys, at Bournville; she was so impressed by their garden suburb that she later called Bournville "the mother of Hampstead Garden Suburb". The Barnetts would have been very aware of all the new developments because they had both been extremely interested and involved in housing problems ever since they started their social work in the 1870s. Their thoughts must have turned to the ideal housing they would like everybody to have, where spiritual and material life could flourish. In 1893 Samuel wrote an article on "The Ideal City", a city of a million people, close to hills and near the sea so foreign visitors would give the inhabitants a knowledge of the world. This was addressed to the people of Bristol. As well as good housing and broad streets lit by electric light, there were to be many open spaces and communal buildings: public libraries, wash-houses, galleries, schools and colleges, prisons (many of them brilliant with mosaic). Everybody would care for his neighbour, and the rich would use their money to build communal facilities. It would be beautiful like Venice and Florence in the Renaissance. This "Ideal City" was mostly about moral and spiritual values and not about the planning of urban space.

One day Henrietta said to Samuel: "If we could only buy a huge estate and build so that all classes could live in neighbourliness together … friendships would come about quite naturally, and the artificial efforts to build bridges need not be made."[13] This was quite a shocking idea. Everybody knew the class characteristic of every district in London. As Kipling observed: "All the people like us are We, and everyone else is They." It is only in the last twenty years that our young people have moved into the East End in force and affordable housing has been built in rich areas, so at last Henrietta's dream is realized. She was taking up Ebenezer Howard's conception of the garden city and uniting it with the educational and social ideals of Toynbee Hall. This remained her central objective: a social ideal as much as a housing development. Brigid Grafton Green has pointed out that in adding housing to the Heath Extension as an objective there was also an important practical consideration: "Mrs Barnett, a good tactician, was quick to realise that councillors might lend a more sympathetic ear to the Heath Extension proposal if it were linked with a plan to improve local working class housing."[14]

In her concise, authoritative booklet *Hampstead Garden Suburb 1907–1977*, Brigid Grafton Green gives an excellent account of the history of the Suburb. I will try to describe Henrietta's part in the story. From 1903 her energies were directed to the creation and development of the Suburb. In July 1903 she wrote to Mr Sanday, manager for the Eton College trustees, asking him to recommend that they should give her the option to buy a further 256 acres for housing on the understanding that there would be no more than eight dwellings per acre. This great new idea possessed her and gave her a new lease of life in her middle age. In a postscript to a letter she wrote: "P.S. I thought the building of our glorious Art Exhib. £25,000 in W'chapel wd be my swan song of public work – but this garden city hope renews my youth."[15]

She describes her meeting with Mr Sanday, the trustees' manager: "Mr Sanday was a tall, grave man, and after I had told him all my hopes, and we had studied maps and discussed prices, he looked down on me and said: "Well, Mrs Barnett, I know you, and I believe in you, but you are *only a woman,* and I doubt if the Eton College Trustees would grant the option of so large and valuable an estate to a woman! Now if you would get *a few men* behind you it would be all right."[16]

Henrietta was amused as well as indignant. If she acted alone she could achieve everything so quickly. "He travels the fastest who travels alone." (Kipling.) But the enterprise was too big for one person and she knew she had to form a committee. She looked round all the people she had met at Toynbee Hall, and she was not afraid of approaching some of the highest people in the land. Remembering the hunting field which she so enjoyed: "Audace, toujours audace, carrying us over some fences,"[17] she chose men who had the same ideals as herself and were likely to succumb to her charms so she could rule the roost. She asked the Earl of Crewe to join her and invited him to lunch with herself and Samuel

**Mr. EBENEZER HOWARD,
The Man Who Invented Garden Cities.**

*Plate 27
Ebenezer Howard,
founder of the garden
city movement..*

at St Jude's Cottage. After lunch Henrietta and Lord Crewe walked across the fields, they climbed the hedges, and toiled through stubbly grass until they reached the central hill. "This is the highest place, and here we will have the houses for worship and for learning, I said; and here they stand."[18]

The other men she recruited were Earl Grey, the Bishop of London, Sir John Gorst, Sir Robert Hunter, Walter Hazell, and Herbert Marnham. Earl Grey was first chairman but had to resign in 1904 as he was made Governor-General of Canada; he was succeeded by the Earl of Crewe. Henrietta described her group as: "Two Earls, two lawyers, two Free Churchmen, a bishop, and a woman – a veritable showman's happy family."[19] What did she mean by "a showman's happy family"? Kit Ikin in his excellent book on the Suburb says: "This has always seemed to me an odd description, and rather rude. I used to assume that it meant the showman with his acrobat, strong man, and wild beast tamer: I have recently discovered that Brewer's *Dictionary* defines travelling menageries as, "the name given to an assortment of animals living together peaceably." Who was the elephant and who the lion?"

These men recruited by Henrietta were long-standing friends or acquaintances, and like-minded people. The Bishop of London, Dr Winnington Ingram, had been their supporter and friend in Whitechapel for many years. In the 1880s the bishop had been warden of Oxford House, a university settlement in the East End, and Bishop of Stepney before he became Bishop of London, so he must have had a real empathy with Henrietta's hope of providing an ideal life for the working class. Sir John Gorst had been her great friend and companion when they both served on the Committee on Poor Law Schools. Sir Robert Hunter, with Octavia Hill and Canon Rawnsley, had founded the National Trust in 1895 and was now its chairman. He was solicitor to the General Post Office and of course his legal knowledge was a great help. He was not a good public speaker, but he was a patient and determined worker. Probably Henrietta had known him for a long time through her friendship with Octavia Hill. Walter Hazell owned a printing firm. He was a member of the Congregational Church and started lunch-time concerts in the City Temple Hall. He did welfare work for women and children in the East End and founded an Emigration Society. Herbert Marnham, a much younger man, was a successful stockbroker. He was treasurer of the Baptist Union and a governor of Mill Hill School and of Mount Vernon Hospital. He was a close friend and a committee member of the Hampstead Heath Extension Council. He was on Hampstead Borough Council and in 1925 became mayor. He must have been a wealthy man for he gave a large sum to the building of the Free Church. Carefully chosen, they were all prominent, influential people who knew Henrietta well and from whom she could expect support for her ideas.

In all her years as a social worker in Whitechapel, Henrietta had mainly dealt with women and had been able to inspire and lead. Now that she had entered into a world of building and finance, publicity and politics, she had to deal with men. Would they accept her leadership? Perhaps she toyed with the idea of finding titled men, not too clever, so she could lead them. But instead she chose clever men who held the same opinions as herself and found herself able to manage them. Writing to a nephew who had emigrated to New Zealand to farm, Henrietta attributed her ability to riding: "Some of the happiest hours of my life were spent in the saddle, & I believe that it was the knowledge of how to ride & rule & <u>love</u> a horse (many horses) wh. makes me now able to manage men – The horse should love one too." She had self-knowledge and humour, but like Mrs Thatcher, she found that a commanding, "unwomanly" style worked with men. She knew she must manage committees to get anything done, although she was constantly chafing against their slow progress for she was always in a hurry to better the world: "Boot, saddle, to horse and away" as Browning said.

Hampstead was very overcrowded and the people and council were very interested in new housing so it was to the *Hampstead and Highgate Express* that Henrietta wrote on 26th November

1903, explaining that Eton College trustees had granted her syndicate of seven men and herself the option to buy the 243 acres "at such a price as will permit a considerable portion of it being used for the erection of houses for the industrial classes". She continued: "The conditions of building are those which ensure the establishment of not a 'garden city,' but a 'garden suburb,' in which every house, however humble, will be surrounded by a garden large enough to be productive as well as pleasurable. The plan, however, will necessitate the provision of some shops, and some houses of larger size and more extensive gardens."

First of all she had to raise the money and buy the land, and this would take years of hard work. With the syndicate (to become the Trust in 1906), Henrietta organised deputations to the London County Council, City companies and Hampstead council, and also to Westminster, St Pancras, Marylebone and Islington councils. From Hampstead they hoped to get £10,000, but the council granted only £5,000.[20] The London County Council gave £8,000 and Middlesex £2,000. Many individuals gave their money and time to help, for Henrietta was now very experienced in whipping up support. She often gave lectures, using the lantern slides of the Cadburys and Raymond Unwin which showed pictures of slums contrasted with the ideal housing of Bournville, Letchworth, New Earswick and Port Sunlight. (These fragile slides and Henrietta's lantern belong to the Hampstead Garden Suburbs Trust and are kept in the London Metropolitan Archives.) Already in December 1903, £17,000 had been raised, and the Princess of Wales (later Queen Mary) headed the subscription list.

There was plenty of opposition to the scheme. There were doubts about the financial viability, about making different classes live together, and whether working-class people could really be interested in gardens. Henrietta knew that there had been many failures, but she was not deterred. Samuel was worried that at the age of 52 she was taking on too much work, and this made her hesitate for a time. He was about to leave Toynbee and be appointed Canon of Westminster Abbey and he was becoming more and more committed to spiritual matters and decided not to get involved with the Suburb, although he always helped her by discussing everything with her and gave her great encouragement.[21] Already she had found her architect, for in September 1904 she read a pamphlet by Raymond Unwin, probably his Fabian Pamphlet 109, *Cottage Plans and Commonsense*. Having read it she said to herself: "That's the man for my beautiful green golden scheme." When they met he reminded her that they had met in Oxford when he was one of Samuel's social service followers. With Henrietta's recommendation, the Trust appointed Unwin as Suburb Architect and Surveyor at a salary of £500 p.a. and commission of 2½% on the outlay of roads supervised by him.[22]

When Unwin was a young man he came to Toynbee to ask Samuel whether he should choose a career in the Church. Samuel had asked him whether he was more troubled by the unhappiness of men or by their wickedness. Unwin replied that he was concerned only with their unhappiness. Samuel advised him not to enter the Church and he had become an architect. Perhaps this student-mentor relationship made it easier for him to accept Henrietta's demands. He was 39 years old when he drew up the first Suburb plan in 1905 and must have seemed young to her. With his partner Barry Parker he had been planner and architect of New Earswick, which was sponsored by the Rowntrees of York, and of Letchworth. He was a Socialist and had been influenced by Ruskin's *Unto This Last,* and by William Morris and James Hinton.[23] These were the same influences that had first come to Henrietta through Miss Carrie, her schoolteacher, and Octavia Hill, and still inspired her thought. So Henrietta and Unwin were very much in agreement in aiming for social improvement and a simple life, closer to nature.

In February 1905 Unwin produced his first plan for the Suburb. Herkomer's portrait of Samuel and Henrietta shows her holding the plan (see pp. 116–117). Friends who called at the house in the Cloisters were drawn into discussing it. Sir Adrian Boult, a young relative of Marion Paterson, wrote:

"I saw the early plans on the floor of their drawing room at the Cloisters. I heard them discussing the possibilities with such different people as Emma Cons of the Old Vic, Sir Robert Hunter of the National Trust, Sir Hubert Herkomer, Sir Edwin Lutyens R.A., and many others."[24]

Henrietta did not alter the road plan, but pencilled comments all over it: "Here will be villas for clerks etc", "Here will be some of the richer houses." The central area was to be like a village with shops, the two churches, institute and club; she planned a library, picture gallery and museum, and a bandstand too. Outside the central area, she had numerous greens for tennis, small gardens with seats and shelters, and two refreshment rooms with tea-gardens. In the artisans' area there was a public bath and wash-house; a pond for paddling, sailing model boats and skating was placed where Queen's Court now stands. Four groups of shops were dotted about. Many of her ideas came from Bournville and Letchworth. There were to be many communal or semi-communal dwellings: associated homes for young men (presumably sharing dining facilities, as happened in Meadway Court), quadrangles of associated or separate dwellings to be homes for widows or single ladies, and a working lads' hostle [sic]. She may have respected her architects' professional knowledge, but she certainly thought she could improve on their plans. She scrawled her directions for communal buildings all over the plan, though she must have discussed the siting with Unwin.

Plate 28 Raymond Unwin was 39 when he made the plan for the Suburb. He moved from Letchworth to live at the Wyldes, where he had his studio and the help of young architects.

*Plate 29
Portrait of Henrietta
and Samuel.
Henrietta is holding
the plan of the
Suburb. Painted
by Sir Hubert von
Herkomer.*

*Plate 30
Photograph of
Henrietta holding
the plan of the
Suburb.*

She pasted the plan into a large album, with many photographs of Suburb land, promising that the trees and hedgerows would be kept wherever possible. She added to the album photos of depressing rows of municipal housing compared with houses in Port Sunlight, New Earswick and Bournville.[25] She circulated this album and another like it to potential investors in the Suburb. With the plan and the photographs the promotion looked convincing.

In June 1906, Unwin moved from Letchworth and rented Wylde's Farm where he lived with his family and had a studio where he was helped by many young architects. From the farm they could look out over the country where their Suburb was to grow. Henrietta got on well with Unwin:

"Of Mr Unwin's rapid adjustment of mind to any and everybody's point of view; of his unsleeping remembrance of the best for everybody; of his fertility of imagination used to provide beauty in out of sight places; of his patience with fools – and their name is a legion! – of his faith in the power of growth in every tiresome insignificant person; of his humility which disliked recognition of his services – (and oh! How I risk the loss of his dear, valued friendship by these sentences) – of his – of his – but I dare not go on! Only I wish it were the world's habit to compel people to add a distinctive addition to their names. I should then choose "None Such" to add to his, but I fear it is already monopolised by an apple."[26]

Unwin may have found the frequent "rapid adjustment" to Henrietta's wishes extremely taxing. After her death he wrote: "As a client Mrs Barnett combined high ideals with a severe sense of economy; and a taste that was often more influenced by picturesque ideas than by very sound aesthetic judgement. When differences of opinion arose between us, we generally managed to come to a mutual solution. We worked together for seven years and soon reached a good understanding."[27] He found that she could deal with opposition: "When her mind was made up, objections and difficulties ceased to exist for her, and largely for those also whom she wished to influence. She had thus great power to persuade other people to help her in the way she wished."[28]

Henrietta was happy with the village centre, but early in 1905 Edwin Lutyens was asked to make another plan for the centre; the central square, the two churches, the Institute, the houses round the square as well as both of the approaches were to be in a grand style by a famous architect. Lutyens was famous for designing many large country

Plate 31
Edwin Lutyens designed the central area of the Suburb. Most of his work on the Suburb was completed by 1911 when he went to India to plan New Delhi.

129

houses and was soon going to design New Delhi, the new capital of India. It is likely that Alfred Lyttleton introduced Lutyens, for he had been working for Lyttleton, designing his house, Grey Walls, in Lothian. In addition to the fee he received for planning Central Square, he was given a retainer fee of 50 guineas a year[29], which does not seem much considering his eminence as an architect. Henrietta could not refuse the services of such an eminent architect. It might be thought that Unwin would have been vexed at having his central area plan scrapped, but architects have to accommodate the wishes and whims of their clients and Unwin and Lutyens were agreeable people. Henrietta was soon writing letters about what she wanted:

> "The great avenues shld be what he calls "closed up" by fine buildings, & I shld like nothing better than for the Church & the Chapel to stand each on the end of one of the two great Avenues, the Church crowned by a Spire. The Chapel by a Tower or if you like it to be 'vice versa.' It would be an outward & visible sign of your & my faith that worship is the highest act of human life, & that the individuality given us by our Creator must find its expression in various methods of worship.
>
> I am however exceedingly anxious to get the worship houses ready <u>soon.</u> We have already 200 people living here, by the end of the year we shall have 1200 & unless we act soon there will be nowhere to pray. I have fixed £10,000 as the kind of Church we need – To be externally beautiful & to hold 400 to 500. I have got £3,250 for it already. Will your Free Church be of a similar class & cost? I shld like each to stand before all men as equal – Oh! <u>What</u> a Canon's wife!!"[30]

There were many other architects involved in designing the houses. Lutyens and Unwin both employed many juniors. Charles Paget Wade, who worked in Unwin's office, prepared plans for Central Square, the Club House (the social centre), and Asmuns Place. Wade lived at 9 Temple Fortune Hill, and dressed in his flowing black cloak, wide-brimmed hat and knee-breeches, he was a familiar sight in the Suburb until he moved to his country house, Snowshill Manor. In 1905 the Country Landowners Association held an exhibition. Henrietta and Unwin went to the exhibition and talent-spotted likely architects whom they invited to work in their Suburb, both to design the cottages and to work for the individual richer clients. In this way they were able to pick architects sympathetic to the Arts and Crafts movement, and involved excellent architects such as Baillie Scott, Courtenay Crickmer and Michael Bunney.[31]

Fortunately Henrietta was content to leave the architecture to the architects, apart from continually reminding them of costs and requiring that "houses will not be put in uniform lines, nor in close relationship". She wanted neighbours to have privacy and hated the uniformity of municipal terraces. She found Unwin's village style of design delightful.

Principles, Publicity and Money

In 1928 Henrietta outlined the main principles of the scheme:-

> "(1) Persons of all classes of society and standards of income should be accommodated, and that the handicapped be welcomed.
> (2) That the cottages and houses should be limited on an average to 8 an acre.
> (3) That the roads should be 40 feet wide, and that the houses should be at least 50 feet apart, gardens occupying the intervening space.
> (4) That the plot divisions should not be walls but hedges or trellis or wire fences.

(5) That every road should be lined with trees, making when possible a colour scheme with the hedges.

(6) That the woods and public gardens should be free to all the tenants without regard to the amount of their ground rent, i.e., the best for all classes.

(7) That noise should be avoided, even to the prohibition of Church or Chapel or Institute bells.

(8) That lower ground rents should be charged in certain areas to enable the weekly wage earners to live on the Estate.

(9) That the houses be so planned that none should spoil each other's outlook or rob its neighbours of beauty."

She stated these principles very clearly in 1928, but she had already formulated them in 1905. It is clear that her interest was not so much in architecture as in community planning and ecology. In her utopia there would be no class conflict, but happy, healthy people living amongst gardens and woodlands, the very opposite of the terrible conditions of Whitechapel. The prohibition of bell-ringing seems odd in a statement of basic principles. Was Henrietta kept awake by the bells of Westminster Abbey and St Jude's in Whitechapel? She had to ask the Bishop of Islington for advice on how to prohibit bells for a certain amount of bell-ringing was required by law.[32]

Temperance was another fundamental principle. Henrietta had seen the drunken men bashing their wives and the frightened and weeping children in the alleys of Whitechapel. She was determined to stop this abuse. Most tenants happily accepted prohibition, for they were trying to save for their house and families and were only too glad if their neighbours were like-minded and there was no temptation. They would busy themselves in the garden and try to forget the Old Bull and Bush, the Spaniards and the Royal Oak just outside the Suburb. There were a few complaints, though the Reverend Basil Bourchier spoke up in favour of beer, and so did a tenant at the Residents Association meeting. Henrietta never saw drunkenness at dinner-parties, for of course the men were careful when ladies were present. One night when she was tucked up in bed my own father was up a lamp-post. When he looked down he saw his friends had scarpered and there was a policeman looking up at him: "Wot are you doing up this 'ere lamp-post?" "I am just lighting the gas and retrieving my top hat, constable." He escaped with a reprimand. Henrietta enjoyed a glass of wine, as we shall discover, and seems to have thought this was quite different from beer-drinking.

Henrietta's most difficult task was to raise more money. The large sum of £200,000 was needed to buy the 243 acres to build the Suburb. This was to be raised by appealing to the public to subscribe to shares in the Trust, either debenture shares yielding 4% or ordinary shares yielding 5%. Applications were to be made to the Honorary Secretary, Henrietta Barnett, at Toynbee Hall. From the start there was an emphasis that this scheme was on a sound financial footing and here Henrietta's experience in management and financial detail was very useful. One recalls her childhood success with mental arithmetic.

Henrietta started a campaign in the press to get support. In March 1905 a long letter from Henrietta, signed by the Trust members, was published in *The Times*. The proposed Suburb would help solve the housing problem and contact with nature would give moral uplift:

"… we believe that in cleaner air, with open space near their doors, with gardens where the family labour would produce vegetables, fruit, and flowers, the people would develop a sense of home life and an interest in nature which form the best security against the temptations of drink and gambling."[33]

The Suburb would be laid out on an orderly plan with small open spaces within reach of every child and old person, and the natural beauty of trees and hedges would be preserved. Of course Big

Wood and Little Wood were sacrosanct and Henrietta planned paths through them. She wanted to open things up and she would not have liked all the brambles that grow now.

Just as she had used the journals successfully to get help for her social work in the past, now she wrote an article for the *Contemporary Review* to explain her scheme. She deplored the way the classes were "divided in the suburbs as definitely as in the towns," with districts for the rich, and districts for the lower middle class with "their small villas side by side, their few yards of garden carefully cherished," and for the industrial classes:

> "... rows and rows of small houses, every one alike, with limited back yards, each only divided from the other by a wall. No gardens, no trees, no open spaces, no public buildings, no children's playgrounds, no spacious thoroughfares, no broad, shady roads, the whole stamped by the landlord's greed, the builder's competition, and the people's helplessness. A combination which has produced miles of 'mean streets', wherein are reared generations of children robbed of their birthright of joyful communion with nature."[34]

She went on to say that in the Suburb there would be small cottages for the industrial classes as well as larger houses for the rich. The overcrowding in urban areas caused a very high death-rate, low vitality, sickness and a disinclination to work, and even an increased number of lunatics. This concern for national health was one of Henrietta's main arguments for better housing, and in 1906 in an article, "Science and City Suburbs", she went into statistical details showing that families living in one-room tenements had a much higher death-rate than those living in three or more rooms. In Manchester health was so poor that during the South African War, of 11,000 men who wished to enlist, only 3,000 passed the low physical standard required. The Boer War was "no end of a lesson". The puny British proved poor adversaries to the tall men who rode the veldt and at this time when there was much talk of national degeneracy it was a telling argument for better housing. "I would venture to affirm that the housing of the people is largely accountable for the evils – spiritual and physical – from which this generation is suffering."[35]

In her *Contemporary Review* article she argued that the separation of classes into separate districts meant that very little money could be raised from rates in the poor districts, moreover, "The English system of government is based on the belief that there is in every district a leisured and cultivated class able to give time and thought to municipal and other public duties, and when such a class is absent the whole suffers both financially and ethically."

In the Suburb, the houses would be carefully arranged so they did not spoil one another's outlook and "the noise of children shall be locally limited". Henrietta had a picture in her mind of all the good things she wanted in her Suburb:

> "A community, however, consists not only of houses. For its higher life it will need houses of prayer, a library, schools, a lecture hall and club houses. For its physical well-being our community will need shops, baths and wash-houses, bakehouses, refreshment rooms and arbours, co-operative stores and agencies for the purpose of fostering interest in gardens and allotments, and the lending of tools which are beyond the means to purchase and unnecessary for everyone to individually possess. It will need also playgrounds for the smaller children and resting places for the aged who could not walk so far as from the end of the estate to the Heath. There will be cottages with individual gardens, and cottages grouped round a quadrangle or common sward, used, perhaps, as a tennis court for teachers before the twopenny Tube carries them to their work in London's centre, and later for their young guests whose joy will be to

'visit teacher' on Saturday afternoons and Summer evenings. There will be the semi-detached two-storied houses, on the ground floor of which will dwell the family, with the man at its head who is ready and capable of working neatly and productively his 1/10th of an acre, and on the first floor the poor lady or working woman who takes no less delight in flowers and grass plots because she cannot dig, and whose refining influence will help the children, while their mother will be glad to earn something by doing her domestic work.

There will be associated residences for young men whose common garden and creeper draped balconies will doubtless be a common joy. There will be, I hope, the convalescent home, the co-operative rest house, the training school and the working lad's hostel – for a community should bear the needy and the handicapped in daily mind. There will be the deep-porched and broad-balconied tenements for the old, the single, and the weakly, whose capacities and infirmities, while hindering action, do not hinder suffering from noise, crowd and dirt, nor the power to enjoy the kinder environment befitting their later days."

This was Henrietta's dream, but anyone reading the article was also made aware that the finances were to be on usual business lines, though with the interest on capital limited to 5%: they wanted investment, not charity. Offprints of the article were sent to all Henrietta's friends and supporters to encourage them to invest.

This article in the *Contemporary Review* was followed by a campaign to get notice in the daily papers. A letter from the Trust resulted in a very long article in *The Times* on "The Garden City Movement" and particularly on the scheme for the Hampstead Garden Suburb, of which it strongly approved. There was wide coverage in the national and provincial press. The *Spectator* was enthusiastic, particularly about the rural qualities which would be retained: "In the 'ideal' suburb it will not be a matter for writing to the papers if the nightingales answer one another across the valley, or the cuckoo calls all the June morning; and the word 'suburban' will take on a new meaning."[36]

In July 1905, Henrietta wrote a long article for the *Daily Chronicle*[37] describing the project and announcing that Raymond Unwin had already made the plan. In reply to critics who said rich and poor would never live together, she said that the industrial classes would be on the western end of the estate, the more expensive housing would be near the Heath Extension. In Germany "under wise laws which govern the laying out of the suburbs" there were zones for the separate classes, which mixed together for educational, musical and social opportunities. Moreover, "a very large number of persons have applied for sites, cottages, villas, houses, or to live in the associated homes which it is hoped to have for working ladies…. Everything would be carried out on the strictest business principles. The money sunk would pay interest, and charity and usury would be alike unknown and equally shunned." Henrietta went on to express the hope that the value of the Suburb would increase and then capital could be released which would be used to create more planned suburbs: "… picture, shall we say, Macclesfield or Manchester or Warrington, with one side laid out as a beautiful spot. What divine discontent it would engender, and gradually the example would raise other quarters of the town."

Henrietta had her feet on the ground, but here we get a glimpse of her utopian dream of solving the national housing problem. Population statistics showed the benefit of good housing, and Henrietta dazzled her readers with statistics: "The birth-rate of England and Wales is declining. It has fallen from 29.6 per thousand in 1897 to 27.9 per thousand in 1904. In Port Sunlight it has risen to 56 per thousand … In England and Wales the death-rate is 15.3. In Liverpool it is 22.6. In Port Sunlight it is 9. The death-rate of babes under one year is in Lancaster 274, in Macclesfield 250, in East London 174, in Bourneville 68, per thousand. Surely the 'cry of the children' can work great reforms." The effect of good housing on the birth-rate was noted more recently when inner London people were decanted to the post-1945 New Towns, and planners were surprised by the high birth-rate. Henrietta finished her article in the *Daily Chronicle* by appealing for more investments, large and small, in the Suburb.

Besides the work of secretary and manager, receiving all the correspondence and applications for shares, Henrietta was promoting the scheme by giving interviews, organising social events and giving talks using her magic lantern and slides. She spoke to 400 people who gathered to hear her at Hampstead public library, and 50 people at the Women's Institute, so interested were they in the new Suburb.[38] Henrietta's nerves could not bear this tremendous pressure of work and in June 1905 she went to the country to rest: "Broken down by incessant work and strenuous thought, Mrs Barnett has had to seek rest and restoration to health by a temporary retreat into the country. That she will not be longer out of work than illness actually compels may be confidently expected."[39]

As explained in Part I, she was manic-depressive, or bipolar as it is called now, so that periods of overactivity with a rushing flow of ideas were followed by deep depression, often combined with some physical illness. At the time it was called neurasthenia. When she was hyperactive, she was gay and "such good fun": this was the greatest compliment that my Edwardian parents could give to their friends. She could say with Browning, her favourite poet:

"I find earth not grey but rosy,
Heaven not grim but fair of hue.
Do I stoop? I pluck a posy.
Do I stand and stare? All's blue."

Henrietta recovered quickly and she was back at work in July, inviting people to a large garden party held in the Hampstead house of Frank Debenham, at which the Earl of Crewe, Sir Robert Hunter and Henrietta all spoke.[40] She was probably still struggling with depression, but determined to carry on.

Henrietta hoped that the money for the Suburb would be invested by rich women and held up the example of Baroness Burdett-Coutts, who had created an estate in Highgate, but she did not manage to interest any rich women. She said some people thought that local authorities should provide new housing, but she pointed out that the 1890 Housing Act only permitted them to provide housing for the industrial classes. The London County Council was building vast one-class estates at Tottenham and Edmonton, estates for about 40,000 people. This policy continued, culminating in the vast estates built in the 1960s. It is only in the last twenty years that councils have insisted on affordable housing being built alongside speculative building and we are beginning to see a mix of classes. Another change is that the youngest generation of middle-class children cannot afford to live near their parents, but find housing in the East End, sometimes in flats previously owned by the council. Perhaps they will bring the uplift and leadership to the people that no amount of social work and public money can effect. Henrietta would have rejoiced in the mix of classes and also in the modern preference for providing small houses instead of the ugly "buildings" that she so hated.

In September 1905, £55,000 had been raised towards the £170,000 of share capital needed. The Trust made it known that Charles Booth, Frank Debenham, W H Lever and George Cadbury supported the schemes, and this wealthy and influential backing made it seem respectable. Indeed the Trust did succeed in impressing people with its financial reliability: the *Morning Post* aptly called the Suburb "Arcadia Limited"[41]. On 1st December there was a fresh appeal for support, launched by a letter from the Trust to the *Daily News* which was reported in other papers.[42]

At this time the nation had more important things to think about, for in December 1905 the Liberals led by Sir Henry Campbell-Bannerman had taken office and in January 1906 he called a general election. (There was a constitutional convention that a government gaining power from a victory in the Commons should call an election.) This was a landslide election, a momentous turning-point, the beginning of the great, reforming Liberal government, later led by Asquith and continuing until 1916. Though Henrietta always remained non-party, her supporters were mostly Liberal, and the change of government could only be beneficial for the Garden Suburb. Despite the prorogation of Parliament, private bill procedure continued and a Hampstead Garden Suburb Metropolitan Electric Supply Company Bill was introduced, the first of several legislative measures which would be needed.[43]

After an initial success in raising money, sales of shares slowed down. But in January 1906 *The Times* carried a long article describing and praising the scheme and ending with an appeal for more investment:

> "It would be difficult to suggest a more salutary application of a fraction of one of the great fortunes of the day than in promoting the formation of such a suburb as that designed at Hampstead. Munificent gifts are now and again made to hospitals and other charities. Here is a benefaction touching the welfare of the nation perhaps even more nearly, yet involving no sacrifice of capital, but only its judicious use."[44]

Strangely, it was more difficult to raise investment for the Trust than gifts for charity. People were unused to a mix of charity and investment. In 1906 Henrietta, after recovering from her depression, made many speeches, as Samuel proudly wrote to his brother: "Yesterday she had another field day. There was a big conference with Bryce & Ld Carrington. She read a paper wh. is to be published. It was very good telling what was behind & before the Garden Suburb."[45] Later in the year she addressed a Congress of 1,000 women at Tonbridge.[46] She was amusing and passionate and becoming a popular speaker.

In 1906 the Hampstead Garden Trust Ltd was floated and a board of directors was formed. Samuel was enormously relieved when the company was formed, for until this time Henrietta as honorary secretary had all the work of administration as well as the responsibility for decisions. She had written the prospectus for the company and sent out 5,000 copies. Now the company secretary became responsible for the detailed work.

The Trust office was at Raymond Buildings, Grays Inn, though after a few months the office was moved to Red Lion Square and a few months later to 32 Theobalds Road. (The Trust office is now at 862 Finchley Road, NW11 6AB.) The Trust had rather different membership from the original syndicate. Henrietta was a director together with Frank Debenham, Sir Robert Hunter (chairman of the National Trust), Herbert Marnham, and Henry Vivian MP (Chairman of the Co-partnership Tenants' Housing Council). The chairman was Alfred Lyttleton MP, for Lord Crewe had to resign on becoming Lord President of the Council in the Liberal government. Lyttleton was a Conservative and had been Colonial Secretary in Balfour's 1903 government. Frank Debenham was a member of the family which owned the department store, and he was a councillor in the LCC. Vivian had already been an important adviser and was to prove a very active member of the Trust. He was a Liberal MP, representing Birkenhead and later Totnes. He steered the Hampstead Garden Suburb Bill and other legislation through the House of Commons. The company secretary was Frederick Litchfield, whom the Barnetts had met in the East End where he did mission work. He had also been a milk inspector, as a result of which he never took milk! He was on the boards of many co-partnership societies, and later he lived in the Suburb at 96 Hampstead Way in the square named after him. He was a very good organizer and a happy person who spread optimism. Litchfield soon resigned to become secretary of the Co-partnership Tenants Housing Council and then G W Rousham was made the secretary. At first the directors of the Trust worked without any payment, but in 1908 a sum of £500 was set aside to remunerate them, presumably for expenses – not much to spread between eight people.[47]

Henrietta now had the help and support of the Trust directors, her new "showman's happy family", but from looking at the Trust committee minutes we can see that she was doing nearly all the work. In 1906, for instance, there were 10 meetings and Henrietta attended every one of them. Vivian attended eight, Hunter four, Marnham four and Debenham two. The meetings were also attended by Unwin, the solicitor and the Trust secretary. So we can see that really only Vivian and the professional advisers were fully aware and participating, and this pattern of attendance continued in the future years.

In May 1906 the Hampstead Garden Suburb Bill was before a select committee of the House of Commons. The main provisions of this private bill were to get powers to make small accommodation roads of 20ft wide, other roads to be 40ft wide, the space between the buildings lining the road to be no less than 50ft and the dividend payable to shareholders to be limited to 5% per annum.[48] The Trust wanted permission to make unusually narrow roads because cul-de-sacs and closes, as at Asmuns Place, were an important part of Unwin's plan. Henry Vivian MP steered the bill through the House of Commons and Sir Robert Hunter represented the Trust to the parliamentary committee so Henrietta did not need to get involved and now that she was freed from the onerous work of secretary, she could spend more time in drumming up support. She gave lectures: in February she was speaking to the Central London Women's Institute[49], and probably used her slides of Bournville and Port Sunlight to show the sort of housing which would be built in the Suburb. She wrote articles for papers and magazines, and in March she got another letter in *The Times* appealing for investors, and read a paper to the Garden City Association conference.[50] At Whitechapel Art Gallery she organised an exhibition on "The Country in Town". She also gave a speech at a sanitary congress in Bristol. She found support by holding drawing room meetings and garden parties. In July, 200 people attended a party at 1 Fitzjohn's Avenue, Hampstead, the house of Frank Debenham and his wife; Lord Crewe spoke and Henrietta drew a delightful picture of the "varied homes, the 'village greens' and the shady avenues". She wrote an article for the *Daily Chronicle* on the "Garden Suburb Trust and the City Charming". Town planning was a hot topic and the speeches and meetings were all well reported in the national press. By July 1906 they had raised £90,000.

Meanwhile, Henrietta had been negotiating the purchase of the land. From 1903 she was carrying on a long correspondence with Mr Sanday of the Eton College trustees. There were many details to negotiate about the exact boundaries of the land as well as the price. It was Mr Sanday who had told Henrietta that "she was only a woman," but Henrietta made him her friend and used her powers of persuasion to convince him that he was not just doing his duty but also doing good:

> "You will allow me kind and patient Mr Sanday to say that I think it would be an excellent thing in itself, & have a deep public influence if the Eton Trustees would show themselves interested in the housing question for the working classes from the artistic as well as ethical point of view. This great body, Trustees for the richest class of the land, might strike a new educational note for other public authorities to follow if it proved that in its business relations it was willing to consider the poor & their needs of the graces of life – which, near towns, require that the rich land owners should be generous & sympathetic."[51]

Mr Sanday was completely charmed and towards the end of the long negotiations when Henrietta wrote to thank him for his help, he wrote that he had a great interest in the scheme, and that "anything I have had to do has been purely a labour of love & has been a real pleasure to me". On 1st May 1907 the purchase of the land was completed.

Henrietta was intrigued that the last time the land had changed hands was under the signature of Henricus Octavius (Henry VIII): "A king who bought with Royal gold for his pleasure – The next time it changed hands the deeds were signed by Henrietta Octavia, a woman who bought it on behalf of a public company, with the people's money to provide the people's homes."[52] She continued to relish this joke, for in 1909 when she employed a new secretary to help with the campaign for the Suburb, it happened that she was called Wolseley, so she nicknamed her "Cardinal" because she worked for Henrietta Octavia![53] There must have been a lot of fun for Henrietta's helpers, as well as very hard work.

Chapter 16

Building the Suburb

"How very little, since things were made,
Things have altered in the building trade."
Kipling

While planning the Suburb a big change had taken place in the Barnetts' lives, for they had been living in Whitechapel since 1873, at first in the Vicarage and then in the Lodge of Toynbee Hall; but now Samuel was appointed a canon of Westminster Abbey and from Christmas 1906 they lived in the Abbey precincts. During the building of the Suburb, Henrietta was either visiting the site from St Jude's Cottage or travelling there from Westminster, usually by car. Henry Ward was a frequent visitor and helper at Toynbee Hall and an admirer of the Barnetts. He was a very rich man and had a Rolls-Royce which he lent to Henrietta most of the time from 1907 onwards.

On 2nd May 1907 Henrietta performed the ceremony of cutting the first sod of the Hampstead Garden Suburb. They had chosen the very next day after signing the deeds and also the nearest day to her birthday, 4th May. The ceremony was organised by Frederick Litchfield, the secretary of the Hampstead Tenants' Co-partnership, who became master of many Suburb ceremonies. The Trust owned the land, but the building was to be done by companies which leased it and Hampstead Tenants leased 70 of the total 243 acres. It was a fine day and a crowd gathered. Children from Brentham (the new co-partnership housing estate in Ealing) sang songs and braided a maypole. Alfred Lyttleton MP, Henry Vivian MP and Sir John Brunner (President of the national Co-partnership Tenants Housing Council), Sybella Gurney and others made lengthy speeches. Then Raymond Unwin presented Henrietta with the spade and she cut the sod, and in her speech she revealed the good news that the Bishop of London had promised £2,000 toward the building of a church in the Suburb. Two little girls, Gladys Bateman and Winnie Hutchings, presented Henrietta with a basket of flowers. The maypole children were each given a box of chocolates (well earned, considering the number of speeches they had heard), then 150 people crossed the road to the Royal Oak and sat down to lunch in the marquee erected in the garden.[54] The Royal Oak pub dated from the mid 19th century and was situated at the junction of Bridge Lane and Finchley Road. Henrietta probably did not like to celebrate in a pub, but it was the only meeting-place nearby. But her main regret was that Samuel could not come to the celebrations: "I have my Canon in bed with a "Flue" or a feverish cold – so he will not be at my cutting – Is not that sad for me?"[55]

A month later, in pouring rain, the first 100 members of the Hampstead Co-partnership Tenants' Society, led by Frederick Litchfield, each laid an initialled Bath stone as the foundation stones of the first two houses. With the rain and mud the building site must have looked extremely bleak; however they were nerved for the ordeal by a preliminary tea given by Mrs Jephson.[56] The stone-laying was widely reported in the provincial press, for at the time there was great interest in co-operative building. Why have housing co-operatives not continued to flourish? Surely there is a need for them today.

On 2nd October 1907 Lord Treloar, the Lord Mayor of London, opened the Suburb by unlocking the first pair of cottages (140–142 Hampstead Way) with a silver key. He said he would like to move from the Mansion House into one of the new houses! Henrietta and Sybella planted lime trees in Asmuns Place: there is a plaque recording the event on the first tree. Henry Vivian presided over this and over the luncheon; he often took the limelight and is always very visible in photographs, so Henrietta did not take all the credit.[57]

Planning went on apace. A plot of two and a quarter acres was laid aside for a school, there were plans for flats for working ladies and for a residential hall for students. The idea for the students' hall came from the University College Students' Christian Association. In August an international housing congress was held at the Caxton Hall and a party of forty came to see the Suburb. There must have been little to see, but Henrietta spoke to them on bringing rich and poor together and Sybella Gurney explained co-operative finances.

The Trust owned the freehold of the land and administered it, but did little building itself and leased parcels of land on 999-year leases to companies and private people to develop. The Trust Development Company did build the charming little houses in Corringway for estate workers. Most of the development was built by co-partnership companies: Co-partnership Tenants Ltd, Hampstead Tenants Ltd, and some by the Improved Industrial Dwellings Company and other companies. This was the same arrangement as in Letchworth. Their principles were commercial return combined with co-operative ownership. Henrietta was convinced of the improving effect on the tenants of investing in their own property. Participants purchased a share, received a dividend and had a say in the management. The initial investment (£5) was beyond the means of the really needy but was possible for skilled artisans, clerks and tradesmen. It had many advantages for men with insecure jobs: "A tenant member pays an ordinary rent, and invests his savings in his Society, for which he receives 5 per cent interest, which is the maximum paid, the rest being divided amongst tenants pro rata to the rent paid, but he remains a tenant with its limited obligations. Thus, should employment prove unsteady, he is at liberty to move without any of the risks he might have had had the house been his own."[58] It seems a pity that the co-operative housing movement did not survive. The partial purchase of council houses does offer some of the same advantages. For the larger private houses near the Heath, the Garden Suburb Development Company had been formed to help richer people building houses for themselves to find the best method of raising capital and select a builder, with the Trust approving or selecting architects.[59]

By Christmas 1908, Hampstead Tenants Co-partnership had 63 houses occupied and 110 being built, with 700 men employed. The Improved Industrial Dwellings Company Ltd was building Waterlow Court, designed by Baillie Scott for spinster ladies with rents they could afford – £1.16s. to £3.3s. per month.[60] Building was progressing rapidly in the northern part of the Suburb and in Hampstead Way, Meadway and Temple Fortune Lane.

Henrietta and Unwin chose the road names, which must have been great fun.[61] They used local names from old maps, such as Asmuns Place, Bunker Hill and Willifield Way, but when these were exhausted they used the names of great lawyers, as in Chatham Close and Erskine Hill, and poets, as in Coleridge Walk and Wordsworth Walk. It is surprising that there is no Browning Way, as Henrietta was so fond of his work. To two of the roads in the artisan area they gave artists' names: Hogarth Hill

and Creswick Walk; and when they came to the more expensive area near the Heath, Henrietta again expressed her enthusiasm for art with the names Turner, Linnell, Reynolds, Constable, Morland, Ruskin, Cotman, Raeburn, all closes. No composers? But Henrietta had hated her piano lessons when she was a child and said she had no ear for music.

Lutyens was already planning the Free Church and St Jude's. Lutyens' relationship with Henrietta was stormy. He wanted to line the grand avenues with tall flats leading up to the central square, and wrote to his wife of his difficulties with Henrietta: "I want a certain height of building in a certain place for the general effect. Mrs B. is dead against this certain height on the ground of the other houses being overshadowed."[62] Their greatest disagreement was over the size of the church, St Jude's. When Henrietta objected to his designs, he dismissed her as a "philistine" with "no idea beyond a window box full of geraniums, calceolarias and lobelias, over which you can see a goose on the green".[63] These were the first churches he had been asked to design, apart from the small one at Knebworth, and he was determined to build really large churches. Stuart Gray tells us: "Mrs B. had asked for both churches to be kept low (in height of course). This Lutyens solved by sweeping their roofs down to ground-floor eaves levels recalling the great barn roofs he had seen in Surrey and especially on his student visits to Normandy."[64] Lutyens was a tease. Luckily for biographers he was a very open man and wrote to his beloved wife that Lyttleton thought: "Mrs B. is a dangerous woman – in that she is a woman! and would not be loyal to a vote, but work up a rumpus at Hampstead about it. Unwin warns me that it will make things difficult between me and Mrs B. in the future. She evidently won't forget it."[65]

They also disagreed over the style of St Jude's church: Henrietta wanted a Gothic church while Lutyens designed a Romantic Byzantine one, much too large and expensive. Lutyens and Unwin had very different styles of architecture. When we walk through Unwin's roads of informally grouped cottages and reach the approach to the central area, we look up Erskine Hill through a symmetrical avenue of terraced houses, Georgian in window design and classical in feeling. We move from the intimate village to a grandeur culminating in the two monumental churches. Today the contrast seems delightful, but one can understand Henrietta's preference for Unwin's village style, particularly as it was cheaper. The early prospectuses and plans had shops in Heathgate and Crickmer Circus but because of the grandeur of Central Square, shops were omitted: today this is regretted because the centre lacks life and in the winter it is bleak, as Nikolaus Pevsner observes: "The omission of shops from Central Square has proved a disadvantage; the square has never become a real social centre. Not only shops, but also cinemas, pubs and cafés have been refused admission. Institute education and divine worship have not proved to be as much of a lively attraction as the social reformers hoped for."[66] There will be more closure now the wings of the Henrietta Barnett School are built (though not quite as Lutyens planned), and a new synagogue arises on the site of the church rooms. It would be jolly if a youth club were built on the empty site west of the Free Church and a little playground, putting green or whatever we all wish in Central Square.

Henrietta found Edwin Lutyens stubborn as compared with Unwin. Money was often the cause of conflict, for Lutyens had grand ideas and wanted expensive materials, whereas Henrietta was faced with the task of raising the money for all their projects. Disagreement over expenditure and style led to delays and Lutyens was undoubtedly offended when Henrietta thought of calling in another architect to complete the work

Plate 32 (opposite) Henrietta (centre) cutting the first sod of Hampstead Garden Suburb, watched by Sir John Brunner, Frederick Litchfield and Henry Vivian, May 2nd, 1907.

*Plate 33
Lutyens' grand,
Georgian style
contrasted with
Unwin's Arts and
Crafts cottages.*

more quickly: "The resolution she passed authorising the Co-partnership people to go to another architect when the delay & fault was on her side is a preposterous piece of cheek. She gets panics and won't let anybody do anything but herself and I believe the bottom of it is that a Ratepayers Association has been formed *against* her."[67] Henrietta called a church committee to try to control Lutyens' extravagances, but it seems that on this occasion she could not make the committee do what she wanted, for Lutyens wrote to his wife:

*Plate 34 (opposite)
Beautiful gardens
in Asmuns Place.
Critics of the Suburb
had believed that
the working classes
would not take
to gardening, but
Henrietta had seen
the joy Whitechapel
people derived from
their window-boxes.*

> "I hear St Jude's is splendid for sound. They tried the choir and Canon Barnett was there exclaiming 'How beautiful, how beautiful'. There is an awful row (secret) going on between Mrs B. and the church committee and as far as I can gather she is not to be allowed in at the opening ceremony to meet Princess Louise and the Bishop. This will make an awful scandal. She is a silly woman though she is nice to me now. The committee was called by her only to annoy me and make my work difficult and has now turned as an old nemesis of the sea upon her back. And Oh what a committee – a committee of bank clerks and curates. I attended the last one and nearly burst when they put questions affecting the appearance of *my* church to the vote – their vote! Luckily it went my way and I was saved from a declaration of my true opinions and beliefs."[68]

Writing in 1928, years after her conflict with Lutyens, Henrietta wrote a kindly reflection on their relationship: "To me he gave time, thought, ideas, innumerable comic

Hampstead Garden Suburb Trust Ltd.   2 March 1909
St Jude's Cottage, Spaniards Road.

I will not apologise for writing to you if we are not
already acquainted, because I feel sure that you desire as I
do to make the garden suburb beautiful and enjoyable to all
who live there or who pass through it.

I have all the winter been greatly interested in planting the
roads and open spaces of the Estate — and, in buying extensively
for them, the opportunity arose of purchasing some apple
trees, some small leaved climbing ivy, and purple
clematis.

Would you like me to instruct the Estate gardener to
plant one of each of the latter on the front of your house, and
the apple tree in the garden?

I know it is not usual to present Tenants with gifts,
but if you think well to accept them you will, I feel sure,
do so in the spirit in which the gifts are offered, and because
it is necessary that we should all work together to make our
Suburb really a garden one.

As you will know, the season for planting is rapidly
drawing to a close, so may I hear from you without
delay.

Yours v truly

Henrietta O. Barnett.

drawings (mainly to illustrate our respective relations of loved tyrant and loving slave) and a friendship that storms cannot shatter. I am grateful."[69]

In September 1908 Henrietta held a garden party at St Jude's Cottage for all the residents of the Suburb to celebrate the planting of gardens.[70] Sir Robert Hunter spoke and Raymond Unwin presented prizes for the best planted gardens. Though Henrietta probably never did any digging, except for first sods, and would have regarded it as man's work, she must have known that the new tenants needed encouragement to tackle their rough gardens consisting of farmland and builders' rubble. Landscaping was a primary concern from the earliest days, and already in 1909 Henrietta reported to the Trust that she and Unwin had organised the planting of street trees and of open spaces.[71] She had to buy many trees and plants for this and "the opportunity arose of purchasing some apple trees, some small leaved house climbing ivy, and purple clematis." At Bournville the Cadburys had arranged that each tenant would receive eight apple and pear trees, 12 gooseberry bushes, a Victoria plum and creepers for the house. Henrietta did not feel that the Trust could afford such lavish expenditure but wrote to all the tenants offering to make the estate gardener plant an ivy and a clematis at the front of their house and one or two apple trees in the back garden. She added: "I know it is not usual to present Tenants with gifts, but if you think well to accept them you will, I feel sure, do so in the spirit in which the gifts are offered, and because it is necessary that we should all work together to make our Suburb a really Garden one."[72] The ivy was soon regarded as a nuisance as it destroyed the brickwork, but some of the apple trees remain a hundred years on. Henrietta was also negotiating with the Tube company about planting climbers over the ugly railway sheds at Golders Green.

The Institute was opened by Canon Barnett in 1909 and the programme of events included every child on the Suburb planting roses and acacias round the new building. In November 1908 Henrietta invited people to tea to discuss forming a horticultural society. It was formed in 1909, the first society founded in the Suburb. At the first meeting on 20th May 1909, a subscription was set at one shilling per year. The Society's first flower-show – for fruit and vegetables – was held on August Bank Holiday in a marquee in Central Square. The Barnetts won a mention for their lovely sweet peas. Subsequent shows were in the Institute hall and sometimes in the Club House by Willifield Green. Henrietta, who had rushed from Oxford, opened the flower-show and was presented with a basket of red rambler roses by the mothers of the first baby girls born on the Suburb – Bessie Stratton and Henrietta Coburn. In her speech, she said this was a red-letter day because it was:-

> "… the first united effort of the tenants to show their own productions. God grant there may be many more. I hope we shall have not only flower shows, but also exhibitions of handicrafts, musical competitions, sketching and photographic club shows, recitation evenings, and many other forms of co-operative competition … But it is my firm belief that besides these flowers the Suburb will grow other flowers – ethical flowers. What do I mean? I mean the flowers of helpfulness, independence and trust. First, the flowers of helpfulness. Such little things as neighbourliness, the exchange of seeds and books and fruits and music, grow to the bigger things of exchange of knowledge and experience, and grow also to the recognition of the duty of helpfulness towards those who are handicapped by physical infirmity or by misfortune or ignorance. Out of the soil of our own happiness we should grow the flower of helpfulness. The second is independence. This is a flower which requires the manure of principle, the watering of thought, and the pruning of plain language."[73]

She urged everybody in the Suburb to retain their independence and not to let the rich pay for the prizes of the poor. Henrietta presented a prize trophy: a copper pot (still owned by the Horticultural

Society) by an artist of the Newlyn school. Today the flower-shows are held in the Free Church Hall, and are always crowded with chatting people.

To encourage the digging and planting of the rough and overgrown ground, there was a competition and prizes for the best laid-out front and back gardens. Meanwhile from 1908 the Hampstead Tenants Co-partnership had been helping people to stock their gardens by forming a small society "for the advantageous buying of plants, and to promote the exchange of vegetables".[74]

There was a very jolly August Bank Holiday in 1909, for cyclists came from Letchworth to join in with sports held in a field near Central Square and see the flower-show. In the afternoon there was a children's pastoral play specially written by Miss A M Tytler and in the evening a concert followed by a dance and the illumination of houses.

Modern planners know that social-meeting places should be built simultaneously with housing, but it is rarely done. Henrietta was determined to open the Institute and the churches as soon as possible so that the new residents of all classes would be meeting and mixing from their first arrival in the Suburb. In March 1909, Samuel Barnett opened the Institute, just one hall, the first part of the big building designed by Lutyens; Henrietta spoke at the opening and lent the Institute a picture which Watts had copied for her "showing the relation of man to knowledge".[75]

Meanwhile, in 1908 Henry Vivian presided at a party given for the Co-partnership Tenants and for visitors from the Co-partnership estates at Letchworth, Wolverhampton and Birmingham. They toured the Suburb and after lunch drove in brakes to the Franco-British Exhibition at the White City, where they were joined by a large number of tenants and workmen from Brentham, the Ealing estate. The tenants had a high regard for Henry Vivian. The first baby boy born on the Suburb was named Vivian. (The first baby girl was

Plate 36
Henry Vivian MP,
was chairman of
Co-partnership
Tenants Ltd which
played a leading role
in the finance of the
artisans' houses.
He piloted the
Suburb bill through
the House of
Commons.

named Henrietta.) Vivian, like Henrietta, was an assertive person and with his strong personality he gave the artisans' area of the Suburb an identity which persisted and sometimes came into conflict with Henrietta's wishes.

Henrietta was immensely busy. She was always watching Trust finances, and she proposed that there should be a monthly report of Trust accounts, a very modern practice.[76] As she was honorary manager a great many of the Trust decisions were passed to her to execute and so her work involved every aspect of the development. During the year1910/11, she was trying to find a housing company that would build on land east of the Institute – which became Bigwood and Southwood Courts.[77] Also she decided the letting fees for the Institute. She reported that a site near the Central Square had been found for the Tea House. She had to decide the charges for letting the Tea House and also for letting the sports pitches. She was to spend £50 in laying out a sports ground on the Heath Extension. She reported that they could not find new offices for the Trust except with an increase of rent, so they had decided to stay in the present offices. However did she cope with the pressure of work?

Meanwhile she was in charge of the Institute, her cherished adult education school which was central to her plan to bring the classes together in pursuit of high culture. She arranged for furniture to be provided and prepared a new Institute prospectus and an accompanying illustrated booklet. She was acting as housekeeper as well as academic head. However in 1910 she engaged a secretary, Mr Fuller, to deal with the detail, while she still took the important decisions.

It was only four years since Henrietta had cut the first sod, yet the greater part of the "old" Suburb had been built, the many communal buildings were built or building and they were buzzing with social life. The "artistic" new houses at reasonable rents were popular and were quickly occupied, while nearer to the Heath more affluent people were buying the leaseholds and commissioning their own houses: "Very many artists, literary people and journalists have gone into residence, but as yet the neighbourhood includes no enthusiasts for rational dress, to go abroad in togas and sandals as [in] another garden suburb near town. Among those who have just settled at Hampstead is Mr F H Townsend, the art Editor of *Punch* and he will have as a near neighbour Mr H G Wells."[78] Others thought the early garden suburbians did have a distinctive look: "… one used to know them by their sunburn and general air of sartorial emancipation, to which the body never seemed quite to have accustomed itself - & that partly because our eyes were deceived by stiff conventional standards".[79]

There was also sexual emancipation. The author H G Wells cycled to see his Rebecca in Denman Drive, a turning off Erskine Hill. There she lived with her mother and two sisters in a little cottage. Maybe he took Rebecca for walks in the nearby Big Wood. H G Wells was 40 and she was only 17, and when she was a little older she moved to a flat and had an illegitimate baby by him.

However, compared with Letchworth which had a reputation for cranks, the people were more mixed:

> "In the Suburb 'almost every trade of London is represented. There are shoemakers, shoesmiths, postmen, gardeners, ordinary clerks, bank clerks (the distinction is carefully made), writers, solicitors, architects, doctors … There are Socialists, Fabians, Communists, Suffragists, anti-vivisectionists, and people who are anti everything else … 'Arty' people abound. There are painters, musicians and sculptors by the score. But 'the suburb' is by no means a 'cranky' place, although the artistic temperament is rampant. There is a very solid element of business people who know a good place to live in when they see it … and so keep Utopia steady."[80]

Many babies had been born and the children were healthy and happy. Henrietta, with her long experience of ill health among the urban poor, was delighted by the health statistics. *The Westminster Gazette* reported:

"The birth-rate is 13.5 per thousand and, not one of the thirty three babies born on the estate having died, the infant mortality rate nil. To those who realise that … the infant mortality rate in certain districts is as high as 180 in the 1000 the statement is almost startling, and shows that the best way of attacking the high rate of infant mortality is to provide healthily built houses, open spaces and gardens which attract the family to pass many hours out of doors."[81]

Henrietta always stressed the connection between housing and health, for she knew the truth of this from her own experience, and also knew that a nation concerned with degeneration would be more concerned with housing if the connection was recognized. At a huge conference in the Albert Hall held by the Pan-Anglican congress on housing in 1908, she said that in Finsbury the death rate among one-room dwellers was 32.7 per thousand, compared with 6.6 per thousand among those who had four-room dwellings.[82]

At this time there was a great fashion for pageants, influenced by the medievalism of the Pre-Raphaelites. In the Suburb pageants were performed each year from 1910 onwards. The Play and Pageant Union was a very important part of local life. Every summer they performed on the Pageant Ground between Northway and Big Wood, later moving to the theatre in Little Wood, and most of the residents took part in one way or another. A new script was written for each pageant, often by the Kelseys of Northway – Mrs Kelsey wore sandals – or by the Chambers or Jewitts. They were full of local jokes that are funny even now. In 1910 they performed *The Masque of Fairthorpe*, written by Paul Jewitt:

"With spade and fork, with rake and hoe, and dibble
We come all armed, a band of eager diggers;
With vaporite, and other insect killers,
With silver sand and scythes, and superphosphates
We join the troop of energetic persons
Who shortly will inaugurate the Suburb …
When London suburbs first arrived
On every vacant space,
The jerry-builder soon contrived
A house to meet the case.
He set it fifty in a row –
Its beauties were but few,
And they were put in front - to show,
In this jolly bad house and new …
But now the garden Suburb's here
Another tale we tell,
Another sort of house we rear,
Wherein a man may dwell.
And all around a garden grows,
And roses on the wall,
Wherein a man may stick his nose
For a jolly good sniff and all."

The characters include architects, gardeners, Asmun, Will o' the Field, the Nymph of the Mead, the Templar, Jerry builder, Folly, fairies, elves and craftsmen.[83] John Garside, the actor, was

Plate 37
Jim and Daisy
Davidson,
Hampstead Way.
This snapshot was
found in a bottle
up the chimney.
Jim and Daisy were
typical of the artisans
who lived in the
north of the Suburb.
Many had moved
from overcrowded
Hampstead, some
from the East End.

one of the producers. Many people were involved in making scenery and costumes for the cast of hundreds. Amazingly, they wove the cloth and dyed it to make the costumes: surely this was the apogee of the medievalism.[84] Practically all the children of the Suburb were dressed up and taking part and many of the grown-ups too, with the Reverend Basil Bourchier in his element as a theatrical lead. After the last night of the pageant there was a torchlight procession all round the Suburb. Some of the Suburb players took part in a national pageant, *Merrie England,* in the Festival of Empire at the Crystal Palace.[85]

New societies were being formed almost every month. The Gilbert and Sullivan Society gave very good performances in the Suburb. The Distaff Guild promoted skilled work and put its members in touch. They met to make baskets, bead chains, children's frocks, Christmas cards and calendars, chutney and jam, coats, confectionery, evening bags and shawls, jewellery, lingerie, pottery, stained glass, stockings and socks, toys and upholstery, and do bookbinding, bookkeeping, crochet, embroidery, fashion drawing, gardening, house decoration, knitting, leatherwork, metalwork, millinery, modelling and casting, painting, raffia work, secretarial work and stencilling. And then there were the Fraternity Weavers who were organized nationally from Dorking. Each craft had a leader and lessons could be arranged. The high mistress of the Distaff Guild, Luie Chadwick, lived at 124 Hampstead Way. The guild was specifically for women, and it would be fun if someone would revive it.[86]

Many of the early residents were Liberals and a Garden Suburb Liberal and Progressive Association was formed. Adult Schools were started for men and women. The Adult School movement was a working-class movement to help literacy and general education. There was an Adult School College, Fircroft, at Bournville. Henry Vivian opened the cricket ground and the first match was played between the Garden Suburb Club and St Jude's. The Reverend Basil Bourchier started a chess club.

The *Daily Chronicle* commented that "The rapidity with which the estate has been developed is unique in the annals of building."[87] While most of the press was full of praise for the Suburb, *The Builder* was very critical: the lines of the roads were inconvenient for access from one part to another:

> "… there is nothing to be said for a wriggling plan … There is something of this artificial picturesque, too in the general treatment of the houses … They have got an exceedingly nice toned tile for the roofs – red but not too red … But high pitched roofs are not the best way of building; they mean either upper rooms with awkwardly shaped ceilings, or they mean large waste spaces which no one gets at … And generally speaking there is too much of the 'hut' order of architecture about these houses; they do not look very solid."[88]

With the exhibition and conference and the efforts of Henrietta and Vivian to get publicity, there was continuing coverage by all the national press, and usually there was nothing but praise. In the *Review of Reviews* there was a character sketch of Henrietta describing her as:

> "A motherly woman who, having no children of her own, has adopted everybody within reach as foster sons and daughters … But for the sex prejudice which still lingers she would be in Parliament and in the Ministry. And even despite that prejudice, I hope to see her appointed by some future President of the Local Government Board as the official mother of all the children of the State."

Chapter 17

Communal Housing

"The wicked, the naughty, the sick, the demented, the sorrowful, the blind, the halt, the maimed, the old, the handicapped, the children are facts – facts to be faced, facts which demand thought, facts which should be reckoned with in town planning – for all, even the first-named, can be helped by being surrounded with 'whatsoever things are pure, whatsoever things are lovely, whatsoever things are of good report.'"[89]

Henrietta was even more concerned with the social provisions than with the family housing. From her intimate knowledge of the East End she understood the special needs of the disadvantaged. Also she thought that people living with "each house surrounded by its own charming garden, in peace and comfort, are in danger of forgetting the sad and poor and the bereft, and so special efforts have been made to settle some of those who are handicapped of all classes and ages in our very midst".[90] To solve the problem of accommodating these people, Henrietta turned to communal housing. This idea was current among her friends, for the Arts and Crafts movement was associated with the idea of communal living, perhaps a return to the medieval hall and *Merrie England*. In *How We Live and How We Might Live*, William Morris wrote:

> "As to what extent it may be necessary or desirable for people under social order to live in common, we may differ pretty much according to our tendencies towards social life. For my part, I can't see why we should think it a hardship to eat with the people we work with; I am sure that as to many things, such as valuable books, pictures, and splendour of surroundings, we shall find it better to club our means together; and I must say that often when I have been sickened by the stupidity of the mean idiotic rabbit warrens, that rich men build for themselves in Bayswater and elsewhere, I console myself with visions of the noble communal hall of the future, unsparing of materials, generous in worthy ornament, alive with the noblest thoughts of our time, and the past, embodied in the best art which a free and manly people could produce; such an abode of man as no private enterprise could come anywhere near for beauty and fitness, because only collective thought and collective life could cherish the aspirations which would give birth to its beauty, or have the skill and I for my part should think it much the reverse of a hardship if I had to read my books and meet my friends in such a place; nor do I think I am better off to live in a vulgar stuccoed house crowded with upholstery that I despise ... Simply because I call it my own, or my house."[91]

Morris was following in the tradition of Owen; he believed in brotherhood and tried to put it into practice living with his artistic friends. Henrietta's approach was practical, not

Group of Mothers from Canning Town Settlement.

Plate 38
The ladies of
Waterlow Court
give a treat
to the Canning
Town visitors.

The Mothers start for a drive round the Suburb

Socialist, though the Barnetts called it Practicable Socialism. She did not envisage exquisite surroundings but just knew that by communal living her disadvantaged folk would live in a much greener place and in much more comfort than could otherwise be afforded. Ebenezer Howard had dreamed of collective ownership, with some houses sharing communal gardens and kitchens and cooperation in building houses, motivated by self help and brotherly love. Letchworth had a quadrangle of cottages with a central green, common rooms, a shared laundry, kitchens, bathrooms and dining room. In Brentham the plan included a men's hostel adjacent to the institute, though it was not built.

In 1901, Erskine House, a large house between St Jude's Cottage and the Spaniards Inn, Hampstead Lane, became vacant and the Barnetts bought it and used it as a home for "sick and weary women from East London". For ten girls from Dr Barnardo's this was a "finishing school" where they were taught to be maids, with much care from Henrietta and Miss Gale, the matron. Mrs Moore, the beloved Nurse, was too tired and elderly for the work. The girls waited on seven old women from Whitechapel, also some tired teachers and a child or two with hip disease. Henrietta's experience of poor-law institutions had taught her that different groups of people should be mixed together, not isolated in institutions. After a time the old women were replaced by convalescents from the London Hospital. The home was run by a committee, but Henrietta was very much in control as she was living next door for a part of every week. She broke down the garden wall between the two houses: "It is of course a great improvement. Destruction of barriers seems almost universally an advantage," observed Samuel.[92] The convalescents were kept busy with lady volunteers teaching patchwork, games and singing. Each week LCC health lecturers instructed the servant girls as well as the convalescents. On Sundays the patients could invite their friends to tea. The patients were taken for drives in the Barnetts' carriage. The chaise pulled by Tom was too small so they bought a landau for this large household, and a phaeton to be driven for pleasure by Henrietta and Samuel in turn.[93] Often they drove about the country toward Harrow, Mill Hill and Totteridge and one day Henrietta took Erskine girls and convalescents to the zoo.[94] She wanted everybody to enjoy life.

Henrietta's intention was to transfer Erskine House convalescent home to the Suburb. She found a site in Wildwood Road where two big houses could be built, one for herself and Samuel and one for Erskine House. She could have continued the same close supervision of convalescents and maids. Unwin prepared plans, and in June 1913 her application for two plots of ground fronting the Heath Extension came before the Trust.[95] But then Samuel died and Miss Gale, the matron, resigned, so in 1913 she closed Erskine House and sold it to the owner of St Jude's Cottage next door.[96]

In the Suburb, a "Haven of Rest" was prepared for old folk who were still able to shop and cook for themselves. Henrietta describes how she met Unwin, Vivian and Litchfield one hot July day to make the plan; Unwin was to design charming quadrangles, Litchfield to find capital at low interest, Vivian to organise the building, and Henrietta to supervise every aspect of the interior design of the flats and raise the money. With Miss Paterson she wrote many letters to ladies asking them to invest capital, with the right to nominate one tenant over 60 years of age for every £50 subscribed. In October 1909 the quadrangle of 57 flats was opened by Sybella Gurney.

Plate 40 (opposite)
A resident of
Waterlow Court,
which was for
spinster ladies.
Teachers and social
workers were poorly
paid and had
to resign if they
married.

Plate 41
Waterlow Court,
c.2000.

Plate 42
Queen's Court was
built in 1927 for
single working
women.

*Plate 43
Emmott Close, 1928,
was for single
working women.*

*Plate 44
Meadway Court
was for bachelors,
with room for a
valet.*

The Haven of Rest was renamed The Orchard: perhaps the old folk were noisier than expected. It had a porter, laundry room, baths and baking ovens and by providing facilities like this communally the rents could be kept very low – from 3s.6d to 4s.6d a week. It was entirely rebuilt to provide individual bathrooms in the 1960s, and still flourishes.

Waterlow Court, off Hampstead Way, was planned by Henrietta to solve the housing problem of poorly paid ladies earning their own living, such as teachers and social workers who usually had to live in lonely and uncomfortable lodgings. The beautiful quadrangle was designed by Baillie Scott to incorporate Henrietta's idea for a collegiate style of living. There were 49 flats, each with a living-room, bathroom, lavatory and scullery, and from one to three bedrooms according to rental. There were tennis and croquet lawns, and "the opportunity of digging in an individually owned plot of land, however tiny". They had a large dining room where meals could be had at a reasonable charge, and a common room. They had a shared staff of servants.[97] The rents were from 36s. up to 63s. monthly. It was opened by Princess Louise, Duchess of Argyll, in 1909. The Princess was shown round the building and entertained with a programme of music – Sousa, Gounod, Puccini. The press described this development as "The Adamless Eden in Hampstead". In the Suburb Archive there is a large album of photographs of Waterlow Court, with signatures of the first 47 residents. The professional ladies are seen in their Arts and Crafts style rooms; another photograph shows them entertaining poor mothers from Canning Town with a coach ride after their tea.[98]

Other "courts" were built, all consisting of flats round a communal open space, and mostly with other communal facilities. The area behind the shops at the junction of Hampstead Way and Temple Fortune Hill was at first used for builders' huts and was intended by Henrietta to be an open space with a pond, allowing a full view of the rear of Temple Fortune House. After the First World War, shortage of money forced the Trust to develop it, but at least it was developed for an underprivileged group. Queen's Court, "79 dainty and restrained cottage flats," was built by the United Women's Homes Association for "thrifty working women": for typists, clerks and nurses. Definitely not the same class as the ladies in Waterlow Court! Queen's Court was opened in 1927 and Emmott Close, off Wildwood Road, also for the same class of women, was opened in 1928. The bathrooms were shared – recently they have been modernized. Henrietta made a virtue of the shared bathrooms: "The bathroom has to be shared by three tenants, but often three friends join up together, and it must be pleasant to have in common one virtue – thrift – and so restful; I find wasteful people so irritating."[99]

Meadway Court, designed by Sutcliffe, was meant for bachelors. Each flat had a room for a servant and there was a communal dining room and indoor as well as outdoor tennis courts. Henrietta had planned more communal rooms, for servants as well as for tenants, and a loggia, and she wanted to have some flats at a low rent, but she did not manage to achieve all this for financial reasons.

Homesfield, off Erskine Hill, was built as a little cul-de-sac with three buildings to provide for "the sad, the poor, the old, or the neglected". One of Henrietta's fundamental principles was that no external features should indicate social distinctions, and in architecture and setting the buildings look like normal houses; indeed it is perhaps the most beautiful group of housing that Unwin designed. Henrietta submitted Unwin's plans for the two houses to the Queen who took a great interest.[100] "Nothing but the best for the worst" was Henrietta's maxim. A maharajah gave her some catalpa trees which she planted at Homesfield and in the grounds of Henrietta Barnett School.

Entering into the Homesfield cul-de-sac: "On the left we find first eighteen young women in what is known as Emma Cottage. These are to be day servants in the Suburb; at least, it is hoped that the inhabitants will so look upon them, and take the opportunity of using them, so helping them to earn something towards their maintenance."[101] Possibly the inhabitants were not very eager

Plate 45
Abbeyfield House,
Homesfield, 2007,
at first called Emma
and Rosemary
cottages.

Plate 46
Ursula and
Henrietta Cottages,
Homesfield, now
Erskine House.

Plate 47
Adelaide Cottage,
Homesfield.

Plate 48 (opposite)
Barnett Homestead

Miss Barnes. Mr. Henry Vivian. Mr. Herbert Marnham. Rev. J. H. Rushbrooke. Lady Bertha Dawkins. Rev. B. G. Bourchier.
THE PRINCE OF WALES.
PRINCESS MARY. THE QUEEN.
Sir Alfred Yarrow, Bart. Lady Lytton. Earl of Lytton. Mrs. S. A. Barnett, C.B.E. Mrs. Maynard. Miss Paterson. Mr. J. C. S. Soutar.

A GROUP TAKEN AT THE BARNETT HOMESTEAD FEBRUARY 1918

Il. 322]

to employ the women of Emma Cottage, for they would have recognised them as girls whom Henrietta had saved from the Whitechapel streets. "Proceeding, we come to Mary Cottage. Here eighteen little girls will in due time be found enjoying the care of the Salvation Army, while they go to school in the Suburb and otherwise seek to get that proficiency which is to fit them for a useful future." These two cottages were paid for by Mrs Knight and her sister, friends of Henrietta, and were named Emma and Mary after them. "Opposite to these two groups Adelaide Cottage is situated, where twelve aged poor people are spending the declining years of their lives in the happy and bright surroundings of the Eventide Home."[102] This cottage was named after the Salvation Army Commissioner Adelaide Cox, and the Army leased it and cared for the old ladies. It was paid for by the contributions of very many ladies, which must have been raised by Henrietta at the cost of much letter-writing. The neighbours were not very happy with the old ladies for they complained of the noise of their hymn-singing.[103] However Henrietta had great sympathy for old people; she thought they were often poorly treated and ideally should be kept within their families:

> "Houses should be planned so as to make family life joyous, and homes surrounded by space, light and air. Is the joy of children considered when large block buildings are run up in which there is no room for 'Granny, that unpaid, uncertificated teacher of reverence, of patience, and the grace of our homes?'
> 'We have no room for her; we are overcrowded,' is again and again the response from the respectable working people when asked if they could take the old people from the workhouse if a pension of 5s a week is granted.
> To bury the old before they had died is a heathen custom, yet here in Christian England we brick up our old people behind walls, or leave them in the isolation of modern institutions."[104]

At the end of the close, behind the two catalpa trees, were two houses, each for twelve children. Each group had a house-mother so that they would live as much like a family as possible, with the children going to Childs Way school. One was financed by Samuel and was named Henrietta, and the other was financed by George Cadbury and named Ursula after his daughter. The Hampstead Board of Guardians hired the houses and under the guidance of Mrs Boon, a house-mother, the children were influenced by "The beauty, the song of birds, the dance of squirrels, and the mystery of growing things". However a Suburb resident who grew up there told Kitty Slack that:

> "The discipline was very strict, punishment frequent, domestic work heavy, with mending and sewing to do after school. There was little or no time for play or to make friends outside the Home. She said that Henrietta often visited the Home with members of the management committee, but after being lined up neat and clean, the children were quickly dismissed out of sight."[105]

In 1924 Emma and Mary cottages were taken on a long lease by the Church of England Waifs and Strays Society and renamed St Catherine's, a home for children, and now they are Abbeyfield House for elderly people. It would please Henrietta that these cottages have always been in communal use. But in 1933 the Trust Board converted Adelaide Cottage into flats, for despite much effort Henrietta was unable to find an

Plate 49 (opposite)
The Wellgarth
Nursery Training
School, opened
in 1915.

*Plate 50
Bigwood
and Southwood
Courts were for
bereaved families
of Army officers.*

organisation which would rent the building for a home for the disadvantaged. Ursula and Henrietta Cottages were also turned into flats for the same reason.

Homesfield is on the north side of the Suburb in Erskine Hill, and further down the hill a house – 110 Erskine Hill – was taken by the Adult School to be used as a mothers' rest house to help mothers from poor homes in the East End recuperate after childbirth. The Adult School, a national movement of working-class self-help education, met in the Club House. Also in Erskine Hill is the Barnett Homestead, twelve little flats for war-widows with young children. Henrietta persuaded Sir Alfred Yarrow to give the money for this in memory of Samuel and it was opened on 24th August 1916.[106] She was concerned at the treatment of ex-servicemen and deplored a plan to house wounded soldiers in block dwellings.[107] Bigwood and Southwood Courts were built in 1923–25 to house the bereaved families of officers. The HGS Archive has a photograph of Queen Mary and Henrietta Barnett at the top of the Institute tower, looking down at the site.

The Nursery Training School in Wellgarth Road was moved to the Suburb from Hackney in 1916 to provide cleaner air for the children and babies. Henrietta was politically correct by nature and conviction: "Believing as I do, in the beneficial influence on normal people of the weak, the handicapped and the young, I gladly welcomed the School." She helped them to find a site and an architect, who designed a delightful building. The neighbours objected to the poor living in their midst. Arthur Waugh, father of Evelyn Waugh, whose house on North End Road (blue plaque) backed onto the site, wrote: "If this can be built, there is no guarantee that a factory will not be erected in Meadway."[108]

But his letter was to no avail as the Suburb was for all classes. There were about 30 little babies and children who had lost their mothers, or whose parents were inadequate, cared for by 30 girls who were training as children's nurses.[109] A few of the babies were black, the first of the few black people who have lived in the Suburb. Neighbours' little children attended the nursery school in the mornings. In recent years the Nursery Training College was closed and the building sold to the Youth Hostel Association which opened in 1981, and now a developer is converting it to luxury houses. One for sale for £6m! Henrietta would be horrified.

Henrietta had further plans for social housing. A boys' hostel was placed near Central Square on the 1905 plan. Also she wanted to build a hostel with low rents for young women, for she was well aware of the problems working girls had in finding accommodation. She wanted to have a convalescent home, and another scheme was a quadrangle for blind people and their families. The blind people were to have a cafeteria which would make food problems easier, and workshops to provide employment. She wanted a boarding-house or simple hotel. But none of this was built for want of money.[110]

Communal living was an essential part of Henrietta's vision. Raising finance for all these buildings must have involved enormous work, with Henrietta aided by Marion appealing to everyone she knew, but she gives us few details. We only know that Henrietta had a wide circle of friends and acquaintances, many rich and influential, and that she was an experienced and brilliant fundraiser and publicist. Today, all her communal dwellings have become privately owned flats with the exception of Abbeyfield and The Orchard. There is a need for more communal housing for old people, but of a higher standard and more spacious. Also the Suburb needs a nursing home. Possibly single mothers would enjoy living in small houses, with no gardens but communal play areas and playrooms.

Chapter 18

Meeting-places

The Institute

Henrietta's great desire was to get the rich and poor to meet together. In Toynbee Hall this had been achieved with the Toynbee residents and visitors from the West End meeting Whitechapel people in the classes and entertainments, conversaziones and tea-parties. These social occasions were famous and could be awkward. J M Barrie satirized them in his play *The Admirable Crichton* written in 1902. Lord Loam is a wealthy aristocrat with a butler called Crichton. Lord Loam has taken up the fashion for equality, and has a monthly tea-party for his servants. As they all come in to the drawing-room he greets them as Mr, Mrs or Miss, shakes their hands and offers them seats: Crichton the butler, Mrs Perkins the housekeeper, Mademoiselle Jeanne the governess, Rolleston, who is Lord Loam's valet, Monsieur Fleury the chef and his assistant Ernest, Miss Fisher, who is Lady Mary's maid, Miss Simmons, a maid, Thomas the footman, the Tweeny maid and a pageboy and a stable-boy. Lord Loam hands round the tea to their evident discomfiture and conversation is very stilted, just as in the Toynbee drawing room. However his Lordship carries on:

Lord Loam: 'Can't you see, Crichton, that our divisions into classes are artificial, that if we were to return to nature, which is the aspiration of my life, all would be equal?' …

Crichton: 'His lordship may compel us to be equal upstairs, but there will never be equality in the servants' hall.'

In the next act, the Loam family, Crichton and Tweeny are shipwrecked on an island; Crichton becomes the leader and the Loam family adapt to low social positions with Lord Loam being very submissive to Crichton.

Henrietta called the play "a kindly satire" and wrote: "The Canon almost choked with laughter, and when we went behind the scenes to thank Mr H B Irving for his sensitive interpretation, he was both pleased and interested that we had recognized so many of the subtleties."[111]

Henrietta's plan was for all Suburb residents to meet in the Club House and in the Institute, in a more natural way than at Toynbee Hall. Planned communities usually have a meeting-place, for instance the Folk Hall at Joseph Rowntree's New Earswick and the institutes at Brentham and Letchworth, and the plentiful allotments, bowling greens, tennis courts and village greens. The Club House was a social club, with numerous societies and sports clubs meeting on the premises, and Henry Vivian played the most important role in creating it. But Henrietta wanted two main meeting-places: a social club for pleasure and an institute for cultural and moral improvement, the "sweetness and light" which Matthew Arnold desired. Hampstead had a subscription library and Highgate had the Literary

Plate 51
Samuel and
Henrietta Barnett.
A contrast in
personalities: Samuel
with his deep insight
and understanding,
Henrietta with her
determination
and inspiration.

and Scientific Institution, founded in 1839. Henrietta wanted to spread high culture and the very core of her plan was the Institute, the home of lifelong learning and culture for young and old. One of Browning's characters said: *"Ignorance is not innocence but sin"*. Henrietta said that the lectures and debates in the Institute brought people together to think and she believed that "the one thing which would unite people was to think together, even if they differed."[112] It was her "big and youngest baby". They were puzzled about finding a name and one suggestion was that it should be called the "Athenaeum"! The problem with "Institute" was that people would think it was a place where only mechanics went to increase their earning powers, as Sir Robert Hunter said, whereas the aim was to bring high culture to everybody. [113] Nevertheless, Institute was the name adopted. In the spring of 1909 Henrietta sent an invitation to the opening to all Suburb residents:

> "Dear Madam or Sir,
> On Saturday, March 27th, it is planned to open the first room of the Institute which is, as you probably know, situated in the Great Central Square.
> It is reached by the pathway (lit by electricity for that evening) which starts from the corner of Willifield Way near where it joins Hampstead Way.
> The Directors of the Trust have built this first room of the Institute, in which there will be it is hoped ultimately a Library, a Studio, and various rooms for Concerts, Meetings, Debates, Social Clubs, Reading parties, the Horticultural Society's Committees and other organizations. The Trust has started the Institute in the hope that as a Centre of common life for <u>all</u> the inhabitants of the Suburb (who will elect persons responsible for its management) it may be the means by which intellectual life will be quickened, social sympathies awakened, and friendly neighbourliness fostered.
> If you agree with these hopes you will, I am sure, like to aid to get them represented on the opening day.
> A small informal Committee has been formed of the inhabitants, under the Chairmanship of Mr F. Litchfield, and this is the programme that it has sketched out for the afternoon.
> At 3 o'clock all who are interested, of every age, will assemble in the Square, when Canon Barnett – who has been asked by the Directors to be the first President of the Institute – will turn the key and open the door.
> All who can get in will then enter, and Mr Herbert Marnham, in the much regretted absence of the Right Honourable Alfred Lyttleton, K.C., M.P., the President of the Board, will take the chair and short speeches will be made.
> At 3.40 all will leave the Hall, and the children will be divided into groups. Each group will then plant a tree, or a shrub, or a creeper, or some growing thing in memory of the glad hopes of the day.
> At 4.30 the children <u>only</u> will re-enter the Hall and have Tea, and after Tea we plan to have a little fun for them, and hear the music of young laughter in our new Hall.
> At 6.15 the children will all go home and remain there!
> At 7.30 all the grown-up people residing on the Estate who care to do so will come to a Conversazione. Mr Henry Vivian, M P, who has been asked by the

Plate 52 (opposite) The opening of the first room of the Institute, March 1909. Henrietta is in the centre with Frederick Litchfield on her left and Henry Vivian on her right.

Board of Directors to be the first Vice-President of the Institute, will take the chair, and there will be, as well as short speeches and music, time for conversation, so that opportunity should be given for people living on the Estate to become better acquainted.

I have set forth the plan fully, because I must ask you to aid the Committee by writing to me and saying if you mean to come, and if so, to which part of the proceedings.

Also, if you have children, will you write and say their names and ages, and if you would like them to help plant some growing thing or to come to Tea. On hearing from you a Planting ticket and a Tea ticket will be sent to each child."

The letter was typewritten, but each was signed personally "Henrietta O. Barnett".[114] She had taken great care with the organisation and detail of the event; it is an example of her meticulous planning. To this personal invitation there was a big response and a crowd assembled, having crossed the muddy expanses of Central Square on planks. They were dressed in their best, and the women in their most ornamental hats, as the photo reveals. They saw the door being opened by Samuel with a silver key presented to him by the architect, Lutyens, and they crowded into the Hall.[115]

The Institute was just a single room, to which three rough huts were soon attached. "The huts" have been a joke ever since, for no matter how often the Institute was enlarged, there were always rough huts attached. In July and August 1909 a Town Planning and Housing Exhibition was organised in a hut erected by the side of the Institute. This was the first of many exhibitions (and the first of many huts). It was organised jointly by the Trust and the Co-partnership. Henrietta asked the Garden City Association to invite the German Garden Cities Association to visit and to attend the conference in the Institute. Two hundred German visitors came! They must have been pleased that there was a model of a German garden city and plans and photographs of Nuremberg and Wiesbaden which had influenced Unwin, as well as exhibits from other cities and from France and America.

The conference was opened with a luncheon when Lyttleton proposed a toast to "The King and Kaiser," and expressed the "profound respect of Englishmen for the versatile genius of the Imperial Ruler of Germany".[116] English town planners certainly respected the system in Germany, where local authorities were empowered to make and enforce town plans. Henrietta was also toasted at the luncheon, and she said they should

"… Recall the services rendered to the movement by women, in the person of Octavia Hill and Emma Cons. If they wished that the good old fashioned virtue of house pride should exist, every woman should have a house in which she could take pride. It was in the garden that the man could work his will quite harmlessly. Speaking for her sex, she said that one of the delights in the possession of a garden was to know their men were healthily and happily employed and out of mischief. She herself always felt perfectly happy when her Canon was occupied, taking plantains out of the lawn."

Herbert Samuel, speaking at the exhibition, described Henrietta as "the Mother of the Hampstead Garden Suburb". During the conference lectures were given by Patrick Geddes and Henry Vivian; a lantern-slide lecture was given by Edward Lovett on "The Educational Value of Public Gardens and Parks"; Councillor Nettlefold of Birmingham Co-Partnership gave a paper on "A Practical Town". Henrietta spoke on "The City and its Relation to Child Life".[117] She said that "children living in large cities were placed under conditions of irksome and unhealthy restraint … They had no freedom, no chance of exercising their will and individuality. For them it was ever 'Do not do this; do not do that/ And wipe your feet upon the mat.'"[118]

The conferences and exhibitions in the Institute attracted national support. In 1912 there was another very successful town planning summer school. It was attended by 51 students, mostly architects and municipal engineers, coming from all parts of the Commonwealth and some from Sweden, Germany, France, Egypt, and the USA. They took a fortnight's course of lectures and visits, and as Henrietta describes this as a full course we may be sure that she organised long hours and hard work for the students.[119] Lectures were given by Unwin, Professor Adshead from Liverpool University, and Pepler the engineer, and Henry Vivian spoke on the financial aspects of town planning. Henrietta gave a lecture on "The Ethics of Suburb Planning".[120]

Soon there were three huts by the Institute in which arts and crafts were taught, and, as these subjects were of great interest to Suburb residents, a flourishing School of Art developed. Henrietta made staff appointments and organised classes and soon there was a very full programme.

In March 1909 Henrietta presided over a meeting to plan the foundation of a Free Church. She also invited groups to visit the Suburb: in May she invited a party of 30 from the committee of the Sweated Industries Exhibition. She met them at the Golders Green tube station, showed them the Institute, gave them a tea-party and took them to see Waterlow Court. This charming quadrangle of flats was officially opened by the Princess Louise, accompanied by her husband, the Duke of Argyll, on 1st July. The Princess said that the Duke had remarked that: "He had always heard of Golders Green as being an ideal spot to be buried in or burnt in, but he must now add to be boarded in."[121]

Henrietta was not musical, but she recognized the spiritual value of music. A choir was organised in the Suburb in the very early days, for in 1909 the Hampstead Tenants' Choral Society gave a concert, singing extracts from *The Merry Widow*; they also sang a cantata entitled *Christmas*. The first concerts took place in the workmen's huts, but for Christmas 1909 they sang *The King Harold Cantata* by F Cunningham Wood in the Institute. Henrietta created a School of Music with Sir Henry Wood as president: she had persuaded this renowned conductor to lend his name. As the musical director at a salary of £50 p.a., she appointed Rosabel Watson, a distinguished musician who conducted choirs in Central Hall and had a national reputation. She organized chamber music concerts in the Institute on Saturdays. Mr Gosling was the conductor of the choral class at a fee of 18 guineas a night; tuition was given individually and in classes, and there were children's classes and a children's choir. Henrietta asked Mr Gosling to maintain more dignity with the choir: "One lady!? Was seen to slap you on the back at the Conversazione, & others were – what shall I say too "larky" to their teacher." He replied that the girl's behaviour was astonishing and painful to him and that "There is a small band of 'free & easy' girls in the suburb – girls perfectly honest, & open-hearted, but, quite impossible, it is a type of new woman that can meet with no one's approval, and the only thing for one to do, is to avoid them." Despite these "free & easy" girls, the music school flourished and could attract such well-known lecturers as Sir Frank Bridge, Vaughan Williams and Holst. In the one year 1910–11 there were 13 concerts of classical music given by Rosabel Watson's orchestra. The Choral Society sang songs by Elgar, Holst and Stanford, and in 1922 sang *Messiah* in the Golders Green Hippodrome.[122]

From 1909 to 1915 the Trust ran the Institute, which really meant it was run by Henrietta. In March 1915 the Trust appointed an Institute management committee with Canon Masterman as chairman and Henrietta as vice-chairman. In 1918 the Institute was made a company and so separated from the Trust; the Institute Council was formed, with Lord Crewe as president and Henrietta as vice-president and continuing to do most of the work. She drafted letters to city companies and charities appealing for funds. She continued to decide policy and kept a control of detailed planning: she was involved with the appointment of teachers, and also with the appointment of other staff, domestics and even details of holiday cleaning.

There is no record of the class composition of people who attended Institute classes and joined the clubs, but it seems probable that they were more likely to be of the leisured class, particularly the middle-class women. Henrietta could have said, like Browning:

"I want to know a butcher paints,
A baker rhymes for his pursuit,
Candle-stick maker much acquaints
His soul with song, or, haply mute,
Blows out his brains upon the flute!"

The Club House

Social life was developing in the hut built for the estate workmen. It was a large hut on the area now occupied by Queen's Court and was organised by Henry Vivian and opened by Sybella Gurney in November 1908. This even had a library presented by Henrietta.[123] In this hut, Canon Samuel Barnett held the first service: the hut was used alternately by the Free Church and the Church of England. From 1909 the services were held in the Institute. Societies were starting up in the huts, but they needed a proper building. Henry Vivian thought this was much more urgent than the building of the Institute and wrote a long and heartfelt letter to Henrietta saying that the people living in the artisans' quarter needed a nearby meeting-place and that soon there would be three to four hundred children and youths "whose social life must be provided for practically every evening in the week & during holidays."[124] Vivian had seen that the Letchworth Hall and the Brentham Club House were great social assets, meeting-places for all sorts of societies and a place for tenants' meetings and to keep sports equipment. Brentham Club House still flourishes, unlike the Hampstead Garden Suburb Club House which was destroyed by a landmine. Brentham never achieved the fame of the Suburb and this was partly due to its small size – only 600 houses – and lack of a brilliant publicist like Henrietta. Also, due to financial problems, Brentham was built very slowly, whereas the speed with which the Suburb was built amazed people and produced ongoing news stories.

Despite Vivian's persuasive arguments, Henrietta gave her cultural Institute priority. Perhaps to calm the conflict, Samuel wrote to Vivian about the use of the Institute and the Club House: "The Hall to be used for Lectures, Meetings, Concerts, Soirees, Tea-fights, Dramatic, Sunday gatherings and At Homes. The Club to be used for Billiards, Smoke and Reading Rooms, Committee Rooms for Sports and Societies. The Tenants' Society to keep the Hall and the Club (as far as possible) for these uses and not compete with one another."[125]

At last, in February 1910, Vivian opened the Club House, a large building with a tower which housed numerous societies and sports clubs. At the opening he was presented with a handsome album of photographs of the estate, for the Co-operative tenants regarded him as an important founder of the Suburb. Henrietta made a speech, advising the listeners that "A good gossip is really very nice, but let it be about things and causes and principles, and not about persons."[126] She preferred meetings with a purpose to social occasions when people just chatted. The Club House was soon flourishing and became "... the scene of many merry meetings – concerts, whist drives and lectures having contributed to dispel any likelihood of gloom; senior and junior choirs have been well supported; the

*Plate 53 (opposite)
The Club House
from Willifield
Green. This was the
social centre of the
Suburb, containing
a restaurant, meeting
rooms, library,
billiard room and
space for sports
equipment.
It was destroyed by a
landmine in 1940.*

Plate 54
The library of the
Club House.

Plate 55 (opposite)
Scout Troop of the
Free Church. St
Jude's also had a
large troop, and there
were Cubs, Brownies
and Guides as well.
Henry Vivian and
Samuel Barnett
wanted to keep all
boys busy after school.

Boys' and Girls' Clubs have been the centres of instruction in handicrafts as well as of recreation; and the Dramatic Society has demonstrated the existence of histrionic ability on the Estate".[127]

In the Club House there was a club for men and one for women, and a reading room, and a library was being formed. There were lectures, concerts, a male voice choir; bridge, whist and cribbage were played (but no other card games were allowed); there was a room for billiards; the tennis courts were very popular and sports equipment was kept for the cricket, croquet, bowling and other clubs. There was a bowling green and a ninepin pitch and other "allurements for the … industrial classes". There were dances and wedding receptions. Vivian entertained his many visitors to the estate in the restaurant.

On 20th September 1912 the Garden Suburb parliament held its first meeting and elected officers, with Mr Thunder as speaker. The procedure closely followed that of the House of Commons. The parliament met on alternate Friday evenings. The Hendon branch of the Women's Franchise Society wrote to protest at the exclusion of women. Women were admitted and in December 1912 Margaret Bondfield spoke in favour of cheap food in a debate on free trade vs. tariffs. The first Cabinet was Liberal, but after a bill to nationalise coal mines was passed by 30 votes to 21 in 1913, a Socialist Cabinet was formed. Margaret Bondfield played the role of Home Secretary.[128] The Suburb parliament was to prove a training ground for her, and perhaps for other budding politicians. She was elected to the Westminster Parliament in 1923 and was Minister of Labour in the 1929–31 Labour government, the first woman to become a Cabinet Minister. She persuaded the Liberal government to introduce a maternity allowance in the 1911 insurance legislation and as Minister of Labour she started family allowances. The Suburb can be proud of providing a political initiation to such a benefactor to women.

Suburb residents, fearful of war, planned a demonstration for the Taft-Grey proposals, really a demonstration for peace.[129] Liberal and Labour Party supporters and suffragettes were very active. The Club House was the centre of political activity as well as social and sporting activities for all ages.

Henrietta's conflict with Vivian continued. She became extremely annoyed when Vivian showed the Suburb to visitors and entertained them in the Club House without showing them her Institute, as when a group of German labour leaders who were visiting Britain came to see co-partnership at work and admire the new style of architecture.[130] In 1914 Henrietta wrote to Lord Lytton:

> "When you told me yesterday that Mr Otto Beit was a large shareholder, I knew, but I did not think well to contradict you at the time, that he is a large shareholder in the Copartnership and not in the Trust. That is one of the difficulties we have with our dear friends the Copartners. They encourage their shareholders to believe that they are the main body. Also, as you probably know, if Mr Beit comes up with Lord Howick, he will be shown the Copartnership side of the Suburb, and will go away, still believing that they are the only body and that the Club is the only central organisation."[131]

Sadly, after the Club House was destroyed during the Second World War, only the small Fellowship House for the elderly was built on the site. A new club house is very much needed.

In the Edwardian period it was understood that boys must be given activities or they would get into mischief. Samuel Barnett left the planning of the Suburb entirely to Henrietta and never interfered, but he did help Vivian to start boys' clubs. Apart from the Club House, there were other leisure activities for children and teenagers in the early years of the Suburb. There were large troops of scouts and guides at both the churches and for young children there were gardening classes. In July 1909 Henry Vivian opened a roller-skating rink in the space between The Orchard, Temple Fortune

*Plate 56
Fellowship House,
with John Hewson,
chairman. Built on
the site of the Club
House after the war,
there is a meeting
room and a club for
people over 60. There
has been no social
centre for children
and younger adults
since the Club House
was bombed.*

Hill and Willifield Way.[132] The skating rink was illuminated several times a week to allow skating at night.[133] The Suburb residents may have felt some "gloom" when trudging to and fro to work through the mud and occasional horse-droppings on unmade roads, perhaps ill lit, and with the noise and other discomforts of major building works all around, but the burgeoning social life reveals the determination and spirit of the pioneers.

The Churches

Henrietta's other great concern was to get the churches built and opened as soon as possible. In January 1909 the Reverend Basil Bouchier was formally welcomed as the first vicar of St Jude's, coming from St Anne's, Soho. Henrietta made a "very happy speech" explaining that £5,000 of the £10,000 required must be raised before the church could be built. From the Bishops of London and Islington they had received £3,250, and she announced a gift of £100 from Sybella Gurney. Subscription forms were passed round the meeting, from which Henrietta received promises of a further £131.15s, the Barnetts giving £25. Henrietta put a great deal of work into raising money for St Jude's.[134]

Henrietta cut the first sod of St Jude-on-the-Hill on 28th October 1909: "The wind blew in a hurricane, the rain fell in torrents, the roads were seas of mud, but many people came." Lord Crewe laid the foundation stone on 25th April 1910 and the church was built so rapidly that on 28th October the Lady Chapel was ready for dedication and the whole church was consecrated on 7th May 1911. Henrietta and others worked hard to raise the money even as the church was being built. Some of the treasures in the church came from Henrietta's friends. Lady Battersea gave the sanctuary lamp in honour of Samuel Barnett. When Alfred Lyttleton, Chairman of the Trust, died in 1913, his friends donated the lectern in his memory.

In the 1920s Walter Starmer painted frescoes on the walls of the church. Evidently Lutyens did not object, but some people prefer the purity of the Free Church where Lutyens' style, unimpeded by painting, can be appreciated. Edward, Prince of Wales, came to unveil Starmer's work in 1924.

Before the churches were built, Samuel held services in the workmen's wooden shanty and then in the Institute. The Reverend Basil Bourchier had been appointed as vicar in December 1908 and continued with services in the Institute until the church was ready. He lived at 27 Temple Fortune Lane while waiting for the vicarage to be built. Henrietta strongly disliked the sound of church bells. In 1909 parishioners, led by the Reverends Chettoe and Bourchier, presented a petition to a court held at St Paul's regarding bell-ringing. It was agreed that St Jude's should not have bell-ringing before 7.55am, nor for longer than five minutes before a service. This must have pleased Henrietta.

The Reverend Bourchier's sermons were being well reported in the local paper.[135] He was acquiring a great reputation in the Suburb and beyond. His sermons were often

Plate 57
The Reverend Basil Bourchier came to the Suburb in 1909 and held services in the Institute until St Jude's was consecrated in 1911.

more political than religious. He defended underpaid workers, attacking employers for growing fat on the "slaves of industry". Evelyn Waugh was taken by his parents to St Jude's and in his autobiography described the "flamboyant" Bourchier:

"He was a man without pretension to doctrinal orthodoxy; a large, florid, lisping man, who was often to be seen in the stalls of London theatres in lay evening-dress. No one could have been more alien to the ideals of Dame Henrietta Barnett and of the general run of the inhabitants of his parish. He was a man of wider claims. His name was constantly in the popular newspapers, giving his wayward opinions on any subject about which he was consulted. He professed an extravagant patriotism and was a friend of Lord Northcliffe and of at least one member of the royal family. He was anathema to the genuine Anglo-Catholics of Graham Street, Margaret Street and St Augustine's, Kilburn. His congregation was not exclusively – nor indeed primarily – local. Personal devotees flocked to him from all parts of London. His sermons were dramatic, topical, irrational and quite without theological content. They would have served, my father remarked – and no stricture was more severe on his lips – as leading articles in the *Daily Mail* …

Mr Bourchier was a totally preposterous parson. When he felt festal he decreed a feast, whatever the season or occasion marked on the calendar. He dressed up, he paraded about, lights and incense were carried before him. When the mood took him he improvised his own peculiar ceremonies. Once he presented himself on the chancel steps, vested in a cope and bearing from his own breakfast table a large silver salt-cellar. 'My people,' he announced, 'you are the salt of the earth', and scattered a spoonful on the carpet before us."[136]

Henrietta found his high church style alien. She was not pleased when he spoke at a meeting of the United Kingdom Alliance at the Free Church and shocked the temperance meeting by proclaiming:

"God Save the King and Beer for the British People."[137]

Also Henrietta must have been worried when she saw his interest in the choirboys. He was transferred back to St Anne's, Soho, in 1930. The Bishop of London knew his sexual preferences and appointed a curate to keep an eye on him at St Anne's. It was found that he was giving expensive presents to the choirboys to ensure that they kept their mouths shut.[138]

> Go practise if you please
> With men and women: leave a child alone
> For Christ's particular love's sake.
>
> Browning.

Henrietta knew about child abuse from her social work in Whitechapel, but the ladies in St Jude's congregation were completely ignorant of such matters and were delighted by Bourchier.

The Free Church was being built at the same time as St Jude's. From the very start of the Suburb, when Henrietta took Lord Crewe to see the land, she was determined that the nonconformist church should have just as prominent a site as the Church of England. Henrietta had seen so many towns where the Church of England had a conspicuous position, while the chapels were in poor buildings in back streets. Lutyens designed them both and gave the Free Church its dome to match and contrast with St Jude's spire. She asked the Free Church Council and other pastors to get together and they agreed that the Baptist Union and the Congregational Union should sponsor the new church. Herbert Marnham raised some of the finance from the London Baptist Association and the annual collection

*Plate 58
Henrietta and
Samuel Barnett
with the Reverend
Basil Bourchier.*

*Plate 59.
Henrietta laying
a foundation
stone of the Free
Church, 1911.*

for new building made in Baptist churches throughout London was allocated to the Suburb church. Marnham himself gave £3,000.[139]

It was the first Free Church in the country for all nonconformists.[140] Henrietta wanted to inscribe her belief on one of the foundation stones: "God is larger than the creeds." While the elders were considering this request in March 1911, Queen Mary came to visit the Suburb: "As the Queen, Frederick Litchfield and I walked across the Central Square, she was told of my wish and Mr Litchfield said: 'There is a divergence of opinion among our Church Elders, but if you, Ma'am, would like those words put on the Stone, it would, of course, be done.' The Queen asked me to repeat the words, and then, after walking the length of the square her Majesty turned at the top of the steps to Mr Litchfield and said in the most queenly manner: 'Yes, I should like those words put on the stone.'"[141] Whatever the elders may have thought, Henrietta had got her way.

She was delighted when the Queen returned in February 1918, this time with Princess Mary and the Prince of Wales on leave from the army, and the Queen related to the Prince the origin of the words on the stone. This was an unscheduled visit and Henrietta had less than a week's notice to organize it. She had to arrange the whole programme, including press, photographs, and the presentation to the Queen of 40 people. Lord Lytton made the speech and announced that £7,000 had already been raised for the school building and a further £26,000 was needed. Henrietta ensured that there were some rich people there. Afterwards she showed the royal party round the Institute, the shops, the staff cottages, garages and chauffeurs' flats, Waterlow Court, Meadway Court, the Addison Way flats, the war-widows flats, the woods, and the houses for the wealthy. The rush to arrange this big programme was a "really stupendous" effort which left her exhausted, but it was a great success and she must have been delighted when the Queen "cared to study estate plans and hear of hopes for the Institute as she drank coffee in my dining-room".

The Queen came officially to lay foundation stones for the Henrietta Barnett School in 1918, and again in 1924, her fifth visit to the Suburb. Henrietta made careful plans for her official visits. In 1924 there was a guard of honour formed by scouts and guides extending from Heathgate to the Institute; all the schoolchildren were cheering, the band of the Middlesex regiment played "God Save the King" and of course all the local clergy, councillors and other important personages, dressed in their finery, were there to receive Her Majesty. The Queen came again in July 1930 to open Crewe Hall, the large building with the clock-tower which joins the first two buildings. Her growing friendship with the Queen might have made Henrietta unfriendly to lesser mortals, but she passed Kipling's test: "If you can talk with crowds and keep your virtue, / Or walk with Kings – nor lose the common touch …".

The Friends Meeting House was opened in October 1913. Henrietta's friends George and Elizabeth Cadbury provided the finance and it was designed by the architect Fred Rowntree. The building had a close resemblance to William Penn's place of worship in Jordans, USA. There were many Friends living in the Suburb in the early years and they played an important part in the development of social services and particularly in welcoming refugees from Germany and later from Uganda.[142]

Other Meeting-places

The Tea House was built after the First World War and was placed where it would be useful for people playing tennis on or near the Square, although it was used by many others and especially by the many visitors to the Suburb. It was rented out to Bickiepegs Limited who provided refreshments and put colourful umbrellas on the front lawn in the summer. Another teahouse was on the ground floor of Arcade House, backing on to the intended pond, now Queen's Court. There were tennis courts, mostly grass, on the squares and in the spaces between the backs of houses as well as many in private gardens, so tennis

Plate 60
Queen Mary
opened the Queen
Mary Hall of the
Institute in 1924.
She was greeted by
guides and scouts,
school-children and a
military band.

must have been a tremendously popular summer pastime in the Suburb and provided an easy way of meeting people. The Reverend Basil Bourchier shocked people by playing tennis on Sundays.[143]

Henrietta met with many disappointments. She was unable to build a Carnegie library because the local authorities wanted the library placed in their town centres, Finchley and Hendon. She had planned to put the library opposite the manse and next door to the Friends Meeting House on North Square. She wanted a theatre, but the Playhouse, now the Everyman, was built in Hampstead instead of in the Suburb. She hoped people would study meteorology and astronomy, but the weather station was vandalised, and though a flat roof was provided, nobody seemed interested in astronomy. She would have liked a swimming bath, and wanted to make Turner's Wood into a bird sanctuary. But her greatest disappointment was over Bunker Hill. After the First World War, she had the idea that the Bunker Hill in the Suburb, at the foot of Hampstead golf course, should become a national monument to Anglo-American friendship. The Bunker Hill in Massachusetts commemorated the battle of 1775 between Britain and America. The Bunker Hill in the Suburb was to be a symbol of peace, with a peace column erected on which were to be the names of all the American soldiers who fell in the war.[144] She got the permission of the Trust to do this and formed a committee with herself as chairman.[145] £15,000 was needed to buy the land and she appealed for it through the wireless and with letters and articles in the press, through speeches and drawing-room meetings and personal appeals. Even though the Prince of Wales came to visit the site, she could not raise enough and the land

Plate 61 (overleaf)
The Tea House
provided teas to
tennis players and
visitors from abroad
and many others.
In the 1950s it was
used by the Henrietta
Barnett Junior
School kindergarten.
From 1973 it was
used as a language
school by the
Institute. In 2010 it
was sold to a private
developer. Another
communal building
privatised!

was sold for building. She was full of wonderful ideas, but they all needed money, and despite her talents she could not always get it.[146]

From the very beginning of the Suburb, Henrietta's greatest desire was to preserve the trees and hedges, the woods and streams. There were to be no more than eight houses per acre on average, so there was plenty of open space. The gardens were hedged and the height limited to six feet in the back garden and three feet in the front garden so neighbours could talk across them and you could see a long vista of gardens and trees, and appreciate the architecture. Henrietta had seen and liked the fenceless "yards" during her travels in America. She was determined to keep the existing farmland hedges and trees, for as part of her publicity she circulated a photo album showing them with a caption saying: "These are some of the trees and hedge-rows which it is hoped to preserve in the proposed Garden Suburb".

Her environmentalism was supported by Unwin, who planned housing to avoid cutting down trees, as in Asmuns Place, Temple Fortune Lane and Lucas Crescent. Hitherto, most builders started by clearing the site of bushes and trees. Small communal open spaces were provided near the houses for young children and old people to use. She could picture the healthy children, living in the cottage homes, with play areas close at hand and for older children the experience of roaming in the woods, blackberrying and picking wild flowers, paddling in the Mutton Brook (it was not encased in concrete): the healing virtues of the country amid the conveniences of town. With Unwin she walked through Big Wood, pushing through the undergrowth, though "I will confess that I was so alarmed of the snakes that I could hardly take in his words as he planned a road here, a pathway there."[147] She delighted in the planning of the public gardens. At first they had gorse in Central Square, which must have looked very rural, but it was pulled up because of the fire risk to the churches. Then they planned a lily pond with a bridge, but this was abandoned. She thought "curly shaped beds would not harmonise with the severe lines of the buildings and unkempt grass would woo noisy boys". Eventually Lutyens, on his way to India, made a rough sketch of the rectangular beds, but his idea of a rectangle of water was never realised. Central Square is now owned by the London Borough of Barnet. Henrietta chose flowering trees and fruit trees to line the roads, enjoying her choice *"Of all the trees that grow so fair, Old England to adorn." (Kipling).* Almond trees were planted on Asmuns Hill, crab trees on one end of Willifield Way and may trees on the other end. But there was vandalism, people breaking the lower branches to get the apples and the flowers, so the trees had to be replaced. To look after the open spaces the Trust employed many gardeners: 29 in 1928. The Trust ran a shop which sold plants and provided labour and tools. Henrietta enjoyed gardening and thought "gardeners are delightful people".[148] Unwin's plan for the Suburb allowed large areas for backlands, with the idea of allowing communal space behind the gardens. In the wealthier areas this was mainly used for tennis courts and in the artisans' quarter it was made into allotments, where the men would be kept busy and away from the pub. Digging the allotment made the men friendly and helped to realise Henrietta's wish for a more communal life:

"Father working, mother watching, children helping, the land yielding with that generosity which under our climate seems to follow spade labour and personal interest. The pennies would not be needed for 'sweeties' as the 'goosgogs' [gooseberries] are enjoyed; the pickles will give place to the lettuces; the hastily

Plate 62 (previous) The children's playhouse in Asmuns Place, one of the small open spaces within walking distance of all children and old people.

Plate 63 (opposite) Everybody should learn to garden and take a pride in the environment. There were prizes for the best gardens. The children's plots were behind the Club House, between Addison Way and Wordsworth Walk.

Plate 64
The tenants' sports
day.

obtained indigestible 'relish' to the 'vegetables we growed', and which is worth more than all the material advantages, the family will be able to take its pleasures together – the pleasure of preparing for, and tending, watching, hoping and wondering about 'the kindly fruits of the earth' which we all enjoy and deserve to enjoy 'in due season'.[149]

It seems strange that the woman is allotted such a passive role, but though Henrietta took great pleasure in planning gardens, she only wielded a spade to dig the first sods of her buildings.

From 1907 to 1911 the national press reported on the smallest events in Suburb life and usually in very complimentary terms. *The Daily News* even gave the Institute programme for the winter season, including the societies such as Henrietta's Novel Literary Club. This honeymoon spell with the press was broken when in-fighting broke out at the Club House. The Club House was owned by Hampstead Tenants, but the members elected a council. The Hampstead Tenants sacked the steward against the wishes of the members, who were so incensed that they boycotted the billiard tables and the bar, and even assembled to demonstrate. Journalists seized on this news of a storm in the Suburb with glee:

"The Golders Green Arcadia ... is just now in the throes of internecine strife. It seems that there are people who don't like other people's children to cry interminably, or to walk on the flower beds. Then there is a squabble about the club, and the outraged members have boycotted the billiard table and the refreshment bar.

188

Plate 65
The tenants' sports day, egg and spoon race.

Yes, it was bound to happen; nevertheless, it is very sad. The Garden City began so auspiciously. Everything was done to ensure concord. No one was allowed to become a tenant whose sobriety and morality was not vouched for, and the members of whose family had not at least three vaccination marks. A respectability as of Upper Tooting was combined with the timid unconventionalism of a demure Bohemia. Propriety of conduct was expected, but it was not compulsory to wear a top hat on Sundays, nor was a man sent to Coventry if he omitted to leave the bottom button of his waist coat unbuttoned. There was a delightful atmosphere of idyllic promise at the start, but now, alas, the serpent of discord has crept into the suburban Eden, and rural serenity is no more."[150]

Chapter 19

The World outside the Suburb

At the turn of the century Henrietta looked young for her age, and had a mature beauty. She continued to dress well, and her body language was graceful. Her voice was strong and she was never at a loss for words. Since the Weir Mitchell treatment for nerves which she had undergone in the 1890s, she had continued overweight. In a letter to his brother, Samuel wrote: "Alice was here last night. She is very jolly & very fat … Yetta is now 10 stone 5 lbs!!!".[151] The exclamation marks seem to denote surprise that her weight is either going up or down, we do not know which. From photographs we can see that she was only about five feet tall so she was very overweight. Certainly it is most surprising that such a considerate husband as Samuel gave away this information, but we are grateful to him. He was worried that her health could not sustain all the work involved in creating the Suburb:

> "Canon Barnett had at first very mixed feelings towards the scheme. Sympathy with it because it was my project, grave doubts as to its success, skepticism as to whether, at fifty-two, I could accomplish the labour inseparable from so large a scheme, and add it to my many other duties; and a firm determination not to share either the work or the responsibility, because he meant to use the years of life that were left to him to teach spiritual truths. For a time therefore I did nothing, for it had always been the practice of both of us, if we did not agree, to abstain from action until we saw eye to eye. But as my hopes developed and crystallized, and he realized that I felt it laid on me to carry out the scheme, he withdrew all opposition and, as was ever his wont, he helped me with his sympathy and counsel when I sought it; but, mindful of his desire to conserve his mind for less mundane matters, worrying details were not laid before him."[152]

Her bouts of illness and depression continued, as one learns from Samuel's letters: "I know all we can do is wait, but it is sad that Y--- makes so little progress. I doubt if she is really one bit better. The last two days she has been at her worst. She lies in the big room by the window, reads simple books, and feels very poorly."[153] But as soon as she recovered she worked very hard, juggling with her many interests and commitments. Until 1907 they lived in the Warden's Lodge at Toynbee Hall and Henrietta was taking part in some of the Toynbee societies and entertaining perhaps more than ever as their fame grew: on one occasion they had 30 people to dinner.[154] They made weekend visits to family and friends, to conferences and to Oxford where they had found so much support for Toynbee. In a postscript to a letter to a friend, Henrietta revealed their dates for November 1903:[155] "Our dates dear are briefly thus 2 – 6 Cheltenham / 7 – 9 Clifton / 9 – 19 Whitechapel / 19 – 23 Oxford 23 – 29

Whitechapel / 10 Leave for Italy / Subject to alteration." They were both leading immensely busy, well-planned lives, discussing their experiences and problems when they were together.

Children of the State

In the late 19th century, "children of the state" was the term used to mean all "cared-for" children. This includes children in national and local government institutions, such as homes and workhouses, children in private homes such as Barnardo's, children at home who are neglected or abused or overworked and lost or vagrant children sleeping out. "Cared-for" children is a ridiculous, loaded term when we all know that there has been much abuse and neglect of these children, and I wish we could return to "children of the state", and once accepted there would be no need to change the phrase every few years, for it is a neutral term.

In 1896 Henrietta and Ernest Hart had founded the State Children's Association to press for reform of the care of pauper children. Ernest Hart died in 1897, and Henrietta fought on. It was an important pressure group and despite all her work for the Suburb, Henrietta became honorary secretary of the association in 1903. She liked this job for it enabled her to determine the agenda and write the important letters, and in this role she could shape its policy and invite the support of many influential people. She and other members of the Association spread its principles and enlarged its influence by speaking at Church congresses, to the National Union of Women Workers, the Charity Organisation Society, political meetings and many other meetings with "audiences ranging from 3,000 to 30," and Henrietta wrote articles for journals and newspapers.[156] The association had started in London but support grew in many other cities and money flowed in. Samuel and Henrietta were among the most generous donors, giving £15 per year. From 1910 they were also supported by City companies: a sign that it was a most respectable pressure group.

At first the office was in a room in Old Broad Street lent by the banker Sir Samuel Montagu MP, but they needed more space as they expanded and so from 1909 they rented an office in Victoria Street, Westminster, close to the hub of government. The association could exert pressure on Parliament through members who were lords or MPs, and when the Liberal Party was elected in 1905 there were high hopes of getting reform. In December 1905 Lord Crewe resigned his post as chairman of the SCA on becoming Lord President of the Council, for, as he wrote: "It will be obvious to the Committee that the close relation which exists between the Local Government Board and the Association's work, makes it impossible for a member of the Government to be responsible for the latter."[157] However, it was helpful to have the ex-chairman in the Cabinet. Lord Lytton became the chairman of the State Children's Association.

In 1903 Samuel wrote to his brother: "On Wednesday Yetta had a very good meeting of 11 MPs in the House who planned all sorts of acts & measures for State Children. She was very pleased."[158] Then Samuel wrote of further success: "My wife got a good three hours' debate in the House on P.L. children."[159] In 1906 she spoke again to a meeting of MPs at the House of Commons. She gave statistics of the large number of children in care. Then she explained their 10 proposals for reform and asked each MP to be present at the Local Government Board estimates and to speak on one proposal: "We will supply full information - & can promise you I hope as good a foundation for you."[160] As usual she worked very hard to prepare for a successful result. In 1907 in a speech to the Church Congress she said there were 602,000 paupers, 220,000 hidden away in monster institutions, the old sitting in rows in workhouses, waiting for death. There were 69,000 children wholly dependent on the state, of whom 20,200 were in large institutions: "disciplined, taught, drilled, controlled, it is true, often with kindliness and conscientious supervision, but for the most part lacking in the music of their lives that one note of love, which alone can turn all from discord to harmony."[161] Measles, diphtheria, ophthalmia and ringworm were a constant threat to the children gathered in such large numbers in the Barrack Schools. Institutional care was extremely costly: the village built for the children of the Bermondsey Union cost £320 per head and each child cost £1.0.6d per week. Henrietta, leading the State Children's Association, worked hard to end the scandal of children in workhouses and barrack schools but she made little headway for she was at loggerheads with Sir John Burns, President of the Local Government Board, who, though a Liberal minister, was very reactionary. Henrietta wanted all state relief to be educational, aiming to strengthen character and make the recipient independent, giving the unemployed worthwhile work instead of stone-breaking and oakum-picking. When she suggested to John Burns that his department could reduce unemployment by founding agricultural colonies, he poured scorn on her: "Woman! When will you learn to mind your own business?"[162] She was convinced that the whole care of children must be taken away from the Local Government Board and placed under the Board of Education.

Amongst the MPs their closest friend remained Sir John Gorst. Henrietta wrote one of her delightful pen portraits:

"When Sir John Gorst was living in Toynbee, he usually sat unobtrusively through any conference, leaning back in his chair, his legs straight out, his pointed beard stiff, his head up, his eyes fixed on the ceiling, gently rubbing the tips of his fingers together, apparently oblivious of all that was going on, and then towards the end he would begin, and in a monotonous, almost sing-song voice sum up the whole position, and ask probing questions. It was masterly, and even when cynically done was always influenced by the desire for reform. He used to chuckle with amusement when we had returned to our quiet clean-aired drawing-room, and recalled how he had taken the humbug out of one speaker, or exposed the rotten foundation of someone else's theories."[163]

Vagrant children became one of her concerns. These were children of tramps or of people with no home who travelled round getting such work as umbrella-mending or chimney-sweeping, their whole family often dirty, ragged, ill-fed and illiterate. In 1902/3 the SCA promoted a Vagrancy Bill and it was introduced by Sir John Gorst as a private members' bill. Gorst was staying with the Barnetts in St Jude's Cottage when Samuel wrote to his brother: "Gorst is in fine form & is making most useful speeches."[164] The Vagrancy Bill was supported by many MPs, including Lloyd George and John Burns, but failed to become law. It was introduced again in 1906 but again failed. The SCA also tried to amend the Infant Life Protection Act 1897 by a private members' bill, and although they were unsuccessful at first they managed to get Parliament to pass the Act in the next session and so strengthen the law against infanticide.

Henrietta was working full out. From 1903 there was so much to plan for the Suburb and at the same time she knew that this was an opportunity for national social change, and with her knowledge and authority she could make a real difference to the care of children. In March 1908, Samuel records: "On Tuesday she took MacNamara to see a Pauper School & opened his eyes. She liked his energy & his enthusiasm for his work. He will not again say such words of praise abt[sic] big barrack schools."[165] Thomas Macnamara was parliamentary secretary to the Local Government Board.

In 1909 the Royal Commission on the Poor Law issued its enormous report which was the foundation of the great social reforms of the Liberal government. Henrietta, well aware of the need to mobilise public opinion and knowing that even educated people would blanch at reading the voluminous report, made a short and simplified version of it. Of course she used every opportunity to make speeches about it, giving an important one to the Political and Economic Circle of the National

Liberal Club. In an article for the *Cornhill Magazine* she quoted parts of the report. In 1908 there were 235,000 children wholly or partially dependent on the state. Of these, 22,500 were in workhouses, 12,000 were in barrack schools, 17,000 in village communities or scattered homes, and 11,000 in other institutions. Only 9,000 were boarded out with families, and 164,000 were receiving relief while remaining with their own families.[166] The village communities consisted of anything from 6 to 40 cottages with from 12 to 30 children living in each cottage. The scattered homes were houses with about 12 children looked after by a stepmother and attending local schools, a system much preferred by Henrietta. In some workhouses 40% of babies died within a year. Why were there any children in the workhouses when the Departmental Committee of 1896 had condemned that system? Where the Guardians supported families at home, the money was sometimes going to mothers who were drunk or immoral and not caring for their children. Some families continued to drag their children in and out of the workhouse frequently – "the Ins and Outs" – as they were called. There had been very little improvement since the 1896 report. And yet, argued Henrietta, these children were very much needed by the state, for the birth rate was declining as middle- and upper-class women were restricting their families, while profligate lower-class people were having unwanted children who became the youth of the future.

In 1910 Henrietta spoke to the Church Congress and outlined her revolutionary scheme for widows with children under the Poor Law. First she explained the current situation. The widows' pension was usually 10s. per week but was means-tested:

> "Mother a seamstress, earning about 9s. a week, and the Board of Guardians granting another 6s. Four children (eleven, nine, six, and two) made happy by the motherly love of a steady, methodical and careful woman, who, however, cannot support them except by working unceasingly, as well as by getting charitable help towards their clothes from the Church, country holidays from the Childrens' Country Holiday Fund, official help in dinners from the Educational Authority, medical help from the health visitor or nurse engaged by the Town Council."

Henrietta was critical of the large number and confusion of sources of help. But her main point was that even a good mother who worked hard could not support a family. Even worse was the situation of the families with inadequate mothers. The Poor Law Report found that in 1908 there were 30,000 poor-law children living in very unsatisfactory homes with careless, slipshod mothers and 20,000 in homes wholly unfit for children with drunk or immoral mothers.[167]

Henrietta had a most remarkable plan for dealing with widows:

1. Children should be boarded out with their own mothers. Women were paid by the State to foster children, so why not pay poor mothers to foster their own children? They could be moved to a healthy suburb and could foster other children as well.

2. Some mothers needed daily supervision. "Some twenty of these women could be placed in small cottages, or tenements in a quadrangle, and employed for part of the day at one of the giant official institutions for the infirm or imbecile which are scattered all over the country. The children could be kept at school for dinner, and care taken that the women's hours of labour were short enough to enable them to home-make morning and evening when the children return from school."

3. Women who were too ignorant to be effective mothers could be in a teaching colony where they would train until they mastered the skill of mothering.

4. Working women should either have short hours, as arranged by Mr Cadbury, or be provided with household assistance.

5. "From other mothers the children should be removed altogether, and for these children I should counsel emigration, for all workers can cite cases of young people, when they reach wage-earning ages, with bad parents claiming rights over them."[168]

With her wonderful imagination, Henrietta could describe even the details of her scheme, which was far ahead of her time. One can imagine the reaction of the assembled clergy and laymen listening to this speech. They would have thought her a madcap Socialist. She thought communal living suited many people and especially single women who were in such a weak economic and social position when alone. This idea was bearing fruit in the Hampstead Garden Suburb.

Juvenile delinquents were other children of the state who were getting more attention at the start of the 20th century. The State Children's Association with the Howard Association, the Waifs and Strays Society and other associations were all demanding the creation of special courts for juveniles. In 1907 Henrietta wrote an article for the *Cornhill Magazine* on "Special Courts of Justice for Children" in which she described how the 668 children arrested in London in one year were treated. They were kept overnight in police cells, and next morning had to stand in dock in the ordinary police court. Then they might be kept in a remand home, perhaps for several weeks, being brought each week before the court, until they were sent to an industrial school. Some were young criminals, but many of them were simply charged with wandering the streets and being destitute, living in houses of ill fame, begging or trespassing, and some were not tall enough to see over the dock! While in court, the children listened to details of domestic violence and prostitution which were unsuitable for them to hear. There was nobody to speak on behalf of the children and the younger ones were frightened and unable to speak for themselves. The magistrates were very varied in their judgements, some discharging more cases than others, some imposing fines, some discharging few and sending more children to industrial schools. Special courts for children had been established in Australia in 1890, in Canada in 1894 and in Massachusetts since 1863; the American system was especially admired by English reformers.

Henrietta was very critical of the industrial schools. Whereas they might suit hardened boys in their teens, young children were subjected to this same hard regime until they were 16. There were 139 such schools in England and Wales, accommodating 13,930 boys and 4,656 girls. The schools came under the Home Office, not the Education Department, and were really prison schools. The schools were very varied, some exploiting the labour of the children to make goods for sale and so contribute to the costs, others putting a proper emphasis on education in trades; some were very harsh, others were kinder. But as the magistrates did not know the schools, they did not send children they dealt with to the ones that would suit them best.

Henrietta with her State Children's Association agitated for special courts for children, and for probation officers to be appointed so that most of the children, instead of being sent to industrial schools, would stay at home and be supervised and perhaps reformed by a woman visitor. Probation already operated in America successfully, and from 1904 the SCA was demanding that special courts and probation should be established here.

The Children Act of 1908 was one of the most important acts of the 20th century. Herbert Samuel, the Home Secretary, asked the SCA to help prepare the bill and this enabled the association to get the reforms for which they had struggled.[169] Part I of the Act strengthened the provisions of the Infant Life Protection Act, making it illegal for foster-parents to insure children. The act made children's courts compulsory, with reform, not punishment, their aim. Part V of the act abolished the death sentence for children and young persons, forbade the sending of children under 14 to penal servitude, made parents responsible for wrongdoing where there was parental neglect, and made compulsory the establishment of remand homes so children would not be kept in prison. No doubt Henrietta, with her role as secretary of the SCA and her great knowledge of cared-for children, must have played a significant part in designing this important legislation. However, the local authorities were slow to establish remand homes and the SCA was soon criticising them and the police for continuing to send children on remand to workhouses.[170]

As children's courts and probation were such an innovation in England, the Home Secretary appointed a departmental committee in 1909 to inquire into the working of the Probation Act, with Lord Samuel as chairman and Lord Lytton, chairman of the SCA, as a member. The SCA was asked to give suggestions for the improvement of the act. But improvements do not seem to have been made, for in 1912 the SCA found that the procedure in the children's courts was the same as that used in adult courts and was much too formal; the ordinary court-rooms, with the dock and boxes for witnesses, were unsuitable; some of the magistrates did not know how to deal with children, and many did not use the probation service. A probation officer could raise the standard of life of a deteriorating family, whereas a fine, strokes of the birch or committal to a reformatory or industrial school tended to lower the family, particularly as they were forced to contribute to the costs of the school. In 1911, of 20,000 children and young persons dealt with by the courts, only 3,600 were placed on probation, so a very inadequate use was being made of it. In many courts no probation officer had been appointed.

The SCA was also concerned with the treatment of mentally disadvantaged children in the care of the state, a subject close to Henrietta's heart on account of her love for her own disadvantaged sister, Fanny. The SCA policy was that they should live in small homes where they could be treated individually, and on no account kept in workhouses or herded into large asylums where they were mixed with the imbeciles and idiots who were not educable. In small homes they could be trained, just as Henrietta had arranged in the home she established in the 1890s. A bill to implement the SCA recommendations was introduced but not passed, so in 1912 the treatment of the mentally disadvantaged was still left to the discretion of the Boards of Guardians.[171]

In all the activities of the SCA, Henrietta as honorary secretary certainly played a leading role. The association's views and policies were those of Henrietta: it was her mouthpiece. One of her publications was a brief leaflet with a remarkable diagram showing the confusion of authorities responsible for children in the care of the state. The diagram is so complex it extends over several pages! It is a very eloquent appeal for bringing all children's services under the control of the Minister of Education. There is no doubt that Henrietta was a driving force in the association, and with the Barnetts' many contacts with MPs she pushed its policies through Parliament. Though "only a woman" and with no vote, she pressed and manipulated MPs and lords to help the children. No wonder that in 1909 when Mr Asquith, the Prime Minister, presented Henrietta and Samuel with their portrait, he called her: "The Guardian of the Children of the State".

Teaching Children about the Countryside

Henrietta was concerned with the health and moral and spiritual well-being of all children, not only cared-for children. She wanted children to be well informed about nature and even about the facts of human reproduction, a controversial idea at that time. Henrietta was invited by Margaret Stephens to write an introduction to her book on *Women and Marriage*. Henrietta praised the author for "telling her sisters simple sex facts," and advocated gradually informing children as well. The book steers clear of any details about intercourse. But women found it really useful and informative: it was first published in 1909 and in 1935 a ninth impression was issued![172]

The Children's Country Holiday Fund had grown very rapidly, from 2,879 children being sent on holiday in 1884 to the peak of 46,402 in 1912. In 1889 arrangements were made for Jewish children to be included and from 1893 Roman Catholic schools participated. In 1908 a schoolmaster and member of the CCHF committee obtained permission from the education authority to take a party of older school boys to Malvern in term-time, the CCHF bearing the cost. Other schools followed suit and later the idea was adopted by the LCC and school journeys became a part of the curriculum. The Barnetts were pioneers in regarding school outings and journeys as an important part of education. The CCHF had great appeal and was supported by many famous people and by the press. The great cartoonists Ernest Shepherd and Sir John Tenniel found it an excellent subject and so added to the publicity.

Henrietta thought all holidays should be educational so that leisure time would not be wasted. She had definite views about leisure. People of all ages wanted excitement, interest and memories, but pleasure should not depend on excitement, should not cause loss or pain to others, nor be founded on greed or gain. Leisure should increase the capacity for enjoyment, strengthen the whole being, enrich memory and call forth effort. How did the current use of leisure measure up to her standards? "The recreations of the rich are found in racing, hunting, shooting, fishing, card-playing, showing their possessions (which includes clothing), sun-seeking, play-going, motoring, dancing and eating. The recreations of the less educated classes are found in races, football matches, music-halls, beach shows, roundabout or switchback movements, sex-romping, and drinking." [173] Has anything changed? She thought that many popular pleasures were over-exciting, based on greed, and caused loss to others: drink, gambling ... inane beach shows, music halls, racing, football matches (betting and possibly brutal conflict), monster school treats, shooting battues and plays which made "a mock of sin" were all condemned. Pleasure should increase the capacities for enjoyment. She recommended:

> "Music, games of skill, books, athletics, foreign travel, cycling, walking-tours, sailing, photography, picture galleries, botanical rambles, antiquarian researches, and many other recreations too numerous to mention call out the growth of the powers, as well as feed what exists; they excite active as well as passive emotions; they enlist the receiver as a co-operator; they allow the pleasure seekers to feel the joy of being the creating children of a creating God."[174]

Most of all she recommended gardening for people of every age as "the purest, deepest and most recreative of pleasures".[175] These pleasures would lift the spirit and develop the mind. She quoted Browning: "From change to change unceasingly, the soul's wings never furled." She gave great value to leisure in the country because of her belief in the spiritual and healing powers of Nature. As the Children's Country Holiday Fund had become such a large organisation it was organized by professionals. But Henrietta saw a need to teach the children to appreciate the country before they went on holiday. For this purpose she founded the Countryside Committee of the Children's Country Holiday Fund, made herself chairman and recruited women helpers from all over London. When they were at their many West End dinner parties and the ladies withdrew after dinner, Henrietta would start telling them about the miseries of East End children. Soon ladies on the other side of the drawing-room would hear someone mimicking a cockney child and they would be

Plate 66 (opposite)
Prime Minister
Asquith presenting
Henrietta and
Samuel with
their portrait
by Herkomer.

drawn into the circle. With her almost masculine authority, her chic apparel and pretty face and hair she was so very attractive. In her hyperactive moods, she spread happiness like Browning's Pippa:

"The year's at the spring
And day's at the morn;
Morning's at seven;
The hill-side's dew-pearled;
The lark's on the wing;
The snail's on the thorn:
God's in his heaven –
All's right with the world!"

Riding home in the brougham carriage, the ladies would gently but firmly seek their husbands' permission to visit poor families and prepare the children for their country treats. They had joined the "Monstrous Regiment of Women". During the winter, they prepared the children for their holiday by lantern-slide talks at their schools on the natural beauties and curiosities they might find in the country. On Saturday afternoons groups of 12 children were taken for a walk, shown what to look for in fields, hedges and woods, given tea and a "romp" before returning home. Her friend Lillian Thompson did a lot of administrative work and provided money, and Henrietta used her usual technique of starting with the support of society women who could influence other women to join in.

Before the children went on holiday, they were each sent a letter with a foreword by Henrietta. She invented questions for the children to answer to make them observant:

"When sheep get up from lying down, do they rise with their front or their hind legs?
Do you think that the big pigs grunt as an expression of pleasure, or pain, or both?
Give the names by which we call the following animals when they are babies: horse, goat, cow, fox, dog, cat, sheep, frog, rabbit, deer."[176]

She asked them to write back about the trees and flowers and creatures and anything that interested them during their holiday. Henrietta delighted in reading their replies, and in using them in her speeches for the fund, no doubt mimicking them:

"Butterflies don't do much work."
"There was no strikes on down there but there was a large number of wasps."
"The cows made a grunting noise, the baa lambs made a pretty little shriek."
"Stinging nettles are a nuisance to people with holes in their boots."

In 1911, 45,000 children were sent on holiday and over 5,000 wrote a letter to Henrietta. She would quote them in her articles for magazines:

"The prettiest flowers a child in the third standard saw were "nosegays" and "tegtoes and garpees" in a garden; but a boy in the fourth standard observed "Vemane, piney, purtunee, genastee, and a stursion" growing. This botanical collection was, however, improved on by a girl in the sixth standard, whose favourite flowers were "Policeman's hats" and "Break your mother's heart", two specimens which, alas, savour more of town and alley memories than country pleasures. Another child in the same standard had enjoyed "Minarets, Holy-oaks, and Chame-oisters".[177]

Some of the children made collections of pressed flowers or leaves. There was nothing compulsory about this nature study, but few children could have remained uninterested with such teaching. Henrietta remarked that the children loved the country, but "were most pleased by getting regular and plentiful meals".[178]

The children who wrote the best reports on their holiday were asked to a prize-giving in the Institute hall in the Garden Suburb. Henrietta expected the mistresses at the Henrietta Barnett School to give up a Saturday to organise the event. The girl-guides provided an entertainment, the children were given tea, and then were taken in groups to see volunteers' gardens, where they were given bunches of flowers to take home to the poor districts of London where they lived. Palmer was required to spend his time off driving Henrietta round – "and that will be his contribution," she said. Miss Harris, who was one of the schoolmistresses dragooned by Henrietta, found her a "forceful person … almost ruthless". (Miss Harris later became headmistress of the Henrietta Barnett Junior School.)[179] In a letter from her joint honorary secretary of the Countryside Committee, we see Henrietta's light and playful approach to children: "In her speeches to the children on prize days she was a joy as she became one of them. On one occasion she wore an English gown a Chinese cloak and a Japanese bonnet and explained to the children that all 3 went well together and so she hoped that the leading Englishmen would be able to bring Japan and China together."[180]

Whitechapel Art Gallery

The Barnetts' great success in attracting crowds of Whitechapel people to their picture exhibitions in St Jude's schoolrooms made them look for a permanent gallery. In 1894 Samuel had the idea of getting the local council to build a town hall with an art gallery as part of it, to be funded under the Public Libraries and Museums Act. But despite "an enormous amount of effort" they did not succeed. In any case, Henrietta disagreed with this idea: "I want it to be only for art … we don't want party politics to be mixed up with it."[181]

During 1896 they were trying to buy the Coin Street Baptist Chapel to convert into a gallery and were making numerous appeals for funds. The Rothschild Bank gave a preliminary donation of £25, Schroeders £200, Hambros £200, Wernher Beit & Co £250 and Messel £50. A group of schoolgirls made a gift and three guineas came from a friend. Truman Hanbury Buxton, the brewers in Brick Lane, gave £100, and Ind Coope, the Romford brewery, gave £50 – conscience money![182]

In April 1897 they were offered a piece of land next door to the Whitechapel Library, an ideal position, but it cost £6,000, so now they had the task of raising it.[183] It was difficult to get money because funds were being raised for the Indian famine. In April 1897 Punch helped with a poem. On 22 May 1897 Samuel wrote an appeal letter to *The Times* and this brought in gifts.[184] An American donor gave £1,000. Mr E Garrett, an artist, sent £25, writing: "it is only by encouraging in them a love of the beautiful and giving them opportunities of seeing something of it that we shall get them to hate evil and all the hideous squalor & misery it brings in its chain." The £6,000 was soon collected for the purchase of the site and Passmore Edwards gave £5,000 for the building. The Parochial Charities Trustees granted £500 per year for upkeep. There were numerous trustees meetings and in 1898 they appointed the architect C Harrison Townsend, a close friend of the Barnetts and architect of Toynbee Hall.[185] Sir Edward Burne-Jones came to dine with the Barnetts and give advice.[186] On 12 March 1901 the Gallery was opened by Lord Rosebery. The Barnetts could not attend the opening because it was the day of the funeral of Dorothy Woods, their adopted child. It was widely reported by the press:

"The gallery was very well filled. The British workman, evidently fresh from work, with corduroy trousers and grimy boots, was conspicuous by his presence. Strange-looking specimens of manhood, with pugnacious features, and formidable looking mufflers, sauntered about, catalogue in hand, studying the pictures with an intentness that would not have discredited a rabid Ruskinite. Factory girls striking incongruous notes of colour in their headgear, perambulated in twos and threes; and if one might judge from their frequent bursts of merriment, they were enjoying themselves to the full."[187]

Samuel was chairman of the trustees from the beginning until his death. Henrietta was a co-opted trustee; however she rarely attended meetings, for Samuel would have discussed everything with her. Besides, when she became engaged with the Suburb, she usually had prior commitments there. She asked the director, Aitken, to give her earlier notice of meetings but evidently he could not do so. Most important was her membership of the Exhibitions Committee, which decided what exhibitions should be held and their content. Unfortunately the minutes of this committee are lost. As the committee consisted of Henrietta and only three other trustees – W M Blyth, the Hon H L W Lawson and Edgar Speyer, and the director, she had a great deal of influence. Some of the early exhibitions were on matters of great interest to her: she must have played a major part in initiating and organizing the "Country in Town Exhibition" 1906, the "House and Home Exhibition" 1911, and the "Housing and Town Planning Exhibition" 1919. To accompany the "Country in Town Exhibition", there was a conference in July on "Suburb Extension", held at the gallery, chaired by Sir John Gorst, who spoke of the evils of unplanned house-building, praised the German example of planning model suburbs and said that the present government with its plans for welfare must see that people were well housed. Henrietta described her new garden suburb and it is clear that she both initiated and organized this exhibition.[188] The exhibition policy was laid down from the beginning of the gallery:

1. Exhibitions of modern Paintings to be held at Easter and in the autumn after the Royal Academy exhibition was closed.
2. Exhibitions of objects from national collections showing trades or a period of history or a foreign country.
3. Exhibitions of work by local children and technical students.
4. Exhibitions on works of art, to give East Londoners a better appreciation of the world's art treasures.[189]

Samuel and Henrietta visited artists and persuaded them to lend paintings, just as they had when exhibitions were held in the schoolrooms. In 1905 Samuel wrote to his brother:

"We have also got on the stocks the next Exhibition, and had an interesting meeting at Holman Hunt's. It was delightful to hear him gathering up his past memories how the Pre-Raphaelite movement began, and to see the reverence of men like Lord Carlisle, Hughes, and others. The Hunts' room is glorious with his work. We shall have a grand and remarkable show."[190]

After Samuel's death, the trustees decided to place a fresco in the entrance hall in his memory. Naturally Henrietta played a large part in deciding the artist and the painting. She was very pleased with the artist chosen and wrote to Ross on 26 January 1914:

"I saw Mr Garrett and found him _most_ wishful to do everything that was wanted. I showed him the "Watts" and the "Herkomer" portraits of the Canon and it made him feel that any commemoration of the Canon must be one that would embody more seriousness and _Dignity_ than his sketch does ... I advised him to spend _hours_ in the Whitechapel Street. Those fancy figures of navies and costermongers would raise hilarity with those who know the real thing."

In 1916 she wrote to Mr Blyth about the Memorial. She had been:

"… in bed for a fortnight first with excruciating lumbago and next at the Doctor's orders for a rest cure … Could the one sketch Mr Garrett made be utilized, and that lady who is such a wonderful fresco painter be asked to do another for the opposite side, carrying out Mr Garrett's idea of the Canon introducing the people in the street to the glories and delights of the Exhibition? I thought the idea splendid and so true, but of course he was not successful with the figure of the Canon. I have thought since that it would be quite possible to have him depicted in the long Italian cloak, the lines of which Mr Aitken specially appreciated. I have the cloak thinking that it might be wanted for some such purpose."[191]

Also in memory of Samuel the Trustees decided to hold an exhibition on "Twentieth Century Art – A Review of Modern Movements". Henrietta saw the paintings chosen and was not at all pleased with some of the modern work:

"May I plead … that you do not get too many examples of the extreme thought of this century, for we must never forget that the Whitechapel gallery is intended for the Whitechapel people, who have to be delicately led and will not understand the Post-impressionists or the Futurists' methods of seeing and representing things. I am so pleased that all are working happily together in the beautiful memorial to my husband."[192]

In the opinion of the author, Henrietta was right. As the gallery continued with the policy of displaying contemporary art, it was pursuing the policy laid down by the Barnetts, but the gallery became distanced from the people of Whitechapel. Today, apart from schools, the visitors all seem to be middle class. Mixed exhibitions, with modern art shown alongside portraits and photographs of celebrities and local people and pretty landscapes, might bring in the Whitechapel people as well as the connoisseurs.

During the war it became very difficult to arrange exhibitions. In 1915 Henrietta suggested that the gallery should have a "Month of Music" and wrote enthusiastically to Rosabel Watson who was the Director of Music at the Institute and was known nationally as conductor of choirs at Central Hall:

"I have had such a good idea – at least I hope you will think so. There has been considerable difficulty in arranging for a Whitechapel Exhibition, as owing to the Zeppelin raid, the rates for insurance are so enormous, and lenders put up the value of their possessions, and in some cases refuse to lend them at all.

My 'good idea' is therefore, that we should have a month of music, and that you should arrange it all …

I think it would be nice to have –

A. Evening Concerts on Tuesday, Thursday and Saturday free, in the big hall of the Whitechapel Exhibition.
B. The Thursday one might be a musical lecture with illustrations. Entrance paid for.
C. A Sunday concert at 3.0.
D. On Monday, Wednesday and Friday, competition singing by local schools say at 5.30 to 7.0 to which Mothers can be invited.
E. Towards the end a concert be given by the schools who have won the test competitions.
F. A concert or two at 3.0 to be given to the inmates of the Workhouse and other local homes, who could travel to the Exhibition.

Round the room though not in any way to interfere with the seating accommodation, I propose to have musical instruments and pictures of them. Such as violins or wind instruments, with some idea of the history and development of their shapes, uses and powers. What do you think of this?"[193]

At first she thought this could be arranged for a cost of only £20![194] Rosabel soon made Henrietta realize that music could not be made so cheaply:

"Dear Mrs Barnett
I am afraid that if the month of music is to be on the same high standard as the picture Exhibitions, £20 would not by any means be an adequate sum. I have thought it out in this way –
The Whitechapel people have plenty of good Chamber Concerts at Toynbee Hall, People's Palace, South Place, and at other places given by the People's Concert Soc. But these do not attract the general public. Also they have quite a fair amount of good Choral singing with the local choirs, but as far as I can find out they very seldom have the chance of hearing a really good orchestral Concert, so I think on Tuesday & Sat evenings, and Sunday afternoons they should have Orchestral Concerts on the lines of the Promenade Concerts and Sunday afternoon Concerts at Queen's Hall, which would be both attractive and educational. Then on Thursday we might as you suggest, have a good popular lecture with illustrations.
Now for the orchestral Concerts I could not manage on less than £10 for each Concert, for an Orchestra of 32 performers, an instrumental soloist, a singer, and myself to conduct, which you will see works out at about 6/- a head but I should offer three Concerts a week to make it sound more. Then the Lecture might be managed for £5. This makes £35 weekly. Any extra Concerts in afternoons could be managed partly by voluntary help or at a cost of, say, £2 each. I would of course organize all the Concerts, but I hope I wouldn't have to look after the running of the "Festival of Music" shall we call it? as I really haven't time to do a great deal of letter writing."[195]

It seems that Rosabel was giving herself only the same salary as the other performers. Henrietta must have appreciated this, especially as she said : "I am, as my own staff know, strongly in favour of paying well."[196] Henrietta asked for £200 and managed to get her scheme accepted by the trustees, though with difficulty for many of them wanted to give the money to the War Loan. They made her cut back the number of concerts.[197] After a great deal of effort the Month of Music began and was no doubt popular at that bleak time.

Henrietta undertook the administrative work for the festival and arranged for the exhibition of musical instruments and instrument making. Ross, one of the directors and a real friend to Henrietta, was worried that the Month of Music would give her too much work. But she threw herself into it and with Rosabel involved local schools to listen, perform and take part in choral competitions. Rosabel contacted the local elementary schools, St Paul's School and North London Collegiate School. Henrietta expected too much of herself and of other people, for at the end of the month it was felt there had been too much music.[198] Undaunted, on 20 December 1918 she proposed to have lectures on communal singing for the public, "with a view to training large masses of people to sing together". She succeeded: there were communal singing lectures in 1920.

From 1918 Henrietta attended trustees' meetings regularly. In 1919 Lord Burnham, her friend and helper with the Institute, became chairman. There was an Exhibition of Housing and Town Planning with the cooperation of the Garden City Association. Henrietta probably played an important part in organizing it and opened the exhibition in 1920.[199] In her speech she said: "in a communication she had received from the Queen her Majesty had declared that she was deeply interested in the smallest detail of the housing question, which just now occupied her mind continually."[200]

In 1919 Henrietta asked Ross to provide one concert a week for children. She suggested inviting people through mothers' meetings, the COS, the London Hospital and its aftercare committee and parents of schoolchildren who came to music evenings. From this list we realise what an immense effort she would make to secure her large audiences.[201]

Of course the gallery was always short of money and from the start the roles of director and secretary had been united. Henrietta had been a friend of both directors, Aitken and Ross. In 1921 an art director was appointed. Henrietta lost no time in advising Mr Duddington that he could go to exhibitions free of charge in every gallery in London. This probably unwanted advice is the last communication we have found between her and Duddington. It is unlikely that she had much further influence on the exhibitions at the gallery, though unfortunately the minutes of trustee meetings from 1919 to 1947 are lost, perhaps in the bombing. However we know that she continued to attend trustee meetings, for Marion Paterson saw that she took a close interest in the gallery: "As Trustee of the Whitechapel Art gallery she seldom missed attending the opening day of its Exhibitions and always took some active part in the ceremony …".[202]

The Barnetts' holidays

In summertime they took short holidays, driving in a trap drawn by their pony, Tom. They visited their London friends in their country houses. In 1902 they were visiting in Buckinghamshire:

> "We left the Markbys on Thursday and drove twenty-two miles to Aylesbury … We found the usual beery, tobaccoey, noisy inn, where we dined well and slept badly. On Friday we visited Hazell, who has established a printing works in the country and occupies a farm himself. The wind was so piercing, I had decided to make my wife return by train, but Hazell pressed us to stay with him, so after a visit to Lady de Rothschild we returned to him. Lady de Rothschild is a very beautiful old lady, living simply in her immense mansion. Lady Battersea was there, and we had some talk – gossip – about the Education Bill. Hazell's we found idyllic, a lovely house and a farm for shorthorns and poultry. We talked much about all things, especially for his plans and doings for his 1,200 workpeople. He has £30,000 of their savings in the business. Yesterday we drove thirty-five miles here, the horse doing admirably, and we enjoyed ourselves although the sun was unkind."[203]

The next summer they visited Arundel Castle, then Chichester, Petersfield, Winchester, Salisbury, Bradford-on-Avon and ended at Bath. Tom "really did very well, so quiet as not to move at any motor, and if necessary able to go nine miles an hour. We did twenty, twenty-seven, and twenty miles in three days, but then all needed a day's rest. We have good memories of the views, the lanes, and the flowers."[204]

In 1905 they visited Evesham where they met Sir William Lever, the rich entrepreneur who created Port Sunlight. They went on to holiday in a hotel at Llandudno and a friend, Dick Batson, drove them in his car through the mountains by Betws-y-Coed and Capel Curig. Samuel wrote: "Dick drives splendidly and is so thoughtful even of chickens, that one has not the entire sense of aggressiveness which belongs to motoring."[205] Henrietta was much more enthusiastic about motoring. In December 1905 they went to the Motor Show at Olympia: "My wife rejoiced in four cylinders, live axles, ignition, etc. Prices are coming down, a landaulette with four cylinders can be got for £400."[206] She embraced modern technology: in 1921 she said she wanted to fly in a plane. She wanted a car, and a member of the council of Toynbee and close friend, Henry Ward, used to bring his car to Bristol and take them to Devon, Wales and Worcestershire, places they could not reach with their pony and trap. Henrietta describes the early days of motoring:

> "Those were the days when motorists were only just released from the restrictions of the law which compelled a 'man with a red flag to precede a mechanically propelled vehicle'; the days when horses went wild with fright, and people in their interest in the new carriage forgot to get rapidly out of the way; the days when the creature often objected to go, and could only be induced to proceed after a long confabulation with a man who lay in the road on his back under its stomach; the days when to ride a motor was a new experience and a great treat."[207]

The speed limit was only 12 miles per hour and Samuel did not approve of breaking the law. However Samuel was not always with them and Henrietta loved speed: "A 28-h.p. Mercedes does not like twelve miles. She does not feel healthy under twenty, and only really enjoys herself at thirty. But during all the years we motored we never hurt a thing – though fowls are strangely bent on suicide."[208] Henry Ward, who may have had several cars, frequently lent both car and chauffeur to Henrietta, so henceforth she was able to use them most of the time. She was such a good horse-rider and enjoyed holding Tom's reins as they bowled along in a chaise, but she always wanted to carry out her impulses immediately and now she could speed round her friends and supporters, for, as Browning said in "The Last Ride Together": "Who knows but the world may end tonight?"

Chapter 20

Westminster

In Whitechapel the Barnetts led a full and varied life, engaging in national events as well as with the poor people around them. Writing to his brother in January 1905 Samuel described Henrietta's activities:

> "My wife has had a very busy week, interviewing people re the Garden Suburb, thinking, planning, etc., and so today she is tired and doing nothing. We have also got on the stocks the next Exhibition, and had an interesting meeting at Holman Hunt's …
> On Thursday Y---- [Henrietta] lectured on Children's Courts, and again did well, so you see what a public wife I have! We have not seen anyone very interesting, but we went to Campbell-Bannerman's on Monday, shook hands with some fifty people and exchanged words."[209]

Campbell-Bannerman was the leader of the Liberal Party and was soon to become Prime Minister. Samuel evidently did not rate this semi-public function and handshaking very highly, yet it shows that the Barnetts had risen to the top of the Liberal Establishment.

In December 1905 the Liberals won the election and Sir Henry Campbell-Bannerman became Prime Minister. In the spring of 1906 he wrote to Samuel offering him a deanery. But the Barnetts did not want to leave London, for Henrietta was involved in the Garden Suburb and they both wanted to stay within reach of Toynbee Hall, so they refused the offer. The Prime Minister asked Samuel what office he would like and he asked for a place at Westminster Abbey "from which he could speak of his religious faith and turn men's thoughts to the condition of East London".[210] In August 1906 he was made a Canon of Westminster Abbey and soon began his work. They were given a house in the Abbey precincts and moved to 3 Little Cloisters in January 1907. The Webbs came to their first lunch party.[211]

Samuel was now 62 and Henrietta 55; they thought a younger man was needed at Toynbee Hall, and T Edward Harvey was able to take on the job of warden. Their friends and admirers and their supporters at Toynbee Hall commissioned Sir Hubert von Herkomer to paint their portrait to commemorate their work. Herkomer lived in Bushey, North London, in a house "built of rocks and lined with gold," said Henrietta and wrote admiringly: "He is a wonderful creature, brimming with life. We talked hard while he studied us, and on 28th, he begins the picture. He interests us, but will he last over six or eight sittings? His house cost £100,000."[212] She may have doubted his persistence because he had so many other interests including teaching and film-making, and he was an eccentric, but the picture was completed during 1908, despite her misgivings. In November 1908 the Prime Minister, Asquith, unveiled the double portrait before them in Toynbee Hall, where it can be seen today.

When they moved into 3 Little Cloisters they found the house cramped, dark and in need of decoration: "the cloistered house was hopelessly insufficient for our somewhat complicated household,

the necessity of accommodation for a secretarial staff and our habits of hospitality". Their household included Aunt Fanny and Nurse and very often visitors staying as well. Henrietta improved the house by pulling down walls, putting in windows and decorating it. Samuel insisted on placing her name with his on the front-door plate, an act which produced "some amusing ecclesiastical remonstrance". The Barnetts' arrival must have created a stir in the stuffy atmosphere. They even had a telephone![213] Henrietta continued to help her husband prepare his sermons, as she had in the past, and these sermons "often annoyed his brother-clergy, who girded at him for his "socialism," his defence of strikes, and his claims for equality for women". Writing to his brother, Samuel reported: "I have just had a talk with the Dean. The University of London is coming to the Abbey on the 8th [May 1907]. The sweet girl graduates want to wear their academicals. This is pain and grief to the Dean – girls in Church with college caps! I have got some shots into his prejudices, and hope they may die before the day is out, or we shall have the women raging about us. Both sides seem to me a bit foolish, but right is with the women."[214] Samuel wanted to widen the congregation by bringing in parties of trade unionists, teachers, co-operators and settlement workers to special services, but the Abbey ecclesiastics were obstructive and the Chapter rejected their ideas. They also opposed the Barnetts' suggestions for a shop at the west door and guides taking organised tours of the Abbey to help people understand its history – reforms which came about much later.

Samuel's opinions were fundamentally upsetting to Abbey clergy. His Socialism was worrying, but there were many respected Socialists among the upper classes. He appreciated the accepted order of services and was devout in communion, although he was carried away by quite unusual religious ideas: he was unpredictable and so very intense. In 1909 he read a book called *Fraternity* which greatly impressed him: "It suggests, I think, that human souls form a sea whose sound ever and anon breaks on men's minds. But each soul is wrapped in a garment woven by individual or social selfishness, so they cry to one another and cannot touch one another."[215] Then he astonished a large audience of young men by speaking of the "idolatry of Christ": "I am sure it is God who has to be preached. God – to give us something which Jews, Moslems, and Puritans had, and which we have lost. We need a crusader to make God known so that every spot of ground shall be holy, and duty the necessity of being."[216] He had been pro-Boer and now he had unusual views about treatment of black people. To friends in Australia he wrote: "I have been learning something of Australia and its fear of the Oriental. My policy would be to admit all who would settle, taking pains to make them Australians, and so form a body of native patriots who would develop the country on approved principles."[217] He often wrote to his nephew who had emigrated to New Zealand. In April 1913 he wrote: "New Zealand is happy in not being able to despise the Maoris, and South Africa is in danger because the whites make the niggers do what they don't like doing."[218]

The unwelcoming, conservative attitude of the Abbey authorities made Henrietta remember Whitechapel with affection: "It is a privilege to live in such a place [as] The Cloisters Westminster Abbey, but I love East London a hundred times better. Our deepest & happiest memories are where we worked & suffered, really loved & struggled, and no place can ever be so dear to me as Whitechapel."[219] They remembered their old friends and every Saturday classes or clubs from Toynbee came from the East End to be shown round the Abbey and entertained by Henrietta: "The Toynbee talk was very refreshing after the

Plate 67 (opposite) Henrietta and Samuel in the Rolls-Royce lent to them by Henry Ward, who is sitting on the running board. Henrietta is in the car, wearing a velvet hat with a large feather.

trivial gossip and consideration of details which seem inseparable from the ecclesiastical mind." They wanted to attract and welcome more visitors to the Abbey and Samuel wrote a penny guide-book, *A Walk through Westminster Abbey*, the first of the many brief guides published. They certainly created a stir in the staid life of the Abbey.

In March 1907, Mrs Moore, Henrietta's beloved Nurse, was found to have cancer. The nature of her illness was kept a secret from Nurse herself, as was usual at that time. They employed a nurse, but when Mrs Moore was in pain she wanted Henrietta, and she was in recurrent pain from August to early November, when she died. During her last weeks Henrietta spent much time with her and was often called to her at night.[220] She grieved for her as for a mother. But although she was motherly she was a servant – perhaps an ideal relationship for a woman? There is a brick archway in Lucas Crescent, Willifield Way, in the Suburb, which has "Moore" written over it and was dedicated to her by Henrietta. Much later, Henrietta wrote of her: "… my old nurse, who was my foster-mother and lived with me fifty six years, taught me to sew, to speak the truth, to fear nothing except sin and snakes, and to consider the poor."[221]

The move into Little Cloisters meant they were living near to some of their friends. Alfred Lyttleton, chairman of the Trust, became a close friend as well as a fellow-worker. He would walk across Dean's Yard from his house at 16 College Street to the Barnetts' house in the Cloister whenever his opinion or advice was needed. He would write her delightfully characteristic little notes: "I have a motor, shut or open as you like; and shall be very proud to drive you up to Hampstead, if you will accept a lift, and tolerate my companionship. April 29. 1907." And another note, presumably when she was ill: "Don't trouble over business take the very nicest novel & hope for the cuckoo & the spring."[222]

Henrietta found their social duties increased: "When we came to live in the centre of London, country friends seemed to have frequent business in town, and our one small guest-room was rarely empty. The constant stream of callers took up much time, and we went out to many parties and receptions."[223] Some of these parties were very grand, such as a Liberal "At Home" where they met the political leaders, and a Foreign Office reception attended by the Prince of Wales. On 15 March 1907 Campbell-Bannerman came from Downing Street to lunch with the Barnetts at their house in the Cloisters; his handwritten note of acceptance is in the Hampstead Garden Suburb Archive.[224] They "were charmed anew by his simple and modest mind".[225] He did not eat meat, and did not drink any wine or spirits, which must have pleased the Barnetts. Living in central London, their dinner parties were more accessible for friends. In November 1907 they had the Beechings, Duncan and the Webbs to dinner: "There was no good general talk, but I think they enjoyed themselves," wrote Samuel.[226] They were relaxing with people they saw often, usually in a work context. Beeching was a fellow-canon, Duncan was to make his mark in South Africa, and Henrietta had many contacts with the Webbs. Dinner parties and weekend house-parties were the basis of social networking in Edwardian society.

They were both very inspired and moved by the Coronation in 1911. Samuel had a part in the ceremony, for he had the duty of carrying the orb and Henrietta was anxious as to whether Samuel's strength would bear the strain of the ceremony. Wearing a low dress with feathers and pearls, she stumbled up the wooden steps to her allotted seat over the muniment room to watch: "The beauty, the colour, the order, the gracious movements, the dignity of repose, the dresses, the jewels, the robes, the fantastic ceremonial, the trumpets, the shouts, all made a golden candle-stick fitted to bear the flame of praise & prayer."[227]

In January 1912 they moved house within the precinct to 4 Little Cloisters, a large and beautiful old house looking out on a garden: "We rejoice in our new house which belongs to the past and was built in the fifteenth century. There is a lovely staircase and the rooms are panelled, but best of all the look-out is over a large garden … The house is full of sun-shine …". Now they had plenty of room for their many friends and visitors. Before February 1912 only Trust subcommittees had been held at the Cloisters and the full Trust committee met in the company offices, but for the next year the full Trust committee met in their spacious house.

Chapter 21

Henrietta at Sixty

The year 1911 was an *annus mirabilis* for Henrietta, for all her efforts were coming to fruition and the Suburb was taking shape. Samuel wrote: "Whenever I go there I burst with pride that Y---- should have created such a place … The suburb is a perpetual joy. The houses increase, and the Central Square, with its fine building, its promenade in the wind and sky, and its flowers, refreshes our hearts."[228]

Henrietta made a special effort to raise the money for the tower and the spire of St Jude's, but then she caught whooping cough and was confined to bed. Her friends rallied round and gave her the tower and spire for her 60th birthday, a wonderful tribute. Has anyone else been given such a birthday present? A brass plaque in the church records this gift:

> THIS TOWER WITH ITS SPIRE
> WAS PRESENTED BY MANY
> FRIENDS OF HENRIETTA <<<
> WIFE OF SAMUEL A. BARNETT
> CANON OF WESTMINSTER
> ON HER 60TH BIRTHDAY
> MAY 4, 1911, TO SYMBOLISE THE
> ASPIRATION OF THE FOUNDERS
> OF THE HAMPSTEAD GARDEN
> SUBURB AND WAS DEDICATED
> BY ARTHUR FOLEY <<<<
> LORD BISHOP OF LONDON
> >>>>>> ON MAY 8 1913 <<<<<<
> SURSUM CORDA

A weathercock was placed on top of the spire and Henrietta used the image of the cock to stamp a red wax seal on her envelopes; it seems an appropriate symbol for her. Lutyens wrote to the Barnetts saying they should both place a message to posterity in the spire. Samuel wrote a message, which included the prediction that the future of Christianity depended on China. The message was engrossed on vellum by Marion Paterson and, with a print of their portrait by Herkomer, was put in a sealed copper cylinder and placed in the tower. Lutyens told Henrietta to write "I, even I, by my indomitable will have built what you see all round you", but she did not comply.

Much of the first part of the Suburb was now built. By September 1911 there were about 1,000 houses and about 5,000 residents. Social life was flourishing. The Institute programme for the autumn

II. 366]

NO. 4 LITTLE CLOISTERS AND THE ABBEY TOWERS, AS SEEN FROM THE GARDEN.
Mrs. Barnett is standing at the gate.

Plate 68
4 Little Cloisters,
where Henrietta and
Samuel lived until
his death in 1913,
was big enough to
be comfortable for
the large household:
Henrietta, Samuel,
Fanny, Nurse, and
various maids, with
Marion Paterson,
the secretaries and
numerous visitors.
They created a stir
in the Cloister.
Henrietta had her
name on the brass
plate by the door!

of 1911 shows that it provided highbrow entertainment and many classes and societies. The Institute had 24 classes, including English Literature, Elocution, Bookkeeping, Shorthand, French, German, Italian, Drawing, Dressmaking, Woodwork, Home Nursing and Hygiene, and Nature Study. There was also a University Extension course. On Wednesday evenings there were public debates, picture talks, conferences, and lectures on musical subjects in rotation. There were 25 debates and conferences, and 8 picture talks in 1910.[229] On Saturday evenings the hall was to be alternately let to local societies and used for music. Many societies met at the Institute, including the Natural History Society, the Shakespeare Society, and the Philosophical Society. For children there were classes in French and in History Taught by Drama. There was woodwork for boys, and St Ursula's Club for Girls offered morris dancing, Shakespeare and games. Also there were classes for the workmen building the Suburb, one of Henrietta's egalitarian ideas. Well, it was egalitarian for Henrietta and her contemporaries, who would not have thought it proper to have the workmen mix with the artisans and clerks. Indeed they might have been in their dirty work clothes and not wished to mix.

In December Henrietta reported that there were 750 fees paid at the Institute.[230] Annual fees were 5/- per subject and 2/6 for each further subject. However there was a total of only 304 students, as some students attended several classes; the most popular classes were French and Dressmaking.[231] In the 1910–11 session at the Institute there were 15 public debates, including debates on Women's Suffrage, Home Rule, Payment of MPs and The Modern Sunday, and there were 16 conferences and 16 slide talks. Numerous local societies were formed and had their meetings at the Institute or at the Club House. Two societies were run by Henrietta: the Child Study Society, and the Novel Literary Club which discussed modern novels, a forerunner of our book groups.[232] These two societies attracted many people. The Child Study Society was formed in October 1910, when a headmaster from the Home School, Highgate, spoke on Children from the Teachers' Viewpoint. In 1913 there was a lecture on The Influence of Alcohol on Mothers – before and after childbirth. There was a lecture on The Nursing of Sick and Ailing Children and in 1915 on War Orphans. Dudley Heath, Head of the Art School, spoke on Self Expression and the Development of Character. Other subjects were Sex Education, Punishment and its Effects, Cheap Food for Children, The Effect of War Games on Children and Youthful Prisoners. Henrietta undertook the work of writing letters of invitation to lecturers. One lecturer asked about the audience and was told: "the audience numbers between 30 and 40, and are women of all Classes of Society but of exceptional intelligence. They as a rule have one servant or perhaps occasional help as all the inhabitants of the Garden Suburb prefer to live in the simplest way". Henrietta inspired the members of her society to take an active interest in poor children through visiting juvenile courts, children's hospitals and workhouse schools. To help the Children's Country Holidays Fund they gave small groups of East End children teas in their Suburb homes and took them on nature walks so they would appreciate the country better when they were taken on holiday.[233]

Although her societies were very successful, Henrietta was disappointed at the poor attendance at the University extra-mural classes, which were more demanding. She kept the fees uneconomically low, and the Co-partnership subsidised their tenants, but still they did not attend as she hoped. In 1915 there were over 1,000 entries for classes, but many people were going to two or three classes so only 268 students were registered.[234] It is not surprising that the Suburb "pioneers," after struggling home on the unmade roads, many to young families, preferred to rest, or go to the Club House for lighter entertainment. Also housed in the Institute building was a kindergarten for 100 children, boys and girls.

In addition there were 60 students at the arts and crafts classes controlled by Middlesex County Council. These were extremely popular from the start and were housed in the huts. Most Suburb people had furnished their houses in the Arts and Crafts style, as advertised in the *Suburb Record*. Some could afford William Morris fabrics and Heal's furniture and most could find cheaper imitations. At least one of the artisans could make his own. The pottery class at the Institute must have produced many teapots (possibly bad-pourers), and there were many houses with kilns, embroidery frames, upholstery needles, spindles and weaving looms. There was a busy social life, and they were starting a sketching club and tennis and croquet clubs.[235] Henrietta as Honorary Manager was responsible for creating the Institute programme and for staff appointments and had complete control until 1915 when a committee was formed. The programme was very much the same as the programme of classes and societies organised at Toynbee Hall, providing high culture for all. Many of the early residents of the Suburb had left school at 14 but wanted to better themselves and, despite the pressures of young families, new houses, gardens and allotments, they responded eagerly to educational opportunities.

One might suppose that Henrietta had created most of the social life of the Suburb by creating the Institute, but the Club House at the heart of the artisans' quarter provided a whole range of more easily enjoyable activities. Here Henry Vivian was the initiator and chief organiser and it was more informal and democratic, run by a committee of worthy men, mainly from the artisans' area. It is not surprising that the Club House was more popular.

Henrietta could be immensely proud of the new community she had created. Royal recognition of success was given by the visit of Queen Mary and George V in 1911. At the Queen's insistence the King found time for an informal visit and they came by car on the afternoon of Saturday, 18 March 1911. The landscape was blurred by a misty rain so part of the time the royal party had to open umbrellas, but they "spent nearly two hours visiting the institutions of the colony, its artistic homes,

Plate 69
The Reverend Alan
Walker, Vicar of St
Jude's. Henrietta's
friends donated the
money to build the
tower and spire as
a 60th birthday
present for her.

and the convenient and picturesque Harbour of Rest provided for the old people."[236] They were met by Henrietta, Henry Vivian, Frederick Litchfield and Lord Howick and visited the Estate Office to see the plans. Then they were taken to St Jude's, the Club House, Waterlow Court and the Orchard and some of the smaller houses. Queen Mary spent some time talking to the working ladies at Waterlow Court. King George "expressed his warm approval of the equipment of the club house which contains spacious billiard-rooms, reading and card rooms, and has a well laid out tennis court attached."[237] The visit was a genuine surprise, so when "their Majesties walked into the Club premises several of the members, without taking the slightest notice, went on playing billiards, chatting or reading.[238]

At the Orchard the King talked to Mr Hosgood, a veteran of the Crimean War, congratulated him on his medals, shook hands and asked him what regiment he was in; this was reported in the *Sunday Times*. In Henrietta's "The Story of the Growth of Hampstead Garden Suburb 1907–1928", she gives an account of their meeting with Mrs Channell:

> "… among my fragrant memories is the talk Her Majesty had with old Mrs Channell, who having been a fur sewer had made a cloak for the Duchess of Teck. When the King offered his hand to the old lady she looked amazed and then said enquiringly:
> 'And you are King George?'
> 'So they usually call me' replied the King and then asked her to explain her room, its bed recess, scullery, cupboards, bath and little garden.
> 'Mrs Barnett she give me the apple tree and "the old man's love,"' she said, humorously and pathetically adding:
> ''Tis all the old man's love I got now.'"[239]

The Queen noticed a defect, the top larder shelf was too high to reach.[240] Mrs Channell showed how she stood on a box and went on to tell the Queen how she had worked for a West End furrier and had lined many fur coats for the Queen and the royal family. They were genuinely very interested in housing reform and at the time the King was taking a personal interest in the rebuilding of the Duchy of Cornwall estate at Kennington. George had become king only a year previously, in May 1910, and the coronation was to be on 22nd June 1911, so he would have been pleased if he had read the comment in the *Evening Times:* "The King and Queen's visit to Hampstead Garden Suburb, and the interest they displayed in the comfort of the inhabitants, is only another instance of their Majesties' thought for their humble subjects. King George has inherited the shrewd common sense of his great father, and not a little of the humanity of his mother – a happy combination of qualities."[241] The national press reported the visit to the Suburb in glowing terms both in the Sunday papers and on Monday. This Saturday afternoon talking to the contented people of the Suburb must have been relaxing compared with the stressful affairs of state, for England was in a state of crisis with the Irish Home Rule problem, the new challenges of the trade unions and the Labour Party, the House of Lords having its powers reduced and the violence of the suffragettes. Some people were predicting revolution.

Hampstead Garden Suburb benefited from many royal visits, partly because it was easily reached from central London, but also because Henrietta was developing a real friendship with Queen Mary, and other royals followed in her footsteps. Henrietta knew how to treat them with respect combined with a friendly openness. She knew how to stage a public event and summon the press to give national coverage. Miss Paterson's newspaper cuttings of the 1911 visit take up 32 pages of her scrapbook; they used a cutting service, but nevertheless the pasting was quite a job.

Princess Louise, Duchess of Argyll, attended the consecration of St Jude's on 7th May 1911 and afterwards unveiled a memorial tablet to King Edward VII. The Bishop of London took for his text "A city that is set on a hill cannot be hid." He said that the whole idea of the Garden Suburb was becoming known throughout the world. Many of the ornaments for the church had been given from abroad: the processional cross had been given by Canada. "They were taking part that day in a permanent thing, and those who had toiled so long in Bethnal Green or Whitechapel would rejoice in the idea of a Garden Suburb. If such a thing had existed long ago there would have been none of those horrible slums, which are such a disgrace to London."[242] The service was followed by a lunch at which Henrietta proposed the toast of "The architect and builders" and said the church was beautiful and a source of joy, and "she was grateful for renewed health, and for the privilege of being present on this the greatest day of her life – except her wedding day."[243]

Two days later the Duke and Duchess of Connaught spent two hours in the Suburb. The Duke had been appointed Governor-General of Canada and wanted to be well informed about planning and building new towns. These royal visits were quite informal and often led to encounters which made amusing snippets for the press. The *Daily Express* reported that the Duke met a house-painter who told him that Buckingham Palace could do with a paint. "I agree with you," laughingly replied the Duke.[244] Then he was greeted by a little boy swinging on the gate in front of his house who proved to be Vivian Litchfield Parker, the first baby born in the Suburb. "Hullo," said Vivian. "Hullo," said the Duke, and they gravely shook hands. Then Vivian, acting as a guide, showed the royal visitors

Plate 70 (opposite) King George V and Queen Mary visit the Suburb, 1911. Henry Vivian is accompanying them as they leave The Orchard, the Queen is behind him.

over the house, and 'after all the sights had been seen conducted them to the door with all the solemnity of an Abbey guide.'[245] From the Suburb they went on to Brentham.

In June 1911, Princess Marie Louise came to open a fair in Central Square in aid of the St Jude's Fund.[246] There was fun for all with a pageant, archery, games, maypole dances, fortune-telling, pierrots, Unwin's Planning Exhibition and a demonstration of an electric telegraph apparatus. The Reverend Basil Bourchier presided, with the Princess and Henrietta sitting either side of him, and in his speech he revealed that the Queen had sent goods to be sold at the fair worth no less than £50. Henrietta was given a picture of St Jude's and in a long speech she said: "I feel as if my later life is one high, deep, prolonged giving of thanks – continual thanks to fellow women, fellow men, fellow workers, fellow idealists, and thanks to God, the Author of all."[247] In August 1911 Henry Vivian added to the jollity by organizing a national Co-operative Festival in the Suburb. Choirs came from many parts of the country and there was a flower-show from the gardens of Co-partnership estates. He organized a similar festival in July 1913. The *Daily Sketch* gave it a big headline: "THE IDEAL PLACE TO BE BORN IN; The Hampstead Garden Suburb was Merrie England on Saturday … The great event of the day was the judging of the children for health and fitness". The boys and girls competing were all dressed in white and looking very jolly. There were bands, a choral contest and the pageant, *Merrie England*. The festival was opened by the Hon. Neil Primrose MP, and Vivian gave a speech. It was reported nationally, even in the *Glasgow Herald*.

Among the early residents of the Suburb there was a preponderance of young married couples, as is usual on any new housing estate, and soon there were a great many children. In 1908 Henrietta met Sir Robert Morant, Permanent Secretary of the Board of Education, and his officials, to discuss her scheme for a secondary school for girls to occupy a building on a site of six acres at the top of Meadway, as the early maps show.[248] She hoped the Dame Alice Owen's School would occupy the site, but in the end that school went further north. She could not find the funds for a new building so she decided that the school must be in the Institute until another site could be afforded.[249] In January 1912 she held a conference at 4 Little Cloisters with representatives of the HGS Trust and of the North London Collegiate School which led to the founding of the High School, later called the Henrietta Barnett School. Some of the pupils at the School were girls from elementary schools who had won scholarships; two were funded by Henrietta, one in memory of her old nurse, Mary Moore. But most of the girls' parents were paying fees. Henrietta was not worried by the division of children between working-class and middle-class schools, nor were her contemporaries. The school motto was "No endeavour is in vain," and it became a very successful school. She chose a bright red tunic for the uniform, which seems to express her own vitality and the brilliance she hoped for the girls. In the 1920s the colour was changed to the usual navy-blue. When Henrietta breezed in one day she saw one of the girls wearing her red uniform. "Ah" she said, "The last of my little red geraniums." The girl, Ailsa Hoblyn, still remembered her acute embarrassment eighty years later. On the annual Speech Day she would address the girls, and Ruth Cass recalled that she would make some slightly risqué remark which would make Miss Hutchings, the headmistress, blush, much to the delight of the older girls.[250] Miss Harris, who was a teacher, remembers that on Speech Day she would always say: "You have to remember that the Henrietta Barnett School has to be A1 Top Dog. Now what does it have to be?" And all the girls would shout: "A1 Top Dog." They were very conscious of her living just across the Square and it was known that she woke early and had a rest after lunch, so the girls were made to be quiet during their lunch break in the playground. At Christmas she gave the staff copies of the books she had written and one Christmas gave them all a copy of Watts' "Hope".

Royal visits had set the highest seal of approval; everyone in England who could read a newspaper knew about the Suburb. Its fame had spread to Germany, America and the Dominions. From Canada came news that a new suburb was to be built following the example of the Hampstead Garden Suburb: they had heard about it when Henry Vivian had visited Canada on a lecture tour.[251] The Suburb was proving so successful that in April 1912 the Co-partnership Tenants' Society bought another 300 acres to enlarge the estate.[252] In July 1912 a large party of MPs with some lords and bishops came to see the Suburb.[253] In August there was a two-week Summer School of Town Planning at the Institute, run by London University. Then a party of 150 town planners and architects who were touring the country came to visit the Suburb and were conducted round by Mr Greenhalgh, who spoke German, and by Mr Litchfield who took them for tea at the Club House. Henrietta spoke to them and "attributed some of the qualities that have helped her in developing the work of the Suburb to inherited German tendencies,"[254] presumably the hard work and thoroughness attributed to Germans at that time. This is a rare reference to her German family background.

In June 1910 there was a public meeting at the Institute in support of women's suffrage, with speeches by H W Nevinson, and Mrs Brailsford. Mrs A J Webbe took the chair and Mrs Kelsey took the names of those wishing to march under the Hampstead Garden Suburb banner in a procession for women's suffrage to be held in London. Henrietta did not participate in this and like most people would have been deeply shocked when in 1913 some militant suffragettes started small fires in the Institute and two private houses, and a really dangerous fire in the Free Church.

In 1913 the summer school was supported by Henrietta's distinguished friends – the Bishop of London, Earl Grey, John Burns, Lord Henry Bentinck, Sir John Gorst and Sir Henry Miers. Henrietta gave talks on the Suburb to audiences at central London societies such as the National Liberal Club.[255]

The gardens and allotments were being cultivated and there were prizes for the best gardens, and children were learning to garden. This was a very quiet place: no leaf-blowers or drills, few telephones and no alarms. There was the clip-clop of horse's hooves as the coalman and baker made their rounds, but few people could afford a horse to ride and there was no stable. If someone was seriously ill, the householder put straw on the street to muffle the sound of horse's hooves. There were very few cars, so the roads were free for adults to walk and children to play on. They played freely in the open spaces and the woods. They picked blackberries from the hedges and gathered bluebells in the woods. Picking bluebells was permitted then and they grew more plentifully. They paddled in Mutton Brook and built dams, and older boys roamed over the Heath. Parents were not afraid to let them explore. In those days there was not a paedophile down every street and an exhibitionist behind every tree. Even when my children were young in the 1960s, we allowed our six-year-old son and daughter to bike from 11 Erskine Hill to play with their friends in the little wood below the tennis courts in the Square. There was only the one exhibitionist who lived in the Lutyens housing on the Square, and when he made his appearance in the wood the children would point at him and run back home.

Henrietta had achieved all the publicity she had wanted for the Suburb and the Institute. She always emphasized the mix of classes in the Suburb, with flats from 3s/3d (17p) per week to houses up to a capital value of £3,500. Keeping the Suburb in the news was made more easy by the fact that for journalists it was within a twopenny tube journey of Fleet Street, so much easier to access than Letchworth. Samuel wrote to his sister-in-law: "It is very delightful to watch the common life growing – the admiration of Yetta – She has come into a Kingdom."[256] She could have become conceited and more autocratic with all this attention. But she soon found she was not an absolute monarch and there were some problems in the utopian scene. Her chief disappointment was that they could not achieve the very low rents she hoped to have for some houses. *The Record*, the Suburb paper founded by Henrietta, complained: "contrary to the understanding upon which this land was let at somewhat less than its market value, the poor class had not been catered for; the rents of the cottages

Plate 71
1911, an eventful
year in the Suburb.
Queen Mary leaving
Waterlow Court,
two photos of the
royal party, roller
skating rink behind
Willifield Way,
Henrietta laying
a foundation stone
of the Free Church,
interiors of St Jude's
and the Free Church.

in those areas which the Trust had originally leased for cottages at 5/6d (27½p) and 6/6d (32½p) a week being now 8/- and 9/-."[257] This was to be Henrietta's major worry for many years. But residents had other concerns.

Henrietta was very knowledgeable about the working-class of Whitechapel, their lifestyles and abilities, but she did not have so much experience of the skilled workers and clerks who filled the Suburb houses. The pioneers had courage, initiative and imagination to make the move to a muddy new estate with unmade roads and gardens. They were literate and could express their views, and they had experience of organising themselves, especially those in trade unions or involved in the nonconformist churches or running societies in the Club House. Since 1908 there had been an agitation for a local elementary school. Only the younger children were accommodated in the elementary infant school in the Institute. All the children over seven had to walk to school at Hendon or Finchley. In 1910 a deputation of residents met the Trust directors with the intention of forming a residents association, but the directors said it was too soon to form a residents association because the population was as yet only one-third of the expected population and it might "provoke the hostility" of new residents; also many people would be deterred from taking houses on the estate by the existence of such an association.[258] These were absurd excuses and the truth was that Henrietta thought that her Trust was in touch with residents and understood their needs, and she was not at all pleased to have her authority challenged. The Suburb was an estate, for it was private and the gate at the junction of Hampstead Way and Finchley Road was closed once a year to denote it.[259] Perhaps she almost regarded it as her estate; after all, she had bought it and built it. However the residents were stirring. Samuel Barnett and Henry Vivian tried to form a Trust residents association, but this was not what the residents wanted. In July 1911 the parents held a protest meeting on Willifield Green outside the Club House, and threatened to withdraw their children from school as a sort of strike.[260] People were also very critical of the state of the roads and paving and the Trust was blamed for not putting sufficient pressure on Hendon council. On 17th January 1911 there was a meeting of delegates from all the Suburb societies to elect a council with the remit of fostering the activities of the societies and residents and publishing a journal. Their council met in March and on 19th October a large meeting of residents accepted the Residents Association Constitution. They produced a Suburb magazine, *The Town Crier,* which reported the work of the association, gave a calendar of events at the Club House, reported on the churches and the political parties, and had a lively boys' and girls' page. This soon made Henrietta produce *The Record* to publicise the Institute and her own views. One question that provoked correspondence in *The Town Crier* was the renaming of the Hampstead Garden Suburb, for this was thought a cumbersome title. One person suggested "Finch-Hampstead" and another suggested "Wyldes". She had brought the Suburb to life and it was going to grow in ways she had not anticipated.

Chapter 22

The Death of Samuel

Samuel was not well. Indeed he had been suffering from heart attacks since 1909. In 1910 the doctor told Henrietta that he was unlikely to last longer than three years. Following the medical practice of the time, Samuel was not to be told of the likely outcome of his illness, so Henrietta had to keep it to herself and she found it very hard to bear when they had shared all their joys and sorrows in the past.[261] His condition grew worse, and by 1912 he was not allowed to go for walks or go to meetings or attend evening parties, but he tried to carry out his other duties and could sometimes preach. Samuel probably knew he could not last long. People with terminal illness often guessed the truth and so the ban on talking about it would become distressing and absurd. In February 1913 when Henrietta was ill with influenza, Samuel wrote his last letter to her:

> "MY OWN DEAR WIFE
> Wife of my young days, wife of my old days, always inspiring, always protecting, God bless you and give you a restful day. I am very well, and I will take care, judging care by your standard, i.e. not lifting a book or even lifting my eyelid too quickly.
> There is a delightful hush about today. It is a day for peaceful thinking, a day for turning over old photos and living again old times. We have had a good life. Bless you, is the chief word of your old lover. Oh, how I miss you, how I shall miss you when the lights come and there is no one to read to. I shall rest and you must be very restful about me …
> Oh, my dear one, as you lie still let the memories of what have been revive, comfort, and strengthen you. All we endure is just meant to teach us how to love, and the lesson is infinite. Get well soon.
> Yours and yours and yours, S.A.B."[262]

On 30th March Samuel managed to preach in the Abbey, and this proved to be his last sermon.[263]

In January 1913 they had sold St Jude's Cottage in Hampstead, for the large house had become a burden, and bought a small house in Hove, 12 Wish Road. In April they went to Hove, but presumably the house in Wish Road was not ready for they stayed at 69 King's Esplanade, Frank Debenham's flat. They intended to stay for a few days, but Samuel had another heart attack. Henrietta wrote to Jane Addams:

> "… we were only just settled into here on April 8th when he had an attack. Another on the 11th. A third on the 18th & a fourth on the 19th. From that two doctors said he could not recover, but he did, … Dear friend I don't think he will live. He is so very very ill, & there is

some mischief in a nerve centre of the brain wh. prevents him sleeping unless he has morphia, & be so fearfully restless when he is not under the drug that he wears himself out. He has been in bed more than 7 weeks, & gets worse. Today he is quite childish in his talk & pleads with his nurse that he is trying to keep still. On other days his brain is as clear & beautiful & nobly hopeful as ever. I will not dwell on my own pain. The sorrow is more than I can bear, but the incessant nursing keeps one ever busy, & whatever the end one loves to be with him now."[264]

He suffered intense pain; Henrietta wrote to her friend, Lillian Thompson : "I wanted you to know that my Canon is very <u>very</u> ill … I have never seen him suffer so – but he moves the nurses to tears with his goodness – Dear please pray for us."[265] After eight weeks of suffering Samuel died at King's Esplanade in Hove on 17th June 1913. He had left a letter asking for cremation and a simple and cheap funeral in St Jude's, Whitechapel, and Henrietta carried out his wishes. His ashes, enclosed in a copper casket, were carried by Toynbee Hall wardens and followed by a long procession of Toynbee men past and present. He was their Lost Leader: the funeral was attended by many others associated with Toynbee Hall, by invited Whitechapel folk and by many famous people. On the same day as the funeral there was a memorial service at Westminster Abbey, held by the Dean and Chapter. The casket was taken to St Jude's in the Garden Suburb, where a large congregation gathered for a service conducted by the Reverend Basil Bourchier. Later the ashes were interred in a grave at Hangleton Church on the Downs above Hove. Henrietta received so many letters of condolence that it was impossible to reply to them individually. Instead she sent a compilation of Browning poetry which seemed to describe the Samuel they were all mourning.[266] The first extract was:

> This world's no blot for us,
> Nor blank; it means intensely, and means good.

And the last:

> Let our God's praise
> Go bravely through the world at last!
> What care
> Through me or thee?

All the newspapers had obituaries and there was a move to make a public memorial such as a statue or by making contributions to one particular charity. Henrietta checked this by writing a letter to *The Times* saying Samuel would not have liked a statue or that people should give support to some existing charity. He would have preferred groups of friends to have new ideas, establish new scholarships, put mosaics on public buildings, take the young to galleries and concerts, provide lectures and oratorios in the churches in poor areas. The idea of having one memorial was abandoned, and instead eleven memorials were created by groups of friends. The Chapter of Westminster Abbey put up a tablet to Samuel, on which there was space to add Henrietta's name. Barnett House, Oxford was established to investigate social conditions, with Henrietta as a member of its council. A Barnett fellowship was created for Toynbee Hall. A tablet was placed in St Jude's, Whitechapel. At Whitechapel Art Gallery two long tiled panels were placed in the entrance hall. They commemorate the work of both Samuel and Henrietta: one panel related to the Children's Country Holiday Fund and the other to the picture exhibitions at St Jude's School. These charming panels have been removed by the Gallery in recent years. The warden of Wadham presented a copy of Watts' portrait of Samuel to hang in the college hall. Henrietta had wanted him to use the Herkomer portrait of them both. The warden was clearly embarrassed by this, for he wrote saying that Wadham had never had a portrait including the wife, and he suggested that they might use a copy of the part of the painting which portrayed Samuel! Fortunately the Watts portrait offered a compromise.[267]

In the Suburb, a clock was placed in the Institute tower in memory of Samuel. This was funded by collections taken at the annual thanksgiving service when the vicar of St Jude's and the minister of the Free Church exchanged pulpits, an expression of the spirit of unity in the Suburb and in memory of Samuel.[268] Lady Battersea gave a silver lamp to St Jude's in the Garden Suburb. "It was, as the *Westminster Gazette* pointed out, typical of his catholicity: for it came from a Roman Catholic Cathedral, was given by a Jewish lady to a Protestant Church, and was dedicated on All Saints' Day, November 1st, 1913". Of course Henrietta was consulted and in some cases played a part in the making of all these memorials. In 1915 she persuaded Sir Alfred Yarrow to give the money for a group of flats off Erskine Hill, to be called the Barnett Homestead.[269] The flats were for war-widows and their children, the rents to be used for scholarships for the Institute and for Barnett House, Oxford. She also hoped to raise the money for a secondary school for girls, and for boys up to ten, to be built on the east side of the Suburb in the Holne Chase area. Lutyens prepared a plan, but Henrietta could not raise sufficient money for the building.[270] To ensure that Samuel was not forgotten she placed an annual "In Memoriam" in The Times until 1935. But when Marion asked her if she wanted to place a notice in 1936, when she was dying, she refused: she must have been too ill to think of a suitable quotation to go with it.[271]

Henrietta was exhausted by nursing her husband through his final illness. The nurse and Marion Paterson helped, but Samuel wanted Henrietta when he was so ill and in pain. Her grief was extreme for their lives had been so close, much of their work was shared and when they were apart they wrote to each other frequently and exchanged all their experiences when they met. Samuel had drawn on Henrietta's originality and her boundless enthusiasm and energy, and she had found in him the security to help her through her times of over-activity and depression. "Never glad confident morning again!" (Browning) Her deep grief must have been shared by Marion Paterson who had worked for them for thirty years and perhaps Marion could comfort her, or at least share in her reflections on the past.

Three weeks after Samuel's death she wrote to Jane Addams of her feelings:

> "I might tell you I was broken hearted, but that is too common place a description of what I feel. I have known for nearly 4 years that he wld not be long with me, & I kept it absolutely to myself & away from him but it has made me treasure every word & act & know the inevitable – What now I feel chiefly is <u>torture of memory</u> of his long illness & all he suffered, & almost a terror in case it remains foremost & that the dear bright loving spirit shld be hidden by it. So I strive to re-vivify his spirit. I shld like to write his life. Do you think I am equal to it? Wld the American Settlements like me to do so? I think if I wrote his life myself it wld help me to bring him back as he was before the illness. He, the man, my lover, the humble Christ follower – The keen seer into things behind the surface & beyond the present time …
> We have so interwoven in our work that I feel <u>uncertain</u> of what I can do without him, but for the last 3–4 years I have had to decide much without telling him (if things were not pleasant I mean) so I have been weaned – but being so cheap a person comparatively to what he was that in any case the output will be poor in quality."[272]

Despite being deeply affected and uncertain, Henrietta was planning for the future and wrote in the same letter that she would like to come to America. Her way of coping with grief was to plunge herself into work. She was absent from Trust meetings in April and May, but from 30th June she was back at all the Trust meetings.

She had to leave Little Cloisters very quickly as it was a tied house. Her first thought was to move to Toynbee Hall where the management was causing her anxiety. She thought they needed a new warden and strongly recommended Canon Masterman. She wrote to Lord Milner, the chairman:

"The more I have seen of Toynbee & its mismanagement the more I have been amazed and saddened … I would go again & live in the Lodge, & put the house right & on an economical basis, & give that confidence to the habitués (societies, clubs, associates etc) & the <u>subscribers</u> which you pardon me saying of myself, but which I cannot but know my presence wd. create … I do not mean that I will return with an outrider & a flourish of trumpets. No! I am too sad to make that possible, even if it were desirable. I just propose … to furnish my old Lodge upper room & a cupboard to sleep in, & slip back to be an out-of-sight general servant – as the one person who can link up the old & new & bridge the gulf wh. now exists."[279]

Her offer was not accepted, which must have distressed her. Lord Milner must have found it difficult to write a refusal to Henrietta when she was so recently widowed, but anyone who knew her would doubt whether she could be "an out-of-sight general servant"!

She decided to live in her Garden Suburb. She rented a house, 12 North Square, and moved there on 8th September 1913. In a letter to Jane Addams she described it as

Plate 72
12 North Square, where Henrietta lived from 1913 to 1915. She found it a small house compared with 4 Little Cloisters where she had lived before.

"this little house on the top of the Hill".[274] It is a terraced house, much smaller than 4 Little Cloisters and the house in the Suburb which they had intended to build, but with six bedrooms it would not be regarded as small today. She lived there for two years, from October 1913 to 1915. This must have been a busy place with numerous callers, and Marion Paterson and another secretary helping with the work. From this time, Trust committee meetings were held in her house, though the Trust met in the London office.[275] The house next door, 13 North Square, was used for Institute classes during 1914 because there had been a fire in the Institute hut, damaging three classrooms.[276]

So she settled down to live in the Suburb, with frequent stays in Hove. The house in Hove was very close to the sea-front, very healthy, and Henrietta found it a good place to write, and to paint, for there were fewer distractions than in London. But she wanted other people to enjoy the sea air and she frequently lent the house to friends and probably to poor people in need of a holiday. While in Hove she visited a psychiatrist, Dr Helen Boyle. Dr Boyle was the first doctor to treat borderline cases of insanity who hitherto had been locked up with chronic cases. The Maudsley Hospital is famous in the history of mental illness, but Dr Boyle was providing holistic treatments for recoverable patients twenty years before the Maudsley. She kept a hospital for the poor, and two large nursing homes for the rich. Besides this she had a large general practice in Brighton and a consulting room in London to which the London doctors took their cases. She was also on the medical committees for this branch of work, both in relation to the Ministry of Health and the British Medical Association. Dr Boyle may have helped Henrietta to gain some insight into her bipolar problem, but what started as a professional relationship soon became a friendship. Henrietta must have admired Dr Boyle for her work and compassion, and Dr Boyle admired Henrietta for her vitality and ability to inspire. In her will, Henrietta bequeathed her beloved coral necklace to Dr Boyle. Marion wrote: "This coral necklace was one of the very few of her possessions she really cherished – A gift from her Father when a girl."[277]

Henrietta turned her attention to perpetuating the work of Samuel and writing his biography. Editing his books and negotiating with publishers must have entailed a great deal of work. From his death to the Armistice in 1918 she worked on tributes to Samuel's life and thought as she said in her *Canon Barnett, His Life, Work and Friends*:

> To spread my husband's thoughts has been my memorial for him, and since June 17th 1913, I have issued a little volume of his pithy paragraphs, *Worship and Work,* November 1913; a new volume of *Practicable Socialism,* 1915; *Vision and Service,* July 1917; and this book, November 1918. The war, the masses of material, my uncertain health, and his oft-expressed desire that I should not, when I was alone, give up public work, have to my regret combined to delay the issue of the present volumes.[278]

She was working hard to keep Samuel's ideas alive in England and abroad. She wrote an article about him for Jane Addams to publish in the *Survey,* but so uncertain did she feel about it that she gave it to four friends to read first: "I have been too sad to trust my own judgement & dear 'I'll ask Samuel' has been to me the refrain of 41 years, as 'I'll talk to my Missus' has been his – & so I feared to make a mistake in this the first thing I had written of him."[279] In this letter she addresses Jane Addams as "My dear friend and counsellor" and after Samuel's death Henrietta confided in her. Jane did help to get Samuel's writings distributed in America, but she almost never replied to Henrietta's heartfelt letters: "I feel almost hopeless in writing to you, for I never get a reply. And yet I do want you to know that I am bearing you in most affectionate admiration. I wonder why you do not write to me. Do you know I think you have only written once in the six years during which I have been alone. Your Secretary wrote once, but usually I get silence to the letters I launch to you in your great country."[280] Possibly Jane found Henrietta too intense. Asking Jane to dictate a letter to her secretary about distributing *Canon Barnett His Life, Work and Friends,* she added: "& dear will you add a tiny line in your own writing to tell me you still remember me & still care for me. I have had to keep a very un-fed faith since I last saw you from the door of the Cadbury's house at Northfield Manor." She signs the letter: "Dear, I love you – Henrietta O.Barnett"[281] At last a letter arrived: "I was so delighted to get your letter of Feb. 3rd. I nearly wept with joy! And especially at the 'devotedly yours' at the end."[282]

Jane Addams' life story is remarkably similar to that of Henrietta. Jane (1860–1935) was the eighth child born to a well-to-do family, with the father successful in trade. Her mother died when she was only two and a half. She was a sickly child, had a spinal curvature and suffered from chronic ill health throughout her life. In 1881 when Jane was 21, her father died. After this she suffered a depression and in 1883 she went on a trip to Europe as a cure. She was influenced by Ruskin and became keen to improve the lot of the poor. When she came to Europe she saw the poverty of London: she was particularly moved by seeing a crowd of people bid for stale vegetables after a market and one man instantly devour an uncooked dirty cabbage.[283]

In 1889 when she came back to Europe, she saw Toynbee Hall and was inspired by the Barnetts' work. She returned to Chicago to found Hull House on the same model, although the settlement workers included women as well as men. Like the Barnetts she considered that art was very important and held art exhibitions in Hull House, one being opened by Henrietta.[284] The importance of her work was widely recognised in America and numerous other settlements were opened. Jane also investigated the working conditions of women and children, sanitary conditions, midwifery, milk supplies and narcotics consumption in Chicago. She was more radical than Henrietta: she was an ardent feminist and worked for votes for women, she was a pacifist, and she was a member of the National Association for the Advancement of Colored People.

Jane had an influence on Henrietta in regard to the importance of international affairs and the promotion of peace and they shared a compassion for the poor, but Jane's pacifism had no influence on Henrietta and was quite alien to her personality. It is clear that Henrietta was passionately fond of Jane, and Jane's lack of response may have been due to lack of time but was more likely to be a rebuff. Henrietta did not recognize her own feelings as lesbian; in fact it is most unlikely that she knew the word. Modern women cannot imagine how ignorant women were before the 1960s.

Chapter 23

The War Years

"Mrs Barnett herself, magnificent in her determination, refused to allow the military authorities to occupy the Institute, assuring the High Command that cultural activities were as important a national work as any other. She herself tells the story of the day of the great daylight German raid when the sky was full of German aeroplanes, making for London. When one young woman hysterically announced that she was going to faint, the redoubtable Mrs Barnett replied, 'Then you must faint alone for I am going to see the battle!'" … "She also entertained homeless soldiers; gave refuge to Belgians; served on Tribunals; was ever at the service of neighbours in Air-raids."[285]

Marion Paterson gives us this account of Henrietta's reaction to the dangers and difficulties of War. Four bombs fell on the Suburb and two zeppelins were seen to come down in flames, an astonishing sight. Many people showed their fear, but not Henrietta. Many of the men who worked for the Suburb were called up, so in her role as honorary manager of the Trust she took on more administrative work. She managed to keep some gardeners to work on the public land by using it to grow vegetables. She designed a colourful display of cabbages, beetroot and so forth for the Square. She helped to find accommodation for the Belgian refugees. In 1914 a Belgian hospitality committee was formed and a large part of the Club House was made into a hostel. In all, 130 people were cared for up to 1916, when the Club House was turned into a military hospital.[286] Then Henrietta arranged for some of the Belgians to live at 13 North Square, the house next door to her own. She did not enjoy their proximity. She was president of the North London Society for Entertaining Overseas Soldiers from 1918 to 1919. Many of the soldiers were American; presumably she spent a lot of time and thought on this, although we do not have any account of her work.

But Henrietta's chief interest was in writing *Canon Barnett, His Life, Work and Friends,* her biography of Samuel. The "Dear Book", as she called it, was chiefly written at Hove to ensure freedom from interruption, and where Mrs Boyle, the secretary who helped in its compilation, was within easy reach and where the precious manuscript was safe from raids.[287] Another reason for staying in Hove was that "Raids do not agree with Fanny," as she wrote in a letter to Lord Milner.[288] Marion Paterson, who saw her writing the "Dear Book", noticed: "She consulted friends whose opinion she valued & not infrequently followed their suggestion. Mrs Sidney Webb told her to be more 'dynamic', & this caused her to be even more daring in her fearlessness."[289] She worked very hard, for in a letter from Hove to a friend in 1916 she wrote: "I am still here working 6–7–8 hours a day on the Book. I must finish it ere long. I do love doing it. Just now I am set fast with lumbago but usually I am <u>much</u>

Plate 73
The memorial tablet in Westminster Abbey, sculpted by Sir George Frampton. This was given by members of Parliament after Samuel's death; Henrietta arranged to have her own name added when she died.

stronger."[290] Since Samuel's death her health had been poor, but she was dealing with her grief by reflecting on her husband's life and working tremendously hard. She took few holidays: in the autumn of 1917 she stayed with the Cadburys and Lady Markby and went to Clifton for a niece's wedding, but this was her first holiday for a year.[291]

While she was writing the biography, her publisher was taken over by another firm and she did not like the new publisher "... who is old, crabbed, & indifferent to social reform of any sort, has been most difficult ... & I have had to pay many hundreds of pounds to get the book out at all! ... But now how is it to get to America? The publisher refuses terms wh. will allow a firm to produce it".[292] It was published in November 1918. She apologized for taking so long to issue it after Samuel's death. Really no apology was necessary for this is a biography of 415 pages. She must have been immensely pleased by the wonderful reception given to the book. She wrote to Jane Addams: "Over 60 reviews, many of them over a col. long, & though I have only the courage to read a few, Miss Paterson & others tell me they are warmly appreciative."[293]

It is still a very readable and interesting biography. Speaking at Henrietta's birthday party in 1928, celebrated in Toynbee Hall, G P Gooch, the historian, said: "That book will live long after the authoress has died, as an example of what a biography should be; & as a vivid picture of the life of the times." Indeed the book does paint a vivid picture of Whitechapel slums and its degraded people, and gives an amusing insight into the anachronisms of life in Westminster Abbey. We learn about networking at Edwardian dinners and house-parties, and realise the significance of the great Liberal government of 1906 to 1916. We see the Barnetts' laissez-faire liberalism in the 1870s change to the welfare liberalism of Hobhouse. We see the neglect and severity toward children in late Victorian England softening with the recognition of children's rights in the early 20th century. And we realize that the Barnetts were playing very significant parts in these great changes.

Henrietta hoped that the Dean and Chapter of Westminster Abbey would place a considerable memorial to Samuel in the Abbey. There were many deliberations and much delay. After much consideration of precedents they advised her not to ask them for a contribution as they had only made contributions to a memorial for one dean in the past fifty years![294] But they did sanction the placing of a memorial in the Abbey. Eventually members of both Houses of Parliament subscribed for a tablet. It was sculpted by George Frampton, and was the subject of much discussion between Henrietta and the sculptor. Her first idea was to include a group of children in the sculpture, but Henrietta thought Frampton's sketch showed a girl who could be seen as a prostitute and objected because Samuel had never saved prostitutes. Frampton was dismayed by this criticism, writing her many letters in his large artist's handwriting. Eventually they decided to cut out the children and simplify the design. The quotation on the tablet, "Fear not to sow because of the birds;" (Luke viii, 5–8) was from one of Samuel's favourite parables, and Henrietta had it written over her fireplace in 1 South Square. Its meaning is rather like the motto which Henrietta chose for her School: "No endeavour is in vain". The tablet was placed in the Abbey, on the north wall of the south aisle of the choir, and dedicated on 8th February 1916. As she had requested, a vacant space was left on the tablet for the addition of "and also Henrietta Octavia, his wife".[295]

In 1915 Henrietta moved from her rented house in North Square to her newly-built house, 1 South Square. From the back windows she could see the view she loved, over the houses and young trees to Harrow-on-the-Hill. Neighbours noticed with amusement that

Plate 74
1 South Square, where Henrietta lived from 1915 until her death in 1936. The author with her daughter Julie and grand-daughter Miranda.

the lower halves of the rear windows were of large sheets of glass, whereas all other houses had glazing bars on their windows as required by the Trust. In October a Trust Committee meeting was held at 1 South Square and now this became the usual venue.

Changes were taking place in the Suburb. In 1913 Lyttleton died; he had been Henrietta's close friend and neighbour in the Cloisters as well as president of the board of directors of the Trust. Hunter died in the same year; since the beginning of the Suburb she had relied on him for his steady advice and firm environmental views:

> "He combined in a rare degree a deep love of beauty, legal acumen, and unfathomed patience. To him I turned in every difficulty – and there were very many in the early days – and never did he fail to give his experienced learning to the movement, or lose perseverance in unravelling petty or wearisome details. He was not an effective speaker, and therefore the world did not know what it owed him, but those of us at whose service he placed his powers appraised truly his great gift and honoured him for his lavish disinterestedness."[296]

Losing the advice and friendship of Lyttleton and Hunter must have added to her intense loneliness after the death of Samuel. Frank Debenham died in 1916: he had given financial help and offered the use of his house and garden in Hampstead for charity garden parties, and it was in his Hove house that Samuel had died. Sutcliffe, the Co-partners' architect, died in 1915 and J S Birkett, solicitor to the Trust, died in 1916. Hubert Von Herkomer, their eccentric portrait-painter, died in 1914. Their generation was dying, in addition to all the young men lost in the war, leaving millions of lonely widows.

Raymond Unwin left the Suburb to become chief technical officer in the Housing and Town Planning section of the Ministry of Health, and from 1st January 1915 John Soutar replaced him as the chief architect to the Suburb. Soutar is regarded as a good architect, but he lacked the flair, originality and above all the social purpose of Unwin. Another blow was to come, for Vivian resigned from the Trust while remaining chairman of the Co-partnership. After this there was no director with a seat on both boards. Brigid Grafton Green observes:

> "Relations with Mr Vivian, the Trust minutes suggest, may have been strained for some time. In March 1916, for instance the Trust Board discussed plans for the extension of the Suburb into the land acquired in 1912. Mr Vivian accepted that the two companies had fully agreed in 1912 to the layout of the 'new' Suburb being planned in conjunction with the 'old'; but, he added, it had never been suggested that the Trust had a right to control the designs or construction of buildings on the Co-partners 300 acres."[297]

After this the Co-partners became commercially minded and deviated from Trust policy, building for the wealthy and for profit.

During the war Henrietta must have thought sometimes of the many young men she had known at Toynbee, and what was happening to them. She was unhappy about the management of Toynbee and had a very poor opinion of the warden, Mr Heath, who was a conscientious objector: "They are such contemptible creatures who gather round him, full of isms & fads & cranks – & feminist tendencies." By feminist she probably meant feminine or homosexual, for she wanted manly men at Toynbee. She thought that they should open six or eight rooms at Toynbee so that they could have a few residents despite the war.[298]

Henrietta was asked to become a member of the sub-committee on co-operative and communal arrangements of the Housing Advisory Council of the Ministry of Health, possibly at the suggestion of Unwin. This was public recognition, and indeed Henrietta was now known nationally as one of "the great and the good". She knew many Establishment figures personally, as a letter written to Jane Addams in 1915 reveals:

"Dear Miss Addams
I cannot help thinking you should talk to some big folk.
Would you like to see the Queen? She is quite a good sort.
I could write to her – if you cld leave some engagements loose enough for her to choose.
Then there is Lord Haldane, Lord Milner, Lord Grey, Lord Crewe, The Archbishops, Sir Albert Spicer, Dr Orchard, Dr Horton, Dr Clifford
All these are my friends & would be grateful to hearken to you – if I told them. You will understand that the purpose of your seeing them wld not be so much to report but to inspire them. To me the main thing now is to get England into the right attitude of mind – & when I came home last night I felt so sorry you had wasted your time on me when you cld. have told the really influential.
There are the Labour leaders too. Snowden, MacDonald, Burns. The latter in the cold now but with a very forcible tongue, wh. might as well say your say. Let me know if I can be of any use. I shall be down near you at 12.15 tomorrow.
Love H.O. Barnett[299]

A rather intimate way of referring to the Queen! With these eminent friends, her creation of the Suburb and her record with children of the State and her War work for service men, it was not surprising that when the CBE was created in 1917, she was on the first list.

In 1918 the King and Queen visited the Suburb to see the Garden of Remembrance with the Calvary, a stone crucifix copied under Lutyens direction from a Velasquez figure. Below the crucifix were two large marble slabs on which are engraved the names of parishioners who died in the war. The King and Queen planted two trees in the garden, which is at the east end of St Jude's, and now obscured by bushes. Queen Mary came yet again in 1918 to lay the foundation stone of the High School, an extension of the Institute building. She broke protocol which required that the finance for the building must be raised before a royal would lay a foundation stone, for Henrietta had only raised a part of the money needed. The Queen was very fond of her and "a good sort".

Chapter 24
A Visit to America 1920–1921

On 4th September 1920 Henrietta accompanied by Marion and Dr Kingston, sailed on the Meganatic from Liverpool for Canada. Dr Boyle was very fond of Henrietta and admired her:

> "Dame Henrietta! Delightful pictures this name brings up of a vivid, gay personality. Emotionally rapidly responsive, with capacity for earnest thought & with business-like acuity; & withall a child-like simplicity.
> Apart from glimpses of her and of Canon Barnett I really only knew her after her husband's death; & her founding of Hampstead Garden Suburb. She took a little house at Hove, for recruiting holidays & asked me to see her professionally. Nevertheless her youthful eagerness to have friends, & her lively interest in anything to help those in distress, enabled us to make up for lost time. Her true generosity of soul was shown, when, full of imaginative schemes & keen as ever to acquire all she could for her beloved Suburb, she yet induced a personal friend to give £500 to the Lady Chichester Hospital, then in great financial straits.
> I rejoiced in being able to go to America with her & Miss Paterson; Miss (now Dr) Kingston was also with us. I combined it with a tour I had long wished to take in connection with my own subject.
> Many of Mrs Barnett's friends remonstrated saying she was too old, & not strong enough to undertake the journeying; even saying that she could not survive it; but I felt, & rightly as it proved, that the mental & moral stimulus of seeing the triumph of her husband's & her own ideas across the world, would be worth the physical strain. She was as good a traveller as any of us. Her courage was sublime in every direction. Not to mention big enterprises, at one time during the trip she was so keen on her 'dear Patser' looking her best that she made an onslaught on Miss Paterson's evening dresses, to bring them up to date, as she thought, & having cut up & pinned & <u>not</u> sewn them left her with hardly anything to wear!
> She took pleasure in simple things. On starting for America, she could hardly say goodbye to her friends who came to see her off, so great was her desire that they should see & admire the beautiful accordion pleated cloak she had bought at the last minute. Was it perhaps too for happiness rather than emotion. She never wallowed in sadness; nor did she ever pose; once with her big blue eyes very wide, she gravely said: 'I am not good enough to have family prayers every day.' Vital, human, large-hearted was Dame Henrietta, with inspiring enthusiasm which lit fires of energy all around her."[300]

What a wonderful tribute from her kindly psychiatrist.

Henrietta and Marion were to make a three-month tour of Canada and the United States. Queen Mary, hearing of this tour, asked a lady-in-waiting to write to Henrietta: "Her Majesty desires me to tell you that she is much interested in your every success. As one already knows the Queen takes a personal interest in the housing question, & hopes that the beautiful houses for all classes which you have inaugurated so successfully in the Hampstead Garden Suburb may be adopted with equal success in Canada."[301] The Canadian government had invited her to be its guest for a lecturing tour on Housing, and the American Federation of Settlements had invited her to talk on town planning, garden cities and garden suburb ideals. The tours had been thoroughly planned with speaking engagements arranged, fees agreed and accommodation and travelling expenses provided for Henrietta and for Marion Paterson, who accompanied her everywhere. Henrietta was armed with 17 letters of introduction from Lord Bryce, and many introductions from Lord Grey, who had been Governor-General of Canada. Marion tells us that Henrietta always enjoyed sea voyages, and their seven-day crossing was especially enjoyable because two academics, Professor Cunliffe of Columbia University and J Baker of Harvard, invited them to sit at their table, where the "conversation is excellent, informative, amusing & altogether fresh".[302]

They landed at Quebec to a warm welcome from Mr Buckley, secretary to the Ottawa Adviser of Town Planning, who presented her with a book; on the flyleaf was written

> "Quebec was taken by the Sword September 13th 1608:
> May you take Quebec once more September 13th 1920
> By the divine instrument of your great & beautiful love for men, women & children.
> Most Gracious Lady welcome to our land!
> The seeds hundred fold, & blown
> Across the mighty water to our shores
> We give you blossoms for your sowing,
> Hearts are not barren ground: Sweet flowers are blowing
> And hearts are gardens, just because you gave
> From yours the wealth you could not save."

With such an emotional welcome, and armed with a letter from the Queen and all her introductions, Henrietta was sure to have a good tour. Her first lecture was The Making of the Home. "I was very nervous," she reported, "but to my surprise I delighted my audience." From Quebec they went to Ottawa, Montreal and Toronto, speaking to packed audiences. By the end of her first week in Canada she had "spoken four times, been interviewed twice; stayed in the homes of four kind friends; seen three towns; attended three parties given for me; & written three lectures". Not surprisingly, while at Ottawa she "got a bad fatigue cold necessitating some days in bed". However she recovered and they were shown all over Government House. At Montreal, "The Lecture Hall was crowded; people stood up all along the sides, & dozens were turned away." In Toronto they had a "wonderful hostess," Sarah Warren, who took Henrietta to the civic reception given for her. She was the first woman to be given a civic reception. At the end of her lecture the Attorney-general, who was on the platform, said that he would see that the Town Planning Bill, which had been very delayed in Parliament, would go through. It pleased Henrietta very much to think she had forwarded the progress of housing in Canada. Before leaving Canada she was taken to see the Niagara Falls and shown the plan for preserving the beauty of the river banks above and below the falls. She was taken over the rapids and the whirlpool in "an ariel car", with lightning flashing around.

Toronto to Chicago was a long and tiring journey:

"We were both half-dead when at 10.45 pm. we were met at Chicago station by Miss Jane Addams, & whirled to Hull House 'the shell of a good woman's soul'. She had given up her own bedroom for me, but the noise of all night trains was so terrible that we both arose, after a sleepless night, utterly done up, and dear Miss Addams decided we should have the use of a palatial flat, in part of this wonderful Hull House, so we moved our things, tumbled on to our beds, & slept all afternoon!"[303]

In Chicago she gave several lectures and visited a University settlement in the squalor of the stockyard where the workers had to endure the nauseating smell. During their tour of America, Henrietta and Marion usually stayed in the Settlement in each town they visited, for now 440 settlements had opened following the success of Hull House. She would get the opportunity to see the local housing and meet the people. Of course she used this opportunity to the full:

"In every town I went, either with the official inspectors or someone well acquainted with the neighbourhood, to see the very worst condition that prevailed, then those homes or hovels which had been repaired, and then such examples of 'model' dwellings as existed. Then I drove around the neighbourhoods where the well-to-do and the rich lived, so that I could ascertain the standard of home-making when money permitted it to be reached."[304]

In Detroit Henrietta gave a lecture and stayed with the Fords:

"After my lecture at Detroit I was tired through, from our journey from Chicago, & Mrs Henry Ford carried us off to her beautiful house 15 miles out, where in perfect quiet I gratefully slept, though it is difficult to get six hours of train din out of one's ears. Next day we visited Mr Ford's Factory where we were met by the Revd. Dr Marquis, the Director of the Ford Social Welfare Department. After an interesting talk with him he took us over the Works where in 45 minutes we saw the beginning of a motor car with a plate & a screw, & then we ourselves rode in it out of the 'fluid' yard, all in readiness for the road. The noise in the Factory was infernal."[305]

She gave further lectures at Washington and Philadelphia:

"I can never forget the alleys of Washington where the coloured people live. I stood there having just turned my back on the glistening palace buildings of that wonderful city, and bore indescribable stinks while the officials explained that the houses on one side of the alley were condemned and that therefore the drains had not been connected with the sewers. I am haunted by the faces of those kindly people degraded by their conditions, which they are, by the facts of modern civilization, helpless to remedy."

But she saw a different aspect of Washington when Julia Lathrop invited them to see her Children's Bureau, which considered the whole welfare of children and the effect of legislation, and afterwards to her home. Then they saw the Arlington Cemetery and the newly built Cathedral where she was blessed by the Bishop.

At New Haven she gave a lecture in a fashionable ballroom. The room was crowded: professors of Yale, members of the Chamber of Commerce, heads of large firms, fashionable ladies, welfare workers all came to hear her. She was anxious that her lecture should be good enough "But God, in his Mercy, aided me & I held them for an hour & ten minutes". They spent two days in New Haven and saw the slums and the housing plans as well as Yale University. They were staying with Mr and Mrs Robert Woods, who introduced Henrietta to Mr and Mrs Kennedy:

"It was gladdening to be told by Mr Kennedy that he heard from every Town that my lectures had done untold good in awakening my listeners to ideals & to face their National duty of considering the terrible condition of their slum dwellers. I was very grateful to hear this from the man who had it all in his hands."

They travelled on to Boston:

"As I had two lectures to give in our five days at Boston I refused the "honour luncheon" & many other hospitalities, only accepting what would give me opportunities for quieter & more intimate relation with people who could explain for me much that is difficult to understand in this great country

We went to luncheon with Professor & Mrs Baker at Harvard (our fellow passengers in crossing the Atlantic). Mrs Baker is the Dean of the Radcliff Girls' College, & one of the most charming of these charming cultivated women. After being shown much of the beauty & interest of Harvard University I went to see the far-famed ex-President, Dr Elliott, with an introduction from Lord Bryce. Dr Elliott is a very remarkable man of 86; he had prepared questions to ask me on housing, on labour, & on other social matters in our country."[306]

On 8th November they arrived in New York, where they stayed in the Ladies Club. One night they dined in the Mary Elizabeth restaurant on Fifth Avenue so they could see the Republican Party procession passing. A weekend was spent at Greenwich, 20 miles from New York, as guests of Mr and Mrs Vincent. Mr Vincent was head of the Rockefeller Foundation.[307] Professor Cunliffe, whom they had met on the *Meganatic*, showed them round Columbia University. One evening they were invited to dine with Mr Cleveland Dodge who was a friend of Lord Bryce. At dinner she sat between Mr Dodge and John Rockefeller Jnr. After dinner she went to the library with the millionaires to talk with them about housing. But Henrietta also used the opportunity to appeal to John Rockefeller to support her Hampstead Garden Suburb Institute.[308] Unfortunately he sent a polite refusal. She then tried Mr Rosenwald, but with no success. But Rockefeller was impressed. In 1930 he gave Henrietta £5,000 to use as she wished. She spent £4,000 on Crewe Hall, the completion of the Institute, and the other £1,000 was spent on her many good causes, including £49 to Dr Helen Boyle and a gramophone for the Henrietta Barnett School. In her letter of thanks she already asked Rockefeller "to give me & the Queen & the people £15,000" to build the new School of Art.[309] Despite this reference to the Queen, Rockefeller did not comply; however he wrote several letters in a very friendly and admiring manner to Henrietta.

She was shocked by the housing conditions in all the big cities:

"Pittsburgh, with its smoke, its dust, its appalling houses, never did I see anything so shocking. I stood in the terrible alleys so horrified & indignant that I wept. I could do nothing but weep, like a child when its doll is broken, for in that rich prosperous town my life was broken, in a Nation that could give its people worse houses to live in from what is given to cattle."[310]

The Federation of Settlements had postponed their meeting from April to September so that Henrietta could attend it, and now, meeting at Buffalo, they made her president of the association. She gave them a lecture on Samuel's life and on Toynbee Hall which was the inspiration of Hull House and the other American settlements. During her travels she promoted her *Canon Barnett, His Life, Work and Friends*. She also saw children's courts which favourably impressed her, and admired the tribunals which dealt with the prostitutes, handling cases with a firm sympathy.

The "Baltic"
Nov. 21st 1920

Dear dear DEAR.
I had a little
"cry" when I had the news
that I should not see you –
I was so deeply disappointed.
For I had treasured a
thousand things which I had
seen & learnt, to ask you
about. – & I am really

In mid-November they sailed on the *Baltic* back to England. She had given 33 speeches, and turned down invitations to make many more. She was invited to return to America "at a handsome remuneration" to develop schemes like the Garden Suburb. At every town they were met by "new friends, with flowers, by photographers & motors," and were given most generous hospitality, and in each town she had met the rich and important people. Lecturing to such big audiences made her nervous; she was very relieved when she gave her last lecture: "Next morning I rose like a child out of school for we were to have a picnic! & my lectures were behind me with all their anxieties & responsibilities." For a 69-year-old this must have been an exhausting tour, but Henrietta was buoyed up by the welcome and the enthusiastic audiences and her increasing fame. She loved America: she found skyscrapers "exciting as they stirred the imagination and made beauty by their mysterious shadows". Her American tour was a triumph. She had the great pleasure of staying with Jane Addams, but was disappointed that Jane did not meet her again before she left. Going home on the *Baltic* she wrote her a ten-page letter, starting

> "Dear dear DEAR
> I had a little cry when I had the news that I should not see you – I was so deeply disappointed, for I had treasured a thousand things which I had seen and learnt to ask you about, – and I am really puzzled over the large non-local matters such as emigrants & their treatment; the unremunerative importance given to the

party government system; the habit of flattering their visitors; the continual harping on the "revolution", & all the petty details of long ago fights – The dull acceptance of religion & the absence of enthusiasm about it as a reforming force: the pride in their charities whether they be individual, or by great Trusts – The positive worship of wealth, & the undercurrent of – ? What can be said? – Dear – I am puzzled & both hopeful & unhappy – Then the Jew! Still more strongly for America than for England am I a "passionate Zionist". – A talk with you would have straightened out lots of my difficulties, & I am returning a poorer woman because I did not get it."[311]

Henrietta's longing for Jane grew with her disappointment with missing her, though in the sure knowledge that there could be no physical intimacy, emotional longing became even more intense until it became a romantic passion. She longed for Samuel, but in his absence found someone else to love. If you are tired of looking, you are tired of loving, if you are tired of loving, you are tired of living.

When she arrived back home, she wrote six articles on America Today for the *Daily Telegraph*.[312] The first two articles were on Charity and Government and show that she was very impressed by the numerous large hospitals, the fact that 440 settlements had been established on the model of Toynbee Hall, the large sums spent on playgrounds, parks, recreation clubs in schools and the vast charities. However she was critical of the lack of thought given to the reasons for poverty and attributed this to the youthfulness of America: "When human beings are young their first impulse is to cure what they see is injured, to mend what they recognise as broken. In later life they ask who broke the damaged article, and what caused the injury, and the deeper thought which follows age and experience produces the further resolve to prevent the injury taking place …". The Americans were not investigating why there were so many patients with nervous diseases or tuberculosis and they were not tackling the causes.

She was full of praise for the care for children:

"There may be truth in the statement that a nation's enlightenment is measured by the interest she exhibits in her children. If so, the high-water mark in child care attained in the United States of America is a tribute to her intelligence, humanity and far-sightedness, for, in spite of the fact that people of all nationalities and from many different climates reach her shores, in spite of their poverty and the change of their conditions, the standard of child prosperity reached is very high."

She praised the work of the Juvenile Protective Association of Chicago as effectively guarding children against vice and exploitation and admired the Federal Children's Bureau for its thorough statistics of children. Her greatest praise was for American education. The kindergartens had spacious buildings and the teachers had "the conviction that the tiniest child has personality". School buildings and libraries were generally the most "conspicuous structures" and schools "show both in design and equipment a freshness of thought." The elementary schools taught geography, history, physiology and hygiene. Henrietta was very keen on the last two subjects, having taught them herself. She found that the children were allowed "self-determination": they were permitted to choose poems to recite at school and choose books to borrow from the library. However she deplored the lack of religious teaching in the public schools and praised the holy atmosphere she found in the best of the private schools.

She was impressed by the large number of colleges and universities and the vast number of undergraduates, and even more impressed by the eagerness to learn:

"Whatever likenesses or differences exist between English and American education there is one factor which is universal there and absent with us. I mean the eagerness to learn. There it pervades all classes of people of every nationality. It seems to come from the air. Teachers in the elementary schools and secondary schools tell tales of children who study late at night, and forsake play to keep up with their class-mates; of youths who deprive themselves of adequate sustenance to buy books; and of girls who adopt cotton overalls to save dollars to obtain extra lessons. This same desire to acquire information must be the cause of the readiness of the average adult person to attend lectures … the humbler folk hardly need officers to enforce school attendance, and the richer people pour vast sums into the coffers of educational centres, or into the laps of noted pioneer educationists."

In an article for the *Teacher's World* she again admired the importance Americans gave to education: "Part of the reason of the American's care for education is the conviction that each child has an individuality to be honoured, and potentialities to be watched for and either stimulated or repressed, but in all cases to be guided and helped". Teachers were encouraged to experiment with different methods. One school took their children to the art gallery once a month, another allowed children to choose their own essay subjects to write at home, children were allowed to select an instrument to learn and play in the school orchestra. This individual treatment helped to make the children eager to learn.

In an article for the *Contemporary Review* she compared the American university system with the British: "… the numbers who take advantage of the opportunities of learning between the ages of seventeen and twenty-one, when they could be either earning or idling, gives one occasion 'furiously to think' whether we in England are right in keeping higher education for the richer classes … In America there are 110,000,000 people and 349 Universities. In England there are 47,000,000 people and 20 Universities."[313] Many American students were earning while they were learning, and there were innumerable opportunities for adult education.

Her last two articles for the *Telegraph* were on Homes for the People and she was very critical. She found that though there were city planning commissions which prepared many plans, they were concerned with the infrastructure – roads, drainage and so on – not with regulating housing: "The result of this freedom is manifest in every town, where the houses are of all sizes, materials and colours, often dumped down wherever the owner fancies, without any relation to other houses or the appearance of the street."[314]

In Europe and in Britain the municipal authorities were now building low-rental housing for the poor, but not in America. In Washington she had seen filthy and insanitary slums. In New York the tenements were five stories high and built so close that there was neither light nor air. In Chicago housing was even worse. The tenements were "built without plan or design, just run up anyhow as the pressure on house-room showed a fresh opportunity for the owner to make more dollars out of the poor. They are of all sizes and shapes and conditions of unrepair, with quite inadequate sanitary accommodation, and have no beauty, no peace, nor any of the constituents of a home, which is the birthright of civilised mankind". She softened this severe criticism of Chicago by prefacing it with praise of its parks, libraries and art gallery, evidently aware that she could greatly offend American readers. She appealed to the women of America to reform the housing, to limit the size of cities and to plan and build beautiful suburbs.

She admired the work of the courts dealing with prostitution in Chicago and New York, and their work to achieve reform by considering each woman as an individual:

"The many methods adopted to abolish commercialised vice and save the vicious can only be briefly mentioned here, but they include: (1) the abolition of fines: (2) the indeterminate sentence, so that liberty depends on conduct, and on the evidence of self-management; (3) power to detain those whose health requires detention; (4) exhaustive inquiry into each case,

Plate 76
"Dame Henrietta Barnett, D.B.E. Taken when addressing a large audience recently." Henrietta was a popular public speaker and broadcaster.

DAME HENRIETTA BARNETT, D.B.E.
Taken when addressing a large audience recently   [*Frontispiece*

and all the physical, mental, social, moral, family, and environment conditions; (5) if freedom seems likely to forward reform, the accused is released, and then enclosed in the wonderful network of the probation system; (6) if requiring discipline, she is referred to one of the many reformatory agencies worked by volunteers in union with the State, and, if possible, given the character-developing influence of dealing with the land."[315]

She admired the "park system". In Chicago there were 66 parks, and in Boston and Philadelphia there were thousands of acres of park. She admired the Federal Children's Bureau in Washington that made surveys and ascertained all the facts about American children. Of course she praised Prohibition and found that it had caused an improvement in health; there were fewer people in mental hospitals. Americans who gave up drinking were able to save money and buy cars.

When the Barnetts visited America in 1891 they were not well known there and they were not given great receptions. They were critical of the uncultured people of the West and the vulgarity of Coney Island. They seemed rather dazed by their experiences. When Henrietta went to America in 1920, she was famous and her progress from one settlement to another and her lecture circuit were all well planned. "The whole tour was mapped out for us; we were saved all trouble, and at every place we were met at the station by new friends, flowers, photographers, and motors."[316] Wherever she spoke she was greeted by admiring audiences and with great hospitality and she met the most important people. She said she was "almost buried under evidences of kindness and good feeling". It is no wonder that she was delighted and found much to admire in America. But she also recognised that the settlement workers had problems peculiar to America:

"First, that a great number of those who need social service are coloured people, with whom it is against normal human nature (whatever a few angelic characters may believe) to feel on terms of absolute equality. Secondly, that the population is composed not only of Americans, but of masses of people from Southern and Central Europe who have different standards of life, different ideals for conduct, and a different attitude to the State. And lastly, there is the Jew, who avowedly keeps himself to himself, is filled with tribal spirit, and often considers, as his forbears did, that his neighbours are Philistines, and fit objects to borrow from or to best."[317]

Henrietta herself had worked in the "dirt, smoke, darkness, noise, smells, crowded streets" for her own "countrymen and co-religionists, who have, below the surface, the same ideals, the same religion, and the same intentions as yourself. But it requires a higher devotion to do it for aggressive people, whether Gentiles or Jews, who don't care twopence for the country of their adoption, whose sole aim is to get rich and move away from the neighbourhood in which they first find themselves, whose sense of public spirit is non-existent, and who don't even pretend to gratitude".[318] These comments were written in 1921, long before the era of political correctness, and would have been acceptable to most of those who read them in the *Cornhill Magazine*. If Samuel had been alive, he would probably have influenced Henrietta to feel more generously to immigrants and Jews and soften her comments. She was now regarded as an authority on America and was frequently asked to speak and write about it.

Chapter 25
The 1920s

I still cling to the poets who put the Golden Age in front of us, and I can quote with emphasis Browning's words:

> Grow old along with me!
> The best is yet to be,
> The last of life for which the first was made
> Our times are in His hand
> Who saith "A whole I planned,
> Youth shows but half; trust God: see all nor be afraid!"[319]

In 1924 Henrietta was made a Dame of the British Empire and now in her seventies she achieved the success and fame she deserved. She was one of the most famous women in England, and she was well known in America and in Commonwealth countries. She had first served on a Government committee in the 1890s, and from 1919 to 1921 she was a member of the Central and Trusts committees to administer the Profiteering Acts.[320] These Acts were passed in 1919 and 1920 to enable the Board of Trade to prosecute people who had made illegal profits out of wartime shortages, and the Board of Trade appointed committees to administer the Acts. Though not many people were fined, the Acts had a powerful deterrent effect.

She was asked to be patron of many organisations. In 1922 the Social and Political Education League asked Henrietta to be their president: she was the first woman president, following such distinguished men as Sir Oliver Lodge and T H Huxley. Her presidential address was on Social Reforms in America. She was honorary president of the American Federation of Settlements throughout the 1920s, president of the International Conference on Settlements from 1920 to 1928, vice-president of the Council of Barnett House from 1914 till 1936, vice-president of the National Union of Women Workers, trustee of Whitechapel Art Gallery from 1901 to 1936, as well as having many roles in the Suburb. She knew her limitations, for when asked to be president of a Suburb music society she refused on the grounds that she knew nothing of music.[321] She made broadcasts, was asked to chair meetings and gave many lectures and speeches. She was asked to speak so often that she had to turn down most of the requests. In 1926 she wrote in a letter: "I refuse 5 out of every 6 requests for speeches". She wrote articles for the newspapers and periodicals, and if she wrote to the papers, her letters were published. In 1921 she wrote to the *Manchester Guardian* on the problem of prostitution: the solution was to reform the men who used prostitutes, to improve the moral atmosphere: "… should not the men who create the demand be treated with the same scorn as the women who supply what is demanded, and be meted

THE GARDEN SUBURB'S MOST FAMOUS PORTRAIT PAINTER

Mr. Maurice Codner is the Hampstead Garden Suburb's most famous portrait painter, and each year claims some space on the Academy walls and has his claims allowed. This year it is with a portrait of Field Marshal Lord Milne, and another year it was with a portrait of Sir Seymour Hicks. Having dealt with Mr. George Robey complete with bowler and arch expression, he has just painted another of the famous comedian as Falstaff. His public fame is matched by local appreciation, for he has recently finished a portrait of Mr. A. J. Reynolds, the Mayor of Hendon. His landscapes are less well-known than his portraits, but they are so full of the joy of craftsmanship that one wonders whether he is not a portrait painter by profession and a landscape painter by choice. He has been the "victim" almost as often as he has been the "executioner." Mr. George Belcher has put him on the spot twice in PUNCH, and in the present Academy has used him as a model in "Painting at Wiston."..Mr. Codner can make a good speech, turn an apt phrase, hold his own as an amateur actor, and is an able critic of other people's work. He is a man of infinite resource and abiding charm, who carries his honours lightly, for he makes modesty his watchword.

Plate 77
Maurice Codner.
An affable man
and famous portrait
painter, he lived in
Temple Fortune Hill.

with the same social ostracism?"[322] It would be wise to follow the example of 14 towns in America which had abolished their houses of ill fame, cleared their streets of temptation and thereby reduced venereal disease. This was a daring letter for a woman to write.

Queen Mary sent Henrietta a telegram on 4th May 1920: "I send you my best wishes on your seventieth birthday".[323] Henrietta must have been delighted, despite the telegram being a year early, and their friendship and mutual admiration deepened.

William Ward and other friends subscribed to have her portrait painted by Maurice Codner, a well-known portrait-painter who lived locally at 27 Temple Fortune Hill, where he had a studio behind his house. He was a very likeable man; he had painted Sir Seymour Hicks the actor, Field Marshall Lord Milne, and George Robey the comedian. Evidently Henrietta's portrait was a good likeness for Marion Paterson wrote that the look in her eyes, caught in the painting, showed that "she never turned back, however difficult the path might

Plate 78
Two portraits
of Henrietta by
Maurice Codner.
Henrietta disliked
this portrait, for
she said it made
her look like a
businesswoman.

Plate 79
So Codner painted
this other portrait,
which reveals
her kind and
loving nature. He
successfully portrayed
the two sides of her
character.

be".[324] But Henrietta did not like it, as she wrote in a letter to Harold Lacey: "Mr Codner wishes to send my portrait?!!? into the Academy. He said you said it was splendid – I can not let it go to RA with my name unless it is less like a successful business woman, & more like, I hope, me, to whom God has given some visions of ideals." Nevertheless it was shown in the Summer Exhibition of the Royal Academy and was presented to the Institute by Lord Burnham on 7th July 1928. It was hung on the wall of the Institute hall, which was used as the School hall. Now it is in the Institute in East Finchley.

She was open to new ideas and eager to try new things. She had always enjoyed making sketches, particularly of landscapes, but she found she needed more colour to express the landscape of Madeira which she visited in 1923, so she tried oils.

> "And each in his separate star,
> Shall draw the Thing as he sees it for the God of things as they are
> When the Earth's last picture is painted and the tubes are twisted and dried."
>
> (Kipling)

She showed her work to Dudley Heath at the Institute, who said it was very good and advised her to try the Spring Exhibition at the Royal Academy. Her painting "Towards the Light" was accepted in 1923 and sold on the opening day. In 1924 she had another painting accepted: "Dawn from Funchal". Evidently she continued painting and submitting her pictures to the Academy, for in 1927 she wrote "My portrait is in the R.A. but my 3 pictures all out!!! The first time all are refused."[325]

She gave some of her paintings away: she gave one to Queen Mary, and to the Whitechapel Art Gallery she gave a painting, also two statues and the Doulton font which had been outside St Jude's.[326]

When asked to name her leisure activities for the *Dictionary of National Biography*, Henrietta listed painting, writing and sewing. The last is rather surprising for though we know Nurse taught her to sew, she does not mention it elsewhere. She had a high regard for craft work and perhaps she found it relaxing, or perhaps she was mischievously claiming this woman's occupation as just as worthy of mention as hunting and fishing. She was comfortably established in her house, 1 South Square, where Fanny lived with her until her death at Easter 1926. She had two maids living in (quite usual at that time), while Marion Paterson and a secretary helped with her work. Marion wrote:

> "In planning her days Dame Henrietta would spend two hours, 7.30 to 9.30 am. quietly alone; carefully planning the work for her secretaries; & in making her own time table." Her very efficient secretary, Miss Alice Cole, wrote: "I knew Dame Henrietta from 1926. Our first interview was on the telephone: "How old are you? What a lovely age – Come & see me this afternoon." Alice's first job was to work on saving Bunker's Hill from the builders. "I never knew anyone work so hard as Dame Henrietta excepting MP & myself trying to keep pace with her. I learned more from the Dame than from anyone else I know – She taught me a great deal & was generous in imparting her knowledge which was on an amazing variety of subjects. We had our disagreements. Sometimes it seemed serious when it came to 'Miss Cole, you & I will have to part.' But quite soon might come her voice calling "Magpie, do come & look out of my window, such a sunset."[327]

She would not tolerate opposition and could be commanding, autocratic to get her way. As Marion wrote: "To her fellow workers, Dame Henrietta would at times appear egotistical, self-assertive – yet it was but her protective armour donned to enable her to attain her goal – however great the opposition – however many the obstacles." And what could they say when Henrietta pronounced: "It is not me but a thought given me by God."?

On committees, Henrietta always preferred to be the secretary, for then she could determine the agenda and censor the minutes. Marion Paterson described her method of dealing with committees:

"She had a reliable memory which she supplemented by a series of note-books, one for each official. These interviews were also carefully planned beforehand.
On the left-hand page of the note book she wrote each subject she meant to discuss.
On the right hand page answers & discussions were noted.
One soon learnt to be ready with facts & figures to support statements; for she would, suddenly, turn to a previous page & ask why one's answer differed from one given twelve months previously."

Except in periods of depression, she was usually cheerful and fun:

"The Dame made friends wherever she went; in shops, in buses. I remember her starting a guessing game of each other's ages in a Brighton bus. She gave presents to people she met: a book to the gas man, some plants for his garden to a porter she met at Victoria Station. At Christmas time she gave coal and groceries to the old people of the Suburb."[328]

A woman who grew up in the house next door remembered her as "A small, stout, handsome old lady, who must not be disturbed by noise and parties, but who could be relied on for sympathetic interest when one engaged in an intelligent activity like music or painting".[329]

Sometimes girls from Henrietta Barnett School were asked to take a message to the Dame. They would cross the Square and approach the front door of 1 South Square in trepidation, but Henrietta would be delighted to see them and as with all her little friends she would give them chocolate – Cadbury's, of course. When she wanted quiet for her writing she would go to 12 Wish Road in Hove. For instance in 1927 she made four visits and spent six weeks there between February and July. She sometimes let the little house, or gave friends a week's holiday there.[330]

Her visit to America had given her an insight into the limitations of some aspects of England, and she thought emigration should be encouraged. "Whenever people talk to me of birth control and the dangers besetting our crowded England, I recall wide stretches of vacant land, glorious mountain ranges, the clean air and scintillating sunshine of Canada, and wish the birth-controllers could go and see it. Our Empire is not half populated, let alone overcrowded."[331]

Henrietta's views on the role of the state had changed with the times. In the 1920s she wrote: "I rejoice that the State now recognises that it is its duty to deal with education, infant welfare, open spaces, sanitation, pensions, unemployment."[332] This was far removed from the Charity Organisation Society ideas that Henrietta and Samuel had embraced in the 1870s. Her mind was flexible, and she continued to juggle with her many interests, national and local. In 1930 Henrietta published a collection of her articles and speeches with the title *Matters That Matter*. The title was politically neutral compared with *Practicable Socialism*, the title Henrietta and Samuel had given to similar publications. Most of the articles were previously published in the 1920s and give an insight into Henrietta's activities and thoughts on social issues during that decade.

Ethical Issues

She found the postwar moral standards difficult where they touched sexual matters. In 1919 there was hope of opening a theatre in the Suburb, although it was soon decided to open it in Hampstead, where it was named *The Everyman* and became a cinema. Henrietta had hoped for a Suburb theatre to show plays which "would improve the general tone of the suburban theatre. Good dramas and plays will be produced, in opposition to the banal productions at present served up on two-thirds of the suburban stages. They will be plays appealing to the intellect, and not those mere exhibitions of legs and shoulders, with no plot to speak of, which chiefly appeal to the senses".[333]

On the other hand her views on more general moral issues were greatly changed from her ideas in the 1870s when she was a young Victorian woman. In 1921 she wrote a remarkable article for the *Westminster Gazette* on The Ethics of Punishment. At that time the Irish problem was the most important issue and the London parks were being used to recruit volunteers, distribute uniforms and even for gun practice. This use of public parks was partly to impress the Irish. Henrietta wrote:

> "Daily we all read about Ireland, to learn with pain fresh facts about her unhappy inhabitants and about her unhappy governors. Daily we find ourselves doubting what we read, feeling that there must be some unknown explanation for one part of the nation behaving as Ireland is doing, and for the methods adopted by another part of the 'United' Kingdom to restrain her wrong action. We ask ourselves with incredulous amazement, 'Is punishment the main duty of Government?' ... Punishment for offences not yet committed seems to have been the spring message sent by the Government, via the parks, to the people. Was it wise? Such evidence that force is relied on must arouse resentment, and suggest acts of violence."

She goes on to say that the government should explain and conciliate to resolve conflict, for instance between miners and mine-owners. Women can play a large part: "As I sat the other day in Lady Astor's beautiful room, among the able and often eloquent representatives of the organisations which collectively number hundreds of thousands of women, I wished they would organise themselves with all despatch into a talking body of explanation, and thus perhaps do woman's work of peace-making. Women can talk."

She thought flogging and caning in schools did not reform character: "... punishment should be dictated by the law of love, and not directed so much to kill evil as to create good. In this complicated world there is a place for punishment. And it should be visible and disagreeable, so as to act as a deterrent, and thus aid the wobbler to walk in the strait and narrow path, but its ultimate object should be the reconstruction of the character of those who would have strayed off the road".[334]

Henrietta was becoming a guru, and in 1923 the *Daily Telegraph* published four articles by her on moral issues. She urged people to give more, and to more imaginative charities, she extolled the virtue of aspiration, particularly to be more creative and cultured.

She loved her nephews and nieces, but sometimes they shocked her, for fashions were changing and skirts could be surprisingly short. One niece related that she had seen a blackbird in the garden who gave her a look just like Aunt Henrietta.[335] Perhaps she looked at the girl with a mix of disapproval and amusement. Blackbirds can give a very beady-eyed, pursed-mouth, quizzical look.

The State Children's Association

Henrietta's leadership of the SCA continued until her death, which brought the association to an end. As she said, the great and far-reaching aim of the State Children's Aid Association was "to urge upon Guardians of the Poor, and all those who deal with large numbers of children, that they should consider each child as an individual, and study its habits, tastes, characteristics, and antecedents, with a view to placing it in the surroundings best suited to the development of its individuality".[336]

During the 1920s the SCA continually pressed for reforms, and had a strong council including the Archbishop of York, the bishops of London and Oxford, seven lords, and many other well-known people such as Sydney Webb. Henrietta was always able to find a lord to support her interests and the association had been chaired by Lords Peel, Herschell, Grey, Crewe, Lytton and lastly Lord Stanmore. As honorary secretary, Henrietta could control proceedings, helped by her friend Colonel Thomson, who was the committee accountant. From the mid-1920s, Henrietta shared the job of secretary with J A Lovat-Fraser MP. They had many friends in Parliament and were successful in asking questions, engineering debates, speaking on the estimates and keeping in touch with departments.[337]

Henrietta and the SCA were determined to get children out of big institutions and into the loving care of foster-parents, or as second choice, the care of house-mothers with groups of no more than 12 children. They also favoured emigration to foster-care in Australia or Canada. With individual care, children would get the affection they needed, and learn to shop and look after a house: "… the worst education that teaches self-reliance is better than the best that destroys it. That is the principle that our State Children's Association lives to uphold, for life under the rules and regulations necessary in institutions tends to sap self-reliance".[338] By the 1920s public policy was to move children out of institutions, but progress was slow: 560,000 children were supported by the state and of these 62,000 were in institutions such as workhouses, barrack schools, industrial schools and reformatories.

The SCA campaigned for a reform in the treatment of juvenile offenders, and this was a particular interest of Lovat-Fraser. They wanted a wider use of probation instead of detention, the establishment of clinics for the examination of juvenile offenders, and the development of after-care.[339] But in 1920 Henrietta reported that the probation of children had not progressed: "According to official figures, twenty-two out of thirty-three county divisions dealt with 7,807 proved charges against children and did not place a single offender on probation. Ten counties with 42,256 proved charges placed only 115 girls and boys on probation, and 189 Courts of Summary Jurisdiction have not yet taken steps to appoint probation officers."[340]

In her Shaftesbury Lecture of 1921, Henrietta stressed the need for education of young offenders:

"In 1920 36,065 children and young persons were brought before the Juvenile Courts, of whom 49 were sent to prison under sentence, or on remand, or while awaiting removal to other institutions; and 2,461 were committed to goal for one month – too short a sentence for remedial discipline, but long enough to rob the boy or girl of self-respect and stamp him or her as a criminal. Last year 67,000 people were sent to prison, of whom over 5,000 were under twenty-one years of age, and of these only 70 could read and write well. What an opportunity for the WEA.[341] Now that there are women magistrates and jurors, we can hope that they will demand a reform of prisons to make them less punitive and more educational."

Henrietta was concerned with strengthening the grass-roots of the association as well as with policy. She recruited many lady supporters, such as Lady Emmott, to the SCA, and spoke to them at tea-party meetings. At one such meeting at Lady Sydenham's house in Onslow Square she encouraged the ladies to visit the barrack schools and reformatories, see the conditions, and befriend an individual child, giving him or her care and friendship. She said that society was changing with the introduction of the dole and widows' pensions and that the SCA must change to keep up with these social changes.

Henrietta remained Honorary Secretary until her death, though she was unable to attend meetings from 1935. With her death the Association came to an end, showing how much it owed to her work and inspiration. It had been the mouthpiece for her own opinions about child care.

The League of Nations

Henrietta took a great interest in the peace movement and in this she was probably much influenced by Jane Addams. Jane was a follower of Tolstoy, had read his books and went to visit him;[342] she believed in non-resistance and the curative power of love, and was a committed pacifist. From the outbreak of the First World War she spent even more time working on the peace movement than on her Chicago settlement, Hull House, despite being attacked for pacifism. In 1915 she formed the Women's Peace Party and opposed American entry to the war, for which she aroused so much hostility that she was expelled from the Daughters of the American Revolution! In May the Peace Party sent delegates to the International Conference of Women at The Hague. They were not allowed to land in England, being denounced as "Pro-Hun peacites". At one point "a British gun-boat came alongside and trained a machine gun on the ship".[343] At the conference, Jane was chosen as one of the delegates to visit Berlin, Vienna, Budapest, Rome, Berne, Paris and London to try to negotiate a peace. Evidently their reception in the European countries gave them respectability and Jane now came to London where she met Asquith, the Prime Minister, and Sir Edward Grey, the Foreign Secretary. As this was only two days after the sinking of the *Lusitania* it is unlikely that her arguments were very well received.

In 1919 there was a Women's Peace Conference in Zurich, attended by 150 people from 16 countries. Coming to London, Jane was entertained by Sydney and Beatrice Webb, Lady Courtney, Graham Wallas and Henrietta. The conference formed the Women's International League for Peace and Freedom and Jane was made the president. The aim of the WILP was to get a revision of the peace treaties which were known to punish the German economy. She presided over annual conferences in Vienna, The Hague, Dublin, Honolulu and Prague, but then resigned on account of her bad health. She had achieved great fame and was awarded the Nobel Peace Prize in 1931.

In 1920, while Henrietta was in Chicago staying with Jane Addams, she said in one of her lectures: "Nationalities are but flimsy & clumsy methods of organising mankind; the whole human race is one. Oh! Why ever fight?! Let those, who dare be brave, anticipate the future, & become internationalists at once." It seems that she was very strongly influenced by Jane's views. During the war, Henrietta was already planning for peace. In 1917 she organised a summer school on Reconstruction and the New Era. It was held in the Suburb, but attracted people from a much wider area. Over 1,200 people paid fees and Henrietta, president of the executive committee, summoned a remarkable array of notable people to attend. The summer school was from August 3rd to 17th and was held in the Institute hall. The daily programme started at 9.30 am and continued until 9.30 pm. With their young men fighting in the trenches, the participants would be intense and willing to work hard. Each day started with a religious service which "CALMED, STIMULATED AND REJOICED all who were present". Lord Crewe was chairman of the organising committee, and Sophie Bryant, Dudley Heath and R H Tawney, the historian, were also involved. Sir Herbert Samuel, Lord Bentinck, Lord Lytton, Lord Burnham, Lord Leverhulme, Sidney Webb, Canon Carlisle, the Bishop of Birmingham, Professor Graham Wallas and three other professors were among the many important speakers at the conference.[344] Large audiences came; Sir Oliver Lodge's audience was so big that his lecture was given from the pulpit in the Free Church.[345] He was Principal of

Plate 80 (opposite) Outside a house in Asmuns Place, a group of children gathered to see Henrietta in the Rolls-Royce.

A SNAPSHOT OF A GROUP OF HAPPY CHILDREN WHO, ATTRACTED BY THE MOTOR HORN, WERE HOPING FOR A SCAMPER.

Taken by Mrs. Barnett outside a Co-partnership cottage in Asmun's Place.

Il. 320j

Birmingham University and a great scientist who had worked on the development of the radio and was the first person to transmit a radio signal – even before Marconi. But he was most famous for his spiritualism, claiming to communicate with the dead and especially with his son who had died in the war. Henrietta had some sympathy with his views. Interest in spiritualism was widespread at the time; moreover she had learned about spiritualism from her schoolteachers. The conference was of national importance, a triumph of organization for Henrietta and of immense significance to her with her relatives in Germany.

Henrietta had high hopes for the League of Nations, although she thought it should have an army to police law and order between nations. She founded the Suburb branch of the League of Nations Union and was its president from 1920 to 1929. She also started a branch in her school. She planned a League of Nations procession in the Suburb for August Bank Holiday 1920. The procession started but heavy rain brought it to an end.[346] The League of Nations Union attracted support from people of all parties and in 1928 there were 1,225 members in the Suburb branch.

Between the two world wars Armistice Day was mainly about remembrance, but for Henrietta it was also about peace: "If during the two minute silence we each willed that friendship should flourish it might spiritually strengthen the League of Nations."[347] In this, as in so many other ways, she was in advance of her time. Even to her last Henrietta still cared deeply about peace. When she was nearing her death, the nurse asked, seeing her closed eyes – "Are you asleep?" She replied "No; I am praying for the peace of the world."[348]

Housing

With the success of the Hampstead Garden Suburb, Henrietta was in demand as an adviser and lecturer on housing. In the postwar years there was a great shortage of housing and much talk of "homes for heroes". The government responded with legislation; there were housing acts in 1919, 1923 and 1924 to promote both local authority and private building. Henrietta was an acknowledged authority and spoke and wrote on housing, using statistics to prove her point. She said that by 1925, 203,019 local authority and 265,236 private houses had been built, a total of 468,255, but this was a million houses short of the need.[349] (She usually quoted statistics to the precise digit, a habit which is both arresting and amusing, and may have impressed her audiences.) Terrible overcrowding continued, and she could use telling examples of conditions she had seen herself, for instance in Sheffield where there was an estimated shortage of 20,000 houses: "In one bedroom are sleeping husband and wife, daughter aged twenty-six, and two sons aged twenty-one and nineteen. Daughter goes to bed first, then the husband and wife, and lastly the sons, who have to climb over the other beds to get to their own." In Manchester there was a "House of two bedrooms, living-room, and kitchen; tenant, wife, and four children, two males twenty-one and fourteen, two females nineteen and sixteen, all in one bedroom, and in the other bedroom a married man, his wife, and two babies."[350]

Henrietta welcomed the power given to local authorities to build houses, but warned against building one-class estates such as Dagenham. She was very critical of the layout of estates, found some of the houses very ugly, and particularly disliked the tall blocks of flats, for how could mothers protect their children if they were living five stories high? She wanted the best for poor people: "Cottages surrounded with gardens; fruit trees; open spaces; rest-arbours for the old, and playing fields for the young; flowering hedges, tree-lined roads."[351] In fact she wanted garden suburbs, or satellite garden cities. She always hoped that the Suburb would be copied throughout Britain and abroad and she was a member of the council of the Garden Cities Association.[352] She was more than ever convinced that bad housing caused crime and vice:

"... death, disease, crime, drunkenness and vice are all higher in neighbourhoods where people are badly housed; all lower in Satellite Towns, Garden Cities, Industrial Villages or Garden Suburbs, the inhabitants live in houses that can be called homes, where they can see the sky and feel the wind and the sunshine, and obtain innocent gladness from the possession and use of a garden."

She was asked to lecture by the Chadwick Trust, the Ministry of Health, the Church Congress, the London Council of Social Service, and Barnett House, Oxford. She spoke in London, and also in provincial towns: "At each town I have visited the condemned areas, the areas which ought to be condemned, the proposed sites for new cottages, studied the plans, talked to the officials, then lectured and publicly answered questions."[353] She spoke at many conferences, such as the Inter-Allied Housing Conference and the International Housing Congress. She used her knowledge of the statistics of child health to enforce her argument for better housing. In articles for the *Cornhill Magazine* she wrote:

"Sir George Newman has shown that the death-rate per 1,000 from respiratory disease, excluding phthisis, was as follows:
In homes consisting of only one room, the figure is 8.3; in two rooms, 4.8; in three room, 2.9; and where the family occupied four or more rooms, 1.2. In the northern suburbs of London the death-rate of babies under one year is 101.3 per 1,000. In the Hampstead Garden Suburb it is 11. Thus by hygienic and happy surroundings it might be possible to save almost nine in ten of the babies who die in the neighbouring districts."[354]

She continued to rejoice in the good health of the Suburb children:

"... the medical officer had weighed and measured the children at the Hampstead Garden Suburb, and found that the Suburb children were taller, heavier, and broader than those of the same age in the neighbourhood. 'It sounds like boasting,' said Mrs Barnett, 'but it is not; it is just gratitude. My grandmotherly heart beams over these lovely children.'"[355]

She could impress by referring to Queen Mary's interest in housing, and revealing that she herself knew the Queen. In an article for the *Cornhill Magazine* she described how she took the Queen to The Orchard to see the rooms for the elderly:

"'You must be very comfortable,' said our Queen to the old lady, 'in such a charming little flat.'
'Oh yes, ma'am,' said old Mrs Chandler (who is no longer on this earth), 'I like it all, and my little garden too, except the windows, but there, there, dear Mrs Barnett is such a draughty lady.'"[356]

She was made a member of the sub-committee on communal dwellings of the Advisory Housing Board of the Ministry of Health. She realised that one of the advantages of local authority house-building was that the authorities could build communal housing: "It is part of the strong individual spirit of the age that girls want to be independent, earn their own living, have freedom from parental control, and yet enjoy the pleasures of friendly converse. Young men demand similar advantages. Also the present-day reluctance to enter domestic service has caused many families to seek associated dwellings."[357]

She was convinced that a poor environment was responsible for moral degradation and criminality: "Statistics show, with painful, penetrating force, that the criminal classes come from slums, and that inhuman social surroundings give opportunities for the growth of depravity, whether it be violence, robbery, prostitution or drunkenness. Bad surroundings are the forcing-houses of the seeds of sin, and are preventable."[358]

Education

Henrietta was first interested in education when she was 17 and met the orphanage children who visited her school. When she was 18 she taught in a night-school and canvassed for the election of Miss Garrett (later Dr Garrett-Anderson), who was the first woman to be on a school board.[359] In her twenties she and Samuel opened the church school behind St Jude's and experimented with new methods. Finding the classrooms bare, she founded the Art for Schools Association. She had founded and organised the Association for Pupil Teachers into which she put so much work. And then in 1912 she founded the Henrietta Barnett School for girls (at first called the High School). She had observed American schooling and been very impressed by it. So now she felt able to speak with authority on education to the many people who came to her lectures, read her publications and listened to her broadcasts.

Henrietta's philosophy of education was much influenced by Samuel. They thought education was a lifelong process and must include the adult as well as the child. The aim of education was to draw forth the best and develop the capabilities of every single person. Vocational education, though necessary, was not nearly enough: "The claim of education is now primarily to fit a child to earn a living, and therefore he is taught to read and write and learn a trade. But if it were seen that it is equally important to fit a child to use well his leisure, many changes would be made."[360]

Henrietta interpreted education in a very broad sense and thought the home, the press, music and art, and broadcasting important, as well as schools. Her American journey had given her the opportunity to see a nation more enthusiastic for education and with a different style of teaching. Her own views became radical and progressive. She wrote an article for the *Contemporary Review* on "Co-operative Education" by which she meant cooperation between all those involved in education: children, teachers, parents, employers and the press. She liked the Montessori system for its democracy, allowing children choice, and had opened a Montessori kindergarten at the Institute in 1922 but was unable to keep it open for long because of lack of money. She believed that children should cooperate with teachers as in the Montessori schools, where the children could choose their tasks. In America children had a voice in selecting their subjects: "In some schools in America such large choice of liberty on their lessons is given to the children that they not only select their own recitations, subjects for drawing, topics for lectures, but decide which lines of study to pursue, and which to abandon."[361] When children were given choice they came willingly to school and there was no need for the school attendance officer. She found that school reports were a string of conventional platitudes and suggested that children should write their own reports!

Cooperation between teachers and parents would be fostered by more parents' meetings when teachers would explain their hopes and standards, and discuss subjects such as holidays, punishments, rewards, homework, sex facts, discipline and fees. Such meetings were unusual at the time, and "sex facts", if this means sex education, very unusual.

Employers in America and Europe know that education pays, said Henrietta, but in England this was only understood by enlightened employers such as Mr Cadbury. There was child labour in the mines, factories, fields and streets. When employers saw the advantages of educated "hands" they would clamour for more education. They could arrange shift-work to enable workers to attend classes.

Cooperation between parents and children could improve if they all came together to lectures on nature study, historical events or other subjects that would interest all ages. Children should be encouraged

HIS BIRTHRIGHT.

By JACK WALKER.

to criticise one another's work, and also to write their own plays. She wanted much better communication between everyone engaged in education, some of which has happened in the last few decades. Her desire for individual choice would have made her very critical of today's national curriculum.

In a broadcast dialogue with Lord Burnham, Henrietta said the press should do far more for education by publishing really interesting articles on the subject. People in England considered going to school a compulsory duty and the school attendance officer was required, whereas in America he was non-existent. Royalty asked for holidays to signify approval, as if to escape a day's school is sure to be a gain and a joy to every child.[362] The press could change this attitude by showing that England was falling behind such countries as America, Canada and Australia, where education was valued. The press should report again and again on education, and here she used one of her little stories: "It would be wise to remember the tale of the Counsel who, on having stated his arguments more than once, was called to account by the Judge, who interrupted him. 'You have already said that three times, Mr So and So.' 'Yes, my Lord, I know,' replied the barrister, 'but there are twelve jurymen.'"[363]

When she was young she had approved of corporal punishment, but now her opinion had changed. She wrote to her nephew: "The cane is useful to everybody at every age who has no imagination."[364] She disliked punishment and believed children should be praised when they did right. Positive reinforcement, to use a modern term. However she did not like prizes as she thought they might encourage "the baneful instinct to glory in possessions". Henrietta's educational ideas were half a century before their time. When there were complaints about child vandals on the Heath, she suggested they should make a play zone with "sand-pits, paddling pond, hills to scramble up and down, timbers for see-saws, seats not too high for small bodies, and a long open shed for shelter when it rains".[365]

She loved teaching and speaking, and at the Wembley Exhibition of 1924 she gave spontaneous talks to little groups on what they saw – reminding her of early days at the Whitechapel Gallery. Soon the little groups swelled until she had to find refuge in the cinema. In a letter to *The Times* she suggested that a gramophone recording could be played to inform people at the Exhibition, yet another of her ideas which was developed

*Plate 81
Cartoon in the Daily Graphic, 6th October 1921, ridiculing Henrietta's disapproval of nursery rhymes and fairy stories. She thought that children should be told nothing but the truth and should not be misled by fantasy.*

later. When asked what career she would choose if she could start again, she said she would teach astronomy. Surely she would have made an inspiring headmistress.

In her Shaftesbury lecture of 1921, Henrietta disapproved of giving guns, tin soldiers and tanks to children, and of competitive as opposed to cooperative games. Any nursery rhyme was nonsense and it "neither develops sympathy, stimulates imagination, nor nourishes a sense of humour." She quoted as an example of nonsense: "Hey Diddle Diddle / The Cat and the Fiddle, / The Cow jumped over the moon / The little Dog laughed to see such sport / And the dish ran away with the spoon." She also disapproved of fairy tales and nursery rhymes. In her Shaftesbury Lecture of 1891 she said that "Hey diddle diddle, the Cat and the Fiddle" was utter nonsense and children should only be taught what was truthful. She was ridiculed in the Press:

> "A Mrs Barnett does protest
> Against the Nursery Rhyme,
> As being too nonsensical
> For these enlightened times."

Despite the ridicule she continued with this opinion. In fact she did not mind if people laughed at her, so long as they took notice of her opinions. She had a sense of fun and enjoyed giving her girl pupil teachers a good time as well as moral lessons. Her commitment to moral improvement sometimes made her too serious. We have seen that she disapproved of pantomimes and the polka, and she also disliked fairs. In 1906 she tried to get the Home Secretary, Herbert Samuel, to stop Mitcham fair, which he declined to do saying that the life of the working class was so drab and the fair gave them pleasure.

Her view of nursery rhymes provoked a great deal of press comment, many letters and even cartoons (the final accolade of fame). In an article in the *Queen* she explained her view: children should be taught what is true to the facts of nature and life, and young children were very receptive and believed what they were told so should not be taught nonsense.[366] The importance of speaking truthfully to children and of answering their questions was the subject of an article by Henrietta in the *Daily Mail*.[367] When she was a child she was told "it is rude to ask questions". Adults should answer children seriously, and if they do not know the answer, say that they or other people will try to find answers and so encourage the child. She had a very matter-of-fact approach, and once admitted that she did not understand *Alice in Wonderland* at all. To her annoyance the press ignored the rest of her Shaftesbury lecture in which she said that in 1920, 2,461 children were sent to prison for one month only and 49 for a longer period, and 1,323 boys were birched. None of this was curative. She hoped that now women were on the bench and in juries there would be a reform. She also spoke of prostitution, saying that the men who used prostitutes should be socially ostracized and brothels should be closed. Rescuing girls was but a palliative: the national conscience must be raised as in some American cities.

Children could be taught to appreciate pictures: she had interested a four-year-old in a collection of Bernardino Pinturicchio. On the subject of kissing, grown-ups liked kissing children, but: "'Kiss your grandfather like a good little girl,' is said by an affectionate daughter, and the little maiden puts up her sweet, soft, flower-like face, and endures an unemotional embrace from an ancestor who has a coarse stubbly chin and smells of tobacco." In Japan kissing is unknown; it is unhygienic and gestures are used to express emotion.

Samuel had thought that elementary schools should have no holidays, but should continue all through the year. During the summer months the children would learn handicrafts, nature study, drawing, dancing, acting, the lessons to be in the playground or the park or a picture gallery.

Also children would be sent for country visits during the spring and summer, while teachers would get longer holidays and at times when they could travel.[368] Holidays should be educational, said Henrietta in a broadcast. She disapproved of idling away time on the beach, and of noisy charabanc parties. Surprisingly she did approve of the noisy carnival days in the south of France. She thought people should prepare for a holiday by reading about the place they were to visit. When building sandcastles, the children could be helped to name the water as the Thames or the Severn and so it could be a time of learning. Some people would pursue a hobby or take an important book to read, though it was disappointing if we only accomplished half what we set out to do. This reminded her that

> "The tale of the continental sausage maker aptly illustrates this point. He made such excellent rabbit sausages that the supply of rabbits fell short, so he added horse-flesh. On this the customers complained, and he had to meet the judge, and in defence stated he supplied fifty to fifty in his sausages.
> 'What do you mean by fifty to fifty?' asked the judge; to which the vendor replied:
> 'What I mean is fifty to fifty equals one rabbit to one horse.'"[369]

In "*The Servant as Citizen*" Henrietta said servants should be encouraged to attend political meetings and listen to lectures on local history; this would make them recognise their rights as citizens. In the home:

> "A daily paper might be taken solely for the kitchen use, a bookshelf kept in the pantry — the books chosen to suit low standards with powers of progression. The servant's individual tastes — music, gardening, art, animal pets, or cycling — and her personal convenience should be studied, so that she could make her own plans and feel secure about her engagements. Labour-saving appliances must be provided and greater use made of temporary help so that her hours of recreation should not be followed by the burden of extra work."[370]

Did Henrietta ever put her radical ideas into practice? A Montessori school, with Olive Smee as headmistress, was opened in the Club House in 1913. When the Club House became a military hospital in March 1916 the whole building was requisitioned to provide 46 beds for injured soldiers. The Montessori school was moved to Arcade House, and later bought by King Alfred School.[371] In 1922 Henrietta started a Montessori kindergarten in the Institute, but it did not last long on account of lack of money.[372] As a governor of the Henrietta Barnett School, she took a part in choice of staff. However Sophie Bryant, headmistress of North London Collegiate School, had the real authority in choice of the headmistress and other staff and to decide the syllabus and organization of the School. It turned out to be very like the other good grammar schools for girls, so Henrietta's radical ideas bore little fruit.

Barnett House

Henrietta established Barnett House as one of the memorials to Samuel and it was opened in 1914. It was in a large redbrick building at the corner of Broad and Turl Street. It was a busy place with lectures and conferences and students mixing with people from trade unions and from Oxfordshire villages, as they all used the library. Henrietta listed its work and aims:

> "(1) A centre for economic information
> (2) A distributor, by lectures, conferences, books, and pamphlets of economic information.

(3) A school of social training.

(4) A bureau of advice for the settlement movement.

(5) A home for the W E A and the Councils of Social Service.

(6) A sort of aunt to Village Institutes.

(7) A general servant to those who are eager to help forward the work of social reform (or reconstruction, as it is now the fashion to call it).

This, then, is the work Barnett House has set itself to do. To garner with one hand; to scatter with the other."[373]

In 1920 Henrietta decided they should add a social research department.[374] She thought they should research the effect of lowering the age of pensions on the labour market, the influence on homemaking of factory work for girls, the result of equal pay for equal work, the influence on families of soldiers' widows' pensions, how far paying women to look after their children had been met with conscientious responsibility, or whether the result had been to create a large number of indolent women. This seems as much like an expression of Henrietta's views as a list of topics for research. She was concerned that benefits were paid to all who qualified, irrespective of character, so that in some cases they encouraged indolence and to stop this she wanted individual assessment of applicants.[375] Social research became the most important part of the work of Barnett House.

As with all her other enterprises, Henrietta helped to raise the necessary money. She wrote to Jane Addams:

"The hope that the Carnegie Trust, on your side, might give substantially towards the lectureships on <u>modern</u> economic (& social) conditions, wh. we are very desirous to start in Sept. at Barnett House – So as to catch the men of all sorts who, of all ages, in their war broken careers will begin again then to study in Oxford. What is wanted there is £25,000, towards wh. a friend has given £2,000 & my £500 will show you I think the scheme sound and <u>needed</u>."[376]

Barnett House soon became very well known as a centre for research and attracted good lecturers such as Arthur Greenwood, who became a Labour minister, and R H Tawney and G M Trevelyan, both famous historians. The subjects ranged from Rural Administration and Welfare to Nationalisation. Conferences were held on Public Ownership and Control of the Liquor Trade and on the Industrial Section of the League of Nations, matters close to Henrietta's heart. Advice and training was given to men and women who wanted to take up social work. It was also a centre for the League of Nations Union, Oxfordshire Women's Institutes, Village Clubs and Workers Educational Association, and through them organised educational and social work throughout the county. Henrietta must have been very pleased by the way Barnett House was developing.[377]

The first president of Barnett House was the master of Balliol, and Lord Bryce was the Visitor; both were old friends of the Barnetts and presumably they were chosen by Henrietta. She must have received all the Reports, and probably read many of them, and no doubt she kept in touch with developments and she usually spoke at the Annual Meeting. It must have pleased her that when Oxford University started an Economics degree the authorities sought the advice of Barnett House.[378]

However in 1928 she became very dissatisfied with Barnett House. In a letter to Mr Catchpool, the sub-warden at Toynbee Hall, she wrote: "the B. House folk are dead in their self satisfaction & so don't move."[379] She had many ideas for development: a Poor Man's Lawyer Service, Travellers Club,

Rotary Club, Housing and Town Planning Study Group and Exhibitions and the Oxford branch of the Children's Country Holiday Fund should all be established there – urgently. She also thought that Oxford University should have a Department of Town Planning and Architecture.[380] She tried to get Mr Catchpool appointed as secretary of Barnett House, but was unsuccessful. It seems she was on a high after the Coming of Age celebrations. Today, Barnett House is the home of the Social Research and Social Administration departments of Oxford University, a fitting memorial to Samuel and a fulfilment of Henrietta's wishes.

In October 1920, Oxford decided to admit women graduates to degrees and Queen Mary received the first honorary degree ever conferred on a woman. After the ceremony at the Sheldonian Theatre, Henrietta was delighted that the Queen came to visit Barnett House. Henrietta's friendship with the Queen increased, as did her admiration: "At public occasions when the toast of 'the King' is given, I always add in a loud voice, 'And the Queen.' Some who hear glare at me, some smile, but no one has yet rebuked my audacity, and in their hearts I know they all echo, for those of us who love her beautiful character both pray for, and drink to, her happiness."[381]

God is Larger than the Creeds

From November 1908 when the Established Church and the Free Church held services in a hut on alternate Sundays, the tradition arose of holding joint services every November, using St Jude's and the Free Church in alternate years. In November 1914 the Reverend Basil Bourchier asked Henrietta to write a message to be read to the congregation to include "woman's thought". She wrote in terms of what her husband would have said had he lived "in the midst of this sad and cruel war," but surely these are her own thoughts:

> "He undoubtedly would have welcomed the union of feeling that the War has produced, breaking down barriers between rich and poor, tutored and ignorant, Tory and Radical, Established and Free Churchmen, who have all united to show their love for their country and their detestation of the principle that might is right … I think my husband would now warn us to beware of indulging in the sin of hate. 'For what shall it profit a man if he shall gain the whole world and lose his own soul?'"[382]

During the war many clergymen served as army chaplains so a few women were allowed to preach, and Henrietta was the first woman accredited as a lay preacher by the Bishop of London. She preached at St Botolph's, Aldgate, in October 1916, St Jude's in the Suburb in November 1918, and at Portslade Church, Sussex, in April 1919.[383] One of her sermons in St Jude's was on 'Humility', rather a surprising subject for Henrietta. Another sermon was on 'Angels': "I saw a very fashionable, superior-looking congregation before me – the kind of people who are spiritually conceited. I was dressed very quietly indeed. I did not go into the pulpit, because I don't like to be above people; but I stood before the congregation, and, raising my great voice, announced as my text, 'And the ass it was who saw the Angel of the Lord.'"

In June 1921 the Convocation of Canterbury decreed that women must only preach to women and children and not to a general congregation. Henrietta was incensed: "Only to preach to children & to their own sex … how ludicrous, just after the War when women were permitted to share the work & all the danger, that the clergy should declare them unfit to speak on the deepest things of life to men."[384] She suggested that if sex mattered so much, men should only preach to men. She hoped the Church would be reformed: "Sooner or later the Church is sure to adopt the ways of common-sense, but it will be after she has once again lost power by delay."[385]

In June 1923 she gave a sermon on board the *SS Arcadian* on a trip to see the midnight sun, and probably she preached to men and women on her many cruises where she was outside the limits of any convocation's powers. At the request of Mr Marnham she gave a sermon to children at the Baptist church in Heath Street, Hampstead.[386] She was a much better speaker than most of the clergy but was forced to give up.

In 1923 St Jude's Whitechapel was closed and then pulled down and the congregation was united with St Mary Matfelon in Whitechapel High Street. There was no need for St Jude's as the area had become predominantly Jewish, and the church organ was given to St Jude-on-the-Hill at Henrietta's suggestion. The Bishop of London asked her to give an address to mark the occasion. In her address she appealed to the people of the Suburb to remember the sorrows of the slum-dwellers in the East End; she feared the comfort of Suburb life might make them forget the poor. Madame Clara Butt sang and no doubt filled the church with her powerful voice. The Bishop of London had progressive views and sympathised with Henrietta in her desire to preach. In 1926, after visiting her, he wrote her a letter beginning "Dear Friend and Clergywoman"![387] Henrietta usually replied to him as "Your affectionate clergywoman".[388]

The film producer Cecil B de Mille was impressed by Henrietta's religious views and in 1927 he asked her to attend a special showing and comment on his film *King of Kings*. She saw it again in the studio, where it was slowed down and shown with pauses so she could study it and make comments and suggestions, many of which were carried out in the cutting-room before its public release.[389] She liked films, but thought they could be a force for bad as well as good: "The cinema has a bad influence when deeds of violence are treated as bravery or grown-ups are ridiculed."[390]

Was Henrietta still as critical of the Church of England as she had been in her youth? To judge from a speech she gave at Barnett House in 1920, she was just as iconoclastic as ever:

> "The first time I met Mr Asquith was at a small dinner given by Dr Bridges at Wimbledon, when Mr Frederick Harrison, Mr Asquith, and my husband were the only guests. Mr Asquith and me (he and I are nearly the same age, and were then both about 27) left to return by train, and the South Western Railway, behaving as we all know it does from Jerome's story of 'Three Men in a Boat', if not from our own experience – (laughter) – we had a long time to wait, and I recall the conversation as we walked up and down that long, lean platform at Raynes Park. It was on the place political economy should fill in education, and I, believing then, as I believe now, that the majority of men want to be good, to do right, and to humanise justice, argued that the most powerful preachers of the future would be the political economists, who would by study and experience learn the laws of God as they work through action and consequence, and so guide and control, not only individuals, but corporate conduct towards goodness and happiness.
>
> 'In short', said Mr Asquith, 'you propose that the Ten Commandments and the Sermon on the Mount should be translated into terms of political economy and direct mankind?'
>
> 'Yes,' I replied, 'for people think that Moses was too fond of negations to arouse enthusiasm, and the Holy Spirit of the Sermon on the Mount too far off the present condition of civilisation to be practical. What is wanted is a modern rendering of them both, and then to democratise the messages.'"

Her conversation with Asquith was in 1878, and it is apparent that she still held the same views in 1920 when she recalled it.[391] Marion Paterson observed in her *Quasi Autobiography* that Henrietta thought the Bible "ought to be brought up-to-date and re-written in the light of scientific knowledge".[392] She thought there was a deep instinct in mankind to reach in thought the realms of the Spirit. God was ideal good, which is at the root of all forms of religion – the Vedas, the songs of Confucius, the hymns to Zeus, the gods of Olympus and Christianity.[393]

Henrietta kept a small statue of the Buddha on the centre of her mantelpiece; she may have been given it when they visited Sri Lanka on their world tour. In 1928 she gave Suburb residents a New Year greeting, published in the *Institute News*:

"… the best wish that I can send to my neighbours … is that we may all realise with dynamic force the spiritual basis of life. Not necessarily do I advise more attendances at places of worship, for each human soul knows what nourishes him or poisons him. The realisation that I refer to is deeper than can be reached by forms or ceremonies, more subtle than can be obtained by education, more individual than can be transferred by another."[394]

She thought a sense of mystery was important, such mysteries as conception, growth and death. "The unknowable is indispensable to the finite creature with infinite longing."

When the Archbishop of Canterbury spoke at Henrietta's funeral, he acknowledged the unorthodox character of her Christianity:

"Her ardent spirit may not always have found its natural expression in the symbols of faith and worship which are a help and strength to others. But most certainly her faith was that God Himself is the Eternal Source and Perfection of all the ideals which filled her soul, and she found in Him the inspiration of all the endeavours by which she sought to realise them. To her the Good, the True, the Beautiful were not mere abstractions. They were the very life of God. Her loyalty to them was her conscious worship of Him."[395]

Broadcasting

At the beginning of the century Henrietta had been enthusiastic about motor-cars, and at the beginning of the wireless age she bought a set and enjoyed listening. She knew that "Words, of course, are the most powerful drug used by mankind". (Kipling)

Marion Paterson observed that

"She was a constant & untiring listener; the Talks on Science & ethical subjects especially appealing to her. The News, the Sunday Evening Service were never missed; sports occasionally. The 'First News' was a daily item in her life; and although she usually switched off at 'sport' that too was occasionally listened to for 'I must hear what it is that other people like.' … 'Plays she enjoyed. Music? Well, she listened to 'Music for the Ordinary Listener' eager as she always was for instruction …"[396]

She realised the great educational potential of the wireless and she was so keen that others should share in the benefits of listening that she donated a "three valve set of wireless" to the Institute in 1923.[397] She was first asked to broadcast in 1925, and this talk must have been an instant success because she gave three further talks in the same year. Evidently she enjoyed the experience:

"Visits to Savoy Hill gave her much pleasure, where Mr Stobart, & his staff of young ladies, welcomed her. Miss Mary Somerville recalls how the Dame always called me 'grandchild'. I was much attracted by her, particularly because she seemed so extremely modern & moved along with my generation. She used, though, to implore me to hold on to the graciousness of the older generation."[398]

Her talks were on her wide variety of interests and always carefully prepared: "Dame Henrietta broadcasted fifteen times – preparing her talks with the greatest care, regarding them as important, if not more so, than sermons preached in church."

In 1925 she gave four talks:

> March 23 *Children with special reference to the State Children's Association and the Children's Country Holiday Fund*
> July 1 *The House I Want as My Home*
> July 20 *The Art of Taking Holidays* (published in *Matters that Matter*)
> Oct 6 *Discussion with Sir Oliver Lodge on Matters that Matter*

She was asked to give a reading of Browning's poetry: "Oh! The joy and privilege, but I <u>refused</u> because of my plan with you." She had promised Harold Lacey that she would attend a meeting on the Institute.[399]

In 1926 she gave six talks:

> March 4 *The Ideal Home*
> June 6 *Discussion with the Bishop of Gibraltar on The Union of the Eastern and Western Churches*
> June 29 Poetry *Readings of Browning and Tennyson*
> July 27 *Discussion with Lord Burnham on Education by the Press*
> Sept 12 *Religion in Poetry*
> Oct 5 *Two Bunker Hills*

After 1926 she was invited less often, possibly because of BBC policy, or perhaps at the age of 76 she seemed too elderly.

> July 6 1927 *Village Life in France*
> March 12 1928 *The Ideal Home Exhibition*
> July 1 1928 *A reading from "In Memoriam"*
> March 29 1931 *An Appeal for Skilled Employment and Apprentices*
> (One broadcast is omitted from this list)

A discussion on the League of Nations between Dame Henrietta Barnett and Sir Gilbert Murray was prepared for the autumn of 1925, but the Locarno Peace Pact intervened and the discussion had to be abandoned.

"As a Speaker it was said: the voice of the Lady of the Suburb, is as near perfection as is possible for microphone purposes. She seems in a fair way to become a Wireless 'Star'." Unfortunately no recordings have survived. Henrietta greatly valued the opportunity to broadcast: she thought it would create peace in the world, and was a wonderful means of spreading education. "I count it an awe-inspiring privilege to broadcast. There is a celebrated staircase in Rome which the faithful mount on their knees. That is what I feel I should like to do when I go to the Studio in Savoy Hill; mentally and spiritually I do, for only an attitude of prayer can make one fit to speak to thousands of one's fellow mortals."[400] Despite her old-fashioned moralising, she knew how to interest audiences and could make them laugh.

Plate 82 (opposite) Henrietta with Sir Oliver Lodge, broadcasting a discussion from Savoy Hill, the BBC studio, in 1925.

Health and Holidays

"And what should they know of England who only England know."

(Kipling)

According to Marion Paterson, "The 1920s were years of foreign trips; a few weeks in each being set aside for a 'real holiday' i.e. a sea-voyage, a new country, a winter of sunshine & flowers. Two such holidays were taken in 1923. A winter & a summer one. The winter one to Madeira, sailing from Southampton, in the RMSP *Arlanze* on 5th January, reaching Funchal 11th January."

Henrietta wrote this account:

"The voyage has been a week rich in interest, beauty and experience. After leaving Corunna we skirted the coast & enjoyed seeing the many headlands, islands & mountains which were all girded with the dashing surf. At Vigo alas! It really rained, & the interesting town was veiled in mist, & grey clouds, beautiful to sketch but rendering going about impossible.

Lisbon was reached, as planned, 8am on Tuesday. The launches took the passengers still further up the great Tagus, landing us in the heart of the town. We saw in a leisurely way, the streets, the churches, the public buildings. The shops, the Zoological Gardens, & the handsome, often picturesquely clothed Portuguese people.

We lunched with a fellow passenger, who took us to a 'Picturesque' Restaurant where the food & the wine encouraged one's greediness beyond one's hunger.

The first glimpse of Madeira (at dawn) saw both Miss Paterson & me rejoicing in the sight of its wondrous mountains, its gorges, ravines & vegetation.

Lady Rhondda had left the fashionable Hotel & had found a simple one, just as beautifully placed on a ledge of a stair of mountain where we joined her.

Sir David & Lady Ferrier (old friends) were also in Madeira, so with old, & new, friends there were gay tea parties, dinner parties; & many excursions up the steep, hilly roads, accompanied by botanists, by government officials & by hospitable residents … and beauty all around.

I sketch a great deal, & Lady Rhondda, Miss Haif (Lady Rhondda's sister) & I laughingly compete for the award of our productions as the *"chef d'ouvre "*[sic] but no brush can convey the colours of the mass of flowers or the rain that both blurs & reveals; or the mystery surrounding distant islands, or the gorgeous crimsons, yellows, violets, greens & purples of the sunrise & the sunset.

One morning we received a telegram 'I have an order to take you over Blandys Wine Store'.

It was a most picturesque old Warehouse – & in it we were told all about the making of the Malmsey, Madeira & the Tinto wines. Shown the pipe. The Vats, the casks, & the heating chambers, which have now taken the place of the old time journey to & from the West Indies. We tasted brands of 1779, 1870 … & also were given a sip of the grape juice before 'treatment'.

Miss Paterson & I were disappointed to have to give up a trip to Teneriffe & beautiful Arucas (time not allowing a visit to the Canary Isles) so I determined to see as much of this island as time and strength allowed.

Our first move was to the great Hotel, Reids. Here I made arrangements for rooms at their lowest tariff 24/- a day, with many extras; so I was surprised to be given a large room on the first floor, with a private balcony, & containing every luxury of lighting, water etc.

I was even more astonished when on asking for the bill to be told that the Board of Directors requested that I would accept to our being their guests during our four days at the hotel as they felt it 'an honour to entertain so distinguished a lady.'

We also spent some days at the Monti Palace Hotel, 1900 feet up the mountain, amid unforgettable beauty, making me wonder how anyone could stay in the dust & noise of Funchal, rather than in this crisp air, amid silent nature – the only sound the comfortable gobble of a turkey or a distant cock crow.

Miss Hutcheon (a member of the Assyrian mission) was the only other resident, at that time, in the Hotel; a sketcher, a photographer, & a most interesting companion. Many were the talks she & I had over the log & pine cone fire in the evenings.

Before leaving Madeira we accepted the kind hospitality of Mr & Mrs Muller, spending a few days with them in their charming house.

It was indeed a holiday enriched by beauty, rested by the absence of work & responsibility & widened by acquaintances & learning something of the Portuguese problems of Island government."[401]

Henrietta's account ends here, but Marion continued to describe holidays:

"Norway, to see the midnight sun was the summer trip.

A fortnight of comfortable travel, in the R.M.S.P. "Arcadian"; void of the drawback of needing to seek an hotel in the towns visited.

On most days there were land excursions, but Mrs Barnett nearly always chose the quieter pleasure of staying on board, & sketching the unfolding beauty as the ship steamed through the fiords.

At Trondheim a wireless message awaited her, from Mrs Pederson (her husband, head of the Town-planning being absent in Christianse) saying she would meet us.

She, & several others, gave us a warm welcome – & showed us much of Trondheim, not only its building plans but also the University; the Cathedral, & much else, including a visit to her own house where we were feasted on delicious coffee & every variety of cake.

Later there was luncheon at the Britannic Hotel where Mr Holmgrunne (President of the Architectural Society) made Mrs Barnett a very complimentary speech. Nor did this end their hospitality, for everyone of our kind entertainers drove down to the Quay crossing over in the tender, & not leaving us until they had seen us safe aboard the "Arcadian".

At Bergen Dr Geirsvold (Inspector of Health) accompanied by his wife, & the municipal architects met us & Mrs Barnett was shown community houses, schools, the Leprosy Hospital, & many other of Norway's methods of solving the housing problem."

In the winter of 1924, Henrietta suffered another depression and wrote from Funchal, Madeira, to Jane Addams:

"For four months I have been poorly, much worried over a few wrong-notioned people who got onto my large staff – & so tired that every action was an effort. Two doctors say that I have no sort of organic trouble, but 73 & more work than 43 ought to do results in nerve exhaustion; so when poor Fanny was well on the road to her recovery, I just slipped down to Southampton, & got on board one of the Royal Mails, & after 5 days slow steaming over an oily sea, reached here on Wednesday."[402]

The light and brilliant colours of Madeira helped her out of depression, and inspired her to take up oil painting.

In the winter of 1925 they were invited to stay with Mrs Cochrane at her Italian home. They sailed on the *Johan De Witt*, a Dutch ship, to Genoa, where there was a freak snowfall. After a four-hour train journey they arrived at Rezzoli. Henrietta's bedroom overlooked the Bay of Spezia – the house was perched on a hill 150ft up: "This is the most beautiful place I have ever been in. I am very unwell, but crawl about the garden, & can paint, & my great windows give me unending joys … We shall stay here until my heart behaves, surrounded by <u>every</u> care."[403] There were eight guests including the Bishop of Gibraltar and his wife Mrs Grieg. Christmas Day was beautifully celebrated, although Henrietta was too poorly to get up until tea-time. On Sunday the Bishop held a service in the private chapel and they were joined by English visitors from the hotel at Lerici. Another day they had their picnic luncheon in the courtyard of a hotel,

> "… the landlord adding soup & good wine to the dainty provisions brought out by Mrs Cochrane". After lunch they sketched the landscape. Mrs Waterfield, who lived in a nearby palazzo, was very interested in the Fascists and argued that Mussolini was aiming at dictatorship. This Italian holiday lasted seven weeks![404] But her health was still a problem and she decided she must not give long speeches: "Short talks must be my rule now. I am <u>ill</u> with nervous exhaustion after a long one & the colour of this paper for hours."[405]

In the winter of 1926/27 they travelled on a P&O liner to the south of France to stay with one of the Toynbee residents at the Hotel Annonciata in Menton. Henrietta got very painful rheumatism in her right knee. On returning home Henrietta still felt ill and consulted Dr Ensor who diagnosed her usual complaint – "nerve exhaustion wh. has produced severe neuralgia. He commands bed rest, silence, warmth, & no decisions".

But her illness continued throughout 1927, and in August while staying in Hove she found she could not walk or stand for long so she took to sitting out in her bath chair. While in Hove she consulted Dr Helen Boyle, who insisted on a treatment that would build up her reserve of nervous energy.[406]

In March 1928 Henrietta and Marion set forth on a sea trip to the Mediterranean for a short holiday in Naples. A friend of Henrietta, Mrs Cochrane, stayed with them as Henrietta's guest. They were disturbed by noisy traffic, except Marion who was used to it because of "her life on the Chelsea Embankment". In 1929 Henrietta and Marion were planning to join a tour to Holland with 25 people, organised through the Institute. Marion said: "She was a happy traveller, never fussing over trivial discomforts; never sea sick, only disappointed if the seas were too rough for her to be allowed on deck."

Chapter 26

The Suburb in the 1920s

Her Suburb was famous and universally acknowledged as a great success. Henrietta as the honorary manager and a director continued to play the most important part in decision-making and the other Trust members were usually in accord with her. Gerald Balfour, the older brother of the pre-war prime minister, was the chairman of the Trust from 1921 to 1928. In 1929 Captain Reiss became chairman and formed a good relationship with Henrietta. She said he was: "… a brilliant Balliol man, a lawyer and above all, a man of unusual public spirit. She greatly valued his judgement and his co-operation in her enterprises".[407] Reiss was not so generous in describing Henrietta. He said that compared with her young days, her defects had become more marked:

> "The breezy self-confidence had developed into a despotic masterfulness. She did not brook opposition to her views, though she criticized others freely when occasion arose. This made it no easy task for those working with her. But one forgave the faults (and sometimes the violent abuse) because they were so small compared with her essential merits."[408]

Henrietta's great administrative skills were at their height. She preferred to be honorary secretary rather than chairman of her many committees, then she could prepare the agenda and her arguments in advance. With such careful preparation she would carry the day. "What's the good of argifying?" (Kipling)

The other very significant person was Colonel Thomson, who was secretary to the Trust from 1922 to 1936. In a letter of condolence to Marion Paterson he wrote admiringly of Henrietta:

> "In vision and perception of method Mrs Barnett was the leader. No opposition turned her aside from a policy on which she had decided. Her strength of will was helped by a gift of cogent argument which enabled her almost to dominate Board meetings. She had a magnificent and persuasive voice and a very unexpected turn of phrase. On occasions, when she could not persuade her fellow directors to take her view, the meeting would present a certain liveliness, and the proceedings could be called neither dull nor brief.
>
> The directors who guided the Garden Suburb Trust through its early difficulties were chosen by Henrietta from men possessed of the same ideals of social service and of the housing needs of the poorer classes as herself. Nor did she neglect to seek out business ability, which was essential to the success of her scheme.
>
> Later on, when the Suburb was completely planned and approaching full development, the management became more concerned with the preserving of the beauty and the character which she had already created, and with the new problems which the war of 1914–1918 had brought about.

Advancing years made it difficult for her to appreciate the changed conditions of social life & of finance. Consequently she found herself more frequently opposed: but still her proposals, though startling, were often proved to be sound, & were eventually adopted.

Every Board meeting entailed for Dame Henrietta much preparatory work. She reviewed all relevant information about every subject on the Agenda, & she made notes of what she intended to say, her hand on every administrative detail – the lesser matters did not escape her. Almost every day she had lengthy interviews with her various officials. Her capacity for work seemed unlimited; for it must be remembered that the Garden Suburb was one among her many activities …

Such talks were seldom confined to business. She delighted in digressing into what she called 'by-ways'. Religion, politics, social conditions, ethics, books & art were some of the subjects she loved to speak about & in every one of them she uttered original opinions. She showed little patience with the dogmas of the churches; conventional politics, or generally accepted traditions.

At times her conversation would become extremely personal. For example she would have no hesitation in remarking on her visitor's appearance, complimentary, or otherwise, according to the end she had in view for the moment.

Often it was disconcerting to be suddenly asked whether you loved your children. Still more embarrassing when the question was followed by whether you <u>liked</u> them & why you liked them. Probably these personalities come from a desire to probe the character of people who worked with her, for she would watch their effect.

Every conversation with Dame Henrietta was full of variety; & there must have been few minds which were not sharpened by an encounter with hers."[409]

Despite her bossiness, Henrietta had a very good relationship with her colleagues, but she was not fond of the Trust architect, John Soutar, who took over from Unwin in 1915. Writing to Harold Lacey in 1929, she said she hated and despised Mr Soutar at present because he was throwing his weight in favour of a cinema against the vote of Reiss and herself for workmen's dwellings. Her plan was for three-storey flats with two-storey shops in front, to be built and managed by the London Labourers Dwellings Society. She was very distressed when she failed to secure the site, for few empty sites remained. The cinema was built and named "The Orpheum". How pleased she would be if she knew that it had been demolished and replaced by Birnbeck Court, flats for old people with wardens, communal sitting-room, and entertainments.[410]

A big change took place in the management of the Suburb in 1919. Vivian, who organized the co-partnerships, resigned from the Trust. Henceforth the Trust had little control of building and the character of the New Suburb, as the eastern extension from the Institute was called, completely changed. The co-partnerships had to raise more money and their approach became commercial. The new houses were bigger and there was no possibility of Henrietta's poor people finding any place. There were few communal facilities, fewer backlands and allotments and less public open space. House frontages were in straight lines and Unwin's delightful groupings seem to have been forgotten. This was not Henrietta's beautiful green golden scheme.

In 1926/27 the government drove a link from the Great North Road (A1) to the Barnet bypass (Falloden Way/Lyttleton Road) along the line of Addison Way, through the centre of the extended Suburb. Northway and Southway reflect the original scheme, but the Market Square, which would have provided a central focus for the area, had to be abandoned; the differently sited Market Place on Falloden Way is a poor substitute.[411]

Henrietta's big disappointment was that she never succeeded in building the low-rental flats for working-class families. She designated a plot, the space where Holyoake Walk is built. The Trust members were well aware of this and when she died they decided to buy the plot to carry out her wishes as a memorial – only to find that the plot had already been sold. It is quite clear that Henrietta continued to keep her grip on the Trust until her health failed in the last year, and that she worked to her limit on Trust matters.

She saw that the Suburb needed playing fields for all the young people interested in sport. She became a member of the committee of the Greater London Playing Fields Association and so helped to secure the 25 acres for the Lyttleton Playing Fields.[412]

The Institute

Henrietta made the Institute a priority from its beginning until her death. As she grew older she became more attached to it; indeed Mr Lacey, the principal, called it "the darling of her old age". She always had very ambitious plans for expansion and wanted to make it a first-rate centre of adult education for this area of north London, just as Toynbee had been a beacon in East London. In 1928 when she wrote *The Story of the Growth of Hampstead Garden Suburb 1907–1928* she gave 17 of the 77 pages to the Institute, and only two pages to the Club House. She compared it to Greek cultural institutions and hoped to share her enthusiasm for high culture with all the citizens of the Suburb.

She planned a very broad curriculum, based on the curriculum of Toynbee Hall. There was always a University Extension class for more serious students, a literary course, classes in French, German, Italian, Spanish and English as a foreign language (the subject which has attracted the most students in recent years), and classes in bookkeeping, shorthand, mathematics, and household science – cookery, dressmaking and tailoring, costume design, first aid and nursing. Commercial courses in book-keeping, economics, shorthand and mathematics were popular and for children there were play hours and classes in drama, opera, and needlework. The strongest department was arts and crafts, where a very wide range was taught: pattern design, illumination and lettering, fashion design, leatherwork, modelling, pottery, raffia work, basket-making, rug-making, furniture repair and carpentry. The middle-class housewives of the Suburb seem to have spent their time playing tennis and learning arts and crafts, a very agreeable lifestyle which must have made them relaxed and happy mothers.

Besides the classes, there were numerous societies, mainly cultural. There were societies for philosophy, science, drama, opera and music and the choral and orchestral societies. "What I value, as much as anything, are the Societies," said Henrietta, and she ran two societies herself. During the war the societies had lapsed or attendance became very poor; this was attributed to the difficulty of getting servants and the long hours women spent shopping, as the usual deliveries stopped. Henrietta reconstituted the Child Study Society in 1921 and it was run by a committee with three members elected by parents, one each from the Henrietta Barnett School, the Kindergarten and the Montessori School, and Henrietta in the chair. The lectures they chose for the first term were on French Children, Music for Children, Economical Food, Children Governing Themselves and Thoughts on Character Training, all subjects close to Henrietta's heart.

She always had fresh ideas for societies to improve the lot of the poor. She recruited about twenty men to the "Why" Society. The object of this society was to pinpoint certain social problems and do something to solve them. In 1929 Catchpool, the sub-warden of Toynbee Hall, gave a talk on Prisons, and probably asked the men to volunteer to visit prisons. There was also a women's "Why" society, a dozen or so women willing to work in the East End.[413]

Henrietta tried to start good citizenship and astronomy societies but was unsuccessful. How delighted she would have been by the success of the present Astronomical Society. However her Novel Reading Club was very popular from the start in 1924. Members were welcomed to the house at 1 South Square by Marion Paterson and coffee was served "with Mary's far-famed cakes". Mary Blade, Henrietta's cook, made cakes for the Institute socials as well as for Henrietta's many tea-parties. At the first meeting of the Novel Reading Club, she explained the aim of the club:

> "Our aim is greater knowledge of each other's minds. People know each others' looks, circumstances, character. We aim at knowing each other's minds. It is not a class. There is no teacher; we are each of us to teach, to learn and all of us to study. The plan is for each of us to buy the same edition of the book selected (in a cheap edition) to read at home and to mark the passages that strike us."[414]

After reading a few novels, they studied the biography of one of the authors, and in the summer would visit the places to which he had made special reference. They read both classics and modern books. Every third or fourth evening was set aside for each member to read a passage from one of their favourite authors. "To close the evening Dame Henrietta would sum up most delightfully with her usual humour, & generally with sly hits at anything with which she had not agreed." From 1935 Henrietta was too ill to preside, attendance declined and the society ended with her death.

The Music School under Rosabel Watson had continued during the war despite the shortage of male voices, though as with the other courses they were functioning with a deficit. Rosabel had a poor opinion of Suburb people:

> "My own private opinion is that the majority of the Residents are utterly indifferent to the Institute and don't in the least care for, nor appreciate its benefits. Perhaps they might do so if these benefits were withdrawn. With a very few dear exceptions they are the most commonplace and unresponsive set of people I have ever met or worked with."[415]

The Play and Pageant Union and the Amateur Operatic Society flourished after the war, and made good use of the stage built in 1923 in the Institute hall: "We are very proud of our Dramatic efforts & our Play & Pageant Union is an interesting attempt in community effort, designing & making the scenery & the dress as well as producing & acting the plays. They have too an open air theatre in Oak Wood, where a play written by one of the members is performed every summer."[416] The beautiful posters painted to advertise the plays show the skill and enthusiasm of the people who lived in the Suburb in those days.

There were between 9,000 and 10,000 people living in the Suburb in 1919, and there were 810 students at the Institute. The number of students had steadily increased, despite the "competitive attractions" of the wireless and the cinema and the fact that "the greater facilities for locomotion make going into town easy". Henrietta added, "when we have arranged for an omnibus to the Central Square there will be even more students". This idea would take half a century to realise!

All these classes and society meetings were taking place in the single Institute building and a variety of "hideous huts"; more buildings were needed. Moreover, Henrietta was determined to have space for a school of domestic economy and an art school. The Trust

Plate 83 (opposite) Women potters digging clay. There were pottery classes at the Institute and many kilns in houses.

had paid for the first building, but now money had to be found from other sources. In 1918 the Institute council was converted into a company so it could sell shares and raise money.

At this time Henrietta's lawyer, Mr Buckland, had legal difficulties with another solicitor, Mr Winearls. Henrietta advised Buckland as to how to deal with Winearls: "As to Mr Winearls, I think the best thing is to bounce. Can you not take Sir Rbt. Morant, Lord Lytton or me to bounce him? He must be told that a large number of people are really interested and perhaps he ought to be shown Mr Lutyens' great picture. I do not know him but there comes a moment when bounce is an admirable weapon."[417] An interesting insight into her determination and methods.

Lutyens was asked to draw up plans for the future expansion of the Institute, and the total cost of the three buildings planned was estimated at £42,000. In 1920 Middlesex County Council granted £20,000 to the school building fund, but the council would not grant any money for adult education. Henrietta gave £5,000 of her personal money, and used her skill as a fundraiser to get more from her rich friends and acquaintances and from the City guilds. She formed an Institute committee known as BEEC (Building, Educational and Endowment Committee). Marion Paterson kept the BEEC accounts for many years.[418] Its inaugural meeting was held at Lady St Helier's house in 1920. It was addressed by Henrietta: "What we want is an educational centre where besides housing the School, the Classes, Societies, Clubs, the Arts & Drama, people will be united also in social pleasure creating the bond of peace which is friendship & sharing what we value most, our knowledge."[419]

Plate 84
Lutyens' plan was to extend the Institute on both sides. In 2011 extensions were built, but the architect, Hopkins, did not follow Lutyens' style, to the dismay of many residents.

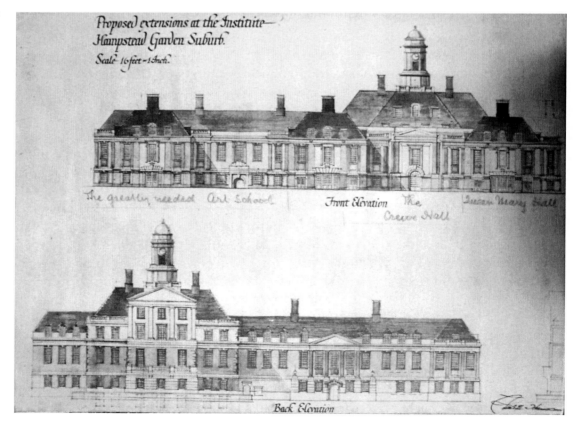

Plate 85 (opposite) Queen Mary with Henrietta after opening the Queen Mary Hall of the Institute, 1924. Marion Paterson is on Henrietta's left.

A drawing-room meeting at the mansion of a lady was the way Henrietta had launched her successful campaigns to raise money in the past. Queen Mary's great interest in the Institute must have encouraged wealthy upper-class people to participate and be generous, and people such as Lord Leverhulme and George Cadbury each gave about £1,000. While she was in America in 1920 Henrietta appealed to Lord Rothschild to give money, but in vain. It was very difficult to raise money in the postwar world, even though she would explain that this institute was to be a model so that other suburbs when they were built would be given institutes.[420] Retrenchment was the order of the day; in 1921/22 the Geddes axe fell, cutting public expenditure, and this policy continued through the 1920s. The war and high taxation had sliced into the fortunes of the wealthy, so private giving was much reduced. Despite these problems, Henrietta eventually raised sufficient money to build the south wing to house the school. Queen Mary came to open the new building and it was named after her.

Friends and supporters helped the Institute with precious gifts. George Watts, the great artist who had often helped Henrietta with her pupil-teachers, gave three copies of his own paintings, "Love and Death", "Death Crowning Innocence", and "The Messenger of Death". In 1927 a group of Henrietta's friends presented the portrait of her painted by Maurice Codner, to hang in the Hall. Two asphalt tennis courts were given by Louis Bartholomew, and Marion Paterson gave two bookcases filled with books. Henrietta founded a library in the Institute, largely staffed by volunteers and with many books donated by residents. Besides raising capital for new building, the Institute was expensive to maintain. Donations to the maintenance fund helped, though they were usually small. Marion Paterson gave the usual one guinea; Henrietta usually gave about £80 annually, but this was the largest donation.

Henrietta intended to have a garden in the space behind the Institute and in 1928 she had a detailed plan prepared by a landscape architect. It included a Shakespeare garden with the plants he cared for, an open-air gymnasium, a rose pergola, open-air classrooms, lawns, children's gardens, seats, and a summerhouse. Behind the Institute building would be a sunken lawn and a terraced slope. This would have been a charming and imaginative garden, but the money for it could not be raised. (The plan for this garden is included in Henrietta Barnett's *The Story of the Growth of Hampstead Garden Suburb 1907–1928.*)

The greatest disappointment was over the art school. Henrietta envisaged a Suburb school of art comparable to the famous Hornsey School of Art. Dudley Heath was the principal of the small school of arts and crafts which flourished after the war and he had five part-time assistants. In 1924 Heath was very disappointed when his salary was cut from £500 to £300. The problem was money: Middlesex County Council was making cuts and stopped financing adult education. In 1926 Heath left to pursue a distinguished career at Hornsey School of Art and the Royal College of Art. But Henrietta was determined to make the art school grow and continued striving to raise the money. (There is a portrait of Dudley Heath in the Henrietta Barnett School entrance area.)

In 1927 an Institute sketching society was founded by Henrietta and at first met at 1 South Square. She was the chairman and Maurice Codner and Helen Copsey criticised the sketches. Henrietta organised visits to National Gallery lectures on artists and arranged for lectures in the Suburb. During 1929–30 the society had 35 members and included photography, organised by Miss Wyld. Henrietta was a keen photographer, and had used slides for her lectures since the 1890s.

She wanted a library for the Suburb and intended to build it on the site between the Friends Meeting House and the Tea House. Henrietta had been personally promised the large sum of £7,000 by Andrew Carnegie himself. But it could not be built because Hendon and Finchley Council refused support, even though Henrietta organised a deputation to meet the councillors. They wanted to site

Low's Topical Budget

POLITICAL NOTES

DEBATE IN THE HOUSE OF SQUAWKS

Lord Blue-nose said they all knew with what love respect and confidence they were held by the whole Zoo. He moved that their cage be made strong enough to resist the throwing of affectionate rocks.

So the new Metropolitan Police College is ready and the tennis courts are in play.

Well, there's nothing more inspiring than to see policemen controlling a set of tennis.

WAR NEWS

Hostilities have broken out between Golders Green and Hampstead Garden Suburb over the demand that the Suburb should be rechristened Golders Green East. The Greens attacked strongly with fixed shopping-bags, and captured the Suburb Institute after desperate fighting, making the enemy very jealous of their fur coats and jewellery. Dame Henrietta Barnett is reported to be retreating to Finchley.

It is evident that yet another noble ideal has been born.

A GREATER GERMANY

A GREATER ARABIA

A GREATER GOLDERS GREEN

A GREATER JAPAN

A GREATER ITALY

PREPARATIONS FOR COURT.

You'll have to curtsey better than that, Joan, or they'll think you're a left-over turn from the Command Performance.

REFLECTION IN TURKISH BATH BY Col. Blimp.

Gad, sir, Lord Beaverbrook is right. The only way to settle the American Debt question is to send a gunboat.

Plate 86
Low used the Suburb and Golders Green to ridicule the nationalism of the dictators. As long as Henrietta was alive, the Suburb was often in the news.

273

the libraries in their own town centres. This was a bitter disappointment and a loss to the Suburb. Nevertheless the small library continued in the Institute building.[421]

From 1910 to 1924 there was a succession of Institute secretaries who headed the work of the Institute under the control of Henrietta. In 1924 she appointed Harold Lacey as secretary and he soon became invaluable. The previous secretary had left the papers and accounts in terrible confusion. Lacey put it all in order while Henrietta went away for Christmas and a six-week holiday in the south of France. She reported to the Institute council that since her return they had worked in "close and peaceful co-operation," a welcome change from the state of affairs with the previous secretary.[422] "I am so deeply grateful that I can write that <u>we</u> about a secretary co-worker," she wrote to him.

His admiration for Henrietta can be seen in the obituary tribute he sent to Marion Paterson:

"I doubt whether anyone was in the presence of Dame Henrietta without recognising her to be a woman of unusual personality.

I remember vividly my own feelings after my first interview with her. It was towards the end of 1924 when she asked me to come & have tea with her in order that we might discuss my becoming Secretary of the Institute.

I left her house feeling I had been in the presence of a human whirlwind, sometimes raising me up to the very heavens, sometimes bringing me back to earth with a disconcerting bump. She questioned me as to my views on philosophy, theology, politics, & art, & at the end summed up in this way:

'Mr Lacey, I hope that the Council will accept my recommendation that you should be appointed Secretary; but you have one great fault which I hope you will not display too strongly when you come before the Council; & that fault is humility. Let the members of the Council see that you are somebody – and be wearing your best clothes!'

I saw a great deal of Dame Henrietta during the next ten years; sometimes we met as often as four times a week, to discuss the future of the Institute & the details of its management: & the impression I have carried away of her is one of the largeness of her personality.

She seemed larger than ordinary men and women: she was larger in her ambitions, in her schemes, her plans, in her courage, her audacity. She was cast in a heroic mode, and no matter what company she was in, she seemed to dominate it without effort.

The Institute was the darling of her old age: she loved it tenderly & showered on it unstinted affection. She was pleased & proud to see its growth; & she found much consolation in reflecting that it had grown sufficiently for its future to be secure. I shall never forget the experience that came from my association with Dame Henrietta in the service of the Institute: & it will remain always as an inspiration to carry on its work for the future."[423]

Henrietta and Harold Lacey formed an excellent working relationship, in which his "humility" was probably a help. He was a man able to cope with her demands, and whom she addressed familiarly as HL. In 1928 he was made principal of the Institute, but Henrietta continued to dominate. She had a rare grasp of administrative detail and interfered with details which should have been left to Lacey. For instance in June 1925 she was prodding him to make better preparations for an event, demanding immediate attention to refreshments and flowers, the programme to be roneoed "<u>nicely</u>", that teachers should wear gowns, "and <u>you too</u>".[424] She drafted letters for him to send out:"I enclose you a) draft of letter for all the staff … b) draft of invitation to all who had attended say 3 times this term".[425]

She was friendly, warm and informal with Lacey. She wrote numerous little notes to him on scraps of paper. Sometimes he dined with her, and in the summer when she went to Hove he would sometimes go down to see her, discuss their work and stay the night. In 1928 she wrote to him:

"Tomorrow Thursday I plan to 1. Leave here at 9 w. Caroline 2. Go to Chelsea Flower Show 3. See Mr Buckland 11.15 4. See Mr Gordon 12 – at Oxford St re Hostels.

Wd. you like to go with me at 9? Or meet me at 12 at Oxford St? R.S.V.P. – by early telephone."

Clearly she was incapable of following her doctors' advice to take things easy. Her hyperactivity led to a spat with Mr Lacey, who was usually so compliant. Finding that he was late in getting out an invitation to a school function she wrote: "I have had a talk with Mr Fowler and Mary and find nothing ready – 220 stamps to meet 1100 letters – nothing done for Miss Hutchings and even the names left for a Teacher to scribble on as she gives the cards!! I am very surprised and very annoyed, and very sad, for you will never succeed when all these matters are late."[426]

This terse note really upset Mr Lacey and he wrote that it had given him extreme and painful surprise to receive such a letter after two and a half years of loyal cooperation; he went on to explain the causes of any delays. Henrietta was unable to see how her note could have caused offence! Nevertheless she apologized and their usual good relationship was resumed.

After the war, Henrietta had revived the Institute Students' Union and was the president. She thought it served a valuable function in bringing together students otherwise separated in different classes and societies. A "talking room" was set aside for it and there were dances and excursions, one to Oxford for a day.[427] She cared a great deal for it and when she spoke to the union she made a meticulous plan, as she did for her other speeches. She told them of her plans for future building and of ways they could help to make money for it. She stressed the importance of friendship between students. On another occasion she asked Harold Lacey to read a message to students saying she was in Hove:

"… to do some writing that had to be done for my wireless talk next Tuesday on International problems – at 10 o'clock … As it is I can only tell you my wish & that is that everyone will begin a friendship tomorrow – Begin a friendship that will grow, and deepen, & strengthen, until you make a real difference to your friend, & your friend makes a real difference to you. The friend must (1) share your ideals; (2) smile with you in great hopes; (3) be ready to help you to sacrifice in the cause."

The Suburb "Coming of Age" Celebrations 1928

In 1928 the Suburb was 21 years old and a week of festivities and performances was planned. The preparations were kept secret from Henrietta, so it was a delightful surprise. The opening ceremony was held on a brilliantly sunny day and a large crowd gathered. Henrietta found herself on the platform flanked by Lord Lytton, Herbert Welch and other Suburb and local council dignitaries, with Sir Philip Cunliffe-Lister in the chair. She was presented with an address, congratulating her on creating the Suburb which was "an example to the world" and praying that she would be long spared to carry on with her "beneficent works". The *Observer* journalist described her as: "A gracious white-haired lady in black, trimmed with delicate white lace, and wearing a feathered black toque". In her speech she asked: "Why should not the Hampstead Garden Suburb adopt a London district where the conditions are the reverse of all that is here, and push and push until in that district slums are abolished, factories made suitable and hygienic, playgrounds used, education adequate?". The journalist remarked: "Still an incurable – and practical dreamer, at seventy seven," and continued: "After the ceremony she saw a procession of the Suburb's buoyant life pass gaily before her in decorated cars and in picturesque costume, with laughing children like foam on the crest of it, and one spectre at the feast – a fearsome dragon labelled 'Bad Housing'".[428] In the evening she saw *The Loom of Time*, written about the Suburb by a local author and performed in Little Wood. A handsome brochure outlined the programme of festivities: eight days of meetings, services, fêtes, functions, flower shows, picture exhibitions, processions, sports, tournaments, plays, and pageants.

The Duchess of York (later the Queen Mother) came to the Suburb during the celebrations; she opened a fete and attended an open-air play by the Play and Pageant Union. Henrietta was delighted that this young member of the royal family was taking such an interest in the Suburb.

Henrietta had been asked to write a history of the Suburb and had worked hard to complete her booklet, *The Story of the Growth of Hampstead Garden Suburb 1907–1928*, which was on sale at the low price of 6d. This is an invaluable account, and a facsimile has been published and is available at the Hampstead Garden Suburb Gallery or the Trust at the low price of £9.95. It will be read for as long as people are interested in town planning.

Chaper 27
The Last Years

Even to her death Henrietta still had plans for further developments; in 1932 she told the local paper that she wanted, "To build a school of art, to build a hostel for women, and to lay out the garden."[429] Lutyens prepared a plan to make two extensions, one on either side of the Institute, to house the school of art and the hostel.[430] Sadly these ambitions remained hopes.

In 1930 she wrote to the Aga Khan saying that if he would give £12,000 she would name the building after him.[431] An Aga Khan School of Art would have been an interesting addition to the Suburb, but unfortunately he did not respond. In 1931 she was writing yet again to the Middlesex Education Committee, asking for a grant toward building an art school on the grounds that they had 184 eager students and a wide range of arts and crafts were taught.[432] In 1934 she appealed to Lord Leverhulme, promising to name the art school after him, and to Lord Harmsworth, both of whom she knew and who were living near in Hampstead, but again with no result. In 1933 when she was ill, she was again hoping that Middlesex would grant the money and even wrote to Queen Mary asking if she would open the school of art if it were built.[433]

Henrietta continued to work at full stretch until her last year, 1935/36, when she was confined to her bedroom. In 1930 a journalist from the *Observer* had an interview with Henrietta:

> "To get an interview with Dame Henrietta Barnett was not an easy matter, because she is still one of the busiest women in England. Apparently the best time to see her is between five and nine in the morning! She told me on the telephone that she rises at five every day. When I suggested a call about noon, Dame Henrietta said that she would still be busy with her secretaries, and that after her midday rest there were usually committees and consultations. However she managed to spare an hour, and when I arrived it was to find her surrounded by pamphlets, plans, sketches, estimates, prospectuses, and reports. Her vitality is amazing: I soon discovered that and I asked her the secret.
> 'Early rising, very little food, and a sense of humour. The strange thing is that I am really a very delicate woman and always have been. I have had pneumonia seven times; but hard work is often the best cure for ill-health.'"[434]

Henrietta had been the weakest child in her family, but she outlived her sisters. Poor Fanny died in 1926. After so many years of care for Fanny, Henrietta must have grieved, but may have been glad to see her go before she herself was too old to look after her. Henrietta showed her great regard for the disabled by putting a notice in *The Times* announcing Fanny's death. Then Alice died on 28th August 1929, and this must have been a great loss after the two sisters had shared so many years of love and confidences and spent so much time together.

To Aga Khan.

June 17. 1930

Dear Sir,

Although you have not been introd[uced]
by a mutual friend to me until 15th —
I think it is quite possible that you m[ay]
like an Art School to the beautiful
buildings on this Estate, & call it The
Aga Khan Hall.

We have built 3 blo[cks]
designed by Sir Edwin Lutyens — at the cost [of]
£63,000.

Her Majesty the Queen l[aid]
the foundation stone & later opened the buil[ding]
which the King allowed to be called the
Queen Mary Hall.

Another block is cal[led]
after the most Hon[oura]ble the Marquess of Crewe — & [if]
you will build the block which is needed [at]
£12,000 it shall be named as you wish.

I enclose you some printed papers, [&]
if you will come, it will give me pleasur[e]
to show the beautiful place to you.

I am, Yours truly

Henrietta O. Barnett

Her health, always a problem, had begun to decline from her late seventies. On 16th April 1926 she wrote to Harold Lacey: "The doctor says my lungs slowly clear, but my 'nerves are frayed' & I can bear nothing – Still I am alive."[435] In May she wrote to Kitty, her sister-in-law: "I have been ill 6 weeks, & nearly died, but am now slowly recovering."[436] Kitty was devotedly looking after Fritz (Frederich), Henrietta's brother. In recognition of her devotion Henrietta sent her a gold brooch which had belonged to Fanny. Her recovery was very slow, for in September she was staying with Lady Markby and was too ill to attend committees. In October of that year she was in pain: "I cannot see you today as lumbago chains me to my bed, but I shall soon be better so don't mention it."[437] And in another letter to Harold Lacey in February 1927 she wrote: "Alas! I am again in bed under a <u>stern</u> doctor, crippled with lumbago." But she could still get around the Suburb, especially with the aid of Palmer, the chauffeur. People saw her as "A white-haired little lady in an old-fashioned poke bonnet and shawl".[438]

Her cycle of overwork and depression continued and perhaps worsened as she aged. In 1929 she had a prolonged depression, which was helped by her visit to Madeira. She was working too hard for someone of her age, and she realised it, for she told Marion that her New Year resolve for 1931 was: "Slowly get out of my work, write, think, pray & live more at Hove. I have three books I wish to write

1. Essays – one of them called 'smaller creed a greater God'
2. People I have known
3. My autobiography. i.e. Lessons I have learnt, & of the work which taught me."

Unfortunately she never found time to write her autobiography, or deal with her other resolves, for she was fully occupied with coping with her many interests until the end.

On her 80th birthday greetings came from all over the world: cablegrams from New York, Boston, Chicago, Pennsylvania, telegrams from Europe and the Commonwealth. There were gifts and masses of flowers, including a huge box of flowers from Windsor Castle with a note personally written by Queen Mary. Some of the flowers from the Queen were made into tiny bunches for the head girls of each class at the Henrietta Barnett School; others were distributed between the East End settlements. There were many presents from Suburb residents, and the gardening staff of the Suburb – all 35 of them – sent rose trees for Henrietta to plant in the Institute garden.[439]

Many journalists were sent to interview her. *The Daily Mail* published Dame Henrietta's replies to "ten very leading questions we would ask our readers to answer as truthfully as possible, as follows: –

1. What makes life worth living? *Loving & working*
2. What is the most loveable quality in the human being for whom you have most affection? *Sympathy*
3. What is the most detestable failing in anyone you dislike? *Lying*
4. What is the most attractive quality in yourself? *Honesty*
5. And the most detestable? *Frequently falling ill*
6. What living celebrity (men & women) do you admire most? *I wish to mention two – a Mrs Baker charwoman in Whitechapel; & Miss Jane Addams of Chicago*

Plate 89 (opposite) Henrietta writing in her workroom. The Vermeer given to her by Queen Mary hangs over the desk.

7. Is either sex superior to the other? If so – Why? *Each sex has qualities which are superior to the other sex*

8. Which gives you most pleasure, a new frock, a new book, or a good meal? *A new book*

9. Do you dress to attract men, to compete with women, or to please yourself? *I dress to keep myself warm – or cool*

10. If you could begin life again what career would you choose? *Studying science; astronomy & teaching it*"

Being asked whether in her opinion one most enjoyed childhood, youth, maternity, or old age, her reply was:

"Surely all stages of life have their advantages. Between twenty & thirty one widens one's field of experience; between thirty & fifty one works & is glad that fresh opportunities are opened for effort & helpfulness; between fifty & seventy, the Harvest is beginning to ripen.

But perhaps the best period is between seventy & eighty; when one cannot work so continuously & there is therefore more time to learn of the fresh discoveries about this wonderful universe. Time to consider the deeper sides of the characters of Nations, movements, friends & neighbours.

One can then be glad, grateful & humble because of the love & care and the consideration of countless kind folk who think that, as you are so clever as to have reached your eightieth year, nothing can be too good for you."[440]

She was interviewed for many of the other papers, and made use of the publicity to air her views on religion: "The longer I live the more I am convinced that religion is the biggest force in the world. When the churches begin to harmonise services & religion, then they will begin to re-assert their place in the life of the country."[441]

She would answer questions on growing old: "I suppose I <u>am</u> growing old, but I know very little about it. That is one of the arts of life: to grow old without feeling that you are doing so." She was continually active and optimistic despite her declining strength. Marion wrote: "She never really rested although she cherished her 'Trappists' days – Sundays when; things I care for are to be considered prayerfully, which are but mine in trust to pass on.' When asked how she had stayed so active, she replied that she had five simple rules: 'Rise at 5.30 a.m., work very hard, read newspapers carefully every day, eat very little, and say your prayers often."[442]

The Queen sent a journalist to interview her and a photographer to take photographs of her and the interior of her house. She is seen working on her dining-room table, as she usually did, surrounded by papers; on the walls hang a Watts portrait of Samuel and the copy of a Vermeer given to her by Queen Mary. There are many paintings on all the walls, some by Henrietta, and one of her pictures of Madeira is on an easel. The house is full of memorabilia. In large letters on tiles across the top of the drawing-room mantelpiece is written "Fear not to sow because of the Birds," the motto on the Barnett tablet in Westminster Abbey. There are ancient Damascus tiles round the fireplace, and at the side the large William de Morgan vase which he made for her to match her tiles. Over the mantelpiece is the carved "mashrabiy" brought back from Egypt in 1880; this is a carved

Plate 90 (opposite) A corner of the drawing-room in 1 South Square showing the Damascus tiles, the de Morgan vase, the Buddha at the centre of the mantelpiece and the motto "Fear not to sow because of the Birds".

wooden panel which covers the wall and extends as a canopy over the settees on either side. A life-size sculptured marble figure of St George of Bologna entitled "The Messenger" stands near the window; it was presented to Henrietta after thirty-three years with the congregation of St Jude's, Whitechapel. There is a humorous Japanese panel of monkeys. There is a crucifix on the wall, but also a Buddha on the centre of the mantelpiece! In the entrance hall Henrietta had stuck on the panels postcard portraits of the many famous people she knew including Ramsay MacDonald (prime minister in 1931), Lord Milner, Lady Courtney, Viscount Haldane, William Morris, George Watts, Thomas Carlyle, Mrs Sidney Webb, Sir John Gorst, Frederick Harrison, Viscount Bryce, Jane Addams, the Archbishop of Canterbury, Asquith, Sir Oliver Lodge and many more.

The article, published 23/12/1931, was given a double-page spread and the journalist called her "probably the most remarkable woman of the day". She always had further goals; as Marion said: "It was said Dame Henrietta's motto was 'Something attempted something done.' But rather should it have been 'Something done but much remains.'"[443]

She had very high hopes of young people: "We must attract the young by offering them the places of honour in the fore-front, & give to them the dignity of bearing responsibility ... We must bear to see our accepted dictums disregarded, our experience set aside. We must, to quote my husband 'lead revolution against ourselves'."

In 1931 she was in bed with sciatica, but worse was to come. In December 1932 she wrote to her lawyer, Mr Buckland:

"It is kind of you to write – but it is difficult to reply – The patient is
1. 81 years old.
2. 7 Times pneumonia.
3. Right lung permanently congested.
4. Heart enlarged and out of place.
5. Takes minimum of food.
6. Is nervous by [?].
7. Worries over her many responsibilities.
8. Caught a severe influenza kind of cough.
9. Has been in bed 5 weeks.
10. Movement agitates the heart.
Now having set out my 10 troubles what can I say. That
1) I have seen 3 doctors including the leading heart specialist. That I obey them
2) That I see no-one but Miss Paterson. Even Miss Cole annoys and agitates me – poor dear!
3) That I am sitting up in the big chair, & have walked twice across the room now, today, with aid.
4) That I say "nothing to nobody", & answer no newspaper enquiries, for my one craving is to be let alone & quiet – and
5) That I often worry over our DHB Board.
6) That I sleep badly & am often alarmed
7) That the doctor hopes that my condition will improve, but much rest needed.
8) I hope I have not bored you with this long letter. Keep it to yourself & pardon your grateful friend."[444]

However, she was still taking on new responsibilities. When Mary Adeney started a branch of the Girls' Friendly Society at the Institute, Henrietta was made presiding associate. The club met several afternoons a week and gave maidservants a meeting-place where they could play games, do needlework, dance to the gramophone and even bring men friends.[445] Henrietta would have enjoyed meeting the girls and giving them a talk, but she was not well enough. In August 1930 she was in Hove and wrote in a letter:

"I came here on Friday, too _too_ played out! But I am recovering, & seeing _no_ _one_, & writing no letters even, nor giving a thought to the packet of letters which ask me for articles." Evidently she was still sketching and painting, for in 1932 Henrietta had a third picture accepted for the Royal Academy: this was entitled "The hard mountains of Madeira softened by entrapped clouds".[446] She was very modest about her achievement, for in a letter to her nephew, Stanley, who was a teacher and artist, she wrote: "I wish I could draw _half_ so well – But my rubbish still gets into galleries & accepted by the RA – So!"[447] She was very fond of Stanley, and sent him money as he was not very successful. He was negligent about sending thank-you letters, even for money, and she had to prod him to get a response:

"Dear Stanley
Will you come to eat a meal with me on Thursday next at 6.45.
I am much better – but 1 half to 2 hours is _all_ I can stand of anyone, so you will be able to get home early.
Yours affectionately
H.O. Barnett
R.S.V.P. at once please dear."[448]

Of course she wanted to watch developments in the Suburb, and in her last years she was driven slowly about by Palmer, the chauffeur, in the large brown Rolls-Royce. She gave her utmost to the Institute, which was flourishing. In November 1932 there were 1,183 students enrolled at the 46 classes and societies at the Institute.[449] The most popular were the French, German, Dressmaking, Bookkeeping classes and the University Extension Course. For children there was a class in gymnastics and a play hour. Societies usually met at 8pm, a very civilised hour allowing time for dinner. Many people preferred the informality of a society and there were many to choose from: sketching, folk dancing, economics discussion circle, London society, literary society, ethics society and the novel reading society. This last was still very popular, with 30 people enrolled, and it was led by Henrietta and met monthly in her drawing-room on Monday evenings. It was so important that it was reported in the local press! They read _Young Anarchy_ by Sir Philip Gibbs, who was a nephew of Henrietta and president of the society, H G Wells' _Mr Britling Sees It Through_, Dickens' _Little Dorrit_ and Hall Caine's _The Manxman_. Sometimes members read extracts from favourite books but usually two members read papers on the chosen novel, followed by a discussion led by Henrietta:

"Dame Henrietta guided these convergent views into a higher and rarer atmosphere, and while encouraging every form of political utterance, kept a firm and gentle hold on the rudder of the good ship Talk until it concentrated on what the author meant to say."

One of the members of the society wrote:

"When she spoke it was in a rather shrill voice, but her magnetic personality and the wisdom of her words more than made up for any peculiarities of speech. Although she was one of the greatest woman social reformers of her time, she never affected sanctimony, but enjoyed a joke and laughed as much against herself as at other people."[450]

Her wonderful voice had become shrill with age and later it would fail her.

She bore physical pain with amazing fortitude. She said "Drugs simply poison me," and although she took what was prescribed she thought it did her no good. She had great faith in her doctors: when her nephew Stanley was ill she urged him to come and see her Dr Ensor who lived half a mile away from her: "He is really wonderful – Taking the most detailed consideration of <u>every</u> case, & then advising what is best, most up to date, & most suitable." Henrietta said she would pay the expenses.[451] Presumably Dr Ensor moved away, for during her last two years Dr Anderson was in constant attendance and became a valued friend; he had a high esteem for her:

"What a treat it was to sit by her bedside, and listen to that interesting & clever woman propounding new ideas & schemes for social development, heedless of the fact that having a first class brain in a well-worn body she would never live to see them carried out. The keynote & standard of her life was truth; & this, I think might have been the reason why she did not make friends easily, for to those in whom she could not see this quality her friendship was denied – or, on the other hand it might be traced to the fact that she did not suffer fools gladly. Above all I was impressed with her originality of mind that was ever emitting a constant stream of new ideas".

Dr Anderson's comment about not making friends easily seems strange when we know she had so many friends and held friendship to be so important. However, Sir William Beveridge who had been a sub-warden at Toynbee Hall when he was young, spoke of "His fear of that earnest – he had almost said austere – lady which her high standards, & ruthless expectations had created in him; 'but perfect love casteth out fear' & he need now only say he was no longer afraid."[452] So to young people and probably to many of her neighbours in the Suburb she may have seemed unapproachable.

From December 1932 she had a prolonged illness. In February 1933 she wrote: "It is 3 months since I took to my bed under a severe attack of nervous exhaustion, which affected all my organs in their administrative action, but especially my heart. Today I have got up and sat in a comfy lounge chair."[453]

In March 1933 a note from Henrietta to the Institute council read: "It seems folly to put on the Agenda as the first item: 'Report of Honorary Director', when it is known that that elderly (82) lady has been in bed 19 weeks."

She was able to keep in touch for: "Mr Lacey, Mr Syrett and various other friends have been kind enough to come and talk to me for short ten minute visits about the Institute, and the hope of its growth in size, efficiency and friendliness is ever with me."[454]

She must have been aware of one important change. The persecution of the Jews in Germany had resulted in a small Jewish community in the Suburb, where they were warmly received by the Quakers. Mr Tanchan thought the Golders Green synagogue was too far to walk, so helped to start a synagogue in a rented room in the Institute.[455] By 1936 the community was sufficiently well established to open the Norrice Lea synagogue, which has grown and flourished ever since then. Henrietta must have approved renting the Institute room to the synagogue even though there was anti-Semitism in the area.

Institute council meetings were held at 1 South Square if Henrietta was well enough to get downstairs. But she had to spend more time in her bedroom, and it was there that the Queen visited her in March 1933: "Dame Henrietta received the honour of a surprise visit from the Queen. Her Majesty drove on to the garden Suburb after a visit to the North St Pancras Nursery Clinic, in order to call and enquire if Dame Henrietta was well enough to see her, and sat with her for nearly half an hour, though the Dame was unable to leave her bedroom." When thanking the Queen for her visit,

Henrietta sent her a copy of *The Brook Kerith* which she evidently found inspirational. "To some of us it appears to be a duty – without being a Luther – to help those who teach religion and to realise that the revelation of the Almighty Goodness did not end at any given date, and is taught by the microscope and the telescope now to those who will watch. To my mind *The Brook Kerith* aids all seekers of the truth to realise the life and surroundings of the Prince of Peace."[456] *The Brook Kerith* (1916) was written by an Irish novelist, George Augustus Moore. It is an imaginative account of the life of Jesus – who survives the Cross.

The Queen sent Henrietta a signed calendar every Christmas. One of these is held in the Hampstead Garden Suburb Archive. In the summer she was invited to a Buckingham Palace garden party. She replied that she was unable to go because she was too weak, but, "I have a new idea which I should dearly like to submit to your Majesty. May I write it one day next week?" In her letter of 22nd July 1933 "To my much loved & deeply honoured Queen," she explained her idea was to establish a Trust board which would ensure that bequests were carried out. She gave as an example of a bequest not carried out, something that made her most indignant: the new vicar of St Jude's had taken down the Watts pictures she had given to the church, unframed them and rolled them up and left them lying in a passage. She asked the Queen to be the patron of the proposed Trust board. The Queen refused.[457] In July 1934 Henrietta must have recovered, for she managed to attend the Trust annual general meeting held at the Holborn Restaurant. This was her last excursion to central London.

In preparation for her death she drew up detailed lists of all her possessions and allocated things to her relatives and many friends. This list was going to give Marion a great deal of work. She had fully come to terms with her own death, and was not perturbed when in 1929 a *Yorkshire Post* journalist mistakenly reported her death. She had written a letter to the editor saying she had not been called upon to take "that interesting step in the journey of the soul … While my body is healthy and my mind as clear as ever it was, I do not want to leave my countless friends, for whose affection I daily thank God".[458]

In a flippant mood she wrote: "when we hang John Brown on a crab-apple tree,' or in other words 'burn Henrietta in the close-at-hand Crematorium,' our souls will 'go marching on' towards progress, educational, mental, moral, and spiritual."[459]

Her last public appearance was in July 1934 at an Institute garden party at "Cartref", Linnell Drive, the home of Sir John and Lady Davies where she sat in the doorway looking out at the lawn. When asked to speak she handed her speech to Mr Lacey to read as "age prevented her from saying anything in person".[460] She continued with her work even when confined to her bedroom:

"During the whole of 1935 she was unable to leave her bedroom, but she managed to keep cheerful. Reflecting on old age she said: 'I think almost the primary duty of old age is to be happy, lively, gay, glad; & thus create an atmosphere of peace, good will & contentment. Old age is the unfolding of the blossoming of youth; the fruits of middle age; the harvest of the years.'"[461]

She kept her interest in life and her humour. In 1935, when the west end of St Jude's was being built:

"She would sit in her bedroom window watching its progress. Mr Thomas the foreman (who had become a friend in the early days of the Church's building) would bring in the architect's plans to discuss with her; & one morning he brought with him two bricks, asking that H.O.B. – M.P. (Marion Paterson) might be inscribed on them as he had reserved a special niche for them.

She had a nodding acquaintance with all the workmen (for whom she provided afternoon cups of tea) & one of them Jack, not much more than a boy, caused her constant amusement by his agile climbing, often turning round, halfway up the ladders, to wave to her."[462]

Marion Paterson's role became more evident as Henrietta declined. She was not lonely for Marion was with her every day, and Miss Cole continued her work as secretary. She chatted with her two maids who were very fond of her: Mary Blades, her treasure, had been with her for many years and Florence Downes was a gifted girl who helped with nursing.[463]

On her last birthday, her 85th, "she was very ill but in spirit as strong as ever," Marion said. Even when she was very tired she still considered it a duty to be dainty in bed. Every morning she liked her hair to be properly done, her lace collar and her coral necklace arranged as she thought they should be. She lost strength, but in her last days she was trying to think of a gift for Queen Mary. On 10th June she was unconscious all day and at 6pm her heart failed and she died. The news quickly spread and a broadcast tribute was paid the same evening. She had been kept to her room overlooking the gardens in the Square for almost a year, but she bore her illness with patience and Marion said she never once complained throughout her long confinement.[464]

The national and local press quickly reported the death of the famous Dame and carried long obituary notices. The obituaries fill 70 pages of newspaper cuttings. The *Manchester Guardian* reporter was the most perceptive: "Dame Henrietta Barnett, who died yesterday, retained in extreme old age the knack, possessed by some Friends and a few others of her sex, of appearing at once extremely gentle and extremely formidable."[465] George Cadbury, whom Henrietta had called "the grandfather of the Hampstead Garden Suburb," wrote "Powerful, yes, and tender and frolicsome and harmless as a lamb, at times. But her dominant mood, reflecting rare depths of feeling, was anything but Lamb-like." The *Hendon Times* paid a fulsome tribute and drew attention to her lifelong energy:

> "It was not until quite recently that Dame Henrietta lost her grip on affairs. In the early stages of her illness, letters, commands, speeches to be read at gatherings, and messages of all kinds literally poured forth from her bedside, and distinguished people attended before her from conferences on matters of importance. About this time too she took a keen interest in the Poetry Reading Society … She also held many telephone conversations with people of all kinds, and generally did everything possible to keep in touch with the world outside, while patiently submitting to her enforced confinement."[466]

As Henrietta had no close relatives, condolences were sent to Marion. Chief of these was a telegram from Queen Mary, who must have regarded Henrietta's death as a personal loss:

"THE QUEEN REGRETS DEEPLY TO HEAR OF THE DEATH OF DAME HENRIETTA BARNETT AND HER MAJESTY WILL ALWAYS REMEMBER THE WONDERFUL SOCIAL AND EDUCATIONAL WORK CARRIED OUT BY HER AT TOYNBEE HALL AND HAMPSTEAD – PRIVATE SECRETARY"[467]

Letters poured in and Marion must have felt overwhelmed. Many of the letters gave long appreciations of Henrietta's work and character and Marion quotes them in her *Quasi-Autobiography*. Elizabeth Cadbury, in the Quaker tradition of telling the whole truth, included a criticism: "Her esteem and admiration were the more valued by knowing how critical she could be, and how caustic sometimes were her remarks on the work or enterprise of others. She was also autocratic." The fact that Marion Paterson quotes this without comment seems to show that she agreed with it. Indeed, the long-suffering Marion had every reason to know about Henrietta's autocratic behaviour. Henrietta's energy made her charismatic and able to attract and inspire devoted workers. However such frenetic energy is difficult to live with, especially when alternated with "nervous exhaustion".

One of the most perceptive appreciations of the Barnetts was written by Dr George Gooch, the Cambridge historian, who had first met them at Toynbee in the 1890s:

"Both belonged to the noble profession of 'Servants of Humanity', but their identity of thought and aim was combined with a striking diversity of temperament. Though there was nothing in the least flabby, or sentimental, about the Canon, he was almost feminine in his gentleness: whereas the inflexible Will of his wife was suggestive of the stronger sex.

The Canon lives in my memory as the embodiment of mellow wisdom: Mrs Barnett of inexhaustible energy.

They had an astonishing power of getting things done; and like so many others of my generation, I owe an equal debt to both.

I saw Mrs Barnett at work at Toynbee; in the first years at Westminster; and more rarely in her wonderful Indian Summer at Hampstead. She changed very little.

There was always something mercive, dominating, Roman, about her, which is rarely found in Women, though she was also capable of deep feeling.

She possessed a powerful and original mind. Without being a great speaker she instantly got in touch with her audience by a direct human appeal. Without being a great writer, her articles were thoroughly readable; and she never wrote on a subject which she had not mastered. She gave us one of the best biographies

THE ARCHBISHOP OF CANTERBURY, who conducted the service at the funeral of Dame Henrietta Barnett at Hampstead to-day, talking to Miss Patterson, a life-long friend of Dame Barnett.

Plate 91
The Archbishop of Canterbury talking to Marion Paterson at the funeral.

in our language (*Life of Canon Barnett*). What were the causes of her enduring influence? I suppose we must answer; brain, will, a shrewd sense of what needed doing, and how it could be done; an almost unique capacity for winning influential support for her projects; a passion for service; an un-faltering faith in God and man."[468]

Gooch's perception of Henrietta as masculine is a reflection of his perception of gender roles. She was a great and courageous woman who had achieved much in a man's world, and it was not possible to achieve in a man's world without appearing dominating and masculine.

Henrietta claimed credit for originating schemes, but her real strength was in carrying out ideas with efficiency and thoroughness. Beatrice Webb wrote "For all the business side of philanthropy, for initiation, advertisement, negotiation and execution, her gifts rose at times to veritable genius." Henrietta discovered the power of informed public opinion and how to influence it through the press, magazines and lectures. She was not interested in party politics or the suffrage movement, and perhaps this was partly due to the influence of Octavia Hill, who thought that the demand for the vote was taking women away from their proper work of helping the poor. Henrietta had found that she could succeed through pressure-group politics. She had won the support of lords, bishops and statesmen. With wealthy and influential backers and access to MPs she could achieve reforms. While claiming that she was not interested in politics, she was using the political techniques of the 20th century. She knew her own strengths and was ready to embark on a new phase in her life – the creation of the Hampstead Garden Suburb.

She was motivated by deep feelings of compassion for the poor, especially the children and girls. Surrounded by the wan, underfed children of Whitechapel and seeing the unloved children in the barrack schools she longed for a better future. She had a vision of healthy, well-loved children frolicking amid flowers and trees, and in the new century she would see this realised in her Suburb.

On 2nd June 1936 in a letter to Marion, the Archbishop of Canterbury offered to speak at the funeral, which was held at St Jude's, and he gave the address at the service conducted by the vicar, the Reverend E D Arundel. The Archbishop said his memory of Henrietta went back fifty-three years and he still had a vivid sense of the impression which she made when she came to Oxford with Samuel. Her ideals were translated into practical action:

"… ideals were never dreams. Once clearly seen they became definite purposes. They had the quality not of light only but of fire – the fire of a courage which at once determined that they must be realised … Once she had clearly conceived the idea of a community in which high and low, rich and poor, could live together as friends and neighbours, she addressed herself with great courage and dauntless determination to the task of its fulfillment.

It may be said that she illustrated rather the active than the passive virtues; rather courage and ardour and resolution than humility and gentleness. But from first to last hers was a truly dedicated life, a life which scorned all that is mean and paltry and frivolous and selfish and strove the utmost for the highest; a life dedicated to the service of her fellow men – she would have liked to have called them her neighbours – and to God."[469]

Later there was a private service at the crematorium and in November her ashes were interred at Hangleton by the side of Samuel's ashes. As she wished, Henrietta's name was added to the tablet that had been placed in Westminster Abbey in memory of Samuel.

Her estate was valued at £34,749. Though generous she had been very prudent and lived economically, maintaining her capital. In her will she left some money to her Rowland and Barnett

**ERECTED BY THE GRATEFUL INHABITANTS OF
THE HAMPSTEAD GARDEN SUBURB
IN HONOUR OF ITS CREATOR AND INSPIRER
DAME HENRIETTA BARNETT, D.B.E.
1851—1936.**

*Plate 92
Lutyens' sketch
of the memorial.
Known as the
architect of the
Cenotaph and the
Thiepval Arch,
he designed the
memorial as a gift for
Henrietta. Although
they quarrelled,
Lutyens admired her.*

nephews and nieces. To Marion Paterson she gave an annuity of £50 per year and requested that she should stay in her house, 66 South Hill Park, Hampstead. The house belonged to Henrietta, and the freehold was sold and the income derived given to Marion, so she was left comfortably off. She left small sums to her secretarial and domestic staff: £15 for each year of service to her secretary, Alice Cole, £250 to her cook, Mary Blades, £25 to her maid, Florence Downes, and £110 to her chauffeur, Palmer.

After the bequests the residue, £16,000, was to be divided into 16 parts. Eight of these were to go to help Henrietta Barnett School girls to go to university to study their chosen subjects, four of them to be at Oxford or Cambridge. The other eight parts were divided: five parts were to provide scholarships at Wadham College, Oxford (Samuel's old college), one part was for a scholarship at Ripon Hall, Oxford, one part for a scholarship at Toynbee Hall and one part for a scholarship for a Mill Hill School boy to go to Oxford. All these scholars were to study social and political economy.

Henrietta left a long list of possessions, naming the person to whom each one should be given. To the Institute she gave her Damascus tiles, with the motto, "Fear not to sow because of the Birds". She also gave the Institute two settees and the "mashrabiy", always a striking picture in her drawing-room.[470] She left her precious William de Morgan vase

*Plate 93
Henrietta Barnett
schoolgirls running
through the
memorial.*

to Mrs George Cadbury: "Because she is the only woman I know to admit the humblest people to her own drawing room. People, nice, good people, often entertain their humbler guests in the kitchen, and I have known them treat the coach-house and the stables as their guest rooms. As if to hurt other people's feelings was not worse than to hurt their own carpets!"[471]

She left all her papers, letters, diaries and literary remains to Marion, also all her furniture and possessions, excluding all at Wish Road which were to be sold. Marion gave all that was not wanted by friends and relatives to the Women's Settlements at Canning Town and at Ratcliff. Pictures and books at Wish Road were given to the Hove Public Library and Museum. She would have many years of work dealing with the literary remains and, as Henrietta had given her the right to destroy any material she thought unwise to keep, she would do it alone. And so the faithful Marion, now in her late seventies, set to work to wind up the estate, to send all the gifts to friends, to answer the numerous letters of condolence, send thanks, and try to write a biography, continuing to work for the wonderful, lovable woman she had served all her life.

In May 1937 a meeting was held at Lambeth Palace attended by the Archbishop of Canterbury, with Lord Crewe in the chair, which established the Dame Henrietta Barnett

Board to administer the Trust to which she bequeathed the residue of her estate – £16,000 – and to issue an appeal for her.[472]

The Hampstead Garden Suburb Trust, Co-partnership Tenants and the Institute formed a committee, chaired by Lord Lytton, to plan a memorial. They asked Lutyens to produce a design and he made several sketches. The committee consulted the Suburb societies and religious communities before making their choice. The residents subscribed to pay for the memorial, and Lutyens gave his design free of charge in her memory. People were very aware that this famous architect had designed the great memorials of the age: the Cenotaph and the Thiepval Arch.

Mervyn Miller describes the memorial: "Its centre is an inscribed Portland stone block, a miniature cenotaph, topped by a laurel wreath, in the centre of interlaced bronze arches, springing from four stone pylons, carrying a central lantern. The inscription reads: 'In fond memory of Dame Henrietta Barnett, D.B.E., 1851–1936, Founder and Inspirer of this Suburb.'" It was surrounded by four Lutyens' benches and placed on the west side of Central Square, from where one could see to Harrow, Henrietta's favourite view. The memorial was unveiled by Lord Lytton in July 1937. He paid tribute to her work and achievements, but also said:

> "She was not always easy to work with. She could be very obstinate at times, bless her, and she was not entirely without her prejudices. She was not divine, but human. With all those qualities she had the faith which moves mountains. Difficulties for her were made to be overcome. They never depressed, they only stimulated.
> She never lowered her flag. She never allowed one of her ideals to be dimmed. Above all she was one of those people who could inspire others."[473]

Queen Mary and the Archbishop of Canterbury sent messages regretting they were unable to attend the unveiling of the memorial.

Chapter 28
Conclusion

So I summed up my new resolve:
Too much love there can never be.
Browning

For thirty years Henrietta and Samuel lived in Whitechapel and battled to improve working class life. They were shocked by the poverty, pollution, rotting houses, ignorance and depravity. They were convinced that cultural deprivation was even worse than economic poverty and were successful in interesting working people in the high culture which would help them spiritually and morally. As they learned more about poverty, they began to see that unemployment was not always due to laziness and could be due to economic factors, and so they became participants in the change in liberal philosophy from laissez-faire to positive liberalism.

The Archbishop of York wrote of the Barnetts' marriage that "It was a singularly beautiful community of mind and spirit"; they shared all their thoughts, their worries and their aspirations. Their marriage was an equal partnership, for Samuel had advanced views about marriage and Henrietta was only willing to marry him on condition she could continue with her social work. They cooperated in parish work and creating and organizing Toynbee Hall and the Whitechapel Art Gallery. But Henrietta created her own world of work when she became a guardian of the barrack school and summoned her women friends to help. She was so vital and charismatic that she found more and more friends and supporters to help her. She plunged into the Lock wards of the Whitechapel workhouse to help the prostitutes and tried to find work for them as maids through the Metropolitan Association for Befriending Young Servants.

The Barnetts both came from families "in trade", but they rose socially as they became famous. Henrietta's friends included many rich or aristocratic women, and with Queen Mary she had a close friendship. This was a great help to her in attracting the support of other women and in raising funds.

Children became her chief interest, particularly the children of the state. She was appointed to the Departmental Committee on Poor Law Schools, the first woman to hold such an appointment. She persuaded the men on the committee that the children needed more love, which they would get from foster-mothers or from house-mothers, but rarely in barrack schools. She knew that there must be continuing pressure to get the policy implemented and so she founded the State Children's Association and entered into pressure-group politics, becoming a successful lobbyist.

Henrietta claimed to be independent politically, although Samuel was known as a Liberal. Liberal governments helped them, for Samuel got preferment when the Liberals were in power, being appointed as Canon in Bristol and then in Westminster Cathedral. Also their causes were Liberal causes: social housing, pensions and welfare. Henrietta makes no comment on the suffragettes. She believed strongly in the advancement of women but thought it would be made by work in local government, social work, and achieving success in the careers they were pursuing.

In her fifties she had a new lease of life and embarked on creating the Suburb, her ideal community, the antidote to the slums of Whitechapel. She believed that bad housing was a source of the poor health and morals of the working class, moreover there were the examples of Bournville and Letchworth pointing to a new world. Perhaps the death of her beloved foster child Dorothy made her look for a new interest to grow and love. When Samuel died in 1913 she plunged into further work as an antidote to grief.

Her idealism, drive and gift for management all found expression in her creation of the Suburb. In a memoir Raymond Unwin wrote:

> "An indefatigable worker, she always prepared carefully for every interview or meeting, and generally had the advantage of knowing more about the affairs under discussion than anyone else present.
> In the creation of the garden Suburb she was a pioneer, exerting considerable influence on the course of town planning, in this country and elsewhere, and helping to promote the introduction of the first Town Planning Act, by John Burns, three years later. In this project Dame Henrietta had a success which has so far proved unique: in no other development have all the combined ideals for which she worked been so fully realised."[474]

Was she satisfied with the Suburb she created? Harold Lacey in a note on *Henrietta Barnett's Thoughts on the Garden Suburb and the Institute* said she was disappointed that:

> "The Garden Suburb expressed only a part of her dream. Her disappointment was for three reasons. In the first place many of the houses were in respect of design and fabric of poor quality. Secondly she was surprised and hurt by the almost complete lack of help from the residents of the Suburb in her social and educational schemes. Her third and greatest disappointment was over the Institute. She had expected to have a very large sum of money at her disposal for the creation of a unique educational centre, extraordinary in its comprehensiveness. On a large area of the Suburb there were to be a Junior School, two secondary schools – one for girls the other for boys, an Art School and a large building specially equipped for technical classes in scientific, commercial and technical subjects. There was to be a large library divided into two departments, one containing books for adults, the other books for children. Some of the large rooms were to be specially designed and equipped for dramatic and musical performances and there were to be gymnasia for adults and children.
> The social work done by Mr & Mrs Barnett at Toynbee Hall in Whitechapel had won the attention and admiration of many rich men not only in England but in America and South Africa; and when she made it known that she was planning to establish in the Garden Suburb an educational centre which would serve as a model in educational organization as Toynbee Hall had been a model for social settlements she received promises from English, American and South African millionaires of donations amounting to well over £250,000. These promises were made in the years before the First World War. When, after the war, she asked that the donations should be sent, all who had promised, with the exception of Mr Rockefeller, replied that the heavy taxation caused by the war had made it impossible for them to implement their promises; and Mr Rockefeller reduced his gift from £50,000 to £5,000."[475]

Lacey went on to say that after the war the Institute became dependent on Middlesex County Council for money and Henrietta had to reduce her aims to only a secondary school for girls with evening classes in art and technical subjects.

If Henrietta were to return to the Suburb today she would be delighted to see the little houses and gardens, the home-making and the healthy children, but soon she would find out that her community plan had been destroyed. Her schemes for communal living have all fizzled out, and Meadway Court and Waterlow Court lost their communal dining rooms during the war and they were never renewed. The Wellgarth Nursery Training College was converted to a youth hostel, but is now luxury homes selling at £6 million.Queen's Court and Emmott Close are available to all, no longer just working women. In Homesfield most of the accommodation has become private flats. Only Abbeyfield House provides communal life for the elderly where once there were "waifs and strays", and The Orchard has triumphantly survived, providing small flats and a warden service for active elderly people; it is still a haven of rest.

Touring the Suburb, she would be astonished at the disappearance of the Club House, scene of so many wedding receptions and society meetings. She would be pleased that old people have a centre, but ask "Why is there no social centre for children and parents?" – and of course she would set about making one.

Henrietta would be most dismayed to see what has become of her Institute. The compulsory purchase of the Institute building by the Department of Education and the London Borough of Barnet showed that those authorities had neither understanding nor appreciation of community. As Lord Lytton said: "The Institute is central to our purpose". The Institute was torn out of the heart of the Suburb, and although it is flourishing in nearby East Finchley, this has wrecked the original community plan, a plan that has been admired by town planners throughout the world. Henrietta would weep; she had hoped that every Suburb would have an adult education institute. But she would rejoice in the new Institute Arts building in East Finchley, the phoenix of the art school she strived to create. With her usual drive and optimism she would raise money to turn it into an even more renowned school of art.

Soon Henrietta would be meeting the residents and would ask: "Where are the clerks and artisans?" She would realize that the mixture of classes, for which she had striven till her death, was no more and that the Suburb had become exclusively middle class. This modern Henrietta would wish that she had interspersed the big houses amongst the small, and would want true social equality.

What of the neighbourliness? She would see the many notices hanging on trees for societies and be delighted by the great success of her Horticultural Society. She would hear people greeting each other in the road, see the crowds at Resident Association and Trust meetings. She would find that the Fellowship was still helping the needy.

She would see the streets planted with trees, just as she liked them, and the men and women busy in their gardens and on the allotments. But she would be critical of the overgrown front hedges which mask the architecture and create divisions between neighbours. She would wonder why no-one was playing tennis in the Square. And what had become of the Tea House?

The 21st century Henrietta would have forgotten anti-Semitism and embrace cultural and ethnic diversity in the hope it would lead to a league of nations. She would be like her Samuel who was unique in being able to love everybody and through Toynbee Hall helped the Jewish immigrants. She would be sad to find that there is a marked division in the Suburb between the growing Orthodox Jewish community centred round the Norrice Lea synagogue and the rest of the community, whether Christian or Jewish. It is difficult to put oneself back into their state of mind, particularly for anyone who wants universal tolerance to reign.

Jewish people began to settle in the Suburb in the early 1930s. A group led by Mr Tanchan, among others, formed a synagogue and hired a classroom in the Henrietta Barnett School for Saturday mornings. This was considerably discussed, and evidently Henrietta approved. Contrast this with the behaviour of estate agents in the 1950s when they would tell Jewish people that there were no houses for sale and so keep them out! Meanwhile all the private schools limited the number of Jewish children by imposing a quota. Despite this anti-Semitism the community grew, and built the Norrice Lea synagogue. They have a social programme for all ages, which is excellent, but means there is little social mix with the rest of the Suburb community. It is ironic that the Jewish population of the Suburb has expanded so much that in the far future St Jude-on-the-Hill may be at risk of closure, like St Jude's in Whitechapel.

Henrietta would be horrified by the sceptical, casual outlook of the English middle class and puzzled that they were copying the working class, following football, listening to pop music and swearing. She was convinced of the superiority of high culture and sure that, given the opportunity to experience great music, poetry and art, working-class people would enjoy it and be ennobled. After all, Whitechapel Art Gallery and Toynbee Hall had attracted the people of the East End to see great art. She worshipped through painting and music, and was confident in pressing everybody to join her.

> "It is the glory and good of Art
> That Art remains the one way possible
> Of speaking truth, to mouths like mine, at least."
> (Browning)

The Suburb is known and has been copied throughout the world. From the start it was reported in detail in the national press and this was largely because of Henrietta's modern understanding of the importance of the media, even knowing how to manipulate the press by writing appropriate text for each paper or magazine. Also the Suburb was only a twopenny train fare away from Fleet Street, a pleasant trip for journalists. Her speeches were tailored to the audience; she had a strong voice and could bring tears and raise a laugh, and use her magic lantern with slides of children in slums, of model housing and comparative statistics.

Letchworth Garden City was started slightly before the Suburb and attracted attention, but not nearly as much as the Suburb. While Brentham was very slowly built, the Suburb arose with amazing speed due to Henrietta's ability as a fundraiser. After 1918 few garden cities or suburbs were built, but the Hampstead Garden Suburb was a model for the council housing, especially with Unwin at the helm in the Ministry of Housing.

Another reason for the fame of the Suburb is that many famous people have lived here. Kitty Slack's unpublished book *People of Fame and Renown* is deposited in the Archive. Now we have the meticulously researched *Who Was Who in the Hampstead Garden Suburb* by Eva Jacobs. It is difficult to choose a few among so many names. During the first twenty-five years in the Suburb you could have met Joan Mary Fry, Quaker, pacifist and relief worker in Germany after the First World War; Archbishop Trevor Huddleston, President of the Anti-Apartheid movement; Eric Coates, who composed the "Dambusters March"; Bernard and Helen Bosanquet, he an idealist philosopher, she a social theorist; Sir John Braithwaite, Chairman of the Stock Exchange and his brother Joseph Braithwaite MP; Marie Goossens, the harpist, whose whole family was musically gifted; Mrs Greenhalgh, a heroic woman who was a member of the Women's Sick and Wounded Convoy Corps in the Balkans during the First World War; Sir Martin Furnival-Jones, a head of MI5. Today's celebs include Jonathan Ross and Richard and Judy, TV presenters, Arab princes, millionaires, and many people important in business and banking;

but most of the professors, civil servants, architects, artists, potters and weavers of yore can no longer afford the houses.

After Henrietta's death she was forgotten by the world. It was a hundred years before two biographies were published in the same year, *Only A Woman* by Alison Creedon and *Henrietta Barnett in Whitechapel* by myself. Why was this famous woman forgotten? After she died it was known that Marion Paterson, her close companion, was writing her biography. Unfortunately Marion was too old to complete the job and left only her *Quasi-Autobiography*, a collection of letters of condolence and information drawn from Henrietta's diary and letters. Marion died just after the Second World War, but by then interest had moved on and Henrietta was no longer famous. In the Suburb she was remembered as an old lady in Victorian dress with a reputation for being very bossy, severe and moralizing. Her character had changed over the years. Beatrice Webb had met her when she was still very attractive, "pretty, witty and well-to-do," and had praised her energy, courage and sympathy. But as she grew older her self-confidence developed into a domineering attitude towards people. There were few memories of her charisma, vigour, and idealism. It is not surprising that no biography was written.

Beatrice Webb said "She would have been conceited but for her admiration for her husband." With the loss of Samuel, and on becoming Dame Henrietta, she became more commanding. She was well known for asking acquaintances to tea and then requiring them to help in one of her good causes. They would find themselves serving cucumber sandwiches to working women in the drawing room ("nothing but the best for the poorest"), or unwillingly entertaining grimy children to a bumper tea and a playtime in the garden, where, hungry for Vitamin C, they could not stop themselves from raiding the raspberries and climbing the apple tree.

Henrietta was inspired by Ruskin, William Morris and James Hinton, whose ideas were taught to her by her schoolteacher. She kept her idealism all her life, and the drive to realise her ideas in practice. Most of all she was inspired by her Samuel's belief that people could bring the Kingdom of Heaven into the sin-stained world:

> "To those who love God, the kingdom of the future means a kingdom of love and peace – of truth and purity. Think of such a kingdom as that. There would be no more war – no more strikes – no more prisons and workhouses. The public houses would no more sell poisonous drink to destroy men's bodies, but books and papers would be given to build up and refresh men's minds. No children would be without their garden full of flowers to play in, no boys without their cricket fields. All men would be pure, all women strong. There would be rest for all who are weary and comfort for all who are sad. That is the Kingdom of the Future, that is the Promised Land to which all humanity is travelling."[476]

Samuel had often said that he was but the mouthpiece of his wife and had the courage of her opinions. Samuel's death was a terrible loss to Henrietta, and yet she continued to work unceasingly and effectively. She embarked on ambitious projects and never lost hope. She was an idealist and the source of energy, while Samuel had judgement and wisdom: an ideal partnership.

Henrietta's dress and morals were old-fashioned, but she embraced modern technology, understood the media, rejoiced in cars and wanted to fly in an aeroplane.

Plate 94 (opposite)
Five girls skipping
along Willifield Way.
Henrietta's dream is
realised.

298

299

She had a great capacity for growth, so she could adapt to changing times. In the 1870s she worked for the Charity Organisation Society with its repressive policies; by the 1920s she supported pensions for all, unemployment relief, municipal housing, and even suggested paying mothers to look after their own children. She fought with depression and used her manic periods to conceive new ideas to better humanity, such as her Children's Country Holiday Fund. She was a superb administrator and fundraiser. She understood pressure-group politics and through her State Children's Association she achieved a big move forward in children's long march from institutional care to individual freedom and love. As Prime Minister Asquith said, she was "The non-official custodian of the children of the State".

She was an iron lady, who decided her aims and overcame most people in her way. Mrs Thatcher had similar qualities; she started in a feminine way, showing television viewers her store cupboard, but soon she lowered her voice and used it to great effect. Like Mrs Thatcher and most prominent women in the past, Henrietta had to adopt male characteristics of strength and aggression to succeed. But with her love of dress, she was very feminine. What difference did her gender make to her success? She was more concerned with the use of buildings and of space than with architecture. With her experience of visiting working-class homes, housing management and the books she had written on domestic arts, she understood what was needed. She planned homes where every house had a bath, even though some were tip-up baths in the kitchen. There were no basements such as Victorian maids had slaved in. Suburb maids were to be given a newspaper to read and encouraged to go to their Daisy Guild at the Institute. Women found many classes to interest them for the arts and crafts were very well taught and Henrietta herself organized the sketching which had always been a woman's pastime. She had hoped for a School of Domestic Science, but failed to find the finance. Frequent small open spaces were planned within walking distance for little children and old people. The battered wives crying in the streets of Whitechapel made her realize the evils of drink, and she hoped that men in her Suburb would spend their time in the garden and allotment, so had no pubs. Her love of flowers led her to encourage Whitechapel women to make window-boxes and she organized flower-shows at Toynbee Hall. In the Suburb she started the Horticultural Society. She planned communal housing specifically for women: Bigwood and Southwood Court were for officers' widows and their families. The Barnett Homestead, Queen's Court and Emmott Close were all for women and The Orchard has always had more widows than widowers. Meadway Court is the only group of flats specifically designed for men, sharing dining-room and games room. Her contribution to community planning was deeply affected by gender and was important in making houses into happy homes for women and children.

Henrietta had two very separate parts to her life: before she was fifty, she was dedicated to social work and lived in the slums; after she was fifty she became a community planner and created a Suburb life which was the antidote to slum life. Her Suburb became a model for the world. In both parts of her life she was successful. Her inner spiritual life informed all she did and she casts a light which will never fail. Unhappy with conventional religion, she found God in Nature, in great paintings and in happy, healthy, children romping around the cottage gardens. Ever an optimist and idealist, the memorial leaflet sent to her many friends quoted Browning:

"Ah! But a man's reach should exceed his grasp,
Or what's a heaven for?"

References for Part Two

1. Grafton Green, Brigid, Heath End House file HGS Archive.
2. Grafton Green, Brigid, *Hampstead Garden Suburb – Vision and Reality* pp. 7–8.
3. Minutes of Hampstead Heath Extension Council 26 June 1903 ACC/3816/01//02/001.
4. Hampstead Heath Extension Council ACC/3816/01//02/001 26 June 1903 first meeting.
5. HB *Canon Barnett II* p. 18.
6. C W Ikin, *Hampstead Garden Suburb, Dreams and Realities* p. 12.
7. Minutes of Hampstead Heath Extension Council 12 May 1903 ACC/3816/01/02/002.
8. Hampstead Heath Extension Council 12 June 1903 ACC/3816/01/02/002.
9. Hampstead Heath Extension Council 14 Aug 1904.
10. HB *Canon Barnett II.*
11. Newspaper cuttings 1903–7 p. 1 *Hampstead and Highgate Express* 15 July 1903.
12. Hampstead Heath Extension Council 14 July 1903 ACC/3816/01/02/002.
13. HB *The Story of the Growth of the Hampstead Garden Suburb 1907–1928*, p. 5.
14. Grafton Green, Brigid, *Hampstead Garden Suburb, 1907–1977* p. 6. Reprinted in HGS Archive Trust Handlist of the Hampstead Garden Suburb Archive 2001.
15. HB *Canon Barnett II* p. 315.
16. HB *Canon Barnett II* p. 41.
17. HB *The Story of the Growth of the Hampstead Garden Suburb 1907–1928* p. 6.
18. HB *Canon Barnett II* p. 316.
19. Newspaper cuttings 1903–7 p. 44 *Hampstead Express* 2 July 1904.
20. HB *Canon Barnett II* p. 316.
21. HB *Canon Barnett II* p. 314.
22. Minutes of HGS Trust 4 May 1906 ACC/3816/01/03/001.
23. Jackson, *Frank Sir Raymond Unwin* pp. 14–16.
24. Boult, Adrian, *My Own Trumpet.*
25. Paterson, Marion Chap XIV.
26. HB *The Story of the Growth of the Hampstead Garden Suburb* 1907–1928 p. 8.
27. 'Dame Henrietta Barnett DBE, a memoir' by Sir Raymond Unwin, Journal of the Royal Institute of British Architects XLII 3ss, 27 June 1936, pp. 885–6. Quoted in Mervyn Miller *Hampstead Garden Suburb, Arts and Crafts Utopia?* Afterword p. 249.
28. *Ibid.*
29. Minutes of HGS Trust Ltd 10 Nov 1908 ACC/3816/01/03/001.
30. Fragment of letter, possibly to Marnham, HGS Archive 'Beginnings of the HGS' file.
31. I am indebted to David Baker for this information.

32. Minutes of HGS Trust 1 Dec 1908 ACC/3816/01/03/001.
33. *The Times* 6 March 1905.
34. HB 'A Garden Suburb at Hampstead', *Contemporary Review* Jan–June 1905 p. 231.
35. Barnett, Mrs S A, 'Science and City Suburbs' in ed. Hand, J E, *Science in Public Affairs 1906* p. 48.
36. Newspaper cuttings 1903–7 p. 91 *Spectator* 24 June 1905.
37. Newspaper cuttings 1903–7 pp. 100–1 *Daily Chronicle* 15 July 1905.
38. Minutes of Hampstead Garden Suburb Trust ACC/3816/01/02/001.
39. Newspaper cuttings 1903–7 p. 87 *Agricultural Economist* June 1905.
40. Newspaper cuttings 1903–7 p. 97 *Echo* 14 July 1905.
41. Newspaper cuttings 1903–7 p. 121 *Morning Post* 25 Jan 1906.
42. Newspaper cuttings 1903–7 p. 112 *Daily News* 1 Dec 1905.
43. Newspaper cuttings 1903–7 p. 119 *Standard* 17 Jan 1906.
44. Newspaper cuttings 1903–7 p. 121 *The Times* 13 Jan 1906.
45. LMA/F/BAR/359 Letter 17.3.1906.
46. LMA/F/BAR/370 Letter 27.10.1906.
47. Newspaper cuttings 1907–10 p. 45 *Daily News* 22 July 1908.
48. HB *The Story of the Growth of Hampstead Garden Suburb 1907–1928* p. 13.
49. Newspaper cuttings 1903–7 p. 123 *The Queen* 17 Feb 1906.
50. LMA ACC/3816/02/01/006 5/5 Letter 19 Aug 1903.
51. Minutes of HGS Trust ACC/3816/01/03/001.
52. HB *Canon Barnett II* p. 316.
53. HB *Canon Barnett II* p. 330.
54. Newspaper cuttings 1903–7 pp. 148–9 *Hampstead and Highgate Express* 4 May 1907.
55. HGS Archive. Letter from HB to Mrs Lillian Thompson 1.5.07.
56. Newspaper cuttings 1903–7 p. 150 *The Leeds Budget* 8 June 1907.
57. Newspaper cuttings 1907–10 p. 24 *Daily Graphic* 3 Oct 1907.
58. Newspaper cuttings 1903–7 p. 151 *Yorkshire Post* 10 June 1907.
59. Newspaper cuttings 1907–10 p. 48 *Sunday School Chronicle* 30 July 1908.
60. Newspaper cuttings 1907–10 p. 67 *Daily Graphic* 8 Dec 1908.
61. HB *The Story of the Growth of the Hampstead Garden Suburb 1907–1928* p. 13.
62. Clayre, Percy & Ridley, Jane (Ed.) *The Letters of Edwin Lutyens to his Wife, Lady Emily* p. 168 Hamish Hamilton 1986.
63. *Ibid.*
64. Gray, A.S. *Suburb Year Book 1981* p. 31.
65. Clayre, Percy & Ridley Jane (Ed.) *The Letters of Edwin Lutyens to his Wife, Lady Emily*, p. 168 Hamish Hamilton 1986.
66. Pevsner, Nicholas, *Buildings of England, London. North* 1988 p. 143.
67. Clayre, Percy & Ridley Jane (Ed.) *The Letters of Edwin Lutyens to his Wife, Lady Emily* p. 184 Oct 15 1909.
68. *Ibid.* pp. 213–14 April 14 1911.
69. *The Story of the Growth of the Hampstead Garden Suburb 1907–1928* pp. 46–7.
70. Newspaper cuttings 1907–10 p. 55 *Hampstead and Highgate Express* 5 Sept 1908.
71. ACC/3816/01/02/005 Minutes of Board of Directors of HGS Trust 16 March 1909.
72. HGS Archive Horticultural Society file.
73. Newspaper cuttings 1907–10 p. 73 *Hampstead and Highgate Express* 1909.
74. HGS Archive Horticultural Society file.
75. Newspaper cuttings 1907–10 p. 76 *Standard* 29 Mar 1909.

76. HGS Trust Minutes 10 Nov 1908 ACC/3816/01/03/001.
77. HGS Trust Minutes 10 Nov 1910 ACC/3816/01/03/001.
78. Newspaper cuttings 1910–11 p. 110 *Glasgow News* 11 May 1911. The "other garden suburb" must have been Letchworth.
79. Pankhurst, E. Sylvia, 'The Home Front' quoted in HGS Archive Pioneers file.
80. Newspaper cuttings 1910–11 pp. 186–7 *Standard* 2 Sept 1911.
81. Newspaper cuttings 1907–10 p. 156 *Westminster Gazette* 16 Feb 1910.
82. HB *Canon Barnett II* p. 323.
83. HGS Archive.
84. Oral evidence of Marjorie Scarfe ACC/3816/09/01/002.
85. Newspaper cuttings 1907–10 p. 184 *Hampstead Advertiser* 7 May 1910.
86. ACC/3816/09/01/026 Oral evidence of Miss Harris.
87. Newspaper cuttings 1907–10 p. 95 *Daily Chronicle* 8 July 1909.
88. Newspaper cuttings 1907–10 p. 122 *Builder* 22 July 1909.
89. 'Of Town Planning', Cornhill Magazine Jan 1911. In *Practicable Socialism* 1915 p. 272.
90. *Ibid.*
91. Morris, William, *How We Live and How We Might Live* Nonesuch Centenary Edition pp. 583–4.
92. HB *Canon Barnett II* p. 181.
93. HB *Canon Barnett II* p. 138.
94. HB *Canon Barnett II* p. 189.
95. ACC/3816/01/02/006 Minutes of Board of Directors of HGS Trust June 1913.
96. Paterson, Marion LMA/4063/006 Chap XVII.
97. HB *The Story of the Growth of the Hampstead Garden Suburb 1907–1928* pp. 14–15 & HGS Archive Waterlow Court file.
98. Photo album ACC/3816/02/05/003.
99. HB *Story of the growth of Hampstead Garden Suburb 1907–1928* p. 65.
100. Newspaper cuttings 1910–11 p. 110 *Hampstead Advertiser* 11 May 1911.
101. *The Record* 1913.
102. *Ibid.*
103. HB *The Story of the Growth of Hampstead Garden Suburb 1907–1928* pp. 21–5.
104. HB *Canon Barnett II* p. 324.
105. Slack, Kitty, *Henrietta's Dream* p. 122.
106. HB *The Story of the Growth of Hampstead Garden Suburb 1907–1928* p. 70.
107. HB *Canon Barnett II* p. 324.
108. *Town Crier* April 1915.
109. HB *The Story of the Growth of Hampstead Garden Suburb 1907–1928* pp. 61–3.
110. HB *The Story of the Growth of Hampstead Garden Suburb 1907–1928* pp. 71–4.
111. HB *Canon Barnett II* p. 85.
112. Newspaper cuttings 1907–10 p. 190 *Hendon Advertiser* 15 July 1910.
113. HB *The Story of the Growth of Hampstead Garden Suburb 1907–1928* p. 43.
114. HGS Archive Institute Papers from 1909 file.
115. The following information about the Institute is from HB *The Story of the Growth of Hampstead Garden Suburb 1907–1928* pp. 43–60.
116. Newspaper cuttings 1907–10 p. 105 *Daily Telegraph* 15 July 1909.
117. Newspaper cuttings 1907–10 p. 86 *Daily News* 9 June 1909.
118. Newspaper cuttings 1907–10 p. 119 *Daily News* 22 July 1909.

119. ACC/3816/01/02/006 Minutes of Board of Directors of HGS Trust Nov 1912.
120. HGS Archive Town Planning Summer School file.
121. Newspaper cuttings 1907–10 p. 113 *The Queen* 17 July 1909.
122. HGS Archive Music file.
123. Newspaper cuttings 1907–10 p. 64 *Daily News* 23 Nov 1908.
124. HGS Archive Clubhouse file.
125. HGS Archive Barnett file.
126. Newspaper cuttings 1907–10 p. 163 *Birkenhead News* 12 Feb 1910.
127. Newspaper cuttings 1907–10 p. 75 'Co-partnership 1909'.
128. *Record* 1913 pp. 47, 103, 138, 149.
129. Newspaper cuttings p. 125 *Daily News* 22 May 1911.
130. HGS Archives Institute Finance file 8 July 1914.
131. Newspaper cuttings 1907–10 p. 123 *The Times* 26 July 1909.
132. Newspaper cuttings 1907–10 p. 164 *Hampstead and Highgate Express* 19 Feb 1910.
133. Newspaper cuttings 1907–10 p. 72 *Guardian* 23 Dec 1908.
134. Newspaper cuttings 1907–10 p. 73 *Hampstead and Highgate Express* 1909.
135. *Ibid.*
136. Waugh, Evelyn, *A Little Learning.*
137. Newspaper cuttings *Westminster Gazette* 1 April 1920.
138. Roe, David, *Standing in the Wings* 1987 p. 34.
139. HB *The Story of the Growth of Hampstead Garden Suburb* p. 37.
140. I am grateful to Mrs Jean Barraclough for helping me with this topic.
141. HB *The Story of the Growth of the Hampstead Garden Suburb 1907–1928* pp. 37–8.
142. Slack, Kitty, *Henrietta's Dream* pp. 62–8.
143. HGS Archive Oral evidence of Molly Trapp.
144. *The Woman Citizen*, Cuttings of Interviews and Articles 1921–22 HGS Archive.
145. ACC/3816/01/02/006 Minutes of Board of Directors of HGS Trust Jan 1919.
146. HB *The Story of the Growth of Hampstead Garden Suburb 1907–1928* pp. 71–4.
147. *Ibid.* p. 61.
148. *Ibid.* p. 61.
149. HB in James Hand *Science in Public Affairs* London 1906 pp. 65–66.
150. Newspaper cuttings 1911–12 p. 7 *Sunday Times* 15 Oct 1911.
151. LMA/F/BAR/284 Letter to Frank Barnett 7.2.1903.
152. HB *Canon Barnett II* p. 314.
153. HB *Canon Barnett II* p. 184.
154. HGS Archive Thompson Family Correspondence.
155. HB *Canon Barnett II* p. 300.
156. State Children's Association. BLPES holds all that remains of the records of this Association.
157. LMA ACC/3816/02/01/003.
158. LMA/F/BAR/296 Letter 2 May 1903.
159. HB *Canon Barnett II* p. 189.
160. ACC 3816/02/01/005 Note in HB's handwriting.
161. HB *Practicable Socialism* pp. 138–141.
162. HB *Canon Barnett II* p. 251.
163. HB *Canon Barnett II* p. 59.
164. LMA/F/BAR/302 Letter 12 June 1903.

165. LMA/F/BAR/404 Letter 7.3.1908.
166. HB *Practicable Socialism* p. 152.
167. HB *Practicable Socialism* p. 206.
168. HB Practicable Socialism pp. 213.
169. State Children's Association Seventh Report, for 1907–9 p. 7.
170. State Children's Association Seventh Report, for 1907–9 p. 17.
171. State Children's Association Eighth Report, for 1910–1912 p. 26.
172. Stephens, Margaret *Women and Marriage* 1909.
173. Mrs S.A. Barnett *Principles of Recreation* in Canon & Mrs S.A. Barnett *Towards Social Reform* 1907 p. 291.
174. HB *Practicable Socialism* p. 92.
175. *Towards Social Reform* p. 296.
176. HB *Towards Social Reform* p. 310.
177. HB *Towards Social Reform* p. 309.
178. HB *Practicable Socialism* pp. 41–52.
179. LMA ACC/3816/09/01/026 Oral evidence from Miss Harris.
180. HB *Canon Barnett II* p. 171.
181. HGS Archive Press Cuttings obituaries p. 99.
182. WAG/EAR/1/1(1)1893–1898.
183. HB *Canon Barnett II* p. 172.
184. WAG/EAR/1/1(1)1893–1898.
185. WAG/EAR/1/1(1)1893–1898.
186. HB *Canon Barnett II* p. 175.
187. Newspaper cuttings *Sunday School Chronicle* 21.3.01.
188. Newspaper cuttings 1903–7 p. 132 *Morning Post* 7 July 1906.
189. HB *Canon Barnett II* p. 175.
190. HB *Canon Barnett II* p. 191.
191. WAG/EAR/2/27 24 July 1916.
192. Quoted in 'Whitechapel Gallery Archives' in *Apollo Magazine*.
193. WAG/EAR Letter to Rosabel Watson 18 June 1915.
194. Trustees' Minute book No1 1899–1919.
195. WAG/EAR Letter from Rosabel Watson 21 June 1914.
196. WAG/EAR/ Letter to Mr Ross 9 July 1915.
197. WAG/EAR/ Letter to Rosabel 9 July 1915.
198. WAG/EAR/2/31919–1947. Trustees' Minute Book No1 1899–1919. 8 July 1915.
199. WAG/EAR/2/25.
200. Newspaper cuttings *Morning Post* 5.11.1919.
201. WAG/EAR/2/29.
202. Paterson, Marion Chap XIX.
203. HB *Canon Barnett II* p. 188.
204. HB *Canon Barnett II* p. 189.
205. HB *Canon Barnett II* p. 192.
206. HB *Canon Barnett II* p. 194.
207. HB *Canon Barnett II* p. 218.
208. HB *Canon Barnett II* p. 218.
209. HB *Canon Barnett II* p. 191.
210. HB *Canon Barnett II* p. 343.

211. LMA/F/BAR/377 Letter 19.1.1907.
212. HB *Canon Barnett II* p. 364.
213. HB *Canon Barnett II* pp. 345–6.
214. HB *Canon Barnett II* p. 349.
215. HB *Canon Barnett II* p. 330.
216. HB *Canon Barnett II* p. 347.
217. HB *Canon Barnett II* p. 337.
218. HB *Canon Barnett II* p. 342.
219. Paterson, Marion Chap XVII.
220. HB *Canon Barnett II* p. 327–8.
221. HB *Matters That Matter* p. 10.
222. LMA/4063/006.
223. HB *Canon Barnett II* p. 353.
224. HGS Archive Barnett file.
225. HB *Canon Barnett II* p. 354.
226. HB *Canon Barnett II* p. 326.
227. Paterson, Marion Chap XVII.
228. HB *Canon Barnett II* p. 320.
229. ACC/3816/01/02/005 Minutes of Board of Directors of HGS Trust 31 Jan 1911.
230. Report to the Lettings Committee of the HGS Trust ACC/3816/01/03/001.
231. HGS Archive Institute Clubs and Societies file.
232. Newspaper cuttings 1911–12 p. 131 *Hendon Advertiser* 6 Sept 1912.
233. *The Record* p. 5 7 Dec 1916.
234. HGS Archive Institute, Clubs and Societies file.
235. Newspaper cuttings p. 124 *Hampstead and Highgate Express* 20 May 1911.
236. Newspaper cuttings 1910–11 p. 49 *Lloyds Weekly Newspaper* 19 March 1911.
237. Newspaper cuttings 1910–11 p. 48 *Sunday Times* 19 March 1911.
238. Newspaper cuttings 1910–11 p. 57 *Daily Telegraph* 20 March 1911.
239. HB *The Story of the Hampstead Garden Suburb 1907–1928* p. 14.
240. Newspaper cuttings 1910–11 p. 66 *Daily Mail* 20 March 1911.
241. Newspaper cuttings 1910–11 p. 65 *Evening Times* 20 March 1911.
242. Newspaper cuttings 1910–11 p. 110 *Hampstead Advertiser* 11 May 1911.
243. Newspaper cuttings 1910–11 p. 119 *Hendon and Finchley Times* 12 May 1911.
244. Newspaper cuttings 1910–11 p. 109 *Daily Express* 11 May 1911.
245. Newspaper cuttings 1910–11 p. 108 *Daily Sketch* 11 May 1911.
246. Newspaper cuttings 1910–11 p. 137 *Hampstead and Highgate Express* 24 June 1911.
247. Newspaper cuttings 1910–11 p. 142 *Hampstead and Highgate Express* 1 July 1911.
248. HGS Trust Minutes 23 Feb 1909 ACC/3816/01/03/001.
249. ACC/3816/01/03/001.
250. HGS Archive. Oral evidence.
251. Newspaper cuttings 1911–12 p. 106 *Winnipeg Telegram* 5 July 1912.
252. Newspaper cuttings 1911–12 p. 81 *The Times* 11 April 1912.
253. Newspaper cuttings 1911–12 p. 107 *Standard* 22 July 1912.
254. Newspaper cuttings 1911–12 p. 128 *Garden Suburb and Golders Green Advertiser* 30 August 1912.
255. Newspaper cuttings 1907–10 p. 87 *Standard* 16 June 1909.
256. F/BAR/420 Letter 4.6.1909.

257. HGS Archive Lettings Committee at 3 Little Cloisters 15 March 1911 HGS Trust Minutes.
258. ACC/3816/01/02/005 Minutes of Board of Directors of HGS Trust.
259. Oral evidence.
260. Newspaper cuttings 1910–11 p. 154 *Daily News* 21 July 1911.
261. HB *Canon Barnett II* p. 371.
262. HB *Canon Barnett II* p. 340.
263. Paterson, Marion Chap XVII.
264. Letters from Henrietta to Jane Addams 1913–34 Swarthmore College Peace Collection. *Jane Addams Papers Series 1, Supplement* (Photocopies held in the HGS Archive).
265. HGS Archive Thompson Family file. Letter undated.
266. HB *Canon Barnett II* p. 385.
267. HGS Archive. Barnett file.
268. Paterson, Marion Chap XV.
269. ACC/3816/01/02/006 Minutes of Board of Directors of HGS Trust July 1915.
270. HB *Canon Barnett II* pp. 390–3.
271. Barnett File in HGS Suburb.
272. *Jane Addams Papers* July 10 1913.
273. A/TOY/6/4 Letter to Lord Milner 20.9.1913.
274. *Jane Addams Papers* Sept 15 1913.
275. ACC/3816/01/03/002.
276. 11 July 1913 Trust Committee Minutes ACC/3816/01/03/002.
277. Paterson, Marion Chap XXX11.
278. HB *Canon Barnett II* p. 393.
279. *Jane Addams Papers* 11 October 1913.
280. Letter to Jane Addams Dec 2 1919.
281. Letter to Jane Addams Jan 28 1919.
282. Letter to Jane Addams Feb 1 1920.
283. Tims, Margaret, *Jane Addams of Hull House* 1961 George Allen and Unwin London.
284. HB *Canon Barnett II* p. 30.
285. Paterson, Marion LMA/4063/006 Chap XX.
286. *Town Crier* Feb.1916 p. 116.
287. Paterson, Marion LMA/4063/006 Chap XVII.
288. LMA/ A/TOY/6/20.
289. Paterson, Marion LMA/4063/006 Chap XVII.
290. HGS Archive Thompson Family file.
291. HGS Archive Thompson Family file Letter 2.11.1917.
292. Letter to Jane Addams Jan 28 1919.
293. Letter to Jane Addams Jan 28 1919.
294. ACC/3816/02/01/003 Letter 18 Oct 1913.
295. HB *Canon Barnett II* p. 390.
296. HB *Canon Barnett II* p. 323.
297. Grafton Green, Brigid *Hampstead Garden Suburb 1907–1977* p. 17.
298. LMA/A/TOY/6/20 Letter to Lord Milner 5.11.1917.
299. Letter to Jane Addams 1915.
300. Paterson, Marion Chap XXII.
301. Letter from Queen Mary 9 July 1920 HGS Archive slide.

302. Paterson, Marion LMA/4063/006 Chap XXI.
303. Paterson, Marion Chap XXIII.
304. HB *Matters That Matter* p. 65.
305. Paterson, Marion Chap XXIII.
306. Paterson, Marion Chap XXII.
307. Paterson, Marion Chap XXI.
308. ACC.3186/02/01/004.
309. ACC/3816/02/01/005.
310. Paterson, Marion Chap XXIII.
311. Letter to Jane Addams Nov 1920.
312. *Daily Telegraph* 29, 30, 31 March 5, 9, 11 April 1921.
313. HB *Matters That Matter* pp. 77, 78.
314. HB Matters That Matter p. 64.
315. HB Matters That Matter p. 80, 81.
316. HB Matters That Matter p. 88.
317. HB Matters That Matter p. 25.
318. HB Matters That Matter p. 27.
319. HB Shaftesbury Lecture 1921 in *Matters That Matter* p. 215.
320. Newspaper cuttings 1921, 1922 *"Who's Who"*.
321. HGS Archive Barnett file. Letter to Mrs Moffit.
322. Interviews and Articles 1921–2 press cuttings HGS Archive.
323. ACC/3816/02/01/005.
324. Paterson, Marion Chap XXX.
325. HGS Archive Portraits file. Postcard to Harold Lacey.
326. Paterson, Marion Chap XIX.
327. Paterson, Marion Chap XXXI.
328. HGS Archive Barnett file.
329. *The Times* 15.1.1962.
330. HGS Archive Barnett file.
331. HB *Matters That Matter* p. 264.
332. HB *Matters That Matter* p. 13.
333. Newspaper cuttings *Daily Express* 13 Jan 1919.
334. Newspaper cuttings HB 'The Ethics of Conduct' *Westminster Gazette* 23 April 1921.
335. Oral evidence of Henrietta's great nephew, Richard Rowland.
336. HB *Matters That Matter* Introduction by John Northcote p. 5.
337. Newspaper cuttings *Golders Green Gazette* 12.4.1935.
338. HB *Matters That Matter* p. 266.
339. Newspaper cuttings *Golders Green Gazette* 12.4.1935.
340. HB *Matters That Matter* p. 115.
341. HB Shaftesbury Lecture in *Matters That Matter* p. 224.
342. Tims, Margaret, *Jane Addams of Hull House* p. 79.
343. Davis, Allen F, *American Heroine. The Life and Legend of Jane Addams* 1973 OUP.
344. HB *The Story of Hampstead Garden Suburb 1907–1928* p. 45.
345. Paterson, Marion LMA Chap XX.
346. Paterson, Marion LMA Chap XX.
347. Paterson, Marion Chap XXX.

348. Paterson, Marion Chap XXX.
349. HB *Matters That Matter* p. 112.
350. HB *Matters That Matter* pp. 109, 110.
351. HB *Matters That Matter* p. 123.
352. HB *Matters That Matter* p. 125.
353. HB *Matters That Matter* p. 104.
354. HB *Matters That Matter* p. 97.
355. HB *Matters That Matter,* Introduction by John Northcote p. 4.
356. HB *Matters That Matter* p. 106.
357. HB *Matters That Matter* p. 103.
358. 'Looking On Helps' *Cornhill Magazine* March 1929 p. 13.
359. HB *Matters That Matter* p. 26.
360. HB *Matters That Matter.*
361. HB 'Co-operative Education', *Contemporary Review* May 1922 Interviews and Articles HGS Archive.
362. HB *Matters That Matter* p. 263.
363. HB *Matters That Matter* p. 279.
364. ACC/3816/02/01/001 Letter to Stanley 15.3.27.
365. Newspaper cuttings p. 126 *Evening News* 22 May 1911.
366. HB *Matters That Matter* p. 234.
367. HB *Matters That Matter* pp. 236–9.
368. HB *Matters That Matter* p. 251.
369. HB *Matters That Matter* p. 358.
370. Newspaper cuttings 1907–10 pp. 126–7 *Review of Reviews* Aug 1909.
371. ACC/3816/01/02/006 Minutes of Board of Directors of HGS Trust.
372. ACC/3816/01/02/006 Minutes of Board of Directors of HGS Trust.
373. HB *Matters That Matter* p. 203.
374. HB *Matters That Matter* p. 204.
375. HB *Matters That Matter* p. 206.
376. Letter to Jane Addams Jan 28 1919.
377. HGS Archive, Barnett House file, Newspaper cutting *Oxford Chronicle* 30 April 1920.
378. HGS Archive, Barnett House file, Newspaper cutting *Oxford Chronicle* 26 May 1922.
379. LMA/A/TOY/24/12 Letter 7.12.28.
380. LMA/A/TOY/24/20 Letter 24.2.1929.
381. HB *Matters That Matter* p. 291.
382. HGS Archive. Barnett file.
383. Newspaper cuttings *"Who's Who"* 1921 HGS Archive.
384. Paterson, Marion Chap. XVIII.
385. *The Church Family Newspaper* 18 March 1921 HGS Archive.
386. Paterson, Marion Chap. XX.
387. HGS Archive Homesfield file. Letter 30 April 1926.
388. HGS Archive Institute correspondence 1916–24 Letter to Bishop of London.
389. Paterson, Marion Chap. XX.
390. Shaftesbury Lecture Oct 1921.
391. HGS Archive. Barnett House file Newspaper cuttings *Oxford Chronicle* 4 June 1920.
392. Paterson, Marion Chap XXI.
393. HB *Matters That Matter* p. 396.

394. HGS Institute News Jan 1928.
395. HGS Archive. Barnett file.
396. Paterson, Marion Chap XV111.
397. HGS Archive Institute papers from 1909 file.
398. Paterson, Marion Chap XV111.
399. LMA ACC/3816/02/01/008(1/6) Letters to Harold Lacey.
400. Paterson, Marion Chap XX11.
401. Paterson, Marion Chap XXVIII.
402. Letter to Jane Addams Feb 8 1924.
403. LMA ACC/3816/02/01/008.
404. Paterson, Marion Chap XXIX.
405. LMA ACC/3816/02/01/008(2/6).
406. LMA ACC/3816/02/01/008(3/6).
407. Reiss, C, *A Memoir* Swindon p17.
408. Quoted in Slack, Kitty, *Henrietta's Dream* p. 8.
409. Quoted in Grafton Green, Brigid, *Hampstead Garden Suburb 1907–1977*.
410. HGS Archive Institute 1909–1929 file.
411. Pevsner, Nicholas *The Buildings of England, London North* 1998 p. 143.
412. HGS Archive Institute Playing Fields file 2.7.1926.
413. LMA A/TOY/7/22–23.
414. Paterson, Marion Chap XXVII.
415. WAG/EAR/2/25 Letter to HB 2 June 1915.
416. Paterson, Marion Chap XV.
417. HGS Archive Institute correspondence 1916–24 Letter to Mr Buckland.
418. HGS Archive Barnett file.
419. Paterson, Marion Chap XV.
420. Letter to Jane Addams 21.11.1920.
421. HGS Institute. Report of the Council 1924–1926. HGS Archive Institute file.
422. LMA ACC/3816/06/01/001 Institute Council Minutes 27 March 1925.
423. Paterson, Marion Chap XV.
424. Letter in HGS Archive. Institute file.
425. LMA ACC3816/02/01/008 (1/6) Letters to Harold Lacey.
426. LMA ACC/3816/02/01/008(3/6).
427. HGS Institute. Report of the Council 1924–1926. HGS Archive Institute file.
428. Newspaper cuttings *Observer* 24.6.1928.
429. HGS Archive Institute Press Cuttings file *Hendon Times* 27.5.1932.
430. LMA ACC/3816/06/01/001 Institute Council Minutes 13 Dec 1929.
431. HGS Archive Institute Art file.
432. Letter to Mr Walton, Secretary to Middlesex Education Committee 28.3.31 HGS Archive.
433. HGS Archive Institute Art file.
434. HGS Archive Press Cuttings file. *Observer* 19.1.1930.
435. HGS Archives. Institute file.
436. LMA ACC/3816/02/01/001 Letter 17 May 1926.
437. HGS Archive. Institute file.
438. Newspaper cuttings *Hendon Times* 12 June 1936.
439. Paterson, Marion Chap XXX.

440. Paterson, Marion Chap XXXI.
441. LMA ACC/3816/02/01/002.
442. HGS Archive Barnett file.
443. Paterson, Marion Chap XXX.
444. HGS Archive Barnett file. Letter 15.12.1932.
445. HGS Archive. Girls' Friendly Society file.
446. HGS Archive Barnett file.
447. LMA ACC/3816/02/01/001 Letter 26.12.30.
448. LMA ACC/3816/02/01/001 Letter 13.12 27.
449. HGS Archive Institute Clubs and Societies file. The following paragraph is drawn from this file.
450. Newspaper cuttings *Hendon Times* 12 June 1936 p. 31.
451. LMA ACC/3816/02/01/001 Letter 24.11.1933.
452. Paterson, Marion Chap XXX.
453. HGS Archive Institute Art & Club file.
454. LMA ACC/3816/06/01/001 Institute Council Minutes 24 March 1933.
455. Oral evidence from Mrs Ellison, daughter of Mr Tanchan.
456. LMA ACC/3816/02/01/005 Letter to Queen Mary.
457. HGS Archive or Paterson Letter 22 July 1933.
458. Newspaper cuttings *Yorkshire Post* 11.6.1936.
459. HB *Matters That Matter* p. 257.
460. HGS Archives Press Cuttings file. *Hampstead Express* 14.7.1934.
461. Paterson, Marion Chap XXXI.
462. Paterson, Marion Chap XXXII.
463. Paterson, Marion Chap XXXII.
464. Newspaper cuttings *Hendon Times* 12 June 1936 p. 31.
465. Newspaper cuttings *Manchester Guardian* 11 June 1936.
466. Newspaper cuttings *Hendon Times* 19 June 1936 p. 72.
467. HGS Archive Barnett file.
468. Paterson, Marion Chap VIII.
469. HGS Archive Barnett file.
470. HGS Archive Barnett file.
471. ACC/3816/02/01/009.
472. Newspaper cuttings *Hendon Times and Guardian* 23.7.1937. HGS Archive Barnett file.
473. Paterson, Marion Chap XIX.
474. 'Dame Henrietta Barnett DBE, a memoir' by Sir Raymond Unwin, Journal of the Royal Institute of British Architects XLII 3ss, 27 June 1936, pp. 885–6. Quoted in Mervyn Miller *Hampstead Garden Suburb, Arts and Crafts Utopia?* Afterword p. 249.
475. LMA ACC 3816/02/04/002.
476. HGS Archive. Quoted by Henrietta in her sermon in St. Jude's 1915.

Bibliography

Books by Henrietta Barnett

Mrs Samuel A Barnett, *The Making of the Home*, Cassell, 1885.

Canon S A Barnett and Mrs S A Barnett, *Practicable Socialism*, Longmans, 1888, 1894, 1915.

Henrietta Barnett, *The Making of the Body*, Longmans, 1894.

Barnett, Canon and Mrs S A, *Towards Social Reform*, Fisher Unwin, London, 1909.

Henrietta Barnett, *Worship and Work*, Letchworth Garden City Press, 1913.

Henrietta Barnett, *Canon Barnett His Life, Work and Friends, by His Wife*. 2 vols. Second edition, John Murray, London, 1919.

Henrietta Barnett, *The Story of the Growth of Hampstead Garden Suburb 1907–1928*, with an introduction by Martin Bell. Facsimile, Hampstead Garden Suburb Archive 2007.

Dame Henrietta Barnett, *Matters That Matter,* John Murray, London, 1930, a collection of speeches and articles.

Articles by Henrietta Barnett

Most of these articles were reprinted in the various editions of *Practicable Socialism, Towards Social Reform*, or *Matters That Matter*.

The Young Women in our Workhouses, *Macmillan's Magazine*, Aug. 1879.

At Home to the Poor, *Cornhill Magazine*, May 1881.

Passionless Reformers, *Fortnightly Review*, Aug. 1882.

Pictures for the People, *Cornhill Magazine*, Mar. 1883.

Vox Clamantis, *Time*, Oct. 1885.

The Poverty of the Poor, *National Review*, July 1886.

The Children of the Great City, *Atlanta*, Apr. 1888.

East London and Crime, *National Review*, Dec. 1888.

The State as Parent, *St. George's Magazine*, Jan. 1898.

The Beginnings of Toynbee Hall, *Towards Social Reform,* Longmans, Feb. 1903.

The Garden Suburb at Hampstead, *Contemporary Review*, Feb. 1905, pp. 231–7.

Science and City Suburbs, in Hand, J E (ed.), *Science in Public Affairs,* 1906, p. 48.

The Hampstead Garden Suburb, *Garden Cities and Town Planning*, Mar. 1908, p. 22.

Some Thoughts on Recreation, *Towards Social Reform,* Longmans, Feb. 1909.

The Babies of the State, *Cornhill Magazine*, July 1909.

Of Town Planning, *Cornhill Magazine*, Jan. 1911.

The Children's Country Holiday Fun, *Cornhill Magazine*, Apr. 1912.
The Ethics of Conduct, *Westminster Gazette*, Apr. 1921.
Co-operative Education, *Contemporary Review*, May 1922, Interviews and Articles HGS Archive.
Looking On Helps, *Cornhill Magazine*, Mar. 1929.

Unpublished sources

BLPES = British Library of Political and Economic Science.
LMA = London Metropolitan Archive.
WAG = Whitechapel Art Gallery.
Barnett Family Papers, Correspondence, LMA ACC/3816/02/01/001–009.
Samuel Augustus Barnett and Henrietta Barnett, 'Our Diary. Canada etc 1890–91', Typescript. LMA: ACC/3816/02/02/001.
Samuel Augustus Barnett, Letters LMA F/BAR/3816/02/01.
Letters to Henrietta and Samuel Barnett, LMA 4266/A.
Blair, Lorraine, 'Comrade Wives, Different Marriages under the Shadow of Toynbee Hall in Late Victorian and Edwardian England', PhD thesis, University of Portsmouth. Copy in HGS Archive.
Blair, Lorraine, 'Dame Henrietta Barnett: Choosing to Settle, Daring to Dream', unpublished ms. copy in HGS Archive.
Cadbury Letters, Birmingham City Archives MS466/69/–18.
Courtney Collection, BLPES Archive.
Hampstead Garden Suburb Archive in Henrietta Barnett School: Letters, memoirs, newspaper cuttings.
Hampstead Garden Suburb Trust, Minutes of Committee Meetings, LMA.
Hampstead Garden Suburb Trust, Minutes of Board of Directors, LMA.
Hampstead Heath Extension Council, Minutes LMA ACC/3816/01/02/001.
Letters from Henrietta to Jane Addams 1913–34, Swarthmore College Peace Collection. Jane Addams Papers, Series 1, Supplement (photocopies held in the HGS Archive).
Letters of Octavia Hill to Canon and Mrs Barnett, BLPES Archive Collection Misc 512.
Paterson, Marion, ms. Quasi-Biography of Henrietta Barnett, LMA/4063/006.
Paterson, Marion, Letters LMA-ACC/3816/02/01.
Paterson, Marion, Journal, 18 Feb. 1891. LMA/4063/005.

Books about the Hampstead Garden Suburb

Grafton Green, Brigid, *Hampstead Garden Suburb, Vision and Reality*.
Grafton Green, Brigid, *Hampstead Garden Suburb 1907–1977, A History pamphlet*. HGS Residents' Association, 1977.
C W Ikin, *Hampstead Garden Suburb, Dreams and Realities*, New Hampstead Garden Suburb Trust and Residents' Association, 1990.
Miller, Mervyn, *Hampstead Garden Suburb, Arts and Crafts Utopia*, Phillimore & Co., Chichester, 2006.
Slack, Kathleen M, *Henrietta's Dream*, Hampstead Garden Suburb Trust, 1997.
The Record, Hampstead Garden Suburb HGS Archive.
The Suburb Year Book, Residents' Association.
The Town Crier, Hampstead Garden Suburb HGS Archive.

Books and other published sources

Aitken, W Francis, *Canon Barnett*, S W Partridge, 1902.

Annual Charities' Register and Digest, 1901.

Borzello, Frances, *Civilising Caliban, The Misuse of Art 1875–1980*, Routledge and Kegan Paul, 1987.

Bosanquet, Helen, *Social Work in London 1869–1912*, John Murray, 1914.

Boult, Adrian, *My Own Trumpet,* Hamish Hamilton, London, 1973.

Briggs, Asa and Macartney, Ann, *Toynbee Hall: the First 100 Years*, Routledge and Kegan Paul, London, 1984.

Clayre Percy & Ridley, Jane (Eds.) *The Letters of Edwin Lutyens to his Wife, Lady Emily,* Hamish Hamilton, 1986.

Clodd, Edward, *Memories*, Watts, London 1926.

Crane, Walter, *An Artist's Reminiscences,* Methuen, 1907.

Creedon, Alison, 'A Benevolent Tyrant? The Principles and Practices of Henrietta Barnett (1851–1936). Social reformer and Founder of Hampstead Garden Suburb', in *Women's History Review*, Vol 11, Nov. 2 2002.

Creedon, Alison, *Only a Woman: Henrietta Barnett – Social Reformer and Founder of Hampstead Garden Suburb,* Phillimore & Co., Chichester, 2006.

D'Arcy Cresswell, *Margaret Macmillan*, Hutchinson, 1949.

Darling, E, *Women and the Making of Built Space in England 1870–1950,* Ashgate Publishing, 2007.

Davin, Anna, *Growing Up Poor*, Rivers Oram Press, London, 1996.

Davis, Allen F, *American Heroine. The Life and Legend of Jane Addams,* OUP, 1973.

Duncan, David, *Life and Letters of Herbert Spencer,* Methuen, 1908.

Edwards, Paul (ed.), *The Encyclopedia of Philosophy,* Macmillan N Y, 1967.

Gorst, Sir John Eldon, *The Children of the Nation,* Methuen, 1907.

Greenwood, James, *The Seven Curses of London*, Stanley Rivers, 1869.

Hopkins, Ellice, *Life and Letters of James Hinton*, Kegan Paul, 1878.

Howard, Ebenezer, *Garden Cities of Tomorrow*, Swann Sonnenschein, London, 1902.

Jackson, Frank, *Sir Raymond Unwin, Architect, Planner and Visionary*, Zwemmer, London, 1985.

Koven, Seth, 'Henrietta Barnett The (Auto)biography of a Late Victorian Marriage', in S Pederson and P Mandler, *After the Victorians*, Routledge, 1994.

Lewis, Jane, *Women in England 1870–1950*, Wheatsheaf Books, Brighton, 1984.

Lowndes, G A N, *Silent Social Revolution,* OUP, 1941.

Lutyens, Mary, *Edwin Lutyens*, John Murray, London, 1984.

Mackenzie, Norman and Jeanne (ed.), *Diary of Beatrice Webb,* Virago, 1982.

Maurice, C Edmund, *Life of Octavia Hill as told in her letters,* Cambridge University, 1913.

Mearns, Andrew, *The Bitter Cry of Outcast London*, a collection of newspaper articles, 1883.

Metropolitan Association for Befriending Young Servants, Leaflet 1876. BLPES.

Moberly Bell, E A C, *Octavia Hill*, Constable, 1942.

Morris, William, *News from Nowhere,* Dover Publications, New York, 2004.

Morris, William, *How We Live and How We Might Live,* Nonesuch Centenary Edition pp. 583–4.

Mowat, Charles Loch, *The Charity Organisation Society*, Methuen, London, 1961.

Nevinson, Henry W, *Changes and Chances*, Nisbet, 1923.

Nevinson, Margaret, *Life's Fitful Fever,* Black, 1926.

Pedersen, Susan & Peter Mandler (eds.), *After the Victorians, Private Conscience & Public Duty in Modern Britain*, Routledge, London, 1994.

Pevsner, N, *The Buildings of England: Middlesex,* Penguin, Harmondsworth, 1951.

Pimlott, J A R, *Toynbee Hall,* J M Dent, 1935.

Prochoska, F K, *Women and Philanthropy in 19th Century England,* Clarendon Press, 1980.

Roe, David, *Standing in the Wings,* Settle Press, 1987.

Ruskin, John, *Sesame and the Lilies,* Routledge, London, 1907.

Seymour-Jones, Carole, *Beatrice Webb, Woman of Conflict,* Alison and Busby, 1992.

Sims, George Robert, *How the Poor Live*, Chatto & Windus, London, 1883.

Sims, George, *How the Poor Live* and *Horrible London,* originally published as articles in the *Daily News,* 1889.

Slack, Kathleen M, *Henrietta's Dream,* Hampstead Garden Suburb Trust & Archive Trust, 1997.

Spencer, Herbert, *Autobiography,* Williams and Norgate, 1904.

Stedman Jones, G, *Outcast London,* Oxford, 1971.

Stephens, Margaret, *Women and Marriage,* Unwin, 1910.

Thomson Hill, William, *Octavia Hill,* Hutchinson, 1956.

Thomson, J A, *Herbert Spencer,* J M Dent, London, 1906.

Tims, Margaret, *Jane Addams of Hull House,* George Allen and Unwin, 1961.

Walkowitz, J, *City of Dreadful Delights,* OUP, 1992/4.

Watkins, Micky, *Henrietta Barnett in Whitechapel, Her First Fifty Years,* Hampstead Garden Suburb Archive Trust, 1905.

Waugh, Evelyn, *A Little Learning,* Chapman & Hall, 1964.

Webb, Beatrice *My Apprenticeship,* Pelican Books, Harmondsworth, 1938.

Young, A F and Ashton, E T, *British Social Work in the Nineteenth Century,* Routledge, 1956.

Journals

Journal of the Chelsea Pupil Teachers' Association. 1892.

Pall Mall Gazette.

State Children's Association Reports in BLPES.

List of Plates

Index